PATTERNS IN LITERARY ART SERIES

The Art of Narration: THE SHORT STORY
A. Grove Day

The Art of Narration: THE NOVELLA
A. Grove Day

Themes in the One-Act Play
R. David and Shirley Cox

The Bible as Literature
Alton C. Capps

The Comic Vision
Peter J. Monahan

Dramatic Tragedy
William McAvoy

The Hero and Anti-Hero
Roger B. Rollin

The Black Experience
Nettye Goddard

Dramatic Comedy
Harry Shanker

Classical Literature
George Kearns

Non-Fiction
George Kearns

The Art of Narration

THE SHORT STORY

The Art of Narration

THE SHORT STORY

Edited by

A. GROVE DAY

Senior Professor of English, Emeritus
University of Hawaii

Buchanan High School
English Department
Read it! Love it! Return it!

WEBSTER DIVISION
McGRAW-HILL BOOK COMPANY

New York St. Louis
San Francisco
Dallas Atlanta

ACKNOWLEDGMENTS

"Red," by W. Somerset Maugham. Copyright ©1921 by Asia Publishing Company. From *The Trembling of a Leaf*, by W. Somerset Maugham. Reprinted by permission of Doubleday & Company, Inc.

"Flowering Judas," copyright 1930, 1958, by Katherine Anne Porter. Reprinted from her volume *Flowering Judas and Other Stories* by permission of Harcourt, Brace & World, Inc.

"The Izu Dancer," by Yasunari Kawabata; translated by Edward Seidensticker. Reprinted from *The Atlantic Monthly*, January, 1955. Copyright 1955 by Intercultural Publications, Inc. Reprinted by permission of the copyright owner.

"The Passover Guest," by Sholem Aleichem, from *Yiddish Tales*, translated by Helena Frank, Jewish Publication Society of America, 1912, reprinted with the kind permission of the Society.

"The Use of Force," by William Carlos Williams, from *The Farmers' Daughters*. Copyright 1938 by William Carlos Williams. Reprinted by permission of New Directions Publishing Corporation.

"Spotted Horses," by William Faulkner. Copyright 1931 and renewed 1959 by William Faulkner. Reprinted by permission of Random House, Inc. An expanded version of this story appears in *The Hamlet* by William Faulkner.

"Her First Ball," by Katherine Mansfield. Copyright 1922 by Alfred A. Knopf, Inc. Renewed 1950 by John Middleton Murry. Reprinted by permission of the publisher from *The Short Stories of Katherine Mansfield*.

"Divorce," by Lu Hsun, translated by Gene Z. Hanrahan, reprinted from *Fifty Great Oriental Stories*, copyright 1965 by Bantam Books, Inc. Reprinted by permission of Paul R. Reynolds, Inc.

"My Old Man," by Ernest Hemingway, reprinted with the permission of Charles Scribner's Sons from *In Our Time* by Ernest Hemingway. Copyright 1925 by Charles Scribner's Sons; renewal copyright 1953 by Ernest Hemingway.

"The Son of Rizal," by José García Villa, reprinted with the permission of Charles Scribner's Sons from *Footnote to Youth* by Jose Garcia Villa. Copyright 1933 by Charles Scribner's Sons; renewal copyright © 1961 by José García Villa.

"The Dead," by James Joyce. From *Dubliners* by James Joyce. Originally published by B. W. Heubsch, Inc. in 1916, copyright © 1967 by the Estate of James Joyce. All rights reserved. Reprinted by permission of The Viking Press, Inc.

"Tobermory," by H. H. Munro (Saki). From *The Short Stories of Saki* by H. H. Munro. All rights reserved. Reprinted by permission of The Viking Press, Inc.

Copyright © 1971 by A. Grove Day. All Rights Reserved. Printed in the United States of America. No part of this publication may be reproduced, stored in a retrieval system, or transmitted, in any form or by any means, electronic, mechanical, photocopying, recording or otherwise, without the prior written permission of the publisher. Library of Congress Catalog Card Number: 79-138991

ISBN 07-016167-4

Editorial Development, Jack R. Dyer; Editing and Styling, Betty Martin; Design, Ted Smith; Production, Richard E. Shaw

Contents

INTRODUCTION	
The Rise of the Modern Short Story	ix
THE MYSTERY OF THE DESERTED HOUSE	
E. T. W. Hoffmann	1
THE PISTOL SHOT	
Alexander Pushkin	17
YOUNG GOODMAN BROWN	
Nathaniel Hawthorne	30
THE FALL OF THE HOUSE OF USHER	
Edgar Allan Poe	43
BARTLEBY: A STORY OF WALL STREET	
Herman Melville	61
THE STUB BOOK	
Pedro Antonio de Alarćon	95
THE FATHER	
Björnstjerne Björnson	101
A PIECE OF STRING	
Guy de Maupassant	105
THE PASSOVER GUEST	
Sholem Aleichem	113
THE MAN WHO WOULD BE KING	
Rudyard Kipling	120
THE REAL THING	
Henry James	152
THE OUTLAWS	
Selma Lagerlöf	176
YOUTH	
Joseph Conrad	193
THE DARLING	
Anton Chekhov	221

THE DEAD		
James Joyce		233
THE CELESTIAL OMNIBUS		
E. M. Forster		271
TOBERMORY		
Saki		286
RED		
W. Somerset Maugham		294
HER FIRST BALL		
Katherine Mansfield		314
MY OLD MAN		
Ernest Hemingway		321
THE IZU DANCER		
Kawabata Yasunari		334
DIVORCE		
Lu Hsun		351
FLOWERING JUDAS		
Katherine Anne Porter		361
SPOTTED HORSES		
William Faulkner		374
THE SON OF RIZAL		
José García Villa		392
THE USE OF FORCE		
William Carlos Williams		400
QUESTIONS		404
APPENDIX A		
Main Questions for the Study of a Story		419
APPENDIX B		
Analysis of "The Man Who Would Be King"		427

The Rise of the Modern Short Story

A cave dweller of ancient times sat by the fire telling his shaggy family and friends about his adventures while hunting a wild pig. Here and there he began adding a few exciting touches to make his listeners hang upon his words. Perhaps the pig became a bison, or even a mammoth. The climax of his victorious struggle was applauded by the listeners. That was the beginning of short fiction.

Everyone is born with an instinctive desire to be entertained by fiction. Among the first sentences a child learns is: "Tell me a story!" There is no need today to justify reading fiction, for its many rewards are widely accepted, and courses in the deeper appreciation of the storyteller's art are found in almost every school.

Reading a piece of literature, of course, differs from reading to obtain facts alone. Fiction reading gives a number of satisfactions, but the main reward it offers the reader is not merely factual and mental, but pleasurable and emotional. Enjoyment is the purpose of all art. But a particular work may not be pleasurable on first acquaintance. We may be able, after further study, to open our minds to the possibility of wider and deeper kinds of enjoyment. One can appreciate best what he more clearly understands. The rewards of fiction are many, as will be shown, and may vary for different readers or for the same reader at different times. One reward that is most important, however, is that understanding fiction can help the reader better to understand life.

Many of the world's best stories not only entertain the reader, but also enable him to realize what it means to be a human being. A complete world history of short prose fiction will probably never be written. The author would have to begin at least as far back as 4,000 B.C., when the Egyptian "Tales of the Magicians" were put down on papyrus. Myths and legends, hero tales of many tribes, stories devised to explain the world to the young people of myriad groups, folk tales and fairy tales—all these have existed since early times, and many have been written down. Fables such as those of Aesop were often used to dramatize a proverb. Animal stories about Reynard the Fox or Old Man Coyote are also of ancient origin.

Certain early pieces of literature resemble the modern short story. The Hindu *Panchatantra,* collected before A.D. 500, included fables and prose fiction. Some of the accounts in the Hebrew Old Testament, such as the Book of Ruth, the adventures of Jonah, and the combat between David and Goliath, have provided plots for many later writers. The parables of the New Testament are stories that offer a memorable lesson. Greek literature includes charming short fiction, like the story of Cupid and Psyche from *The Golden Ass* of Lucius Apuleius and the inserted tales in the *Satyricon* of Petronius. Parts of the epics of Homer, such as the adventure of Odysseus and his friends with the Cyclops, might be taken by themselves and considered as forerunners of the later form. All these, however, can be considered to resemble the modern short story only by accidental invention.

Far away in Japan, around the year 1,000, Lady Shikibu Murasaki strung together a long series of episodes collected as *The Tale of Genji.* During the Middle Ages in Europe, the *Gesta Romanorum* (about 1250) provided many plots. The writings of Giovanni Boccaccio, especially *The Decameron* (1353), containing a hundred tales such as that of Patient Griselda, are still popular. The collection known as *The Arabian Nights' Entertainments,* put together around 1450, included the stories of Ali Baba, Sinbad the Sailor, and many others remembered today. One of the Canterbury Tales of Geoffrey Chaucer, the story of Melibeus, was written in prose before 1400. Toward the end of the Middle Ages, Sir Thomas Malory put together the episodic adventures of King Arthur and his knights, first printed in England in 1485. The pranks of the rascally Dutch folk hero Tyll Owlglass were first published in 1483.

Miguel Cervantes, the Spanish author who was a contemporary of Shakespeare, wrote stories under the title of *Novelas Ejemplares* (1613), and had interpolated in his famous novel *Don Quixote* (1605) some stories which had little to do with the main plot. The rise of the novel, in fact, led to many such insertions. The Englishman Henry Fielding filled out his novel *Tom Jones* (1749) with separate stories—a practice that continued even in the novels of Sir Walter Scott and Charles Dickens. The popular essay sometimes contributed as well to the development of fiction; "The Vision of Mirza," published by Joseph Addison in the *Spectator* in 1711, was an Oriental tale adapted for the entertainment of British readers. Most of these pieces, however, were written without any theory of a planned type of fiction with a tight structure.

The Rise of the Short Story

The romantic "tale" popular in Europe in the early nineteenth century is closest to the modern short story, which evolved from it. Some of these tales, such as those by the German writers Ludwig Tieck and E. T. W. Hoffmann, are still readable. Hoffmann tales like "The Mystery of the Deserted House" can be enjoyed, but such narratives were usually rambling in style, feeble in motivation, whimsical in characterization, and lacking in unity. Many tales were written by Washington Irving, Nathaniel Hawthorne, and Edgar Allan Poe, but these three American authors differed from earlier writers because they slowly developed a new form which might be defined as the modern short story.

The modern short story differs from longer forms of fiction, such as the novel and the novelette, not merely in length. Its particular quality is unity of impression. It aims, in the words of Clayton Hamilton, "to produce a single narrative effect with the greatest economy of means that is consistent with the utmost emphasis." My own definition is: "The short story is a piece of prose fiction which can be read at a single sitting; it presents an artistic and unified impression of life through many devices, especially theme, characters, action involving conflict and crisis, setting, and style." Perhaps we should not, however, attempt to define too rigidly a type of literature whose possibilities still seem great. Another Edgar Allan Poe or Henry James is probably sitting in an American classroom today.

Irving began writing the sketch, which might be described as a form offering setting or characterization but lacking a plot. Aside from a few stories like "Rip Van Winkle" and "The Legend of Sleepy Hollow," he remained a sketch writer or taleteller.

Hawthorne began publishing fiction in 1830, and many of his pieces, such as "Young Goodman Brown," are properly short stories. He never stated any theory of the genre, but Poe, his contemporary, hammered out his gospel of the short story through a study of his fellow craftsman. "If wise," observed Poe in a review of Hawthorne's *Twice-Told Tales* in *Graham's Magazine* for May, 1842, "he [the story writer] has not fashioned his thoughts to accommodate his incidents; but having conceived, with deliberate care, a certain unique or single *effect* to be wrought out, he then invents such incidents—he then combines such events as may best aid him in establishing the preconceived effect. If his very initial sentence tends not to the outbringing of this effect, then he has failed in his first step. In the whole composition there should be no word written of which the tendency, direct or indirect, is not to the one preëstablished design."

Poe, then, recognized that the brevity of this form demands a single striking effect: that the short story differs from longer fiction not only in length but also in purpose; that the writing of magazine stories could be a planned technique; and that such stories would prove immensely appealing—especially in America, where many readers are still attracted by its brevity, the variety of its forms, and its sharp impact. The short story, in fact, has been the most popular type of literature in this country for more than a century, and no other nation can show such a record of creation, on both quantity and quality, in this very modern form.

One of the greatest American short-story writers before the Civil War was Herman Melville, known also as a novelist. The story also evolved in Europe, especially in Russia, France, and Scandinavia, where authors not only adapted and put down folk yarns based on legends, *contes,* or hero tales preserved by oral tradition, but also began writing realistic stories that were marked by a feeling for unified effects. At about the same time that Hawthorne began writing, Alexander Pushkin in Russia published "The Pistol Shot." He and his contemporary Nikolai Gogol showed the way to later Russian masters such as Ivan Turgenev, Fëdor Dostoevski, and Leo Tolstoy. Anton Chekhov began a continuing school of writers interested more in character depiction than in contrived "plot."

Three Frenchmen—Prosper Mérimée, Honoré de Balzac, and Théophile Gautier—by 1830 had also demonstrated that the anecdotal *conte* could be adapted to their needs to reveal contemporary life. They were followed by other French short-story writers like Gustave Flaubert, Alphonse Daudet, Anatole France, and Guy de Maupassant. One story by De Maupassant, "The Necklace," did, in fact, originate a school of imitators who depended upon an ironic, whirligig ending, best exemplified by the American writer O. Henry.

American writers after the Civil War leaned heavily upon the magazine story which emphasized plot, especially "trick endings" of the O. Henry sort. There is a definite limit, however, to the possible dramatic twists of events, whereas the varieties of personality in the human race are almost as unlimited as the total population. Aside from the "local-color" writers, who emphasized regional settings and unusual Americans who spoke in quaint dialects, and aside from the realists and naturalists, who believed that the main function of literature should be to objectively depict their society, the most important group of writers were those who concentrated upon the psychology motivating the actions of their characters. Foremost among these was Henry James, a New Yorker who began publishing stories in 1865. He often used settings in his homeland, but his best work depicted the international scene through the eyes of traveling Americans. He insisted less upon stirring action than upon unraveling complex human relationships in a subtle style. His technical comments, and his insistence that literature was worthy of serious, artistic devotion, influenced a growing number of authors who are still guided by his theories.

The Rise of the Short Story

Prominent among the followers of James in America was Edith Wharton. The naturalist school was well represented around 1900 by Stephen Crane, Frank Norris, and Theodore Dreiser. Their pioneer attitudes survived, with many modifications, in the writings of American novelists who also contributed to the development of the short story. The unprettified narratives of Willa Cather, F. Scott Fitzgerald, Sherwood Anderson, Ernest Hemingway, John Steinbeck, William Faulkner, Eudora Welty, and Katherine Anne Porter showed the world that the technical skills of a Henry James could be applied to a serious, even harsh view of twentieth century American life.

The American and Continental experiments were slow to affect the old tradition of English writing. Scott, Dickens, George Meredith, and Thomas Hardy were novelists who sometimes wrote in the shorter form, but contributed little to the advancement of its techniques. Not until the beginning of our century did the English novelists comprehend the possibilities of the short story. Thereafter, writers like Joseph Conrad (born in Poland), James Joyce (an Irishman), E. M. Forster, D. H. Lawrence, and W. Somerset Maugham aroused the English-speaking world to the realization that a new generation demanded new modes of expressing the age-old emotions of the authors.

Advances in the Western nations also aroused the interest of writers in Asia, the Pacific, and many other parts of the globe. Interest in regionalism became worldwide, inspired by such colorful authors as Rudyard Kipling. The breakup of colonial possessions did not shatter the use of English as a literary language. Writers in countries that had formed the British Commonwealth continued to write fiction that vied with anything produced in London. People in India, Malaysia, Canada, Australia, New Zealand, Africa, and the Caribbean are today putting down words that readers in the rest of the world will enjoy and applaud. Minority groups use literature to make known their problems and plights. The development of the short story—a cosmopolitan form whose potential is still far from exhausted—will continue so long as new writers are born and readers seek new ways of interpreting life.

Greatest of the Tale-tellers

E. T. W. HOFFMANN

Hoffmann was the very spirit of the wild Late Romantic period in Europe. His tales were tossed off with the same fury that possessed him in his roles as lawyer, music critic and composer, and painter.

Ernst Theodor Wilhelm Hoffmann (1776–1822) was born in Prussia. His stunted body had tiny feet and hands and a big head. He had large, deep-set eyes, sharp features, and bristling hair, and through his life he was always making nervous faces and shifting his hands and feet. His spirit, too, was never at rest. He was an infant prodigy as a musician, and as a man, he composed an opera, *Undine*, that was performed in Berlin.

He passed examinations as a lawyer in 1795, but was forced by his excesses to wander around Poland, where he married. He traveled through the German provinces, where he composed music and painted. After the downfall of Napoleon he was restored to his post as a judge in Berlin in 1814, but ironically he turned at that time to writing stories which earned him the title of the foremost German author, after Goethe, of his day. When he was not working with frenzy, he would go to a tavern and lead the conversation all night.

Such a life could not last long, and after suffering much pain from illnesses, his body fell apart like a wornout machine. His fantastic life is reflected in his fiction, which inspired the opera *Tales of Hoffmann* by Jacques Offenbach. He lived and died the Romantic, self-destructive life of such other writers as Percy Bysshe Shelley, John Keats, and Lord Byron.

Hoffmann and other authors of the period did not write the well-plotted fiction that was later developed by Hawthorne and Poe. Their aim was to make supernatural events convincing, but they did not bother to plan structure, reveal motives, or attain the singleness of effect of the modern short story. Their characters were often grotesque, and events were seldom explained. Hoffmann would start a story and ramble along, hoping he might find a suitable ending. Thus, many of his tales leave the reader unconvinced and unsatisfied.

"The Mystery of the Deserted House" is a good example of Hoffmann's art. He has been unfavorably compared with Edgar Allan Poe. In his defense, it may be said that he did not coldly plan ahead the outcome of his story, and we share with him the exploration of a mystery for which he himself is seeking a solution.

E. T. W. HOFFMANN

The Mystery of the Deserted House

THE MANY FINE MANSIONS to be seen in W——, the luxurious productions of art and industry of every kind with which it increases in riches from day to day, are the delight of the sightseer and the admiration of every traveler. The street, lined with magnificent residences leading to the old gate, serves as a continual corridor for the élite of society going to while away the time in one another's houses. The ground floors of the houses are occupied by very elegant shops; the upper stories are divided into comfortable flats. It is the quarter belonging to the upper ten.

I had already gone up and down this avenue a thousand times, when my eyes paused by chance on a building whose strange construction was in strong contrast with its neighbors. Imagine a square block of stone pierced by four windows, forming two stories only, a ground floor and a first floor; its height was hardly more than that of the ground floor of the magnificent mansions flanking it on either side. This building, cracked and decayed, was topped by a roof in exceedingly bad condition, and most of the windowpanes were broken and replaced by squares of gray or blue paper. The four windows were fast shut. Those belonging to the ground floor had been walled up, and you might look in vain for a bell by the front door, which was narrow and low and without a lock. This dilapidation proclaimed utter desolation; the hovel looked as though it had been derelict and abandoned for a hundred years. A deserted house is, after all, nothing surprising; but in so wealthy a quarter, on a site that might have brought its owner a substantial income, it certainly offered grounds for speculation, and I could never again pass the old barrack without building a thousand castles in Spain.

One day, at the hour when the smart folk were jostling one another like ants, I was standing, leaning against a perron opposite the deserted house, lost in reverie, when a gentleman I had lost sight of for a long time suddenly stopped beside me and drew me from my dreaming. This was Count P——, a dreamer at least as fantastic and curious as I could possibly be. Like me, he had speculated tremendously about the mystery of the deserted house. His imaginings had gone far beyond mine, and he had finally invented a legend so extravagant that only the boldest imagination could accept it as real, and that with great difficulty. Judge the disappointment of this poor count when, after elaborating his story to the best of his ability, and in the most tragical fashion, he learned that the famous deserted house was simply the workshop of a fashionable pastry cook whose shop was close by! The windows in the ground floor had been walled up to hide the stoves and the boilers from the passersby; and the windows of the first floor had been stuffed up to preserve the sweetstuffs kept in store there from the sun and from the flies. This accursed piece of information was like an icy douche to me; no more dreams, no more romantics were possible! It was enough to make an emotional and easily excited heart burst with annoyance. However, in spite of the quite commonplace and materialistic explanation I had been given, I could not prevent myself from looking at the quondam deserted house with an inexplicable feeling that gave me a shiver. My spirit, once aroused, wrathfully rejected that idea of bonbons instead of the ghosts that had so powerfully taken hold of me; and I did not despair of one day seeing the fantastic world resume possession of that dwelling. Chance, too, was very soon to launch me once more in the path of speculation.

A few days after my meeting with Count P——, I was passing about noon before the deserted house; I saw a slight movement in a green taffeta curtain that veiled the window next to the confectioner's shop. A white hand, exquisitely shaped, the loveliest finger of which bore a superb diamond, slipped under the curtain; then I saw an alabaster arm, adorned with a gold bracelet. The hand placed a crystal flask on the windowsill, and was withdrawn.

I stayed there staring, nose in air, my feet nailed to the pavement, displaying, it must be believed, so strange an air that in less than ten minutes an innumerable crowd of gapers, and very smart ones, were pressing round about me, and straining their eyes to see what I was looking at; but there was no rosy hand or alabaster arm now; the inquisitive ones discovered nothing by their impertinence. This city populace made me think of the ninnies of a certain village who flocked one morning before a house crying "Miracle" because a cotton cap had fallen from the sixth floor without breaking a single thread. It was a thousand to one that the rose-tinged hand and the alabaster arm belonged in lawful property to the confectioner's wife, or his sister, or his daughter, and that the crystal flask prosaically contained gooseberry cordial. See how a disturbed but logical mind contrives to attain its end by the quickest way! It came into my head to go into the confectioner's shop and cunningly extract some confidences from him.

As I took my chocolate ice, I said to him: "You have chosen an excellent place for your establishment, and I find it particularly convenient for you to enjoy possession of the next house in which you have set up your kitchens." At these words the honest tradesman looked at me with an air of surprise.

"Who on earth," he exclaimed, "could have told you that the next-door house was mine? I would certainly like to have it with all my heart; but in spite of all my attempts the affair never came off. In any case, and all things considered, I am not too sorry for it, for there must be a heap of things going on in that house that would embarrass a peaceful tenant to a singular extent."

Imagine, my dear reader, how excited I was by these words. I tried to get my man to talk freely; but all I could learn from him was that the deserted house belonged to Countess S——, who lived on her estates, and who had not been seen in this residence for a number of years. The house, in any event, had from time immemorial looked exactly as it did today, and no one seemed to trouble to make even the smallest repairs to save it from imminent ruin. Two creatures lived in it, an old manservant and a decrepit dog that never stopped barking. The common folk in the quarter were convinced that the place was haunted by ghosts, for at certain times, and particularly when Christmas was at hand, there were heard fantastic noises disturbing the silent night; sometimes there was a frantic hubbub. Once the broken voice of an old woman essayed a yelping sort of ghostly song, in which a few French words could just be distinguished, mingled with some entirely unknown language.

"Look, sir," said the confectioner, as he brought me through into his back shop, "look at this iron pipe coming through the party wall. Sometimes in the height of summer I have seen huge volumes of smoke coming out of it, as if there was a regular hell-fire inside the house. More than once I have soundly scolded the old servant, who constantly makes us afraid we are going to have a fire; but the slyboots pretends it's his kitchen stove. The devil alone knows what such a creature eats, for the smoke coming out of his den every now and then spreads a stink that is anything but appetizing."

At that moment the shop door opened, setting in motion a little bell with a shrill sharp note. The confectioner excused himself on the score of duty calling him to attend to a customer. As I was coming back in his wake, I divined, from a sly sign he made me with his head, the person we had just been discussing. Imagine, dear reader, a little dry fellow with a skin like yellow parchment, a nose sharp as an awl, lips thin as a knife blade, green-gray eyes, a vacant smile, hair powdered and turned up into a pyramid; his dress was made up of a loose shabby coat, the color of which had once been a dark brown, his tight breeches fitted over gray stockings, and the individual ended in square-toed shoes with imitation gold buckles. From his sleeves emerged two powerful fists that hardly matched a thin whiny voice asking for preserved oranges, marrons glacés, marchpanes, and other dainties.

The confectioner took all pains to serve him; the old man brought out of his pocket a well-worn purse of reddish leather, and took from it, one by one, a few much-rubbed pieces of money, almost defaced and hardly fit for circulation. He paid, grumbling the while, and snarling and murmuring bits of phrases devoid of meaning. "Are you ill, my good neighbor?" said the shopkeeper. "You seem very melancholy; old age, I suppose, old age." "Hoho! hoho! hoho! who says so?" growled the satanic old fellow angrily, with a pirouette so heavy that the shop windows rattled in their frames; as he came down he nearly crushed the paw of the black dog that accompanied him, which set up a shrill yelp. "Accursed brute!" the old man went on, opening his bag to throw a marchpane to the dog, which shut up to gulp it down, and sat on its tail with the grace of a squirrel. "Good night to you, neighbor," said the old servant when the dog had swallowed his allowance, "good night, neighbor. The poor old boy whom old age has broken wishes you good luck and long life!" And saying this, he gripped the shopkeeper's hand with his bony talon, so hard that the other gave a cry of pain.

"You see," said the confectioner to me after his client had gone, "that is Count S——'s factotum, the caretaker of the deserted house. Every so often I call on him to put an end to his nocturnal racket; but he has an answer for everything: he is expecting his master's family, he says, but it has been going on now for so many years that we may believe they will never arrive. That is as much as I know, and I now have the honor to bid you good-day, for this is the hour when our fine ladies lay siege to my shop and compete with one another for the sweet things I invent every day for their pretty little mouths."

When I took leave of the confectioner, I set my brains to work to discover some natural link between the strange and melancholy song that had been heard in the deserted house and the lovely arm I had caught a glimpse of under the taffeta curtain. I persuaded myself that by some acoustical illusion what the confectioner had taken for the wailing of an old woman was the sweet though plaintive song of a beautiful creature persecuted and held prisoner by some detestable tyrant. I thought again of the stinking smoke issuing from the pipe, of the crystal flask on the windowsill; and from this I concluded, without more ado, that the lovely unknown was the victim of abominable enchantments. The old servant turned, in my mind, into a wizard in disguise; my brain soared into flights of imagination, and diabolical shapes haunted my sleeplessness. By some inexplicable magic, the alabaster arm was joined to a snowy shoulder my very eyes seemed to see; then the face of an adorable maiden rose out of this hallucination, white and veiled: it seemed to me that the silvery mist that half concealed from me the features of this angelic being came in endless waves from the crystal flask. For the rescuing of this heavenly creature, I devised the maddest plans; I gave myself up to the most chivalrous soliloquies. Suddenly it seemed that a skeleton hand clapped me on the shoulder, shattered the magic flask to ten thousand fragments, and the apparition vanished, leaving the dying echo of a sweet plaint behind.

The next day I hastened at an early hour to station myself in front of the deserted house. Venetian blinds had been installed since the previous day. The house had all the aspects of a tomb. I prowled round the neighborhood all that day. In the evening I passed it again; the lockless door was ajar, the man in the dark-brown coat was putting his head out through it. I made bold to speak to him. "Does not Councillor Binder live in this house?" I asked, in the politest manner possible. "No," said the old fellow with a suspicious smile; "he has never set a foot in it, and he never will; and everybody knows that he lives a long way from this quarter." As he finished, he pulled his head inside and shut the door in my face. I heard him cough, and then move with slow, heavy tread, accompanied by a jangling of keys, and it seemed as though he was going down an internal staircase. I had noticed through the half-open door that the hall was stretched with old ragged tapestries, and furnished with ancient armchairs covered in scarlet.

The following day, about noon, some irresistible power brought me back to the same place. I saw, or thought I saw, through the first-floor window, the green taffeta curtain half drawn up; a diamond sparkled, then a ravishing creature, leaning her elbows on the inner sill, held out her arms to me with a beseeching air. Hardly believing myself awake, I looked for some spot whence I could continue my watch without attracting the attention of the crowd. There was a stone bench on the other side of the street directly opposite the house; I went over and sat on it, I raised my eyes, I pondered; it was she, indeed, it was the exquisite maiden my imagination had figured so well, only her posture was unchanging and her wild eyes were not fixed upon me. I was tempted to think that my senses were tricked by a beautiful painting. Suddenly there passed by, close to me, a hawker of miscellaneous odds and ends, who begged me to buy something from him "for luck," as he had sold nothing all day. At first, I refused harshly; but he insisted, spreading out all his stock in front of me, and offered me a little pocket mirror, which he held in front of me at a certain distance and in such a way that I could clearly see in it the window of the deserted house and the angelic face of the girl. This article tempted me so strongly that I bought it at the first price he quoted, without bargaining.

No sooner had I begun to use it on my own account than a kind of catalepsy seemed to glue my eyes on the mirror, with no possible power in me to turn them away. I fancied all at once that I saw the lovely eyes of my unknown divinity interpose between the mirror and me; a feeling of ineffable tenderness made my heart beat. "That is a charming pocket mirror of yours," said a voice beside me. I awoke as from a dream; great was my astonishment to see myself surrounded by a ring of people, complete strangers to me, who were smiling at me with an equivocal air, as if they thought I was mad. The same voice presently began again. "That is a most wonderful mirror; but might we know what it is that so powerfully holds your attention? Are you by any chance in communication with spirits?"

The person who put this question to me appeared to be a gentleman. He was clad with elegant simplicity. His kindly, honorable face inspired trust. I could not refrain from frankly telling him my feelings, and asking him if he had not himself observed this admirable figure. "Upon my word, sir," he answered, "I think my eyes are pretty good, and God send I need not take to spectacles till the last possible moment! I have seen the face you speak of, but it is, I verily believe, a portrait in oils executed by an excellent artist."

I hastened to look again, but the curtain had just fallen on the other side of the window. "Good heavens, sir," added my interlocutor, "the

The Mystery of the Deserted House

old servant of the owner of this barrack, Count S——, has just taken down that portrait to dust it, and then he has shut the window." "Are you quite, quite sure?" I cried in consternation. "As sure as I am that I'm alive," he rejoined; "as you looked at it in your mirror you were deceived by an optical illusion; for my own part, when I was your age and had the same burning fancy I might have been caught, too." "But I saw the arm and the hand move!" I exclaimed again in a state of stupefaction hard to describe. "I do not say you didn't," rejoined my neighbor rising with a smile, and fixing upon me a look of polite irony, he went away, adding: "Beware of mirrors of the devil's making. I have the honor to bid you adieu."

Can you conceive, dear reader, what I must have suffered to see myself mystified in this fashion and treated as a visionary idiot? Filled with anger and with shame, I hurried off to shut myself up at home, fully resolved to have nothing more to do with the deserted house.

A few matters of business occupied several days and helped to cool my brain. Only during the night I still, at moments, felt a feverish superexcitement; but I resisted this without great difficulty, and had even come to make use of the mirror that had played me such a trick, when one morning as I was about to use it in my toilet the glass seemed to be tarnished: I breathed on it and wiped it; when I tried to see myself, oh! I still shudder at the memory! I saw, instead of my own face, that of the mysterious unknown lady of the deserted house. Her eyes were wet with tears, and fixed me with an expression more heartrending than the first time.

So violent was my emotion that on the following days I did nothing but pass to and fro before the deserted house. The image of the marvelous maiden had taken possession of all my thoughts; I now lived for nothing but the phantom. I came to feel physical, though invisible, ties taking shape between me and this creature of nature unknown. Gradually I fell into a languid state that sapped at the roots of my life; it was a mixture of pain and pleasure that exhausted me, and I could bring no force to fight the supernatural influence. Fearing I might become mad, and finding myself barely able to drag myself along, I managed with great difficulty to visit a celebrated physician who specialized in the preventive treatment of mental diseases. I told him everything that had happened within me over a certain period, and besought him not to abandon me to a condition worse than death. "Make your mind easy," said the doctor, "your brain is sick, but you know the exact cause of your trouble, and this in itself offers a good chance for cure. In the first place, leave your mirror with me, go back to your home, take up some task that will absorb all your faculties, and when you have worked solidly on it, tire your body out with a long tramp; in the evening see your friends and enjoy yourself with them. To this course of treatment add a generous diet and drink rich wines. Your whole malady lies merely in a fixed idea; if we can once drive it away you will be radically cured."

I hesitated to part with the mirror. The doctor took it, breathed on it, wiped it, and handed it to me, saying, "Do you see anything?"

"I see my own features, nothing else," I replied. "That's good," said the doctor; "well now, try the experiment yourself this time." A cry escaped me, and I became very pale. "'Tis she! 'tis she!" I exclaimed. The doctor took the mirror again. "For my part," he said, "I see nothing, absolutely nothing; but I must confess that at the moment I looked in it I felt an involuntary shudder. So you must have complete trust in me. If there is a charm, we must break it. Would you be so good as to try it again?" Once more I breathed on the mirror, while the doctor placed his hand on my spine. The face appeared again; the doctor grew pale on observing the effect this phenomenon had upon me. He took the mirror from me and locked it away in a box, and sent me away, repeating the advice he had given me; he added that we should see a little later what was to be done.

From that day I gave myself up wholly to a multitude of distractions, and led a noisy existence, well calculated to keep my mind under control by dint of physical weariness. A few evenings later, I found myself in a very lively gathering, and the talk ran on occult sciences and magnetic phenomena, and the most surprising anecdotes were told on this theme. We ran over all the experiments connected with dreams, with hallucinations, with trances, and we asked ourselves most seriously whether some will, existing outside our life, could not in certain conditions exercise a real influence upon our faculties without the help of any material contact. "To admit such a hypothesis," said one of the talkers, "would lead us directly to recognize the truth of the sorceries of the Middle Ages, and all the superstitions long since disposed of by a philosophy enlightened by the progress of the sciences."

"But," said a young doctor in his turn, "must we, under pretext of wisdom and an enlightened philosophy, deny the existence of ascertained facts? Does not nature comprise mysteries that our feeble organs are powerless to fathom and to understand? Just as a blind man recognizes by the rustling of leaves or by the murmur of running water that he is near a wood or a stream, can we not in like manner feel certain things in our existence by means of the invisible communication between certain spirits and our own?" At these words I entered

The Mystery of the Deserted House

the lists. "You do admit, then," said I to the young doctor, "the existence of a nonmaterial principle endowed with a power that in certain conditions our will could not repel?" "Yes," he answered, "that is a fact proved by observations brought together by the most serious students of magnetism." "In that case," I continued, "we must also acknowledge as possible the existence of demons, maleficent beings, armed with a nature superior to ours." "That would be going too far," replied the doctor, smiling. "I do not believe in possession. My opinion is merely that in the chain of creatures there may exist certain nonmaterial principles capable of exerting an irresistible action on others. But I base this idea solely on simple observations, and I believe that only organisms of feeble constitution or debilitated by some excess in living are liable to undergo this kind of experience."

"But," said a gentleman of mature years who had not spoken till then, "if, as you practically agree, there do exist occult powers inimical to our nature, I conclude from this, in accordance with your explanations, that these powers exist solely through the weakness of our minds. If only faculties debilitated from excesses or suffering, or incomplete organs, can be subjected to this physiological phenomenon, I infer that this phenomenon is nothing else but an accidental malady of our mind, and consequently outside of ourselves there do not exist any powers endowed with capability of material action, halfway between God and ourselves. And now here is my own personal opinion with regard to those mental maladies that subject us to passing hallucinations. I think that by reason of its disturbing power over the most delicate fibers of our organism, the passion, or rather the disease, of love is the one affection of the mind that can bring about disorders in the material life, and present the example of a power exercised in irresistible fashion by one individual over another. I have seen in my own house a case, the details of which are a drama in themselves. When the French army was laying waste our provinces under the orders of General Bonaparte, I had billeted in my house a colonel of the guards of the Viceroy of Naples; he was an officer of uncommon distinction, but his features unmistakably betrayed the ravages of either a deep grief or a recent illness. A few days after his arrival, I surprised him in the throes of a paroxysm of distress that filled me with compassion. He was almost choking with sobs that made it impossible for him to speak: he was compelled to throw himself down upon a daybed; gradually his eyes lost their vision and his limbs their power to move; he became as rigid as a statue. Every now and then he had a spasm of convulsions, but without moving from where he lay.

A physician whom I sent for in haste brought him under the magnetic influence, which seemed to afford him a little ease; but he was obliged to discontinue this, for he could not relieve the patient without feeling within himself a sensation of intense suffering impossible to explain. However, on recovering from this attack, the officer, whose confidence he had won by his attentions, told him that in the height of the crises he had seen the image of a woman he had known at Pisa; this phantom had an eye and a look that pierced his very heart, like the burning of a red-hot iron; he escaped this agony only to fall into a kind of lethargy, after which he had unbearable bouts of migraine and complete prostration in every limb, as if he had been indulging in frantic sensuality. At the same time he never told what had passed in the old days between him and the lady of Pisa. The order having been given for his regiment to move to the advance guard, he asked for luncheon to be served while his baggage was being packed. Just as he put a last glass of Madeira to his lips, he fell dead with a stifled cry. The doctor was of the opinion that he had been struck with apoplexy. Two or three weeks after this accident I received a letter addressed to the colonel. I opened it in the hope of finding some information as to the family of my late guest. The letter came from Pisa, and contained only the following words, without any signature: 'My poor friend, this day, the seventh of June, at noon, Antonia died imagining that she was embracing your shadow!' It was the very hour and day of the colonel's death. Explain that if you can."

I could not possibly, dear reader, depict the terror that seized me when I suddenly realized the analogy between my own sensations and those the colonel had endured. A cloud passed over my eyes; a ringing in my ears as dismal as the sound of a passing bell prevented me from hearing the end of the tale; and my imagination at once soaring to delirious heights, I hurried away from the room to go to the deserted house. From afar I seemed to see lights moving behind the closed blinds; but when I reached it, I could see nothing. My hallucination increasing, I threw myself against the door, which yielded, and I found myself in the hall, with a hot and acrid vapor catching me in the throat. Suddenly I heard a woman's cry close at hand, and I somehow found myself in the middle of a drawing room resplendent with lights and most sumptuously decorated in medieval style. Aromatic herbs in perfume burners filled the air with divine fragrances that floated up to the vaulted roof in azure clouds. "O welcome, welcome, my betrothed, for now is the hour for love!" said the same woman's voice I had just heard; and only at that moment did I perceive a young woman in bridal

The Mystery of the Deserted House

attire coming towards me with open arms; when I looked at her closer, I saw the face was yellow and dreadfully contorted by insanity. I fell back in terror, but the woman still advanced, and I then fancied I could see that this hideous face was only a crape mask behind which the enchanting features of my ideal might be divined. Already her hands were touching mine, when she fell moaning on the floor, and I heard behind a growl, "Hu, hu! to bed, my pretty, or beware of the stick!" Turning round I saw the old servant, he of the dark-brown coat, who was making long birch twigs whistle in the air and about to fall upon the poor woman lying on the ground in floods of tears. I sprang forward to stay his arm; but throwing me off with a strength I had not expected from him, he contented himself with saying, "Eh! do you not see that but for me this madwoman would have strangled you! Away, away from here quicker than you came in!"

At these words my vertigo seized me once more, and I rushed from the drawing room feeling for some way out of this fatal house. I heard the shrieks of the madwoman mingling with the sound of the blows the old man was showering on her. I was turning back to rescue her, when the ground gave way under me and I fell from step to step down a stair, falling through a door at the bottom. From the tumbled bed and the dark-brown coat thrown over a chair, I guessed this was the lair that harbored the servant. I had no sooner collected my senses when I heard heavy steps shaking the stairs again. It was the old man returning from his nocturnal execution. "Oh, sir," he cried, throwing himself at my feet, "whoever you are, I conjure you to preserve absolute silence on everything you have seen here; the slightest indiscretion would ruin me, a poor old man who could never know where to turn to earn his bread for the rest of his days. The madwoman has been soundly corrected, and I have tied her down in her bed. Everything is quiet now. So do you also go and take your rest at home, my good gentleman! Sleep well, and try to forget this night."

When he had said this, the old man took a candle and, inviting me to go in front, took me on my feet up the stairs I had gone down on my back, and pushed me out of the house, bolting the door behind me. I hurried off home in a state of stupor hard to describe, and dreaming over the extraordinary encounter I had just been through; it needed almost supernatural efforts to put from my mind the fatal hallucinations the accursed magic mirror had engendered in it.

Some time after, I met Count P—— in a drawing room; he took me aside and told me laughingly that he was on the track of the mysteries of the deserted house. The arrival of a servant to announce supper did not allow time to listen to the account he was about to give me. I gave my hand to a young lady to bring her to the supper room with the proper ceremony observed in good society. Judge of my surprise when, on fixing my eyes on her features, I recognized the face of the ideal shown me by my mirror! When I told her my idea that I had met her somewhere, she replied easily that nothing was less likely, as she had just arrived in W—— for the first time in her life. She accompanied her reply with so charming a look that I was as though electrified. We talked long together, and I introduced into our conversation a certain boldness of expression that nevertheless did not seem to displease her, and on her side she displayed an exquisite wit. When the moment came for champagne, I went to fill her glass; but the English crystal, struck by inadvertence, gave out a high, melancholy note. At once I saw my pretty neighbor's brow turn to a deathly pallor, and I seemed to hear the shrill falsetto of the mysterious old woman of the deserted house.

During the course of the evening I watched for an opportunity to join Count P——. From him I learned that the beautiful lady who had so much occupied my attention was Countess Edwina S——, and that her aunt was shut away as insane in the deserted house. That very day mother and daughter had visited the unhappy recluse. The old servant having been suddenly smitten with a serious illness, the ladies had admitted their sad secret to Doctor K——, who was to employ his celebrated skill in an attempt to cure the poor woman. At that moment Doctor K——, who was passing close beside us, and whom I had myself consulted as to what remedies might combat my hallucinations, stopped to inquire after my health, and by my importunate questions I got from him some details of the story of the woman imprisoned in the deserted house.

"Angelika, Countess of Z——," said the doctor, "was at thirty in the full splendor of her beauty, when Count S——, several years her junior, fell desperately in love with her, and set everything at work to get himself accepted by her family. But on a visit he paid to the Castle of Z—— to ask for the object of his passion in marriage he met Gabrielle, Angelika's sister. This encounter utterly changed his feelings and altered his plans immediately. From that moment Angelika lost all the charms with which she had at first seemed to him to be endowed, and, on the other hand, Gabrielle became lovelier in his eyes with everything her sister no longer possessed. Gabrielle was asked for in marriage instead of Angelika. The poor forsaken one made no complaint; her pride made her look on the affair from a very consoling angle. 'It is not this young spark who is jilting me,' she said to herself, 'it is I who do not want him any longer.' Still, she had suddenly ceased to show herself in society, and she was now rarely to be met with save in the darkest and least frequented part of her father's park.

"One day the servants of the Castle of Z—— were returning from hunting down a horde of thieving gypsies who for some time had been devastating the countryside with pillage and burning; they brought back into the courtyard of the manor a cartful of carefully trussed-up prisoners. Among these bandits, the most remarkable countenance was that of a scrawny, decrepit old woman, bundled up rather than clothed in scarlet tatters, who, as she stood up in the cart, shouted imperiously that she wished to get down. The cords that bound her were untied, and she was allowed to descend. Count von Z——, informed of the capture of the band, had left his apartments, and was busy arranging the cellars of the castle to serve as prisons for the marauders fate had thrown into his hands, when suddenly Countess Angelika rushed all disheveled into the courtyard, and falling on her knees sobbing and imploring, besought pardon for the gypsies; she drew a stiletto from her dress and declared that she would kill herself then and there if the least harm was done to those poor people whose innocence she asseverated. 'Bravo, my lovely,' cried the old woman, 'I knew that you would be an advocate for us whose pleadings would be heard on our behalf!'

"And as Angelika, exhausted by this violent outburst, had fallen in a swoon, the old woman broke the bonds that still held her, and threw herself on her knees beside her, lavishing the most eager attentions upon her. She took from her satchel a flask filled with a liquor in which there seemed to swim a golden fish; directly this flask was laid on Angelika's bosom, the beautiful girl opened her eyes, sprang up as though a new life ran in her veins and, after closely embracing the old gypsy, pulled her headlong after her into the castle. Count von Z——, who had been joined by his wife and his daughter Gabrielle, looked on at this strange scene with a kind of mixed surprise and fear. The gypsies had remained impassive. They were locked away in the underground cells of the castle.

"The next day the council of justice was assembled, and the gypsies were brought before it and subjected to a severe examination; then Count von Z—— himself formally declared that he recognized them as innocent of all misdeeds and all brigandage committed on his domain. They were restored to liberty and passports were granted them to continue their travels. As for the old woman in the scarlet rags, she had vanished, and no one knew whither she had gone. Everyone had his own opinion and his own conjectures upon the count's behavior. It was said that the leader of the gypsies had had a long interview with the count by night, in which extraordinary revelations were exchanged.

"Meantime Gabrielle's marriage was about to be celebrated. On the eve of the day fixed for the ceremony, Angelika had all her possessions put on a coach and left the castle, accompanied in her flight by a single woman who was said to look very much like a gypsy. Count von Z——, to avoid scandal, gave this flight a plausible motive, announcing that his daughter, distressed by a marriage that aroused her jealousy, had asked him to give her a little house in W——; she had declared that she wished to retire to it and end her days in complete solitude. After the wedding, Count S—— went with his bride to a domain at D——, where for a year they enjoyed the most perfect felicity; suddenly the count's health broke down for no cause that could be divined; an internal complaint seemed to eat away his vital organs; he refused all attention, and his wife could not get from him any confession of the hidden malady under which he was becoming exhausted with languor. At length, after long resistance he gave way to the doctors, who prescribed a journey to distract his mind. He went to Pisa. Gabrielle, who was on the point of giving birth to a child, could not accompany him. The little girl she brought into the world disappeared shortly after the birth without a trace, and without its being possible to fix suspicion for the kidnapping on anyone whomsoever. The mother's agony was pitiable, and to add to her distress there arrived a message from her father, Count von Z——, informing her that Count S——, instead of being at Pisa, had just died at W——, in the little lonely house to which Angelika had retired; and Angelika had fallen into a fearful condition of dementia, against which the physicians declared themselves powerless.

"Poor Gabrielle went home to her father. One night as she lay brooding over the twofold loss of her husband and her child the sound of sobbing fell upon her ears. She listened: the feeble sound seemed to come from a room adjoining her bedchamber; she rose up disquieted, took a night light, and softly opened the door. What did she behold! the gypsy of the scarlet rags sitting on the floor, her eye dull and staring; in her arms leaped a baby uttering tiny cries. A mother's instinct is seldom at fault. Countess Gabrielle knew her child at once; she darted forward and seized the babe from the old savage's arms; the other tried to resist, but the violent effort finally broke what little strength was left to her, and she fell back heavily to rise no more. The countess uttered cries of affright. The footmen were on the alert, everybody ran up, but there was nothing left but a corpse to be laid in earth. Count von Z—— betook himself to the little house in W—— to question Angelika with regard to the babe lost and found again. In her father's presence, the poor madwoman seemed to recover a few moments of sanity; but presently the malady reasserted its fatal sway. Angelika began to wander, her features became distorted and assumed a horrible likeness to the face of the old gypsy. She wept and sobbed; then in hoarse and frantic accents she begged everyone to go away and leave her alone.

"The unhappy father gives the world to understand that the madwoman is shut up in one of his castles; but the truth is that Angelika has refused to leave her retreat; she lives alone in the little house where Count S—— came to die beside her. The secret of what took place at the last between those two has remained undivulged and impenetrable.

"Count von Z—— is dead. Gabrielle has come with Edwina to W—— to settle the family affairs. As for the recluse of the deserted house, she is at the brutal discretion of the old servingman whom solitude has turned into a maniac."

Doctor K—— ended his story by saying that my unexpected presence in the deserted house had produced on Angelika's blurred senses a shock the result of which might very well restore equilibrium to her faculties. In any case, the lovely image I had seen reflected in my pocket mirror was that of Edwina, who at the moment of my inquisitive watching was visiting Angelika's retreat. A few days after these happenings, which had so nearly unbalanced my brain, feelings of blackest melancholy forced me to give up residing in W—— for a long period. And this strange influence was not entirely dissipated until after the death of the poor mad lady.

Russian Pioneer of Realism

"The Pistol Shot," written about 1829, precedes in time most of the stories in this book and lacks some of the craftsmanship resulting from the theories of later writers such as Hawthorne and Poe. Pushkin was a daring experimenter, however, and often hit upon a most effective way to tell a modern story. This account of the fate of a duelist is ironic, for Pushkin died at the age of thirty-seven years as the result of wounds received in a duel defending his wife's honor.

ALEXANDER PUSHKIN

The founder of modern Russian literature, by whom most of the later writers of that country were influenced, Pushkin, during his brief life, was outstanding as poet, novelist, critic, and storyteller.

Alexander Sergeevich Pushkin (1799–1837) was born in Moscow of a noble but poor family. He had Negro blood; his mother's grandfather was Abraham Gannibal, son of an Abyssinian prince, who was bought as a slave at the age of eight and became a favorite of Peter the Great of Russia. Alexander was educated at a school later renamed for him. He graduated at the age of seventeen and entered the civil service, but spent much time among the gay social circles of St. Petersburg. His first volume of poetry in 1820 brought him celebrity. Soon after, he was banished by the Czar to southern Russia because of his outspoken poems in praise of political liberty, but he continued to hold government positions until 1824, when he settled on his father's estate and devoted himself to becoming Russia's greatest poet. Influenced by such English authors as Shakespeare and Sir Walter Scott, he forged a new kind of Russian prose noted for its richness of content, brilliant thought, and realistic attitude toward life.

ALEXANDER PUSHKIN

The Pistol Shot

I

"We fired at each other."—*Bariatynski*
"I vowed to kill him, according to the code of dueling, and I still have my shot to fire."—*A Night on Guard*

WE WERE IN CAMP in the village of ——. Everyone knows the life of an officer of the line: in the morning, drill and horseback exercise; then comes dinner with the colonel of the regiment, or else at the Jewish restaurant; and at night drinks and cards. At ——, there were no entertainments of any kind, for no one had a marriageable daughter to bring out. We spent our time in each other's quarters, and at our evening gatherings there were uniforms only.

However, there was one man in our set who was not a soldier. He must have been about thirty-five and consequently we looked upon him as quite old. His experience had great weight with us, and besides his reserve, his grand air and sarcastic manner made a deep impression on us young men. There seemed to be something mysterious about his life. He looked like a Russian, though he bore a foreign name. In days gone by he had been in a regiment of Hussars where he was quite prominent at one time; but suddenly he had sent in his resignation, no one knew why, and had retired to this poor out-of-the-way village, where he fared very badly, while at the same time spending much money. He always wore a shabby overcoat and still he kept open house where every officer was made welcome. To tell the truth, his dinners generally consisted of two or three simple dishes prepared by his servant, an old discharged soldier, but the champagne always flowed. No one knew anything of his circumstances or his means, and no one dared ask him any questions on the subject. There were plenty of books in his house—mostly military—and a few novels. He lent them willingly and never asked for them again; on the other hand, he never returned those he borrowed. His one pastime was pistol shooting. The walls of his room were riddled with bullets, giving it the appearance of a honeycomb. A rich collection of pistols was the only luxury to be seen in the miserable house he occupied. The accuracy of his aim was remarkable, and if he had taken a bet that he could shoot the pompon on a helmet, not one of us would have hesitated to put the helmet on. Sometimes we talked of dueling, but Silvio (I will give him that name) never opened his lips on the subject. If someone asked him had he ever fought a duel, he answered shortly that he had, and that was all; he never entered into any particulars and it was evident that he disliked being asked such questions. We surmised that the death of one of his victims had left a blight on his life. Never for a minute would any of us have thought that he could have been guilty of faintheartedness. There are some people whose very appearance precludes such an idea.

One day eight or ten of our officers were dining at Silvio's. We drank as much as usual, that is, excessively. When dinner was over, we begged of our host to take the bank in a game of faro. After refusing to do so, for he seldom played, he finally called for cards and laying fifty ducats on the table before him, he sat down and shuffled. We formed in a circle about him and the game began. When playing, Silvio never uttered a word, neither objecting nor explaining. If a player made a mistake, he paid out exactly the amount due him or else credited it to himself. We were all familiar with his manner of playing and always let him have his own way. But on the day I speak of, there was with us an officer newly arrived who, through absentmindedness, doubled his stakes on a certain card. Silvio took the chalk and marked down what was due him. The officer, convinced that there was a mistake, made some objections. Silvio, still mute, went on dealing as if he had not heard. The officer, out of patience by this time, took the brush and wiped off the figures. Silvio picked up the chalk and wrote them down again. At this, the officer, excited by the wine, by the play

The Pistol Shot

and the laughter of his comrades, and thinking he had been insulted, took up a brass candlestick and hurled it at Silvio, who by bending aside, averted the blow. Great was the uproar! Silvio rose, pale with rage, and with eyes blazing:

"My dear sir," he said, "you will please leave this room, and be thankful that this has happened in my house."

Not one of us doubted the outcome of this fray, and we all looked upon our new comrade as a dead man. The officer went out saying he was ready to meet the banker just as soon as it was convenient. The game proceeded a few minutes longer, but it was evident that the master of the house was not paying much attention to what was going on; we all left, one by one, and returned to our quarters discussing the while the vacancy in our ranks which was sure to take place.

Next morning, while at riding exercise, we all wondered if the poor lieutenant were dead or alive, when, to our surprise, he appeared among us. We plied him with questions and he answered that he had had no challenge from Silvio, which caused us all much surprise. We called on Silvio and found him in his yard, firing bullet after bullet at an ace nailed to the door. He received us in his usual manner, never mentioning the scene of the night before. Three days went by and the lieutenant was still alive. We kept saying to each other: "Will Silvio not fight?" amazed at such a thing. But Silvio did not fight. He simply gave a very lame explanation and that was all that was said.

This forbearance on his part did him much harm among us young men. A want of courage is never quite forgiven by youth, for to him fearlessness is the greatest quality one can possess and it excuses many faults. Still, after a while, all this was forgotten and by degrees Silvio regained his old ascendency over us.

I, alone, could never feel the same toward him. Being of a romantic turn of mind, I had loved this man, whose life was an enigma to us all, more than anyone else, and I had made him, in my thoughts, the hero of some mysterious drama. And he liked me, of this I felt sure, for when we were alone, dropping his sharp and sarcastic speeches, he would converse on all sorts of subjects, and unbend to me in a fascinating manner. Ever since that unlucky evening I speak of, the fact that he had been insulted and had not wiped out the offense in blood worried me to such an extent that I never could feel at ease with him as in the days gone by. I even avoided looking at him, and Silvio was too clever and quick not to notice and guess at the reason. He seemed to me to feel it deeply. On two occasions, I thought I detected a wish on his part to explain matters, but I avoided him and he did not follow me. After that I never saw him except when others were present, and we never again resumed our intimate talks.

Those happy mortals who live in cities, where there is so much to see and do, can never imagine how important certain small happenings can become in an out-of-the-way village or town. One of these is the arrival of the mail. Tuesdays and Fridays, the offices of our regiment were besieged with men. One expected money, another a letter, and again others looked for newspapers. As a rule, everything was opened and read on the spot; news was given and the improvised post office was full of animation. Silvio's letters were addressed in care of our regiment and he called for them with us. One day a letter was handed to him, the seal of which he broke hurriedly. While reading it his eyes flashed with excitement. None of the officers but myself noticed this, as they were all busy reading their own letters.

"Gentlemen," said Silvio, "business compels me to leave town immediately. I must go tonight. I hope none of you will refuse to dine with me for the last time. I will expect you," said he, turning to me pointedly. "I hope you will not disappoint me."

After saying which he went away in great haste, and we all retired to our own quarters, agreeing to meet at his house later.

I arrived at Silvio's at the hour he had named and found almost the whole regiment there. Everything he possessed was packed and the bare walls riddled with bullets stared back at us. We sat down to dinner and our host was in such a jovial mood that before long we were all in the greatest of spirits. Corks flew about; the froth rose in our glasses, which we refilled as rapidly as they emptied. We all felt great affection for our host and wished him a pleasant journey with joy and prosperity at the end of it. It was very late when we got up from the table and while we were all picking out our caps in the hall, Silvio took me by the hand and detained me as I was about to leave.

"I must speak to you," he said in a low tone.

So I remained after the others went away and, seated facing each other, we smoked our pipes in silence for a while. Silvio seemed worried, and there was no trace of the feverish gaiety he had displayed in the earlier part of the evening. This dreadful pallor, the brilliancy of his eyes, and the long puffs of smoke he blew from his mouth, gave him the appearance of a fiend. After a few minutes he broke the silence.

"It may be," he said, "that we will never see each other again; before we part, I wish to explain certain things to you. You have noticed, perhaps, that I attach very little importance to the average man's opinion, but I like you and I feel I cannot leave without seeing you think better of me than you do."

He stopped to shake the ashes out of his pipe. I remained silent and avoided looking at him.

"It may have seemed strange to you," he continued, "that I did not ask any satisfaction from that drunkard, that young fool R——. You will admit that, having the choice of weapons, he was at my mercy and that there was not much chance of his killing me. I might call it generosity on my part, but I will not lie about it. If I could have given R—— a good lesson, without in any way risking my life, he would not have been rid of me so easily."

I looked at Silvio in the greatest surprise. Such an admission from him was astounding. He went on:

"As it is, unhappily, I have no right to risk my life. Six years ago, I received a blow and the man who struck me is still alive."

This excited my curiosity to an unusual degree.

"You did not meet him?" I asked. "Surely some extraordinary circumstance must have prevented your doing so?"

"I did meet him," answered Silvio, "and here you see the result of our encounter."

He rose and drew from a box near him a cap of red cloth with a gilt braid and tassel such as Frenchmen call *bonnet de police*. He put it on his head and I saw that a bullet had pierced it about an inch above the forehead.

"You know," said Silvio, "that I was in the Hussars of——, and you also know what kind of a disposition I have: I like to rule everyone. Well, in my youth, it was positively a passion with me. In my day, brawlers were in fashion and I was the foremost brawler of the regiment. To get drunk was then considered a thing to be proud of; I could outdrink the famous B——, celebrated in song by D. D——. Every day brought its duel, and every day saw me either the principal actor in one or else taking the part of a second. My comrades looked up to me, and our superior officers, who were constantly being transferred, considered me a plague of which they could not be rid.

"As for me, I kept on quietly (or rather riotously) in my glorious career, when one day there was transferred to our regiment a young fellow who was very wealthy and of good family. I will not name him to you, but never have I met a fellow with such unheard-of luck. Imagine having youth, a fine figure, no end of spirits, a daring which was utterly indifferent to danger, a great name, and unlimited means to do with as he liked, and you may have a faint idea of the impression he created among us. My power was gone in an instant. At first, dazzled by my reputation, he tried to make friends with me; but I received his advances very coldly, seeing which, he quietly dropped me without showing any annoyance whatever. I took such a dislike to him, when I saw his popularity in the regiment and his success with the ladies, that I was driven almost to despair. I tried to pick a quarrel with him, but to my sarcastic remarks he answered with caustic and unexpected wit that had the merit besides of being more cheerful than mine. He was always in jest, while I was in dead earnest. Finally one night, while at a ball in a Polish house, seeing how much the ladies admired him, especially our hostess with whom I had been very friendly, I whispered in his ear some insulting remark which I have long since forgotten. He turned around and struck me. We grasped our swords, some of the ladies fainted, and a few officers parted us. We went out immediately to fight it out right then and there.

"The three witnesses and myself reached the meeting place, and I awaited the coming of my adversary with no ordinary impatience. The sun rose, and its intense heat was being felt more and more every minute when I finally saw him coming in the distance. He was on foot and in his shirt-sleeves, carrying his uniform over his arm—he was attended by only one witness. I went forward to meet him, and I noticed that his cap, which he carried in his hand, was full of cherries. Our witnesses placed us twelve paces from each other. It was my privilege to shoot first, but what with passion and hatred blinding me I feared my aim would be poor, and to gain time to steady my hand, I offered to let him fire first. He refused to do so, and it was then agreed we would leave it to chance. Luck was, as usual, with this spoilt child of fortune. He fired and pierced my cap. It was now my turn, and I felt he was at my mercy. I looked at him with eagerness, hoping to find him at least a little uneasy. Not at all, for there he stood, within range of my pistol, coolly picking the ripest cherries out of his cap and blowing the pits in my direction where they fell at my feet.

" 'What will I gain,' thought I, 'by taking his life, when he thinks so little of it?'

"A diabolical thought crossed my mind. I unloaded a pistol.

" 'It seems,' I said, 'that you care very little whether you die or not at the present moment. You seem more anxious to breakfast instead. It will be as you please. I have no wish to disturb you.'

" 'You will be kind enough to attend to your own business,' answered he, 'and to please fire, . . . but after all you may do as you like.

The Pistol Shot

You can always fire your shot when and where you like. I will always be at your call.'

"I went away with my witnesses to whom I said that I did not care to shoot just then, and the thing ended there.

"I sent in my resignation and retired to this out-of-the-way village. From that day to this, I have thought of nothing but revenge. And now, the time has come . . . !"

Silvio drew from his pocket the letter received that morning. Someone, his lawyer it seemed, had written from Moscow that the *person in question* was soon to be married to a young and pretty girl.

"You can guess, I have no doubt," said Silvio, "who is *the person in question*. I am leaving for Moscow and we will see if he will look at death in the midst of bridal festivities with as much coolness as he did when facing it with a pound of cherries in his cap!"

After saying these words he rose and, throwing his cap viciously on the floor, he walked back and forth the length of the room like a caged tiger. I had listened to him without saying a word, stirred by very contradictory feelings.

A servant entered saying the carriage was at the door. Silvio grasped my hand, which he shook with all his might. He entered a small open carriage where were two boxes already, one containing his pistols and the other his luggage. We said good-bye once more, and he was driven away.

II

Years went by, when family matters compelled me to live in an obscure village in the district of ——. While looking after my interests, I often sighed for the enjoyable life I had led until then. The long solitary evenings of winter and spring were the hardest to bear. I could not become reconciled to their lonesomeness. Until the dinner hour I managed somehow to kill time by chatting with the starosty (Polish landowner) visiting my workmen, and watching the new buildings being erected. But as soon as night came I was at a loss to know what to do. I knew by heart the few books I had found in the ancient bookcases and in the garret. All the stories known to my old housekeeper, Kirilovna, I had asked her to tell me over and over again, and the songs of the peasants saddened me. I drank everything at hand, soft drinks and others, until my head ached. I will even admit that at one time I thought I should become a drunkard from sheer desperation, the worst kind of drunkard, of which this district offered me a good many examples.

My nearest neighbors consisted of two or three of these confirmed inebriates, whose conversations were forever interspersed with sighs and hiccoughs, so that even complete solitude was to be preferred to their society. I finally got into the habit of dining as late as possible and retiring as early as I could afterward, and in that way I solved the problem of shortening the evenings and lengthening the days.

About four versts from my house was a beautiful property belonging to the Countess B——. It was occupied by her steward, the Countess herself never having lived in the place but a month at a time, and that in the first year of her marriage.

One day, in the second year of this lonely existence of mine, I heard that the Countess and her husband were to occupy their residence during the summer months. In the early part of June, they arrived with all their household.

The coming of a rich neighbor is always an event in the life of country people. The owners of property and their servants also speak of it two months before they arrive, and it is still a topic of interest three years after they have left. For my part, the fact that a young and pretty woman would live so near upset me very much. I was dying to see her, and the first Sunday after they were settled, I walked over after dinner to pay my respects to the lady and introduce myself as her nearest neighbor and her devoted slave.

A footman led me to the Count's library and left to announce me. This library was large and magnificently furnished. Against the walls were shelves filled with books, and on each one was a figure in bronze; above a marble mantelpiece stood a large mirror. The floor was covered with green cloth over which were thrown rich Persian rugs. Unused as I was in my hovel to any kind of luxury, it was so long since I had seen anything like this display of wealth that I actually felt timid and experienced inward tremblings while waiting for the Count, such as a country solicitor might feel when asking an audience of a minister. The door opened and a young man, about thirty-two years of age, entered. He greeted me in a most cordial and charming manner. I tried to appear at ease and was just going to make the usual commonplace remarks about being delighted at having such neighbors when he forestalled me by saying how welcome I was.

We sat down and his manner was so cordial that it soon dispelled my unusual timidity. I was just beginning to feel like my old self again

The Pistol Shot

when the Countess appeared in the doorway, and once more I grew desperately shy. She was a beauty. The Count introduced me and the more I tried to be natural and quite at ease, the more I looked awkward and embarrassed. My hosts, in order to give me time to recover from my bashfulness, chatted together, as if to show that they considered me an old acquaintance already and one to be treated as such, so that while walking about the library I looked at the books and pictures. As far as pictures are concerned, I am no connoisseur, but there was one there that attracted my attention. It represented a Swiss scene, and the beauty of the landscape did not attract me quite as much as did the fact that the canvas was pierced by two bullets evidently fired one on the other.

"That is a pretty good shot!" I cried, turning toward the Count.

"Yes," said he, "and rather a peculiar one. Are you a pistol shot?" he added.

"Why, yes, a fairly good one," I answered, delighted to have a chance to speak of something with which I was familiar. "I think I could hit a card at thirty paces, with my own pistols of course."

"Really?" said the Countess, seemingly much interested. "And you, my dear," this to her husband, "could you hit a card at thirty paces?"

"I don't know about that," answered the Count, "I was a pretty good shot in my day, but it must be four years now since I used a pistol."

"In that case, sir," I continued, "I'll bet you anything that even at twenty paces you could not hit a card; because to excel at pistol shooting one requires constant practice. I know this from experience. At home, I was considered one of the best shots in the regiment, but it happened once that I was a month without using a pistol, mine being at the gunsmith's. We were called to the shooting gallery one day, and what do you think happened to me, sir? I missed a bottle standing twenty-five paces away, four times in succession. There was with us at the time a major of cavalry, a good fellow, who was forever joking: 'Faith, my friend,' he said to me, 'this is too much moderation. You have too great a respect for the bottle.' Believe me, sir, one must practise all the time. Otherwise, one gets rusty. The best marksman I ever knew practised every day, firing at least three shots before his dinner; he would no more have missed them than he would have omitted his cognac before dinner."

Both the Count and his wife seemed pleased to listen to me.

"And how did he shoot?" asked the Count.

"How? Let me tell you. He would see a fly on the wall. .... You laugh? Madam——, I swear to you this is true. 'Eh! Kouska! a pistol!' Kouska would bring one loaded. Crack! there lay the fly flattened against the wall."

"What consummate skill!" cried the Count, "and what was this man's name?"

"Silvio, sir."

"Silvio!" cried the Count, starting to his feet. "You have known Silvio?"

"Have I known him? Well, rather. We were the greatest of friends; he was like one of us in the regiment. But it is five years now since I heard of him. And you also knew him?"

"Yes, I knew him well. Did he ever tell you a peculiar thing which happened to him once?"

"How he received a slap in the face, one evening, from a cad?"

"And did he tell you the name of this cad?"

"No, sir, he did not. Ah!" I cried, guessing at the truth. "Forgive me, sir, I did not know. Can it be you?"

"Yes, it was I," answered the Count, in an embarrassed manner, "and that picture with a hole in it is a souvenir of our last interview."

"For God's sake, my dear," said the Countess, "don't speak of it —the thought of it terrifies me to this day."

"No," said the Count. "I feel I ought to tell this gentleman. He knows how I offended his friend and it is only fair that he should learn how he revenged himself."

The Count drew an armchair for me to sit in, and I listened with the greatest interest to the following story:

"Five years ago we were married. We spent the first month of our honeymoon here in this house, and to it clings the memory of the happiest days of my life, coupled with one of the most painful experiences I have ever had.

"One evening, we had both gone out horseback riding. My wife's horse became very restless and she was so frightened that she begged me to lead him to the stables and she would walk back by herself. On reaching the house, I found a traveling coach at the door and was told that a man was waiting in the library. He had refused to give his name, saying he wished to see me on business. I came into this room and in the half light I saw a man with a beard standing before the mantelpiece, still in his dusty traveling clothes. I drew nearer to him, trying to place him in my memory.

"'You do not remember me, Count?' said he, in a voice that shook.

The Pistol Shot

" 'Silvio!' I cried.

"And to be candid with you, I felt as if my hair were standing on end.

" 'Exactly,' he continued, 'and it is my turn to shoot. I have come to fire. Are you ready?'

"I saw a pistol sticking out of his left pocket. I measured twelve paces and stood there in that corner, begging him to be quick about it, as my wife would return in a few moments. He said he wanted a light first, and I rang for candles.

"I closed the door after giving orders not to admit anyone, and once more I told him to proceed. He raised his pistol and took aim.... I was counting the seconds.... I was thinking of her.... All this lasted a full minute and suddenly Silvio lowered his weapon.

" 'I am very sorry,' he said, 'but my pistol is not loaded with cherry pits ... and bullets are hard.... After all, come to think of it, this does not look much like a duel. It is more like a murder. I am not in the habit of firing on an unarmed man. Let us begin all over again. Let us draw lots to see who will shoot first.'

"My head was in a whirl, and it turned out that I refused at first. Finally, we loaded our pistols and we put two papers in the very cap I had once perforated with a bullet. I took one of the papers and as luck would have it, I drew number one.

" 'You are devilish lucky, Count!' said he, with a smile I will never forget.

"I cannot to this day understand it, but he finally compelled me to fire, ... and my bullet hit that picture there."

The Count pointed to the landscape with the hole in it. His face was crimson. There was the Countess as white as a sheet, and as for me I barely suppressed a cry.

"I fired at him," continued the Count, "and thank God, I missed him.

"Then Silvio—at that moment he was positively hideous—stood back and took aim. Just then, the door opened. My wife came in and seeing us facing each other, threw herself in my arms. Her presence gave me back my courage.

" 'My dear,' I said, 'do you not see that we are only jesting? How frightened you are! Go now, get a glass of water and come back to us. I will then introduce my old friend and comrade to you.'

"But my wife knew better than to believe my words.

" 'Tell me, is what my husband says true?' she asked of the terrible Silvio. 'Is it true that this is only a jest?'

" 'He is always jesting, Madam,' replied Silvio. 'Once upon a time he gave me a slap, in jest; again, in jest, he pierced my cap with a bullet; and a few minutes ago, still jesting, he just missed me. Now it is my turn to laugh a little.'

"Saying which, he took aim once more, with my wife looking on. She fell on her knees at his feet.

" 'Get up, Marsha!' I cried enraged. 'Are you not ashamed of yourself? And you, sir, do you wish to drive this poor woman crazy? Will you please fire, yes or no?'

" 'I will not,' answered Silvio, 'I am satisfied. I saw you falter. You were pale with fright, and that is all I hoped to see. I compelled you to fire on me and I know you will never forget me. I leave you to your conscience.'

"He walked toward the door and turning round, he glanced at the picture with the bullet hole and without aiming at all, he fired, and doubled my shot. Then he went out. My wife fainted—none of the servants dared stop him, and the doors opened before him in great haste. On the porch he called for his carriage, and he was already some distance when I recovered from my bewilderment."

The Count stopped.

It was thus I heard the end of a story, the beginning of which interested me much. I have never seen Silvio. It was said that at the time of the insurrection of Alexander Ypsilanti, he was at the head of a regiment of rebels and that he was killed when their army was routed at Skouliani.

Witches in the Wood

NATHANIEL HAWTHORNE

Hawthorne, who along with Poe might be considered the inventor of the modern short story in English, is still widely read and studied in many languages.

Nathaniel Hawthorne (1804–1864) was born in Salem, Massachusetts, the only son of a Puritan family that went back to 1630 in America. After taking a degree at Bowdoin College, he spent a dozen years in Salem, forging his literary art in solitude. A novel published in 1828 was so unsatisfactory to him that he soon destroyed all the copies he could find and turned to the shorter form. He began contributing to gift-books and early magazines, but the rewards were few until the publication of his first series of *Twice-Told Tales* in 1837 brought him a wider audience and appreciation from many fellow craftsmen like Poe, Melville, and, later, Henry James.

During the twenty years when Hawthorne was turning out short stories, he often used fanciful situations such as those found in the German tale-tellers like E. T. W. Hoffmann and Ludwig Tieck, but his deep moral sense and artistic taste usually kept him from their extravagance. His style is clear and harmonious, yet filled with echoing overtones and hints of the supernatural (although he usually offers a rational explanation for hardheaded readers to choose if they wish). On the other hand, his serious purpose sometimes produces characters who are less individuals than walking personifications of some virtue or vice. He is a master of the story of atmosphere, in which setting forms a motivating force. He turned the romantic tale from a toy of wild fantasy to an instrument for suggesting the most important questions of life. He often demonstrated that a story could be a unified study of one intense situation. And he made fiction respectable, even in conservative New England.

The region of Hawthorne's birth and the lore of his ancestors gave him much material for his fiction, such as *The Scarlet Letter* and "Young Goodman Brown." Stories of devil worship had been current in Salem at least since 1692, when Nathaniel's ancestor John was a hanging judge in the famed witchcraft trials. "Hawthorne was the first writer in America," it has been said, "to deal profoundly with the most serious problem that confronts man: the problem of good and evil." Although not himself a Puritan, Hawthorne was haunted by a vision of the original sin that put a curse on humanity, and often must have felt himself surrounded by a witches' sabbath that would condemn him to the loss of heaven and the pains of hell. Yet he considered the greatest sin to be guilty withdrawal from the rest of mankind.

NATHANIEL HAWTHORNE

Young Goodman Brown

YOUNG GOODMAN BROWN came forth at sunset into the street at Salem village; but put his head back, after crossing the threshold, to exchange a parting kiss with his young wife. And Faith, as the wife was aptly named, thrust her own pretty head into the street, letting the wind play with the pink ribbons of her cap while she called to Goodman Brown.

"Dearest heart," whispered she, softly and rather sadly, when her lips were close to his ear, "prithee put off your journey until sunrise and sleep in your own bed tonight. A lone woman is troubled with such dreams and such thoughts that she's afeard of herself sometimes. Pray tarry with me this night, dear husband, of all nights in the year."

"My love and my Faith," replied young Goodman Brown, "of all nights in the year, this one night must I tarry away from thee. My journey, as thou callest it, forth and back again, must needs be done 'twixt now and sunrise. What, my sweet, pretty wife, dost thou doubt me already, and we but three months married?"

"Then God bless you!" said Faith, with the pink ribbons; "and may you find all well when you come back."

"Amen!" cried Goodman Brown. "Say thy prayers, dear Faith, and go to bed at dusk, and no harm will come to thee."

So they parted; and the young man pursued his way until, being about to turn the corner by the meetinghouse, he looked back and saw the head of Faith still peeping after him with a melancholy air, in spite of her pink ribbons.

"Poor little Faith!" thought he, for his heart smote him. "What a wretch am I to leave her on such an errand! She talks of dreams, too.

Methought as she spoke there was trouble in her face, as if a dream had warned her what work is to be done tonight. But no, no; it would kill her to think it. Well, she's a blessed angel on earth; and after this one night I'll cling to her skirts and follow her to heaven."

With this excellent resolve for the future, Goodman Brown felt himself justified in making more haste on his present evil purpose. He had taken a dreary road, darkened by all the gloomiest trees of the forest, which barely stood aside to let the narrow path creep through, and closed immediately behind. It was all as lonely as could be; and there is this peculiarity in such a solitude, that the traveler knows not who may be concealed by the innumerable trunks and the thick boughs overhead; so that with lonely footsteps he may yet be passing through an unseen multitude.

"There may be a devilish Indian behind every tree," said Goodman Brown to himself; and he glanced fearfully behind him as he added, "What if the devil himself should be at my very elbow!"

His head being turned back, he passed a crook of the road, and, looking forward again, beheld the figure of a man, in grave and decent attire, seated at the foot of an old tree. He arose at Goodman Brown's approach and walked onward side by side with him.

"You are late, Goodman Brown," said he. "The clock of the Old South was striking as I came through Boston, and that is full fifteen minutes agone."

"Faith kept me back a while," replied the young man, with a tremor in his voice, caused by the sudden appearance of his companion, though not wholly unexpected.

It was now deep dusk in the forest, and deepest in that part of it where these two were journeying. As nearly as could be discerned, the second traveler was about fifty years old, apparently in the same rank of life as Goodman Brown, and bearing a considerable resemblance to him, though perhaps more in expression than features. Still, they might have been taken for father and son. And yet, though the elder person was as simply clad as the younger, and as simple in manner too, he had an indescribable air of one who knew the world, and who would not have felt abashed at the Governor's dinner table or in King William's court, were it possible that his affairs should call him thither. But the only thing about him that could be fixed upon as remarkable was his staff, which bore the likeness of a great black snake, so curiously wrought that it might almost be seen to twist and wriggle itself like a living serpent. This, of course, must have been an ocular deception, assisted by the uncertain light.

"Come, Goodman Brown," cried his fellow traveler, "this is a dull pace for the beginning of a journey. Take my staff, if you are so soon weary."

"Friend," said the other, exchanging his slow pace for a full stop, "having kept covenant by meeting thee here, it is my purpose now to return whence I came. I have scruples touching the matter thou wot'st of."

"Sayest thou so?" replied he of the serpent, smiling apart. "Let us walk on, nevertheless, reasoning as we go; and if I convince thee not thou shalt turn back. We are but a little way in the forest yet."

"Too far! too far!" exclaimed the good man, unconsciously resuming his walk. "My father never went into the woods on such an errand, nor his father before him. We have been a race of honest men and good Christians since the days of the martyrs; and shall I be the first of the name of Brown that ever took this path and kept—"

"Such company, thou wouldst say," observed the elder person, interpreting his pause. "Well said, Goodman Brown! I have been as well acquainted with your family as with ever a one among the Puritans; and that's no trifle to say. I helped your grandfather, the constable, when he lashed the Quaker woman so smartly through the streets of Salem; and it was I that brought your father a pitch-pine knot, kindled at my own hearth, to set fire to an Indian village, in King Philip's war. They were my good friends, both; and many a pleasant walk have we had along this path, and returned merrily after midnight. I would fain be friends with you for their sake."

"If it be as thou sayest," replied Goodman Brown, "I marvel they never spoke of these matters; or, verily, I marvel not, seeing that the least rumor of the sort would have driven them from New England. We are a people of prayer, and good works to boot, and abide no such wickedness."

"Wickedness or not," said the traveler with the twisted staff, "I have a very general acquaintance here in New England. The deacons of many a church have drunk the communion wine with me; the selectmen of divers towns make me their chairman; and a majority of the Great and General Court are firm supporters of my interest. The Governor and I, too— But these are state secrets."

"Can this be so?" cried Goodman Brown, with a stare of amazement at his undisturbed companion. "Howbeit, I have nothing to do with the Governor and Council; they have their own ways, and are no rule for a simple husbandman like me. But, were I to go on with thee, how should I meet the eye of that good old man, our minister, at Salem village? Oh, his voice would make me tremble both Sabbath day and lecture day."

Thus far the elder traveler had listened with due gravity; but now burst into a fit of irrepressible mirth, shaking himself so violently that his snake-like staff actually seemed to wriggle in sympathy.

"Ha! ha! ha!" shouted he again and again; then composing himself, "Well, go on, Goodman Brown, go on; but, prithee, don't kill me with laughing."

"Well, then, to end the matter at once," said Goodman Brown, considerably nettled, "there is my wife, Faith. It would break her dear little heart; and I'd rather break my own."

"Nay, if that be the case," answered the other, "e'en go thy ways, Goodman Brown. I would not for twenty old women like the one hobbling before us that Faith should come to any harm."

As he spoke he pointed his staff at a female figure on the path, in whom Goodman Brown recognized a very pious and exemplary dame, who had taught him his catechism in youth, and was still his moral and spiritual adviser, jointly with the minister and Deacon Gookin.

"A marvel, truly, that Goody Cloyse should be so far in the wilderness at nightfall," said he. "But with your leave, friend, I shall take a cut through the woods until we have left this Christian woman behind. Being a stranger to you, she might ask whom I was consorting with and whither I was going."

"Be it so," said his fellow traveler. "Betake you the woods, and let me keep the path."

Accordingly the young man turned aside, but took care to watch his companion, who advanced softly along the road until he had come within a staff's length of the old dame. She, meanwhile, was making the best of her way, with singular speed for so aged a woman, and mumbling some indistinct words—a prayer, doubtless—as she went. The traveler put forth his staff and touched her withered neck with what seemed the serpent's tail.

"The devil!" screamed the pious old lady.

"Then Goody Cloyse knows her old friend?" observed the traveler, confronting her and leaning on his writhing stick.

"Ah, forsooth, and is it your worship indeed?" cried the good dame. "Yea, truly is it, and in the very image of my old gossip, Goodman Brown, the grandfather of the silly fellow that now is. But—would your worship believe it?—my broomstick hath strangely disappeared, stolen, as I suspect, by that unhanged witch, Goody Cory, and that, too, when I was all anoited with the juice of smallage, and cinquefoil, and wolf's bane—"

"Mingled with fine wheat and the fat of a newborn babe," said the shape of old Goodman Brown.

"Ah, your worship knows the recipe," cried the old lady, cackling aloud. "So, as I was saying, being all ready for the meeting, and no horse to ride on, I made up my mind to foot it; for they tell me there is a nice young man to be taken into communion tonight. But now your good worship will lend me your arm, and we shall be there in a twinkling."

"That can hardly be," answered her friend. "I may not spare you my arm, Goody Cloyse; but here is my staff, if you will."

So saying, he threw it down at her feet, where, perhaps, it assumed life, being one of the rods which its owner had formerly lent to the Egyptian magi. Of this fact, however, Goodman Brown could not take cognizance. He had cast up his eyes in astonishment, and, looking down again, beheld neither Goody Cloyse nor the serpentine staff, but this fellow traveler alone, who waited for him as calmly as if nothing had happened.

"That old woman taught me my catechism," said the young man; and there was a world of meaning in this simple comment.

They continued to walk onward, while the elder traveler exhorted his companion to make good speed and persevere in the path, discoursing so aptly that his arguments seemed rather to spring up in the bosom of his auditor than to be suggested by himself. As they went, he plucked a branch of maple to serve for a walking stick, and began to strip it of the twigs and little boughs, which were wet with evening dew. The moment his fingers touched them they became strangely withered and dried up as with a week's sunshine. Thus the pair proceeded, at a good free pace, until suddenly, in a gloomy hollow of the road, Goodman Brown sat himself down on the stump of a tree and refused to go any farther.

"Friend," said he, stubbornly, "my mind is made up. Not another step will I budge on this errand. What if a wretched old woman do choose to go to the devil when I thought she was going to heaven: is that any reason why I should quit my dear Faith and go after her?"

"You will think better of this by and by," said his acquaintance, composedly. "Sit here and rest yourself a while; and when you feel like moving again, there is my staff to help you along."

Young Goodman Brown

Without more words, he threw his companion the maple stick, and was as speedily out of sight as if he had vanished into the deepening gloom. The young man sat a few moments by the roadside, applauding himself greatly, and thinking with how clear a conscience he should meet the minister in his morning walk, nor shrink from the eye of good old Deacon Gookin. And what calm sleep would be his that very night, which was to have been spent so wickedly, but so purely and sweetly now, in the arms of Faith! Amidst these pleasant and praiseworthy meditations, Goodman Brown heard the tramp of horses along the road, and deemed it advisable to conceal himself within the verge of the forest, conscious of the guilty purpose that had brought him thither, though now so happily turned from it.

On came the hoof tramps and the voices of the riders, two grave old voices, conversing soberly as they drew near. These mingled sounds appeared to pass along the road, within a few yards of the young man's hiding place; but, owing doubtless to the depth of the gloom at that particular spot, neither the travelers nor their steeds were visible. Though their figures brushed the small boughs by the wayside, it could not be seen that they intercepted, even for a moment, the faint gleam from the strip of bright sky athwart which they must have passed. Goodman Brown alternately crouched and stood on tiptoe, pulling aside the branches and thrusting forth his head as far as he durst without discerning so much as a shadow. It vexed him the more, because he could have sworn, were such a thing possible, that he recognized the voices of the minister and Deacon Gookin, jogging along quietly, as they were wont to do, when bound to some ordination or ecclesiastical council. While yet within hearing, one of the riders stopped to pluck a switch.

"Of the two, reverend sir," said the voice like the deacon's, "I had rather miss an ordination dinner than tonight's meeting. They tell me that some of our community are to be here from Falmouth and beyond, and others from Connecticut and Rhode Island, besides several of the Indian powwows, who, after their fashion, know almost as much deviltry as the best of us. Moreover, there is a goodly young woman to be taken into communion."

"Mightly well, Deacon Gookin!" replied the solemn old tones of the minister, "Spur up, or we shall be late. Nothing can be done, you know, until I get on the ground."

The hoofs clattered again; and the voices, talking so strangely in the empty air, passed on through the forest, where no church had ever been gathered or solitary Christian prayed. Whither, then, could these holy men be journeying so deep into the heathen wilderness? Young Goodman Brown caught hold of a tree for support, being ready to sink down on the ground, faint and overburdened with the heavy sickness of his heart. He looked up to the sky, doubting whether there really was a heaven above him. Yet there was the blue arch, and the stars brightening in it.

"With heaven above and Faith below, I will yet stand firm against the devil!" cried Goodman Brown.

While he still gazed upward into the deep arch of the firmament and had lifted his hands to pray, a cloud, though no wind was stirring, hurried across the zenith and hid the brightening stars. The blue sky was still visible, except directly overhead, where this black mass of cloud was sweeping swiftly northward. Aloft in the air, as if from the depths of the cloud, came a confused and doubtful sound of voices. Once the listener fancied that he could distinguish the accents of townspeople of his own, men and women, both pious and ungodly, many of whom he had met at the communion table, and had seen others rioting at the tavern. The next moment, so indistinct were the sounds, he doubted whether he had heard aught but the murmur of the old forest, whispering without a wind. Then came a stronger swell of those familiar tones, heard daily in the sunshine at Salem village, but never until now from a cloud of night. There was one voice, of a young woman, uttering lamentations, yet with an uncertain sorrow, and entreating for some favor, which, perhaps, it would grieve her to obtain; and all the unseen multitude, both saints and sinners, seemed to encourage her onward.

"Faith!" shouted Goodman Brown, in a voice of agony and desperation; and the echoes of the forest mocked him, crying, "Faith! Faith!" as if bewildered wretches were seeking her all through the wilderness.

The cry of grief, rage, and terror was yet piercing the night, when the unhappy husband held his breath for a response. There was a scream, drowned immediately in a louder murmur of voices, fading into far-off laughter, as the dark cloud swept away, leaving the clear and silent sky above Goodman Brown. But something fluttered lightly down through the air and caught on the branch of a tree. The young man seized it, and beheld a pink ribbon.

"My Faith is gone!" cried he, after one stupefied moment. "There is no good on earth; and sin is but a name. Come, devil; for to thee is this world given."

And, maddened with despair, so that he laughed loud and long, did Goodman Brown grasp his staff and set forth again, at such a rate that he seemed to fly along the forest path rather than to walk or run. The road grew wilder and drearier and more faintly traced, and vanished at length, leaving him in the heart of the dark wilderness, still rushing onward with the instinct that guides mortal man to evil. The whole forest was peopled with frightful sounds—the creaking of the trees, the howling of wild beasts, and the yell of Indians; while sometimes the wind tolled like a distant church bell, and sometimes gave a broad roar around the traveler, as if all Nature were laughing him to scorn. But he was himself the chief horror of the scene, and shrank not from its other horrors.

"Ha! ha! ha!" roared Goodman Brown when the wind laughed at him. "Let us hear which will laugh loudest. Think not to frighten me with your deviltry. Come witch, come wizard, come Indian powwow, come devil himself, and here comes Goodman Brown. You may as well fear him as he fear you."

In truth, all through the haunted forest there could be nothing more frightful than the figure of Goodman Brown. On he flew among the black pines, brandishing his staff with frenzied gestures, now giving vent to an inspiration of horrid blasphemy, and now shouting forth such laughter as set all the echoes of the forest laughing like demons around him. The fiend in his own shape is less hideous than when he rages in the breast of man. Thus sped the demoniac on his course, until, quivering among the trees, he saw a red light before him, as when the felled trunks and branches of a clearing have been set on fire, and throw up their lurid blaze against the sky, at the hour of midnight. He paused, in a lull of the tempest that had driven him onward, and heard the swell of what seemed a hymn, rolling solemnly from a distance with the weight of many voices. He knew the tune; it was a familiar one in the choir of the village meetinghouse. The verse died heavily away, and was lengthened by a chorus, not of human voices, but of all the sounds of the benighted wilderness pealing in awful harmony together. Goodman Brown cried out, and his cry was lost to his own ear by its unison with the cry of the desert.

In the interval of silence he stole forward until the light glared full upon his eyes. At one extremity of an open space, hemmed in by the dark wall of the forest, arose a rock, bearing some rude, natural resemblance either to an altar or a pulpit, and surrounded by four blazing pines, their tops aflame, their stems untouched, like candles at an evening meeting. The mass of foliage that had overgrown the summit of the rock was all on fire, blazing high into the night and fitfully illuminating the whole field. Each pendent twig and leafy festoon was in a blaze. As the red light arose and fell, a numerous congregation alternately shone forth, then disappeared in shadow, and again grew, as it were, out of the darkness, peopling the heart of the solitary woods at once.

"A grave and dark-clad company," quoth Goodman Brown.

In truth they were such. Among them, quivering to and fro between gloom and splendor, appeared faces that would be seen next day at the council board of the province, and others which, Sabbath after Sabbath, looked devoutly heavenward, and benignantly over the crowded pews, from the holiest pulpits in the land. Some affirm that the lady of the Governor was there. At least there were high dames well known to her, and wives of honored husbands, and widows, a great multitude, and ancient maidens, all of excellent repute, and fair young girls, who trembled lest their mothers should espy them. Either the sudden gleams of light flashing over the obscure field bedazzled Goodman Brown, or he recognized a score of the church members of Salem village famous for their especial sanctity. Good old Deacon Gookin had arrived, and waited at the skirts of that venerable saint, his revered pastor. But, irreverently consorting with these grave, reputable, and pious people, these elders of the church, these chaste dames and dewy virgins, there were men of dissolute lives and women of spotted fame, wretches given over to all mean and filthy vice, and suspected even of horrid crimes. It was strange to see that the good shrank not from the wicked, nor were the sinners abashed by the saints. Scattered also among their pale-faced enemies were the Indian priests, or powwows, who had often scared their native forest with more hideous incantations than any known to English witchcraft.

"But where is Faith?" thought Goodman Brown; and, as hope came into his heart, he trembled.

Another verse of the hymn arose, a slow and mournful strain, such as the pious love, but joined to words which expressed all that our nature can conceive of sin, and darkly hinted at far more. Unfathomable to mere mortals is the lore of fiends. Verse after verse was sung; and still the chorus of the desert swelled between like the deepest tone of a mighty organ; and with the final peal of that dreadful anthem there came a sound, as if the roaring wind, the rushing streams, the howling beasts, and every other voice of the unconcerted wilderness were mingling and according with the voice of guilty man in homage to the prince of all. The four blazing pines threw up a loftier flame, and obscurely discovered shapes and visages of horror on the smoke wreaths above the impious assembly. At the same moment the fire on the rock shot redly forth and formed a glowing arch above its base, where now appeared a figure. With reverence be it spoken, the figure bore no slight similitude, both in garb and manner, to some grave divine of the New England churches.

"Bring forth the converts!" cried a voice that echoed through the field and rolled into the forest.

At the word, Goodman Brown stepped forth from the shadow of the trees and approached the congregation, with whom he felt a loathful brotherhood by the sympathy of all that was wicked in his heart. He could have well-nigh sworn that the shape of his own dead father beckoned him to advance, looking downward from a smoke wreath, while a woman, with dim features of despair, threw out her hand to warn him back. Was it his mother? But he had no power to retreat one step, nor to resist, even in thought, when the minister and good old Deacon Gookin seized his arms and led him to the blazing rock. Thither came also the slender form of a veiled female, led between Goody Cloyse, that pious teacher of the catechism, and Martha Carrier, who had received the devil's promise to be queen of hell. A rampant hag was she. And there stood the proselytes beneath the canopy of fire.

"Welcome, my children," said the dark figure, "to the communion of your race. Ye have found thus young your nature and your destiny. My children, look behind you!"

They turned; and flashing forth, as it were, in a sheet of flame, the fiend worshippers were seen; the smile of welcome gleamed darkly on every visage.

"There," resumed the sable form, "are all whom ye have reverenced from youth. Ye deemed them holier than yourselves, and shrank from your own sin, contrasting it with their lives of righteousness and prayerful aspirations heavenward. Yet here are they all in my worshipping assembly. This night it shall be granted you to know their secret deeds: how hoary-bearded elders of the church have whispered wanton words to the young maids of their households; how many a woman, eager for widows' weeds, has given her husband a drink at bedtime and let him sleep his last sleep in her bosom; how beardless youths have made haste to inherit their fathers' wealth; and how fair damsels—blush not, sweet ones—have dug little graves in the garden, and bidden me, the sole guest, to an infant's funeral. By the sympathy of your human hearts for sin ye shall scent out all the places—whether in church, bedchamber, street, field, or forest—where crime has been committed, and shall exult to behold the whole earth one stain of guilt, one mighty blood spot. Far more than this. It shall be yours to penetrate, in every bosom, the deep mystery of sin, the fountain of all wicked arts, and which inexhaustibly supplies more evil impulses than human power—than my power at its utmost—can make manifest in deeds. And now, my children, look upon each other."

They did so; and, by the blaze of the hell-kindled torches, the wretched man beheld his Faith, and the wife her husband, trembling before that unhallowed altar.

"Lo, there ye stand, my children," said the figure, in a deep and solemn tone, almost sad with its despairing awfulness, as if his once angelic nature could yet mourn for our miserable race. "Depending upon one another's hearts, ye had still hoped that virtue were not all a dream. Now are ye undeceived. Evil is the nature of mankind. Evil must be your only happiness. Welcome again, my children, to the communion of your race."

"Welcome," repeated the fiend worshippers, in one cry of despair and triumph.

And there they stood, the only pair, as it seemed, who were yet hesitating on the verge of wickedness in this dark world. A basin was hollowed, naturally, in the rock. Did it contain water, reddened by the lurid light? or was it blood? or, perchance, a liquid flame? Herein did the shape of evil dip his hand and prepare to lay the mark of baptism upon their foreheads, that they might be partakers of the mystery of sin, more conscious of the secret guilt of others, both in deed and thought, than they could now be of their own. The husband cast one look at his pale wife, and Faith at him. What polluted wretches would the next glance show them to each other, shuddering alike at what they disclosed and what they saw!

"Faith! Faith!" cried the husband, "look up to heaven, and resist the wicked one."

Whether Faith obeyed he knew not. Hardly had he spoken when he found himself amid calm night and solitude, listening to a roar of the wind which died heavily away through the forest. He staggered against the rock, and felt it chill and damp; while a hanging twig, that had been all on fire, besprinkled his cheek with the coldest dew.

The next morning young Goodman Brown came slowly into the street of Salem village, staring around him like a bewildered man. The good old minister was taking a walk along the graveyard to get an appetite for breakfast and meditate his sermon, and bestowed a blessing, as he passed, on Goodman Brown. He shrank from the venerable saint as if to avoid an anathema. Old Deacon Gookin was at domestic worship, and the holy words of his prayer were heard through the open window. "What God doth the wizard pray to?" quoth Goodman Brown. Goody Cloyse, that excellent old Christian, stood in the early sunshine at her own lattice, catechizing a little girl who had brought her a pint of morning's milk. Goodman Brown snatched away the child as from the grasp of the fiend himself. Turning the corner by the meetinghouse, he spied the head of Faith, with the pink ribbons, gazing anxiously forth, and bursting into such joy at sight of him that she skipped along the street and almost kissed her husband before the whole village. But Goodman Brown looked sternly and sadly into her face, and passed on without a greeting.

Had Goodman Brown fallen asleep in the forest and only dreamed a wild dream of a witch meeting?

Be it so if you will; but, alas! it was a dream of evil omen for young Goodman Brown. A stern, a sad, a darkly meditative, a distrustful, if not a desperate man did he become from the night of that fearful dream. On the Sabbath day, when the congregation were singing a holy psalm, he could not listen because an anthem of sin rushed loudly upon his ear and drowned all the blessed strain. When the minister spoke from the pulpit with power and fervid eloquence, and, with his hand on the open Bible, of the sacred truths of our religion, and of saintlike lives and triumphant deaths, and of future bliss or misery unutterable, then did Goodman Brown turn pale, dreading lest the roof should thunder down upon the gray blasphemer and his hearers. Often, awaking suddenly at midnight, he shrank from the bosom of Faith; and at morning or eventide, when the family knelt down at prayer, he scowled and muttered to himself, and gazed sternly at his wife, and turned away. And when he had lived long, and was borne to his grave a hoary corpse, followed by Faith, an aged woman, and children and grandchildren, a goodly procession, besides neighbors not a few, they carved no hopeful verse upon his tombstone, for his dying hour was gloom.

Master of the Macabre

EDGAR ALLAN POE

Poe, who did more than anyone else to state the theory of the modern short story, is still widely read in many countries.

The life of Edgar Poe (1809-1849) is in many ways as "romantic" and macabre as the stories written by this genius. The future poet, critic, and short-story author was born in Boston, Massachusetts, son of a pair of traveling actors, both of whom died when he was small. He became the foster son of John Allan, a merchant in Richmond, Virginia, and thereafter signed himself Edgar Allan Poe. In 1826, he entered the University of Virginia. Poe had already begun to write verses and was a brilliant but extravagant student who was forced to leave after one term because Allan would not pay his gambling debts. The breach widened between Poe and Allan, who could not understand why anyone would wish to devote his life to literature.

Poe's first book of poems was printed in 1827. The same year, penniless, he enlisted in the United States Army, and later was given an honorable discharge in order to enter West Point. However, when Allan later disowned him, Poe deliberately neglected his duties and was dismissed in 1831. Thereafter, he was forced to survive by writing or depending upon the help of others. He began getting his stories in print in 1832, and won a place on the *Southern Literary Messenger*, edited in Richmond. There he married his fourteen-year-old cousin, Virginia Clemm, in 1836 and later took her and her mother to live in New York.

Poe was not only a writer, but an excellent editor, who served on the magazines then becoming popular; but instability, worries, and alcoholism always kept him from steady success. At times he went over the edge of sanity. His wife died of tuberculosis in New York in 1847. Less than three years later, Poe died in a Baltimore hospital, having in his relatively short life consumed himself in the Romantic tradition, but having also defined and exemplified the well-made short story aimed at a "single effect."

"The Fall of the House of Usher," first printed in 1839, is considered the most typical of Poe's "arabesque" stories. It has some obvious faults, but is still widely studied as a prime example of the "Gothic" story of character and atmosphere. Many critics differ on its precise meaning; it is as if they, peering into the dark tarn of the story, find themselves reflected, as did the main character, Roderick Usher. As one critic says: "In Roderick Usher ... we get for the first time the archetypal hero of modern fiction."

EDGAR ALLAN POE

The Fall of the House of Usher

Son coeur est un luth suspendu;
Sitôt qu'on le touche il résonne.
—DE BÉRANGER

*D*URING THE WHOLE of a dull, dark, and soundless day in the autumn of the year, when the clouds hung oppressively low in the heavens, I had been passing alone, on horseback, through a singularly dreary tract of country; and at length found myself, as the shades of the evening drew on, within view of the melancholy House of Usher. I know not how it was—but, with the first glimpse of the building, a sense of insufferable gloom pervaded my spirit. I say insufferable; for the feeling was unrelieved by any of that half-pleasurable, because poetic, sentiment with which the mind usually receives even the sternest natural images of the desolate or terrible. I looked upon the scene before me—upon the mere house, and the simple landscape features of the domain, upon the bleak walls, upon the vacant eyelike windows, upon a few rank sedges, and upon a few white trunks of decayed trees—with an utter depression of soul which I can compare to no earthly sensation more properly than to the after-dream of the reveler upon opium: the bitter lapse into everyday life, the hideous dropping off of the veil. There was an iciness, a sinking, a sickening of the heart, an unredeemed dreariness of thought which no goading of the imagination could torture into aught of the sublime. What was it—I paused to think—what was it that so unnerved me in the contemplation of the House of Usher? It was a mystery all insoluble; nor could I grapple with the shadowy fancies that crowded upon me as I pondered. I was forced to fall back upon the unsatisfactory conclusion that while, beyond doubt, there *are* combinations of very simple natural objects which have the power of thus affecting us, still the analysis of this power lies among considerations beyond our depth. It was possible, I reflected, that a mere different arrangement of the particulars of the scene, of the details of the picture, would be sufficient to modify, or perhaps to annihilate its capacity for sorrowful impression; and, acting upon this idea, I reined my horse to the precipitous brink of a black and lurid tarn that lay in unruffled luster by the dwelling, and gazed down—but with a shudder even more thrilling than before—upon the remodeled and inverted images of the gray sedge, and the ghastly tree stems, and the vacant and eyelike windows.

Nevertheless, in this mansion of gloom I now proposed to myself a sojourn of some weeks. Its proprietor, Roderick Usher, had been one of my boon companions in boyhood; but many years had elapsed since our last meeting. A letter, however, had lately reached me in a distant part of the country—a letter from him—which, in its wildly importunate nature, had admitted of no other than a personal reply. The MS. gave evidence of nervous agitation. The writer spoke of acute bodily illness, of a mental disorder which oppressed him, and of an earnest desire to see me, as his best, and indeed his only personal friend, with a view of attempting, by the cheerfulness of my society, some alleviation of his malady. It was the manner in which all this, and much more, was said—it was the apparent *heart* that went with his request—which allowed me no room for hesitation; and I accordingly obeyed forthwith what I still considered a very singular summons.

Although, as boys, we had been even intimate associates, yet I really knew little of my friend. His reserve had been always excessive and habitual. I was aware, however, that his very ancient family had been noted, time out of mind, for a peculiar sensibility of temperament, displaying itself, through long ages, in many works of exalted art, and manifested, of late, in repeated deeds of munificent yet unobtrusive charity, as well as in a passionate devotion to the intricacies, perhaps even more than to the orthodox and easily recognizable beauties, of musical science. I had learned, too, the very remarkable fact that the stem of the Usher race, all time-honored as it was, had put forth, at no period, any enduring branch; in other words, that the entire family lay in the direct line of descent, and had always, with

The Fall of the House of Usher

very trifling and very temporary variation, so lain. It was this deficiency, I considered, while running over in thought the perfect keeping of the character of the premises with the accredited character of the people, and while speculating upon the possible influence which the one, in the long lapse of centuries, might have exercised upon the other —it was this deficiency, perhaps, of collateral issue, and the consequent undeviating transmission, from sire to son, of the patrimony with the name, which had, at length, so identified the two as to merge the original title of the estate in the quaint and equivocal appellation of the "House of Usher"—an appellation which seemed to include, in the minds of the peasantry who used it, both the family and the family mansion.

I have said that the sole effect of my somewhat childish experiment, that of looking down within the tarn, had been to deepen the first singular impression. There can be no doubt that the consciousness of the rapid increase of my superstition—for why should I not so term it?—served mainly to accelerate the increase itself. Such, I have long known, is the paradoxical law of all sentiments having terror as a basis. And it might have been for this reason only that, when I again uplifted my eyes to the house itself from its image in the pool, there grew in my mind a strange fancy—a fancy, so ridiculous, indeed, that I but mention it to show the vivid force of the sensations which oppressed me. I had so worked upon my imagination as really to believe that about the whole mansion and domain there hung an atmosphere peculiar to themselves and their immediate vicinity: an atmosphere which had no affinity with the air of heaven, but which had reeked up from the decayed trees, and the gray wall, and the silent tarn: a pestilent and mystic vapor, dull, sluggish, faintly discernible, and leaden-hued.

Shaking off from my spirit what *must* have been a dream, I scanned more narrowly the real aspect of the building. Its principal feature seemed to be that of an excessive antiquity. The discoloration of ages had been great. Minute fungi overspread the whole exterior, hanging in a fine tangled web-work from the eaves. Yet all this was apart from any extraordinary dilapidation. No portion of the masonry had fallen; and there appeared to be a wild inconsistency between its still perfect adaptation of parts and the crumbling condition of the individual stones. In this there was much that reminded me of the specious totality of old woodwork which has rotted for long years in some neglected vault, with no disturbance from the breath of the external air. Beyond this indication of extensive decay, however, the fabric gave little token of instability. Perhaps the eye of a scrutinizing observer might have discovered a barely perceptible fissure which, extending from the roof of the building in front, made its way down the wall in a zigzag direction, until it became lost in the sullen waters of the tarn.

Noticing these things, I rode over a short causeway to the house. A servant in waiting took my horse, and I entered the Gothic archway of the hall. A valet, of stealthy step, thence conducted me, in silence, through many dark and intricate passages in my progress to the studio of his master. Much that I encountered on the way contributed, I know not how, to heighten the vague sentiments of which I have already spoken. While the objects around me—while the carvings of the ceilings, the somber tapestries of the walls, the ebon blackness of the floors, and the phantasmagoric armorial trophies which rattled as I strode, were but matters to which, or to such as which, I had been accustomed from my infancy—while I hesitated not to acknowledge how familiar was all this—I still wondered to find how unfamiliar were the fancies which ordinary images were stirring up. On one of the staircases, I met the physician of the family. His countenance, I thought, wore a mingled expression of low cunning and perplexity. He accosted me with trepidation and passed on. The valet now threw open a door and ushered me into the presence of his master.

The room in which I found myself was very large and lofty. The windows were long, narrow, and pointed, and at so vast a distance from the black oaken floor as to be altogether inaccessible from within. Feeble gleams of encrimsoned light made their way through the trellised panes, and served to render sufficiently distinct the more prominent objects around; the eye, however, struggled in vain to reach the remoter angles of the chamber, or the recesses of the vaulted and fretted ceiling. Dark draperies hung upon the walls. The general furniture was profuse, comfortless, antique, and tattered. Many books and musical instruments lay scattered about, but failed to give any vitality to the scene. I felt that I breathed an atmosphere of sorrow. An air of stern, deep, and irredeemable gloom hung over and pervaded all.

Upon my entrance, Usher arose from a sofa on which he had been lying at full length, and greeted me with a vivacious warmth which had much in it, I at first thought, of an overdone cordiality—of the constrained effort of the ennuyé man of the world. A glance, however, at his countenance convinced me of his perfect sincerity. We sat down; and for some moments, while he spoke not, I gazed upon him with a feeling half of pity, half of awe. Surely, man had never before so terribly altered, in so brief a period, as had Roderick Usher! It was with difficulty that I could bring myself to admit the identity of the wan being before me with the companion of my early boyhood. Yet the character of his face had been at all times remarkable. A cadaverousness of complexion; an eye large, liquid, and luminous beyond comparison, lips somewhat thin and very pallid, but of a surpassingly beautiful curve; a nose of a delicate Hebrew model, but with a breadth of nostril unusual in similar formations; a finely moulded chin, speaking, in its want of prominence, of a want of moral energy; hair of a more than weblike softness and tenuity; these features, with an inordinate expansion above the regions of the temple, made up altogether a countenance not easily to be forgotten. And now in the mere exaggeration of the prevailing character of these features, and of the expression they were wont to convey, lay so much of change that I doubted to whom I spoke. The now ghastly pallor of the skin, and the now miraculous luster of the eye, above all things startled and even awed me. The silken hair, too, had been suffered to grow all unheeded, and as, in its wild gossamer texture, it floated rather than fell about the face, I could not, even with effort, connect its arabesque expression with any idea of simple humanity.

In the manner of my friend I was at once struck with an incoherence, an inconsistency; and I soon found this to arise from a series of feeble and futile struggles to overcome an habitual trepidancy, an excessive nervous agitation. For something of this nature I had indeed been prepared, no less by his letter than by reminiscences of certain boyish traits, and by conclusions deduced from his peculiar physical conformation and temperament. His action was alternately vivacious and sullen. His voice varied rapidly from a tremulous indecision (when the animal spirits seemed utterly in abeyance) to that species of energetic concision—that abrupt, weighty, unhurried, and hollow-sounding enunciation—that leaden, self-balanced and perfectly modulated guttural utterance, which may be observed in the lost drunkard, or the irreclaimable eater of opium, during the periods of his most intense excitement.

It was thus that he spoke of the object of my visit, of his earnest desire to see me, and of the solace he expected me to afford him. He entered, at some length, into what he conceived to be the nature of his malady. It was, he said, a constitutional and a family evil, and one for which he despaired to find a remedy—a mere nervous affection, he immediately added, which would undoubtedly soon pass off. It displayed itself in a host of unnatural sensations. Some of these, as he detailed them, interested and bewildered me; although, perhaps, the terms, and the general manner of the narration had their weight. He suffered much from a morbid acuteness of the senses; the most insipid food was alone endurable; he could wear only garments of certain texture; the odors of all flowers were oppressive; his eyes were tortured by even a faint light; and there were but peculiar sounds, and these from stringed instruments, which did not inspire him with horror.

To an anomalous species of terror I found him a bounden slave. "I shall perish," said he, "I *must* perish in this deplorable folly. Thus, thus, and not otherwise, shall I be lost. I dread the events of the future, not in themselves, but in their results. I shudder at the thought of any, even the most trivial, incident, which may operate upon this intolerable agitation of soul. I have, indeed, no abhorrence of danger, except in its absolute effect—in terror. In this unnerved—in this pitiable condition, I feel that the period will sooner or later arrive when I must abandon life and reason together, in some struggle with the grim phantasm, *fear*."

I learned, moreover, at intervals, and through broken and equivocal hints, another singular feature of his mental condition. He was enchained by certain superstitious impressions in regard to the dwelling which he tenanted, and whence, for many years, he had never ventured forth—in regard to an influence whose suppositious force was conveyed in terms too shadowy here to be restated—an influence which some peculiarities in the mere form and substance of his family mansion had, by dint of long sufferance, he said, obtained over his spirit—an effect which the physique of the gray walls and turrets, and of the dim tarn into which they all looked down, had, at length, brought about upon the morale of his existence.

He admitted, however, although with hesitation, that much of the peculiar gloom which thus afflicted him could be traced to a more natural and far more palpable origin—to the severe and long-continued illness, indeed to the evidently approaching dissolution, of a tenderly beloved sister—his sole companion for long years, his last and only relative on earth. Her decease, he said, with a bitterness which I can never forget, would leave him (him the hopeless and the frail) the last of the ancient race of the Ushers. While he spoke, the lady Madeline (for so was she called) passed slowly through a remote portion of the apartment and, without having noticed my presence, disappeared. I regarded her with an utter astonishment not unmingled with dread, and yet I found it impossible to account for such feelings. A sensation of stupor oppressed me as my eyes followed her retreating steps. When a door, at length, closed upon her, my glance sought instinctively and eagerly the countenance of the brother; but he had buried his face in his hands, and I could only perceive that a far more than ordinary wanness had overspread the emaciated fingers through which trickled many passionate tears.

The disease of the lady Madeline had long baffled the skill of her physicians. A settled apathy, a gradual wasting away of the person, and frequent although transient affections of a partially cataleptical character were the unusual diagnosis. Hitherto she had steadily borne up against the pressure of her malady, and had not betaken herself finally to bed; but, on the closing in of the evening of my arrival at the house, she succumbed (as her brother told me at night with inexpressible agitation) to the prostrating power of the destroyer; and I learned that the glimpse I had obtained of her person would thus probably be the last I should obtain—that the lady, at least while living, would be seen by me no more.

For several days ensuing, her name was unmentioned by either Usher or myself: and during this period I was busied in earnest endeavors to alleviate the melancholy of my friend. We painted and read together; or I listened, as if in a dream, to the wild improvisations of his speaking guitar. And thus, as a closer and still closer intimacy admitted me more unreservedly into the recesses of his spirit, the more bitterly did I perceive the futility of all attempt at cheering a mind from which darkness, as if an inherent positive quality, poured forth upon all objects of the moral and physical universe, in one unceasing radiation of gloom.

I shall ever bear about me a memory of the many solemn hours I thus spent alone with the master of the House of Usher. Yet I should fail in any attempt to convey an idea of the exact character of the studies, or of the occupations, in which he involved me, or led me the way. An excited and highly distempered ideality threw a sulphureous luster over all. His long improvised dirges will ring forever in my ears. Among other things, I hold painfully in mind a certain singular perversion and amplification of the wild air of the last waltz of Von Weber. From the paintings over which his elaborate fancy brooded, and which grew, touch by touch, into vaguenesses at which I shuddered the more thrillingly, because I shuddered knowing not why;—from these paintings (vivid as their images now are before me) I would in vain endeavor to educe more than a small portion which should lie within the compass of merely written words. By the utter simplicity, by the nakedness of his designs, he arrested and overawed attention. If ever mortal painted an idea, that mortal was Roderick Usher. For me at least, in the circumstances then surrounding me, there arose out of the pure abstractions which the hypochondriac contrived to throw upon his canvas an intensity of intolerable awe, no shadow of which felt I ever yet in the contemplation of the certainly glowing yet too concrete reveries of Fuseli.

One of the phantasmagoric conceptions of my friend, partaking not so rigidly of the spirit of abstraction, may be shadowed forth, although feebly, in words. A small picture presented the interior of an immensely long and rectangular vault or tunnel, with low walls, smooth, white, and without interruption or device. Certain accessory points of the design served well to convey the idea that this excavation lay at an exceeding depth below the surface of the earth. No outlet was observed in any portion of its vast extent, and no torch or other artificial source of light was discernible; yet a flood of intense rays rolled throughout, and bathed the whole in a ghastly and inappropriate splendor.

I have just spoken of that morbid condition of the auditory nerve which rendered all music intolerable to the sufferer, with the exception of certain effects of stringed instruments. It was, perhaps, the narrow limits to which he thus confined himself upon the guitar which gave birth, in great measure, to the fantastic character of his performances. But the fervid facility of his impromptus could not be so accounted for. They must have been, and were, in the notes, as well as in the words of his wild fantasias (for he not unfrequently accompanied himself with rhymed verbal improvisations), the result of that intense mental collectedness and concentration to which I have previously alluded as observable only in particular moments of the highest artificial excitement. The words of one of these rhapsodies I have easily remembered. I was, perhaps, the more forcibly impressed with it, as he gave it, because, in the under or mystic current of its meaning, I fancied that I perceived, and for the first time, a full consciousness on the part of Usher of the tottering of his lofty reason upon her throne. The verses, which were entitled "The Haunted Palace," ran very nearly, if not accurately, thus:

> In the greenest of our valleys
> By good angels tenanted,
> Once a fair and stately palace—
> Radiant palace—reared its head.

The Fall of the House of Usher

In the monarch Thought's dominion,
   It stood there!
Never seraph spread a pinion
   Over fabric half so fair!

Banners yellow, glorious, golden,
   On its roof did float and flow
(This—all this—was in the olden
   Time long ago)
And every gentle air that dallied,
   In that sweet day,
Along the ramparts plumed and pallid,
   A wingèd odor went away.

Wanderers in that happy valley
   Through two luminous windows, saw
Spirits moving musically
   To a lute's well-tunèd law,
Round about a throne where, sitting,
   Porphyrogene!
In state his glory well befitting,
   The ruler of the realm was seen.

And all with pearl and ruby glowing
   Was the fair palace door,
Through which came flowing, flowing, flowing
   And sparkling evermore,
A troop of Echoes, whose sweet duty
   Was but to sing,
In voices of surpassing beauty,
   The wit and wisdom of their king.

But evil things, in robes of sorrow,
   Assailed the monarch's high estate;
(Ah, let us mourn!—for never morrow
   Shall dawn upon him, desolate!)
And round about his home the glory
   That blushed and bloomed
Is but a dim-remembered story
   Of the old time entombed.

>   And travelers, now, within that valley,
>   Through the red-litten windows see
>   Vast forms that move fantastically
>   To a discordant melody;
>   While, like a ghastly rapid river,
>   Through the pale door
>   A hideous throng rush out forever,
>   And laugh—but smile no more.

I well remember that suggestions arising from this ballad led us into a train of thought wherein there became manifest an opinion of Usher's which I mention not so much on account of its novelty (for other men have thought thus) as on account of the pertinacity with which he maintained it. This opinion, in its general form, was that of the sentience of all vegetable things. But, in his disordered fancy, the idea had assumed a more daring character, and trespassed, under certain conditions, upon the kingdom of inorganization. I lack words to express the full extent, or the earnest abandon of his persuasion. The belief, however, was connected (as I have previously hinted) with the gray stones of the home of his forefathers. The conditions of the sentience had been here, he imagined, fulfilled in the method of collocation of these stones—in the order of their arrangement, as well as in that of the many fungi which overspread them, and of the decayed trees which stood around—above all, in the long undisturbed endurance of this arrangement, and in its reduplication in the still waters of the tarn. Its evidence—the evidence of the sentience—was to be seen, he said (and I here started as he spoke), in the gradual yet certain condensation of an atmosphere of their own about the waters and the walls. The result was discoverable, he added, in that silent, yet importunate and terrible influence which for centuries had moulded the destinies of his family, and which made *him* what I now saw him—what he was. Such opinions need no comment, and I will make none.

Our books—the books which, for years, had formed no small portion of the mental existence of the invalid—were, as might be supposed, in strict keeping with this character of phantasm. We pored together over such works as the *Ververt et Chartreuse* of Gresset; the *Belphegor* of Machiavelli; the *Heaven and Hell* of Swederborg; the *Subterranean Voyage of Nicholas Klimm* by Holberg; the *Chiromancy* of Robert Flud, of Jean D'Indaginé, and of De la Chambre; the *Journey into the Blue Distance* of Tieck; and the *City of the Sun* of Campanella. One favorite volume was a small octavo edition of the *Directorium Inquisitorum,* by the Dominican Eymeric de Gironne; and there were passages in Pomponius Mela, about the old African Satyrs and Aegipans, over which Usher would sit dreaming for hours. His chief delight, however, was found in the perusal of an exceedingly rare and curious book in quarto Gothic—the manual of a forgotten church—the *Vigilae Mortuorum Secundum Chorum Ecclesiae Maguntinae.*

I could not help thinking of the wild ritual of this work, and of its probable influence upon the hypochondriac, when, one evening, having informed me abruptly that the lady Madeline was no more, he stated his intention of preserving her corpse for a fortnight (previously to its final interment) in one of the numerous vaults within the main walls of the building. The worldly reason, however, assigned for this singular proceeding was one which I did not feel at liberty to dispute. The brother had been led to his resolution (so he told me) by consideration of the unusual character of the malady of the deceased, of certain obtrusive and eager inquiries on the part of her medical men, and of the remote and exposed situation of the burial ground of the family. I will not deny that when I called to mind the sinister countenance of the person whom I met upon the staircase, on the day of my arrival at the house, I had no desire to oppose what I regarded as at best but a harmless, and by no means an unnatural, precaution.

At the request of Usher, I personally aided him in the arrangements for the temporary emtombment. The body having been encoffined, we two alone bore it to its rest. The vault in which we placed it (and which had been so long unopened that our torches, half smothered in its oppressive atmosphere, gave us little opportunity for investigation) was small, damp, and entirely without means of admission for light; lying, at great depth, immediately beneath that portion of the building in which was my own sleeping apartment. It had been used, apparently, in remote feudal times, for the worst purposes of a donjon keep, and, in later days, as a place of deposit for powder, or some other highly combustible substance, as a portion of its floor, and the whole interior of a long archway through which we reached it, were carefully sheathed with copper. The door, of massive iron, had been, also, similarly protected. Its immense weight caused an unusually sharp grating sound, as it moved upon its hinges.

Having deposited our mournful burden upon trestles within this region of horror, we partially turned aside the yet unscrewed lid of the coffin, and looked upon the face of the tenant. A striking similitude between the brother and sister now first arrested my attention; and Usher, divining, perhaps my thoughts, murmured out some few words from which I learned that the deceased and himself had been twins, and that sympathies of a scarcely intelligible nature had always existed between them. Our glances, however, rested not long upon the dead —for we could not regard her unawed. The disease which had thus entombed the lady in the maturity of youth had left, as usual in all maladies of a strictly cataleptical character, the mockery of a faint blush upon the bosom and the face, and that suspiciously lingering smile upon the lip which is so terrible in death. We replaced and screwed down the lid and having secured the door of iron, made our way, with toil, into the scarcely less gloomy apartments of the upper portion of the house.

And now, some days of bitter grief having elapsed, an observable change came over the features of the mental disorder of my friend. His ordinary manner had vanished. His ordinary occupations were neglected or forgotten. He roamed from chamber to chamber with hurried, unequal, and objectless step. The pallor of his countenance had assumed, if possible, a more ghastly hue—but the luminousness of his eye had utterly gone out. The once occasional huskiness of his tone was heard no more; and a tremulous quaver, as if of extreme terror, habitually characterized his utterance. There were times, indeed, when I thought his unceasingly agitated mind was laboring with some oppressive secret, to divulge which he struggled for the necessary courage. At times, again, I was obliged to resolve all into the mere inexplicable vagaries of madness, for I beheld him gazing upon vacancy for long hours, in an attitude of the profoundest attention, as if listening to some imaginary sound. It was no wonder that his condition terrified—that it infected me. I felt creeping upon me, by slow yet certain degrees, the wild influences of his own fantastic yet impressive superstitions.

It was, especially, upon retiring to bed late in the night of the seventh or eighth day after the placing of the lady Madeline within the donjon, that I experienced the full power of such feelings. Sleep came not near my couch, while the hours waned and waned away. I struggled to reason off the nervousness which had dominion over me. I endeavored to believe that much, if not all, of what I felt was due to the bewildering influence of the gloomy furniture of the room—of the dark and tattered draperies, which, tortured into motion by the breath of a rising tempest, swayed fitfully to and fro upon the walls, and rustled uneasily about the decorations of the bed. But my efforts were fruitless. An irrepressible tremor gradually pervaded my frame; and, at length, there sat upon my very heart an incubus of utterly causeless alarm. Shaking this off with a gasp and a struggle, I uplifted myself upon the pillows and, peering earnestly within the intense darkness of the chamber, hearkened—I know not why, except that an instinctive spirit prompted me—to certain low and indefinite sounds which came, through the pauses of the storm, at long intervals I knew not whence. Overpowered by an intense sentiment of horror, unaccountable yet unendurable, I threw on my clothes with haste (for I felt that I should sleep no more during the night) and endeavored to arouse myself from the pitiable condition into which I had fallen, by pacing rapidly to and fro through the apartment.

I had taken but few turns in this manner when a light step on an adjoining staircase arrested my attention. I presently recognized it as that of Usher. In an instant afterward he rapped, with a gentle touch, at my door, and entered, bearing a lamp. His countenance was, as usual, cadaverously wan—but, moreover, there was a species of mad hilarity in his eyes—an evidently restrained hysteria in his whole demeanor. His air appalled me—but anything was preferable to the solitude which I had so long endured, and I even welcomed his presence as a relief.

"And you have not seen it?" he said abruptly, after having stared about him for some moments in silence—"you have not then seen it? —but, stay! you shall." Thus speaking, and having carefully shaded his lamp, he hurried to one of the casements and threw it freely open to the storm.

The impetuous fury of the entering gust nearly lifted us from our feet. It was, indeed, a tempestuous yet sternly beautiful night, and one wildly singular in its terror and its beauty. A whirlwind had apparently collected its force in our vicinity; for there were frequent and violent alterations in the direction of the wind; and the exceeding density of the clouds (which hung so low as to press upon the turrets of the house) did not prevent our perceiving the lifelike velocity with which they flew careering from all points against each other, without passing away into the distance. I say that even their exceeding density did not prevent our perceiving this; yet we had no glimpse of the moon or stars, nor was there any flashing forth of the lightning. But the under surfaces of the huge masses of agitated vapor, as well as all terrestrial objects immediately around us, were glowing in the unnatural light of a faintly luminous and distinctly visible gaseous exhalation which hung about and enshrouded the mansion.

"You must not—you shall not behold this!" said I, shudderingly, to Usher, as I led him, with a gentle violence, from the window to a seat. "These appearances, which bewilder you, are merely electrical phenomena not uncommon—or it may be that they have their ghastly origin in the rank miasma of the tarn. Let us close this casement; the air is chilling and dangerous to your frame. Here is one of your favorite romances. I will read, and you shall listen; and so we will pass away this terrible night together."

The antique volume which I had taken up was the *Mad Trist* of Sir Launcelot Canning; but I had called it a favorite of Usher's more in sad jest than in earnest; for, in truth, there is little in its uncouth and unimaginative prolixity which could have had interest for the lofty and spiritual ideality of my friend. It was, however, the only book immediately at hand; and I indulged a vague hope that the excitement which now agitated the hypochondriac might find relief (for the history of mental disorder is full of similar anomalies) even in the extremeness of the folly which I should read. Could I have judged, indeed, by the wild overstrained air of vivacity with which he hearkened, or apparently hearkened, to the words of the tale, I might well have congratulated myself upon the success of my design.

I had arrived at that well-known portion of the story where Ethelred, the hero of the *Trist,* having sought in vain for peaceable admission into the dwelling of the hermit, proceeds to make good an entrance by force. Here, it will be remembered, the words of the narrative run thus:

> "And Ethelred, who was by nature of a doughty heart, and who was now mightly withal, on account of the powerfulness of the wine which he had drunken, waited no longer to hold parley with the hermit, who, in sooth, was of an obstinate and maliceful turn, but, feeling the rain upon his shoulders, and fearing the rising of the tempest, uplifted his mace outright, and, with blows, made quickly room in the plankings of the door for his gauntleted hand; and now pulling therewith sturdily, he so cracked, and ripped, and tore all asunder, that the noise of the dry and hollow-sounding wood alarmed and reverberated throughout the forest."

At the termination of this sentence I started, and for a moment, paused; for it appeared to me (although I at once concluded that my excited fancy had deceived me)—it appeared to me that, from some very remote portion of the mansion there came, indistinctly, to my ears what might have been, in its exact similarity of character, the echo (but a stifled and dull one certainly) of the very cracking and ripping sound which Sir Launcelot had so particularly described. It was, beyond doubt, the coincidence alone which had arrested my attention; for, amid the rattling of the sashes of the casements, and the ordinary commingled noises of the still increasing storm, the sound, in itself, had nothing, surely, which should have interested or disturbed me. I continued the story:

> "But the good champion Ethelred, now entering within the door, was sore enraged and amazed to perceive no signal of the maliceful hermit; but, in the stead thereof, a dragon of a scaly and prodigious demeanor, and of a fiery tongue, which sate in guard before a palace of gold, with a floor of silver; and upon the wall there hung a shield of shining brass with this legend enwritten—
>
> *Who entereth herein, a conqueror hath bin;*
> *Who slayeth the dragon, the shield he shall win;*
>
> And Ethelred uplifted his mace, and struck upon the head of the dragon, which fell before him, and gave up his pesty breath, with a shriek so horrid and harsh, and withal so piercing, that Ethelred had fain to close his ears with his hands against the dreadful noise of it, the like whereof was never before heard."

Here again I paused abruptly, and now with a feeling of wild amazement—for there could be no doubt whatever that, in this instance, I did actually hear (although from what direction it proceeded I found it impossible to say) a low and apparently distant, but harsh, protracted, and most unusual screaming or grating sound—the exact counterpart of what my fancy had already conjured up for the dragon's unnatural shriek as described by the romancer.

Oppressed, as I certainly was, upon the occurrence of the second and most extraordinary coincidence, by a thousand conflicting sensations, in which wonder and extreme terror were predominant, I still retained sufficient presence of mind to avoid exciting, by any observation, the sensitive nervousness of my companion. I was by no means certain that he had noticed the sounds in question; although, assuredly, a strange alteration had, during the last few minutes, taken place in his demeanor. From a position fronting my own, he had gradually brought his chair so as to sit with his face to the door of the chamber; and thus I could but partially perceive his features, although I saw that his lips trembled as if he were murmuring inaudibly. His head had dropped upon his breast—yet I knew that he was not asleep, from the wide and rigid opening of the eye as I caught a glance of it in profile. The motion of his body, too, was at variance with this idea —for he rocked from side to side with a gentle yet constant and uniform sway. Having rapidly taken notice of all this, I resumed the narrative of Sir Launcelot, which thus proceeded:

> "And now, the champion, having escaped from the terrible fury of the dragon, bethinking himself of the brazen shield, and of the breaking up of the enchantment which was upon it, removed the carcass from out of the way before him, and approached valorously over the silver pavement of the castle to where the shield was upon the wall; which in sooth tarried not for his full coming, but fell down at his feet upon the silver floor, with a mighty great and terrible ringing sound."

No sooner had these syllables passed my lips, than—as if a shield of brass had indeed, at the moment, fallen heavily upon a floor of silver —I became aware of a distant, hollow, metallic, and clangorous yet apparently muffled reverberation. Completely unnerved, I leaped to my feet; but the measured rocking movement of Usher was undisturbed. I rushed to the chair in which he sat. His eyes were bent fixedly before him, and throughout his whole countenance there reigned a stony rigidity. But as I placed my hand upon his shoulder, there came a strong shudder over his whole person; a sickly smile quivered about his lips; and I saw that he spoke in a low, hurried, and gibbering murmur, as if unconscious of my presence. Bending closely over him, I at length drank in the hideous import of his words.

"Not hear it?—yes, I hear it, and *have* heard it. Long—long—long —many minutes, many hours, many days, have I heard it—yet I dared not—oh, pity me, miserable wretch that I am!—I dared not—I *dared* not speak! *We have put her living in the tomb!* Said I not that my senses were acute? I *now* tell you that I heard her first feeble movements in the hollow coffin. I heard them—many, many days ago—yet I dared not—*I dared not speak!* And now—tonight—Ethelred—ha! ha!—the breaking of the hermit's door, and the death cry of the dragon, and the clangor of the shield!—say, rather, the rending of her coffin, and the grating of the iron hinges of her prison, and her struggles within the coppered archway of the vault! Oh, whither shall I fly? Will she not be here anon? Is she not hurrying to upbraid me for my haste? Have I not heard her footstep on the stair? Do I not distinguish that heavy and horrible beating of her heart? *Madman!*" Here he sprang furiously to his feet, and shrieked out his syllables, as if in the effort he were giving up his soul— *"Madman! I tell you that she now stands without the door!"*

The Fall of the House of Usher

As if in the superhuman energy of his utterance there had been found the potency of a spell, the huge antique panels to which the speaker pointed threw slowly back, upon the instant, their ponderous and ebony jaws. It was the work of the rushing gust—but then without those doors there *did* stand the lofty and enshrouded figure of the lady Madeline of Usher. There was blood upon her white robes, and the evidence of some bitter struggle upon every portion of her emaciated frame. For a moment she remained trembling and reeling to and fro upon the threshold—then, with a low moaning cry, fell heavily inward upon the person of her brother, and in her violent and now final death agonies, bore him to the floor a corpse, and a victim to the terrors he had anticipated.

From that chamber, and from that mansion, I fled aghast. The storm was still abroad in all its wrath as I found myself crossing the old causeway. Suddenly there shot along the path a wild light, and I turned to see whence a gleam so unusual could have issued; for the vast house and its shadows were alone behind me. The radiance was that of the full, setting, and blood-red moon which now shone vividly through that once barely discernible fissure of which I have before spoken as extending from the roof of the building, in a zigzag direction, to the base. While I gazed, this fissure rapidly widened—there came a fierce breath of the whirlwind—the entire orb of the satellite burst at once upon my sight—my brain reeled as I saw the mighty walls rushing asunder—there was a long tumultuous shouting sound like the voice of a thousand waters—and the deep and dank tarn at my feet closed sullenly and silently over the fragments of the *House of Usher.*

The Eternal "Nay"

HERMAN MELVILLE

A great novelist, Melville was also one of the most powerful writers of short stories, several of which have become world classics.

Herman Melville (1819–1891) was born in New York City. He went to school in that city until his father's business failed and the family moved to Albany, where the boy got further schooling. When his father died in debt in 1832, young Herman worked as a bank clerk, helper on his uncle's farm, and assistant in his brother Gansevoort's fur store, which business also failed. Herman taught school, and then shipped aboard a sailing ship across the Atlantic.

Early in 1841 he began his greatest adventure. As a substitute for suicide, he shipped as a foremast hand on the whaler *Acushnet*, bound on a far cruise of several years. On July 9, 1842, Herman and a friend deserted at the Pacific island of Nukahiva in the southern Marquesas group. His adventures there and later in Tahiti are told in his first books, *Typee* (1846) and *Omoo* (1847). He enlisted before the mast on an American naval frigate at Honolulu in order to return home, and after being mustered out in 1844 began writing his great stories. No less than six volumes, including his masterpiece *Moby Dick*, are set in the Pacific region, and often reflect his Romantic desire to escape to a more primitive world than that of complex, nineteenth-century "civilization."

Melville in 1847 married the daughter of the chief justice of Massachusetts, and they had three children. In order to support his family, he wrote many novels and short stories, and also published poetry. His writing became increasingly symbolic and obscure, however, and having lost a popular audience, he took a post in 1866 in the customs office in New York City, where he worked for almost twenty years. He continued to write, chiefly for his own satisfaction, and at his death in 1891, the manuscript of one of his great novellas, *Billy Budd*, was found on his desk. He had been almost forgotten by historians of literature when, in 1921, the first full-length biography was published.

Melville's situation in the year 1853, when he wrote "Bartleby," may help us to understand one level of the story's meaning. Having exhausted himself in pouring out novels, Melville, a literary artist of high integrity, here announced to the perceptive reader that he would no longer willingly misemploy his talents as a writer, grinding out marketable fiction and drudging to copy the work of others or even his own. Herman probably felt that the life of the story's narrator was almost as barren as that of his scrivener Bartleby. Undoubtedly the contrast between the moneymaking employer and his grotesque copyists reflects a feeling that Melville had been rejected by a dollar-grubbing world. But there are other levels of meaning. The richness of this story, although the detail is apparently commonplace, routine, even dull, has not yet been exhausted by the many critics who have studied it.

HERMAN MELVILLE

Bartleby: A Story of Wall Street

I AM A RATHER ELDERLY MAN. The nature of my avocations, for the last thirty years, has brought me into more than ordinary contact with what would seem an interesting and somewhat singular set of men, of whom, as yet, nothing, that I know of, has ever been written—I mean, the law copyists, or scriveners. I have known very many of them, professionally and privately, and, if I pleased, could relate divers histories, at which good-natured gentlemen might smile, and sentimental souls might weep. But I waive the biographies of all other scriveners, for a few passages in the life of Bartleby, who was a scrivener, the strangest I ever saw, or heard of. While of other law copyists I might write the complete life, of Bartleby nothing of that sort can be done. I believe that no materials exist for a full and satisfactory biography of this man. It is an irreparable loss to literature. Bartleby was one of those beings of whom nothing is ascertainable, except from the original sources, and, in his case, those are very small. What my own astonished eyes saw of Bartleby, *that* is all I know of him, except, indeed, one vague report, which will appear in the sequel.

Ere introducing the scrivener, as he first appeared to me, it is fit I make some mention of myself, my employees, my business, my chambers, and general surroundings; because some such description is indispensable to an adequate understanding of the chief character about to be presented. Imprimis: I am a man who, from his youth upwards, has been filled with a profound conviction that the easiest way of life is the best. Hence, though I belong to a profession proverbially energetic and nervous, even to turbulence, at times, yet nothing of that sort have I ever suffered to invade my peace. I am one of those unambitious lawyers who never address a jury, or in any way draw down public applause; but, in the cool tranquillity of a snug retreat do a snug business among rich men's bonds, and mortgages, and title deeds. All who know me consider me an eminently *safe* man. The late John Jacob Astor, a personage little given to poetic enthusiasm, had no hesitation in pronouncing my first grand point to be prudence; my next, method. I do not speak it in vanity, but simply record the fact, that I was not unemployed in my profession by the late John Jacob Astor; a name which, I admit, I love to repeat; for it hath a rounded and orbicular sound to it, and rings like unto bullion. I will freely add that I was not insensible to the late John Jacob Astor's good opinion.

Some time prior to the period at which this little history begins, my avocations had been largely increased. The good old office, now extinct in the State of New York, of a master in chancery, had been conferred upon me. It was not a very arduous office, but very pleasantly remunerative. I seldom lose my temper; much more seldom indulge in dangerous indignation at wrongs and outrages; but I must be permitted to be rash here and declare that I consider the sudden and violent abrogation of the office of master in chancery, by the new Constitution, as a —— premature act; inasmuch as I had counted upon a life lease of the profits, whereas I only received those of a few short years. But this is by the way.

My chambers were upstairs, at No. — Wall Street. At one end, they looked upon the white wall of the interior of a spacious skylight shaft, penetrating the building from top to bottom.

This view might have been considered rather tame than otherwise, deficient in what landscape painters call "life." But, if so, the view from the other end of my chambers offered, at least, a contrast, if nothing more. In that direction, my windows commanded an unobstructed view of a lofty brick wall, black by age and everlasting shade; which wall required no spyglass to bring out its lurking beauties, but, for the benefit of all nearsighted spectators, was pushed up to within ten feet of my windowpanes. Owing to the great height of the surrounding buildings, and my chambers being on the second floor, the interval between this wall and mine not a little resembled a huge square cistern.

At the period just preceding the advent of Bartleby, I had two persons as copyists in my employment, and a promising lad as an office boy. First, Turkey; second, Nippers; third, Ginger Nut. These may seem names the like of which are not usually found in the Directory. In truth, they were nicknames, mutually conferred upon each other by my three clerks, and were deemed expressive of their respective persons or characters. Turkey was a short, pursy Englishman, of about my own age—that is, somewhere not far from sixty. In the morning, one might say, his face was of a fine florid hue, but after twelve o'clock, meridian—his dinner hour—it blazed like a grate full of Christmas coals; and continued blazing—but, as it were, with a gradual wane— till six o'clock, P.M., or thereabouts; after which I saw no more of the proprietor of the face, which, gaining its meridian with the sun, seemed to set with it, to rise, culminate, and decline the following day, with the like regularity and undiminished glory. There are many singular coincidences I have known in the course of my life, not the least among which was the fact that, exactly when Turkey displayed his fullest beams from his red and radiant countenance, just then, too, at that critical moment, began the daily period when I considered his business capacities as seriously disturbed for the remainder of the twenty-four hours. Not that he was absolutely idle, or averse to business then; far from it. The difficulty was, he was apt to be altogether too energetic. There was a strange, inflamed, flurried, flighty recklessness of activity about him. He would be incautious in dipping his pen into his inkstand. All his blots upon my documents were dropped there after twelve o'clock meridian. Indeed, not only would he be reckless, and sadly given to making blots in the afternoon, but, some days, he went further, and was rather noisy. At such times, too, his face flamed with augmented blazonry, as if cannel coal had been heaped on anthracite. He made an unpleasant racket with his chair; spilled his sandbox; in mending his pens impatiently split them all to pieces and threw them on the floor in a sudden passion; stood up, and leaned over his table, boxing his papers about in a most indecorous manner, very sad to behold in an elderly man like him. Nevertheless, as he was in many ways a most valuable person to me, and all the time before twelve o'clock, meridian, was the quickest, steadiest creature, too, accomplishing a great deal of work in a style not easily to be matched—for these reasons, I was willing to overlook his eccentricities, though, indeed, occasionally, I remonstrated with him. I did this very gently, however, because, though the civilest, nay, the blandest and most reverential of men in the morning, yet, in the afternoon, he was disposed, upon provocation, to be slightly rash with his tongue —in fact, insolent. Now, valuing his morning services as I did, and resolved not to lose them—yet, at the same time, made uncomfortable by his inflamed ways after twelve o'clock—and being a man of peace, unwilling by my admonitions to call forth unseemly retorts from him,

I took upon me, one Saturday noon (he was always worse on Saturdays) to hint to him, very kindly, that, perhaps, now that he was growing old, it might be well to abridge his labors; in short, he need not come to my chambers after twelve o'clock, but, dinner over, had best go home to his lodgings, and rest himself till teatime. But no; he insisted upon his afternoon devotions. His countenance became intolerably fervid, as he oratorically assured me—gesticulating with a long ruler at the other end of the room—that if his services in the morning were useful, how indispensable, then, in the afternoon?

"With submission, sir," said Turkey, on this occasion, "I consider myself your right-hand man. In the morning I but marshal and deploy my columns; but in the afternoon I put myself at their head, and gallantly charge the foe, thus"—and he made a violent thrust with the ruler.

"But the blots, Turkey," intimated I.

"True; but, with submission, sir, behold these hairs! I am getting old. Surely, sir, a blot or two of a warm afternoon is not to be severely urged against gray hairs. Old age—even if it blot the page—is honorable. With submission, sir, we *both* are getting old."

This appeal to my fellow feeling was hardly to be resisted. At all events, I saw that go he would not. So, I made up my mind to let him stay, resolving, nevertheless, to see to it that, during the afternoon, he had to do with my less important papers.

Nippers, the second on my list, was a whiskered, sallow, and, upon the whole, rather piratical-looking young man, of about five-and-twenty. I always deemed him the victim of two evil powers—ambition and indigestion. The ambition was evinced by a certain impatience of the duties of a mere copyist, an unwarrantable usurpation of strictly professional affairs, such as the original drawing up of legal documents. The indigestion seemed betokened in an occasional nervous testiness and grinning irritability, causing the teeth to audibly grind together over mistakes committed in copying; unnecessary maledictions, hissed, rather than spoken, in the heat of business; and especially by a continual discontent with the height of the table where he worked. Though of a very ingenious mechanical turn, Nippers could never get this table to suit him. He put chips under it, blocks of various sorts, bits of pasteboard, and at last went so far as to attempt an exquisite adjustment, by final pieces of folded blotting paper. But no invention would answer. If, for the sake of easing his back, he brought the table lid at a sharp angle well up towards his chin, and wrote there like a man using the steep roof of a Dutch house for his desk, then he

Bartleby: A Story of Wall Street

declared that it stopped the circulation in his arms. If now he lowered the table to his waistbands, and stooped over it in writing, then there was a sore aching in his back. In short, the truth of the matter was Nippers knew not what he wanted. Or, if he wanted anything, it was to be rid of a scrivener's table altogether. Among the manifestations of his diseased ambition was a fondness he had for receiving visits from certain ambiguous-looking fellows in seedy coats, whom he called his clients. Indeed, I was aware that not only was he, at times, considerable of a ward politician, but he occasionally did a little business at the justices' courts, and was not unknown on the steps of the Tombs. I have good reason to believe, however, that one individual who called upon him at my chambers, and who, with a grand air, he insisted was his client, was no other than a dun, and the alleged title deed a bill. But, with all his failings, and the annoyances he caused me, Nippers, like his compatriot Turkey, was a very useful man to me; wrote a neat, swift hand; and, when he chose, was not deficient in a gentlemanly sort of deportment. Added to this, he always dressed in a gentlemanly sort of way; and so, incidentally, reflected credit upon my chambers. Whereas, with respect to Turkey, I had much ado to keep him from being a reproach to me. His clothes were apt to look oily, and smell of eating houses. He wore his pantaloons very loose and baggy in summer. His coats were execrable; his hat not to be handled. But while the hat was a thing of indifference to me, inasmuch as his natural civility and deference, as a dependent Englishman, always led him to doff it the moment he entered the room, yet his coat was another matter. Concerning his coats, I reasoned with him; but with no effect. The truth was, I suppose, that a man with so small an income could not afford to sport such a lustrous face and a lustrous coat at one and the same time. As Nippers once observed, Turkey's money went chiefly for red ink. One winter day, I presented Turkey with a highly respectable-looking coat of my own—a padded gray coat, of a most comfortable warmth, and which buttoned straight up from the knee to the neck. I thought Turkey would appreciate the favor, and abate his rashness and obstreperousness of afternoons. But no; I verily believe that buttoning himself up in so downy and blanketlike a coat had a pernicious effect upon him—upon the same principle that too much oats are bad for horses. In fact, precisely as a rash, restive horse is said to feel his oats, so Turkey felt his coat. It made him insolent. He was a man whom prosperity harmed.

Though, concerning the self-indulgent habits of Turkey, I had my own private surmises, yet, touching Nippers, I was well persuaded that, whatever might be his faults in other respects, he was, at least, a temperate young man. But, indeed, nature herself seemed to have been his vintner, and, at his birth, charged him so thoroughly with an irritable, brandylike disposition, that all subsequent potations were needless. When I consider how, amid the stillness of my chambers, Nippers would sometimes impatiently rise from his seat, and stooping over his table, spread his arms wide apart, seize the whole desk, and move it, and jerk it, with a grim, grinding motion on the floor, as if the table were a perverse voluntary agent, intent on thwarting and vexing him, I plainly perceive that, for Nippers, brandy-and-water were altogether superfluous.

It was fortunate for me that, owing to its peculiar cause—indigestion—the irritability and consequent nervousness of Nippers were mainly observable in the morning, while in the afternoon he was comparatively mild. So that, Turkey's paroxysms only coming on about twelve o'clock, I never had to do with their eccentricities at one time. Their fits relieved each other, like guards. When Nipper's was on, Turkey's was off; and vice versa. This was a good natural arrangement, under the circumstances.

Ginger Nut, the third on my list, was a lad, some twelve years old. His father was a carman, ambitious of seeing his son on the bench instead of a cart, before he died. So he sent him to my office, as student at law, errand boy, cleaner, and sweeper, at the rate of one dollar a week. He had a little desk to himself, but he did not use it much. Upon inspection, the drawer exhibited a great array of the shells of various sorts of nuts. Indeed, to this quick-witted youth, the whole noble science of the law was contained in a nutshell. Not the least among the employments of Ginger Nut, as well as one which he discharged with the most alacrity, was his duty as cake and apple purveyor for Turkey and Nippers. Copying law papers being proverbially a dry, husky sort of business, my two scriveners were fain to moisten their mouths very often with Spitzenbergs, to be had at the numerous stalls nigh the custom house and post office. Also, they sent Ginger Nut very frequently for that peculiar cake—small, flat, round, and very spicy—after which he had been named by them. Of a cold morning, when business was but dull, Turkey would gobble up scores of these cakes, as if they were mere wafers—indeed, they sell them at the rate of six or eight for a penny—the scrape of his pen blending with the crunching of the crisp particles in his mouth. Of all the fiery afternoon blunders and flurried rashnesses of Turkey was his once moistening a ginger cake between his lips and clapping it on to a mortgage for a seal.

I came within an ace of dismissing him then. But he mollified me by making an oriental bow, and saying:

"With submission, sir, it was generous of me to find you in stationery on my own account."

Now my original business—that of a conveyancer and title hunter, and drawer-up of recondite documents of all sorts—was considerably increased by receiving the master's office. There was now great work for scriveners. Not only must I push the clerks already with me, but I must have additional help.

In answer to my advertisement, a motionless young man one morning stood upon my office threshold, the door being open, for it was summer. I can see that figure now—pallidly neat, pitiably respectable, incurably forlorn! It was Bartleby.

After a few words touching his qualifications, I engaged him, glad to have among my corps of copyists a man of so singularly sedate an aspect, which I thought might operate beneficially upon the flighty temper of Turkey, and the fiery one of Nippers.

I should have stated before that ground-glass folding doors divided my premises into two parts, one of which was occupied by my scriveners, the other by myself. According to my humor, I threw open these doors, or closed them. I resolved to assign Bartleby a corner by the folding doors, but on my side of them, so as to have this quiet man within easy call, in case any trifling thing was to be done. I placed his desk close up to a small side window in that part of the room, a window which originally had afforded a lateral view of certain grimy backyards and bricks, but which, owing to subsequent erections, commanded at present no view at all, though it gave some light. Within three feet of the panes was a wall, and the light came down from far above, between two lofty buildings, as from a very small opening in a dome. Still further to a satisfactory arrangement, I procured a high green folding screen, which might entirely isolate Bartleby from my sight, though not remove him from my voice. And thus, in a manner, privacy and society were conjoined.

At first, Bartleby did an extraordinary quantity of writing. As if long famishing for something to copy, he seemed to gorge himself on my documents. There was no pause for digestion. He ran a day and night line, copying by sunlight and by candlelight. I should have been quite delighted with his application had he been cheerfully industrious. But he wrote on silently, palely, mechanically.

It is, of course, an indispensable part of a scrivener's business to verify the accuracy of his copy, word by word. Where there are two or more scriveners in an office, they assist each other in this examination, one reading from the copy, the other holding the original. It is a very dull, wearisome, and lethargic affair. I can readily imagine that, to some sanguine temperaments, it would be altogether intolerable. For example, I cannot credit that the mettlesome poet, Byron, would have contentedly sat down with Bartleby to examine a law document of, say five hundred pages, closely written in a crimpy hand.

Now and then, in the haste of business, it had been my habit to assist in comparing some brief document myself, calling Turkey or Nippers for this purpose. One object I had, in placing Bartleby so handy to me behind the screen, was to avail myself of his services on such trivial occasions. It was on the third day, I think, of his being with me, and before any necessity had arisen for having his own writing examined, that, being much hurried to complete a small affair I had in hand, I abruptly called to Bartleby. In my haste and natural expectancy of instant compliance, I sat with my head bent over the original on my desk, and my right hand sideways, and somewhat nervously extended with the copy, so that, immediately upon emerging from his retreat, Bartleby might snatch it and proceed to business without the least delay.

In this very attitude did I sit when I called to him, rapidly stating what it was I wanted him to do—namely, to examine a small paper with me. Imagine my surprise, nay, my consternation, when, without moving from his privacy, Bartleby, in a singularly mild, firm voice, replied, "I would prefer not to."

I sat awhile in perfect silence, rallying my stunned faculties. Immediately it occurred to me that my ears had deceived me, or Bartleby had entirely misunderstood my meaning. I repeated my request in the clearest tone I could assume; but in quite as clear a one came the previous reply, "I would prefer not to."

"Prefer not to," echoed I, rising in high excitement, and crossing the room with a stride. "What do you mean? Are you moonstruck? I want you to help me compare this sheet here—take it," and I thrust it towards him.

"I would prefer not to," said he.

I looked at him steadfastly. His face was leanly composed; his gray eye dimly calm. Not a wrinkle of agitation rippled him. Had there been the least uneasiness, anger, impatience, or impertinence in his manner; in other words, had there been anything ordinarily human about him, doubtless I should have violently dismissed him from the premises. But as it was, I should have as soon thought of turning my pale plaster-of-paris bust of Cicero out of doors. I stood gazing at him awhile, as he went on with his own writing, and then reseated myself at my desk. This is very strange, thought I. What had one best do? But my business hurried me. I concluded to forget the matter for the present, reserving it for my future leisure. So, calling Nippers from the other room, the paper was speedily examined.

A few days after this, Bartleby concluded four lengthy documents, being quadruplicates of a week's testimony taken before me in my High Court of Chancery. It became necessary to examine them. It was an important suit, and great accuracy was imperative. Having all things arranged, I called Turkey, Nippers, and Ginger Nut from the next room, meaning to place the four copies in the hands of my four clerks, while I should read from the original. Accordingly, Turkey, Nippers, and Ginger Nut had taken their seats in a row, each with his document in his hand, when I called to Bartleby to join this interesting group.

"Bartleby! Quick, I am waiting."

I heard a slow scrape of his chair legs on the uncarpeted floor, and soon he appeared standing at the entrance of his hermitage.

"What is wanted?" said he, mildly.

"The copies, the copies," said I, hurriedly. "We are going to examine them. There"—and held towards him the fourth quadruplicate.

"I would prefer not to," he said, and gently disappeared behind the screen.

For a few moments I was turned into a pillar of salt, standing at the head of my seated column of clerks. Recovering myself, I advanced towards the screen, and demanded the reason for such extraordinary conduct.

"*Why* do you refuse?"

"I would prefer not to."

With any other man I should have flown outright into a dreadful passion, scorned all further words, and thrust him ignominiously from my presence. But there was something about Bartleby that not only strangely disarmed me, but, in a wonderful manner, touched and disconcerted me. I began to reason with him.

"These are your own copies we are about to examine. It is laborsaving to you, because one examination will answer for your four papers. It is common usage. Every copyist is bound to help examine his copy. Is it not so? Will you not speak? Answer!"

"I prefer not to," he replied in a flutelike tone. It seemed to me that, while I had been addressing him, he carefully revolved every statement that I made; fully comprehended the meaning; could not gainsay the irresistible conclusion; but, at the same time, some paramount consideration prevailed with him to reply as he did.

"You are decided, then, not to comply with my request—a request made according to common usage and common sense?"

He briefly gave me to understand, that on that point my judgment was sound. Yes: his decision was irreversible.

It is not seldom the case that, when a man is browbeaten in some unprecedented and violently unreasonable way, he begins to stagger in his own plainest faith. He begins, as it were, vaguely to surmise that, wonderful as it may be, all the justice and all the reason is on the other side. Accordingly, if any disinterested persons are present, he turns to them for some reinforcement for his own faltering mind.

"Turkey," said I, "what do you think of this? Am I not right?"

"With submission, sir," said Turkey, in his blandest tone, "I think that you are."

"Nippers," said I, "what do *you* think of it?"

"I think I should kick him out of the office." (The reader of nice perceptions will here perceive that, it being morning, Turkey's answer is couched in polite and tranquil terms, but Nippers replies in ill-tempered ones. Or, to repeat a previous sentence, Nippers's ugly mood was on duty, and Turkey's off.)

"Ginger Nut," said I, willing to enlist the smallest suffrage in my behalf, "what do *you* think of it?"

"I think, sir, he's a little *luny,*" replied Ginger Nut, with a grin.

"You hear what they say," said I, turning towards the screen, "come forth and do your duty."

But he vouchsafed no reply. I pondered a moment in sore perplexity. But once more business hurried me. I determined again to postpone the consideration of this dilemma to my future leisure. With a little trouble we made out to examine the papers without Bartleby, though at every page or two Turkey deferentially dropped his opinion that this proceeding was quite out of the common; while Nippers, twitching in his chair with a dyspeptic nervousness, ground out, between his set teeth, occasional hissing maledictions against the stubborn oaf behind the screen. And for his (Nippers') part, this was the first and the last time he would do another man's business without pay.

Meanwhile Bartleby sat in his hermitage, oblivious to everything but his own peculiar business there.

Some days passed, the scrivener being employed upon another

lengthy work. His late remarkable conduct led me to regard his ways narrowly. I observed that he never went to dinner; indeed, that he never went anywhere. As yet I had never, of my personal knowledge, known him to be outside of my office. He was a perpetual sentry in the corner. At about eleven o'clock, though, in the morning, I noticed that Ginger Nut would advance toward the opening in Bartleby's screen, as if silently beckoned thither by a gesture invisible to me where I sat. The boy would then leave the office, jingling a few pence, and reappear with a handful of ginger nuts, which he delivered in the hermitage, receiving two of the cakes for his trouble.

He lives, then, on ginger nuts, thought I; never eats a dinner, properly speaking; he must be a vegetarian, then; but no; he never eats even vegetables, he eats nothing but ginger nuts. My mind then ran on in reveries concerning the probable effects upon the human constitution of living entirely on ginger nuts. Ginger nuts are so called because they contain ginger as one of their peculiar constituents, and the final flavoring one. Now, what was ginger? A hot, spicy thing. Was Bartleby hot and spicy? Not at all. Ginger, then, had no effect upon Bartleby. Probably he preferred it should have none.

Nothing so aggravates an earnest person as a passive resistance. If the individual so resisted be of a not inhumane temper, and the resisting one perfectly harmless in his passivity, then, in the better moods of the former, he will endeavor charitably to construe to his imagination what proves impossible to be solved by his judgment. Even so, for the most part, I regarded Bartleby and his ways. Poor fellow! thought I, he means no mischief; it is plain he intends no insolence; his aspect sufficiently evinces that his eccentricities are involuntary. He is useful to me. I can get along with him. If I turn him away, the chances are he will fall in with some less indulgent employer, and then he will be rudely treated, and perhaps driven forth miserably to starve. Yes. Here I can cheaply purchase a delicious self-approval. To befriend Bartleby; to humor him in his strange wilfulness, will cost me little or nothing, while I lay up in my soul what will eventually prove a sweet morsel for my conscience. But this mood was not invariable with me. The passiveness of Bartleby sometimes irritated me. I felt strangely goaded on to encounter him in new opposition—to elicit some angry spark from him answerable to my own. But, indeed, I might as well have essayed to strike fire with my knuckles against a bit of Windsor soap. But one afternoon the evil impulse in me mastered me, and the following little scene ensued:

"Bartleby," said I, "when those papers are all copied, I will compare them with you."

"I would prefer not to."

"How? Surely you do not mean to persist in that mulish vagary?"

No answer.

I threw open the folding doors near by and, turning upon Turkey and Nippers, exclaimed:

"Bartleby a second time says, he won't examine his papers. What do you think of it, Turkey?"

It was afternoon, be it remembered. Turkey sat glowing like a brass boiler; his bald head steaming; his hands reeling among his blotted papers.

"Think of it?" roared Turkey. "I think I'll just step behind his screen, and black his eyes for him!"

So saying, Turkey rose to his feet and threw his arms into a pugilistic position. He was hurrying away to make good his promise when I detained him, alarmed at the effect of incautiously rousing Turkey's combativeness after dinner.

"Sit down, Turkey," said I, "and hear what Nippers has to say. What do you think of it, Nippers? Would I not be justified in immediately dismissing Bartleby?"

"Excuse me, that is for you to decide, sir. I think his conduct quite unusual, and indeed, unjust, as regards Turkey and myself. But it may only be a passing whim."

"Ah," exclaimed I, "you have strangely changed your mind, then—you speak very gently of him now."

"All beer," cried Turkey; "gentleness is effects of beer—Nippers and I dined together today. You see how gentle *I* am, sir. Shall I go and black his eyes?"

"You refer to Bartleby, I suppose. No, not today, Turkey," I replied; "pray, put up your fists."

I closed the doors, and again advanced towards Bartleby. I felt additional incentives tempting me to my fate. I burned to be rebelled against again. I remembered that Bartleby never left the office.

"Bartleby," said I, "Ginger Nut is away; just step around to the post office, won't you?" (it was but a three minutes' walk) "and see if there is anything for me."

"I would prefer not to."

"You *will* not?"

"I *prefer* not."

Bartleby: A Story of Wall Street

I staggered to my desk, and sat there in a deep study. My blind inveteracy returned. Was there any other thing in which I could procure myself to be ignominiously repulsed by this lean, penniless wight—my hired clerk? What added thing is there, perfectly reasonable, that he will be sure to refuse to do?

"Bartleby!"

No answer.

"Bartleby," in a louder tone.

No answer.

"Bartleby," I roared.

Like a very ghost, agreeably to the laws of magical invocation, at the third summons, he appeared at the entrance of his hermitage.

"Go to the next room, and tell Nippers to come to me."

"I prefer not to," he respectfully and slowly said, and mildly disappeared.

"Very good, Bartleby," said I, in a quiet sort of serenely-severe self-possessed tone, intimating the unalterable purpose of some terrible retribution very close at hand. At the moment I half intended something of the kind. But upon the whole, as it was drawing towards my dinner hour, I thought it best to put on my hat and walk home for the day, suffering much from perplexity and distress of mind.

Shall I acknowledge it? The conclusion of this whole business was that it soon became a fixed fact of my chambers that a pale young scrivener, by the name of Bartleby, had a desk there; that he copied for me at the usual rate of four cents a folio (one hundred words); but he was permanently exempt from examining the work done by him, that duty being transferred to Turkey and Nippers, out of compliment, doubtless, to their superior acuteness; moreover, said Bartleby was never, on any account, to be dispatched on the most trivial errand of any sort; and that even if entreated to take upon him such a matter, it was generally understood that he would "prefer not to"—in other words, that he would refuse point-blank.

As days passed on, I became considerably reconciled to Bartleby. His steadiness, his freedom from all dissipation, his incessant industry (except when he chose to throw himself into a standing revery behind his screen), his great stillness, his unalterableness of demeanor under all circumstances, made him a valuable acquisition. One prime thing was this—*he was always there*—first in the morning, continually through the day, and the last at night. I had a singular confidence in his honesty. I felt my most precious papers perfectly safe in his hands.

Sometimes, to be sure, I could not, for the very soul of me, avoid falling into sudden spasmodic passions with him. For it was exceeding difficult to bear in mind all the time those strange peculiarities, privileges, and unheard-of exemptions, forming the tacit stipulations on Bartleby's part under which he remained in my office. Now and then, in the eagerness of dispatching pressing business, I would inadvertently summon Bartleby, in a short, rapid tone, to put his finger, say, on the incipient tie of a bit of red tape with which I was about compressing some papers. Of course, from behind the screen the usual answer, "I prefer not to," was sure to come; and then, how could a human creature, with the common infirmities of our nature, refrain from bitterly exclaiming upon such perverseness—such unreasonableness? However, every added repulse of this sort which I received only tended to lessen the probability of my repeating the inadvertence.

Here it must be said that, according to the custom of most legal gentlemen occupying chambers in densely populated law buildings, there were several keys to my door. One was kept by a woman residing in the attic, which person weekly scrubbed and daily swept and dusted my apartments. Another was kept by Turkey for convenience' sake. The third I sometimes carried in my own pocket. The fourth I knew not who had.

Now, one Sunday morning I happened to go to Trinity Church to hear a celebrated preacher, and finding myself rather early on the ground I thought I would walk round to my chambers for a while. Luckily I had my key with me; but upon applying it to the lock, I found it resisted by something inserted from the inside. Quite surprised, I called out; when to my consternation a key was turned from within; and thrusting his lean visage at me, and holding the door ajar, the apparition of Bartleby appeared, in his shirt sleeves, and otherwise in a strangely tattered deshabille, saying quietly that he was sorry, but he was deeply engaged just then, and—preferred not admitting me at present. In a brief word or two, he moreover added that perhaps I had better walk round the block two or three times, and by that time he would probably have concluded his affairs.

Now, the utterly unsurmised appearance of Bartleby, tenanting my law chambers of a Sunday morning, with his cadaverously gentlemanly nonchalance, yet withal firm and self-possessed, had such a strange effect upon me that incontinently I slunk away from my own door, and did as desired. But not without sundry twinges of impotent rebellion against the mild effrontery of this unaccountable scrivener. Indeed, it was his wonderful mildness, chiefly, which not only disarmed me, but unmanned me, as it were. For I consider that one, for

Bartleby: A Story of Wall Street

the time, is a sort of unmanned when he tranquilly permits his hired clerk to dictate to him, and order him away from his own premises. Furthermore, I was full of uneasiness as to what Bartleby could possibly be doing in my office in his shirt sleeves, and in an otherwise dismantled condition of a Sunday morning. Was anything amiss going on? Nay, that was out of the question. It was not to be thought of for a moment that Bartleby was an immoral person. But what could he be doing there?—copying? Nay again, whatever might be his eccentricities, Bartleby was an eminently decorous person. He would be the last man to sit down to his desk in any state approaching to nudity. Besides, it was Sunday; and there was something about Bartleby that forbade the supposition that he would by any secular occupation violate the proprieties of the day.

Nevertheless, my mind was not pacified; and full of a restless curiosity at last I returned to the door. Without hindrance I inserted my key, opened it, and entered. Bartleby was not to be seen. I looked round anxiously, peeped behind his screen; but it was very plain that he was gone. Upon more closely examining the place, I surmised that for an indefinite period Bartleby must have eaten, dressed, and slept in my office, and that too without plate, mirror, or bed. The cushioned seat of a rickety old sofa in one corner bore the faint impress of a lean, reclining form. Rolled away under his desk, I found a blanket; under the empty grate, a blacking box and brush; on a chair, a tin basin, with soap and a ragged towel; in a newspaper a few crumbs of ginger nuts and a morsel of cheese. Yes, thought I, it is evident enough that Bartleby has been making his home here, keeping bachelor's hall all by himself. Immediately then the thought came sweeping across me, what miserable friendlessness and loneliness are here revealed! His poverty is great; but his solitude, how horrible! Think of it. Of a Sunday, Wall Street is deserted as Petra; and every night of every day it is an emptiness. This building, too, which of weekdays hums with industry and life, at nightfall echoes with sheer vacancy, and all through Sunday is forlorn. And here Bartleby makes his home; sole spectator of a solitude which he has seen all populous—a sort of innocent and transformed Marius brooding among the ruins of Carthage!

For the first time in my life a feeling of overpowering, stinging melancholy seized me. Before, I had never experienced aught but a not unpleasing sadness. The bond of a common humanity now drew me irresistibly to gloom. A fraternal melancholy! For both I and Bartleby were sons of Adam. I remembered the bright silks and sparkling faces I had seen that day, in gala trim, swanlike sailing down the Mississippi of Broadway; and I contrasted them with the pallid copyist, and thought to myself, Ah, happiness courts the light, so we deem the world is gay; but misery hides aloof, so we deem that misery there is none. These sad fancyings—chimeras, doubtless, of a sick and silly brain—led on to other and more special thoughts, concerning the eccentricities of Bartleby. Presentiments of strange discoveries hovered round me. The scrivener's pale form appeared to me laid out, among uncaring strangers, in its shivering winding sheet.

Suddenly I was attracted by Bartleby's closed desk, the key in open sight left in the lock.

I mean no mischief, seek the gratification of no heartless curiosity, thought I; besides, the desk is mine, and its contents, too, so I will make bold to look within. Everything was methodically arranged, the papers smoothly placed. The pigeonholes were deep, and removing the files of documents, I groped into their recesses. Presently I felt something there, and dragged it out. It was an old bandanna handkerchief, heavy and knotted. I opened it, and saw it was a savings bank.

I now recalled all the quiet mysteries which I had noted in the man. I remembered that he never spoke but to answer; that, though at intervals he had considerable time to himself, yet I had never seen him reading—no, not even a newspaper; that for long periods he would stand looking out, at his pale window behind the screen, upon the dead brick wall; I was quite sure he never visited any refectory or eating house; while his pale face clearly indicated that he never drank beer like Turkey, or tea and coffee even, like other men; that he never went anywhere in particular that I could learn; never went out for a walk, unless, indeed, that was the case at present; that he had declined telling who he was, or whence he came, or whether he had any relatives in the world; that though so thin and pale, he never complained of ill health. And more than all, I remembered a certain unconscious air of pallid—how shall I call it?—of pallid haughtiness, say, or rather an austere reserve about him, which had positively awed me into my tame compliance with his eccentricities, when I had feared to ask him to do the slightest incidental thing for me, even though I might know, from his long-continued motionlessness, that behind his screen he must be standing in one of those dead-wall reveries of his.

Revolving all these things, and coupling them with the recently discovered fact that he made my office his constant abiding place and home, and not forgetful of his morbid moodiness; revolving all these things, a prudential feeling began to steal over me. My first emotions had been those of pure melancholy and sincerest pity; but just in proportion as the forlornness of Bartleby grew and grew to my imagination, did that same melancholy merge into fear, that pity into repulsion. So true it is, and so terrible, too, that up to a certain point the thought or sight of misery enlists our best affections; but, in certain special cases, beyond that point it does not. They err who would assert that invariably this is owing to the inherent selfishness of the human heart. It rather proceeds from a certain hopelessness of remedying excessive and organic ill. To a sensitive being, pity is not seldom pain. And when at last it is perceived that such pity cannot lead to effectual succor, common sense bids the soul be rid of it. What I saw that morning persuaded me that the scrivener was the victim of innate and incurable disorder. I might give alms to his body; but his body did not pain him; it was his soul that suffered, and his soul I could not reach.

I did not accomplish the purpose of going to Trinity Church that morning. Somehow, the things I had seen disqualified me for the time from churchgoing. I walked homeward, thinking what I would do with Bartleby. Finally, I resolved upon this—I would put certain calm questions to him the next morning, touching his history, etc., and if he declined to answer them openly and unreservedly (and I supposed he would prefer not), then to give him a twenty-dollar bill over and above whatever I might owe him, and tell him his services were no longer required; but that if in any other way I could assist him, I would be happy to do so; especially if he desired to return to his native place, wherever that might be, I would willingly help to defray the expenses. Morever, if, after reaching home, he found himself at any time in want of aid, a letter from him would be sure of a reply.

The next morning came.

"Bartleby," said I, gently calling to him behind his screen.

No reply.

"Bartleby," said I, in a still gentler tone, "come here; I am not going to ask you to do anything you would prefer not to do—I simply wish to speak to you."

Upon this he noiselessly slid into view.

"Will you tell me, Bartleby, where you were born?"

"I would prefer not to."

"Will you tell me *anything* about yourself?"

"I would prefer not to."

"But what reasonable objection can you have to speak to me? I feel friendly towards you."

He did not look at me while I spoke, but kept his glance fixed upon my bust of Cicero, which, as I then sat, was directly behind me, some six inches above my head.

"What is your answer, Bartleby?" said I, after waiting a considerable time for a reply, during which his countenance remained immovable, only there was the faintest conceivable tremor of the white attenuated mouth.

"At present I prefer to give no answer," he said, and retired into his hermitage.

It was rather weak in me, I confess, but his manner, on this occasion, nettled me. Not only did there seem to lurk in it a certain calm disdain, but his perverseness seemed ungrateful, considering the undeniable good usage and indulgence he had received from me.

Again I sat ruminating what I should do. Mortified as I was at his behavior, and resolved as I had been to dismiss him when I entered my office, nevertheless I strangely felt something superstitious knocking at my heart, and forbidding me to carry out my purpose, and denouncing me for a villain if I dared to breathe one bitter word against this forlornest of mankind. At last, familiarly drawing my chair behind his screen, I sat down and said: "Bartleby, never mind, then, about revealing your history; but let me entreat you, as a friend, to comply as far as may be with the usages of this office. Say now, you will help to examine papers tomorrow or next day: in short, say now, that in a day or two you will begin to be a little reasonable:—say so, Bartleby."

"At present I would prefer not to be a little reasonable," was his mildly cadaverous reply.

Just then the folding doors opened, and Nippers approached. He seemed suffering from an unusually bad night's rest, induced by severer indigestion than common. He overheard those final words of Bartleby.

"*Prefer not,* eh?" gritted Nippers—"I'd *prefer* him, if I were you, sir," addressing me—"I'd *prefer* him; I'd give him preferences, the stubborn mule! What is it, sir, pray, that he *prefers* not to do now?"

Bartleby moved not a limb.

"Mr. Nippers," said I, "I'd prefer that you would withdraw for the present."

Somehow, of late, I had got into the way of involuntarily using the word "prefer" upon all sorts of not exactly suitable occasions. And I trembled to think that my contact with the scrivener had already and seriously affected me in a mental way. And what further and deeper aberration might it not yet produce? This apprehension had not been without efficacy in determining me to summary measures.

Bartleby: A Story of Wall Street

As Nippers, looking very sour and sulky, was departing, Turkey blandly and deferentially approached.

"With submission, sir," said he, "yesterday I was thinking about Bartleby here, and I think that if he would but prefer to take a quart of good ale every day, it would do much towards mending him, and enabling him to assist in examining his papers."

"So you have got the word, too," said I, slightly excited.

"With submission, what word, sir?" asked Turkey, respectfully crowding himself into the contracted space behind the screen, and by so doing, making me jostle the scrivener. "What word, sir?"

"I would prefer to be left alone here," said Bartleby, as if offended at being mobbed in his privacy.

"*That's* the word, Turkey," said I— "*that's* it."

"Oh, *prefer?* oh, yes—queer word. I never use it myself. But, sir, as I was saying, if he would but prefer—"

"Turkey," interrupted I, "you will please withdraw."

"Oh, certainly, sir, if you prefer that I should."

As he opened the folding door to retire, Nippers at his desk caught a glimpse of me, and asked whether I would prefer to have a certain paper copied on blue paper or white. He did not in the least roguishly accent the word "prefer." It was plain that it involuntarily rolled from his tongue. I thought to myself, surely I must get rid of a demented man who already has in some degree turned the tongues, if not the heads, of myself and clerks. But I thought it prudent not to break the dismission at once.

The next day I noticed that Bartleby did nothing but stand at his window in his dead-wall revery. Upon asking him why he did not write, he said that he had decided upon doing no more writing.

"Why, how now? what next?" exclaimed I, "do no more writing?"

"No more."

"And what is the reason?"

"Do you not see the reason for yourself?" he indifferently replied.

I looked steadfastly at him, and perceived that his eyes looked dull and glazed. Instantly it occurred to me that his unexampled diligence in copying by his dim window for the first few weeks of his stay with me might have temporarily impaired his vision.

I was touched. I said something in condolence with him. I hinted that of course he did wisely in abstaining from writing for awhile; and urged him to embrace that opportunity of taking wholesome exercise in the open air. This, however, he did not do. A few days after this, my other clerks being absent, and being in a great hurry to dispatch certain letters by the mail, I thought that, having nothing else earthly to do, Bartleby would surely be less inflexible than usual, and carry these letters to the post office. But he blankly declined. So, much to my inconvenience, I went myself.

Still added days went by. Whether Bartleby's eyes improved or not, I could not say. To all appearance, I thought they did. But when I asked him if they did, he vouchsafed no answer. At all events, he would do no copying. At last, in reply to my urgings, he informed me that he had permanently given up copying.

"What!" exclaimed I; "suppose your eyes should get entirely well —better than ever before—would you not copy then?"

"I have given up copying," he answered, and slid aside.

He remained, as ever, a fixture in my chamber. Nay—if that were possible—he became still more of a fixture than before. What was to be done? He would do nothing in the office; why should he stay there? In plain fact, he had now become a millstone to me, not only useless as a necklace, but afflictive to bear. Yet I was sorry for him. I speak less than truth when I say that, on his own account, he occasioned me uneasiness. If he would but have named a single relative or friend, I would instantly have written and urged their taking the poor fellow away to some convenient retreat. But he seemed alone, absolutely alone in the universe. A bit of wreck in the mid-Atlantic. At length, necessities connected with my business tyrannized over all other considerations. Decently as I could, I told Bartleby that in six days' time he must unconditionally leave the office. I warned him to take measures, in the interval, for procuring some other abode. I offered to assist him in this endeavor, if he himself would but take the first step towards a removal. "And when you finally quit me, Bartleby," added I, "I shall see that you go not away entirely unprovided. Six days from this hour, remember."

At the expiration of that period, I peeped behind the screen, and lo! Bartleby was there.

I buttoned up my coat, balanced myself; advanced slowly towards him, touched his shoulder, and said, "The time has come; you must quit this place; I am sorry for you; here is money; but you must go."

"I would prefer not," he replied, with his back still towards me.

"You *must*."

He remained silent.

Now I had an unbounded confidence in this man's common honesty. He had frequently restored to me sixpences and shillings carelessly dropped upon the floor, for I am apt to be very reckless in such shirt-button affairs. The proceeding, then, which followed will not be deemed extraordinary.

"Bartleby," said I, "I owe you twelve dollars on account; here are thirty-two; the odd twenty are yours— Will you take it?" and I handed the bills towards him.

But he made no motion.

"I will leave them here, then," putting them under a weight on the table. Then taking my hat and cane and going to the door, I tranquilly turned and added—"After you have removed your things from these offices, Bartleby, you will of course lock the door—since everyone is now gone for the day but you—and if you please, slip your key underneath the mat, so that I may have it in the morning. I shall not see you again; so good-bye to you. If, hereafter, in your new place of abode, I can be of any service to you, do not fail to advise me by letter. Good-bye, Bartleby, and fare you well."

But he answered not a word; like the last column of some ruined temple, he remained standing mute and solitary in the middle of the otherwise deserted room.

As I walked home in a pensive mood, my vanity got the better of my pity. I could not but highly plume myself on my masterly management in getting rid of Bartleby. Masterly I call it, and such it must appear to any dispassionate thinker. The beauty of my procedure seemed to consist in its perfect quietness. There was no vulgar bullying, no bravado of any sort, no choleric hectoring, and striding to and fro across the apartment, jerking out vehement commands for Bartleby to bundle himself off with his beggarly traps. Nothing of the kind. Without loudly bidding Bartleby depart—as an inferior genius might have done—I *assumed* the ground that depart he must; and upon that assumption built all I had to say. The more I thought over my procedure, the more I was charmed with it. Nevertheless, next morning, upon awakening, I had my doubts—I had somehow slept off the fumes of vanity. One of the coolest and wisest hours a man has is just after he awakes in the morning. My procedure seemed as sagacious as ever —but only in theory. How it would prove in practice—there was the rub. It was truly a beautiful thought to have assumed Bartleby's departure; but, after all, that assumption was simply my own, and none of Bartleby's. The great point was, not whether I had assumed that he would quit me, but whether he would prefer so to do. He was more a man of preferences than assumptions.

After breakfast, I walked down town, arguing the probabilities pro and con. One moment I thought it would prove a miserable failure, and Bartleby would be found all alive at my office as usual; the next moment it seemed certain that I should find his chair empty. And so I kept veering about. At the corner of Broadway and Canal Street, I saw quite an excited group of people standing in earnest conversation.

"I'll take odds he doesn't," said a voice as I passed.

"Doesn't go?—done!" said I, "put up your money."

I was instinctively putting my hand in my pocket to produce my own, when I remembered that this was an election day. The words I had overheard bore no reference to Bartleby, but to the success or non-success of some candidate for the mayoralty. In my intent frame of mind, I had, as it were, imagined that all Broadway shared in my excitement, and were debating the same question with me. I passed on, very thankful that the uproar of the street screened my momentary absentmindedness.

As I had intended, I was earlier than usual at my office door. I stood listening for a moment. All was still. He must be gone. I tried the knob. The door was locked. Yes, my procedure had worked to a charm; he indeed must be vanished. Yet a certain melancholy mixed with this: I was almost sorry for my brilliant success. I was fumbling under the doormat for the key, which Bartleby was to have left there for me, when accidentally my knee knocked against a panel, producing a summoning sound, and in response a voice came to me from within —"Not yet; I am occupied."

It was Bartleby.

I was thunderstruck. For an instant I stood like the man who, pipe in mouth, was killed one cloudless afternoon long ago in Virginia by summer lightning; at his own warm open window he was killed, and remained leaning out there upon the dreamy afternoon, till some one touched him, when he fell.

"Not gone!" I murmured at last. But again obeying that wondrous ascendancy which the inscrutable scrivener had over me, and from which ascendancy, for all my chafing, I could not completely escape, I slowly went downstairs and out into the street, and while walking round the block considered what I should next do in this unheard-of perplexity. Turn the man out by an actual thrusting I could not; to drive him away by calling him hard names would not do; calling in the police was an unpleasant idea; and yet, permit him to enjoy his cadaverous triumph over me—this, too, I could not think of. What was to be done? or, if nothing could be done, was there anything further that

I could *assume* in the matter? Yes, as before I had prospectively assumed that Bartleby would depart, so now I might retrospectively assume that departed he was. In the legitimate carrying out of this assumption, I might enter my office in a great hurry, and pretending not to see Bartleby at all, walk straight against him as if he were air. Such a proceeding would in a singular degree have the appearance of a home thrust. It was hardly possible that Bartleby could withstand such an application of the doctrine of assumptions. But upon second thoughts the success of the plan seemed rather dubious. I resolved to argue the matter over with him again.

"Bartleby," said I, entering the office, with a quietly severe expression, "I am seriously displeased. I am pained, Bartleby. I had thought better of you. I had imagined you of such a gentlemanly organization that in any delicate dilemma a slight hint would suffice—in short, an assumption. But it appears I am deceived. Why," I added, unaffectedly starting, "you have not even touched that money yet," pointing to it, just where I had left it the evening previous.

He answered nothing.

"Will you, or will you not, quit me?" I now demanded in a sudden passion, advancing close to him.

"I would prefer *not* to quit you," he replied, gently emphasizing the *not*.

"What earthly right have you to stay here? Do you pay any rent? Do you pay my taxes? Or is this property yours?"

He answered nothing.

"Are you ready to go on and write now? Are your eyes recovered? Could you copy a small paper for me this morning? or help examine a few lines? or step round to the post office? In a word, will you do anything at all, to give a coloring to your refusal to depart the premises?"

He silently retired into his hermitage.

I was now in such a state of nervous resentment that I thought it but prudent to check myself at present from further demonstrations. Bartleby and I were alone. I remembered the tragedy of the unfortunate Adams and the still more unfortunate Colt in the solitary office of the latter; and how poor Colt, being dreadfully incensed by Adams, and imprudently permitting himself to get wildly excited, was at unawares hurried into his fatal act—an act which certainly no man could possibly deplore more than the actor himself. Often it had occurred to me in my ponderings upon the subject that had that altercation taken place in the public street, or at a private residence, it would not have terminated as it did. It was the circumstance of being alone in a solitary office, upstairs, of a building entirely unhallowed by humanizing domestic associations—an uncarpeted office, doubtless, of a dusty, haggard sort of appearance—this it must have been, which greatly helped to enhance the irritable desperation of the hapless Colt.

But when this old Adam of resentment rose in me and tempted me concerning Bartleby, I grappled him and threw him. How? Why, simply by recalling the divine injunction: "A new commandment give I unto you, that ye love one another." Yes, this it was that saved me. Aside from higher considerations, charity often operates as a vastly wise and prudent principle—a great safeguard to its possessor. Men have committed murder for jealousy's sake, and anger's sake, and hatred's sake, and selfishness' sake, and spiritual pride's sake; but no man, that ever I heard of, ever committed a diabolical murder for sweet charity's sake. Mere self-interest, then, if no better motive can be enlisted, should, especially with high-tempered men, prompt all beings to charity and philanthropy. At any rate, upon the occasion in question, I strove to drown my exasperated feelings towards the scrivener by benevolently construing his conduct. Poor fellow, poor fellow! thought I, he doesn't mean anything; and besides, he has seen hard times, and ought to be indulged.

I endeavored, also, immediately to occupy myself, and at the same time to comfort my despondency. I tried to fancy that in the course of the morning, at such time as might prove agreeable to him, Bartleby, of his own free accord, would emerge from his hermitage and take up some decided line of march in the direction of the door. But no. Half-past twelve o'clock came; Turkey began to glow in the face, overturn his inkstand, and become generally obstreperous; Nippers abated down into quietude and courtesy; Ginger Nut munched his noon apple; and Bartleby remained standing at his window in one of his profoundest dead-wall reveries. Will it be credited? Ought I to acknowledge it? That afternoon I left the office without saying one further word to him.

Some days now passed, during which, at leisure intervals I looked a little into "Edwards on the Will," and "Priestley on Necessity." Under the circumstances, those books induced a salutary feeling. Gradually I slid into the persuasion that these troubles of mine, touching the scrivener, had been all predestinated from eternity, and Bartleby was billeted upon me for some mysterious purpose of an all-wise Providence, which it was not for a mere mortal like me to fathom. Yes, Bartleby, stay there behind your screen, thought I; I shall persecute

Bartleby: A Story of Wall Street

you no more; you are harmless and noiseless as any of these old chairs; in short, I never feel so private as when I know you are here. At last I see it, I feel it; I penetrate to the predestinated purpose of my life. I am content. Others may have loftier parts to enact; but my mission in this world, Bartleby, is to furnish you with office room for such period as you may see fit to remain.

I believe that this wise and blessed frame of mind would have continued with me had it not been for the unsolicited and uncharitable remarks obtruded upon me by my professional friends who visited the rooms. But thus it often is, that the constant friction of illiberal minds wears out at last the best resolves of the more generous. Though to be sure, when I reflected upon it, it was not strange that people entering my office should be struck by the peculiar aspect of the unaccountable Bartleby, and so be tempted to throw out some sinister observations concerning him. Sometimes an attorney, having business with me, and calling at my office, and finding no one but the scrivener there, would undertake to obtain some sort of precise information from him touching my whereabouts; but without heeding his idle talk, Bartleby would remain standing immovable in the middle of the room. So after contemplating him in that position for a time, the attorney would depart, no wiser than he came.

Also, when a reference was going on, and the room full of lawyers and witnesses, and business driving fast, some deeply occupied legal gentleman present, seeing Bartleby wholly unemployed, would request him to run round to his (the legal gentleman's) office and fetch some papers for him. Thereupon, Bartleby would tranquilly decline, and yet remain idle as before. Then the lawyer would give a great stare, and turn to me. And what could I say? At last I was made aware that all through the circle of my professional acquaintance a whisper of wonder was running round, having reference to the strange creature I kept at my office. This worried me very much. And as the idea came upon me of his possibly turning out a long-lived man, and keep occupying my chambers, and denying my authority; and perplexing my visitors; and scandalizing my professional reputation; and casting a general gloom over the premises; keeping soul and body together to the last upon his savings (for doubtless he spent but half a dime a day), and in the end perhaps outlive me, and claim possession of my office by right of his perpetual occupancy: as all these dark anticipations crowded upon me more and more, and my friends continually intruded their relentless remarks upon the apparition in my room; a great change was wrought in me. I resolved to gather all my faculties together, and forever rid me of this intolerable incubus.

Ere revolving any complicated project, however, adapted to this end, I first simply suggested to Bartleby the propriety of his permanent departure. In a calm and serious tone, I commended the idea to his careful and mature consideration. But, having taken three days to meditate upon it, he apprised me that his original determination remained the same; in short, that he still preferred to abide with me.

What shall I do? I now said to myself, buttoning up my coat to the last button. What shall I do? what ought I to do? what does conscience say I *should* do with this man, or, rather, ghost. Rid myself of him, I must; go, he shall. But how? You will not thrust him, the poor, pale, passive mortal—you will not thrust such a helpless creature out of your door? You will not dishonor yourself by such cruelty? No, I will not, I cannot do that. Rather would I let him live and die here, and then mason up his remains in the wall. What, then, will you do? For all your coaxing, he will not budge. Bribes he leaves under your own paper-weight on your table; in short, it is quite plain that he prefers to cling to you.

Then something severe, something unusual must be done. What! surely you will not have him collared by a constable, and commit his innocent pallor to the common jail? And upon what ground could you procure such a thing to be done?—a vagrant, is he? What! he a vagrant, a wanderer, who refuses to budge? It is because he will *not* be a vagrant, then, that you seek to count him *as* a vagrant. That is too absurd. No visible means of support: there I have him. Wrong again: for indubitably he *does* support himself, and that is the only unanswerable proof that any man can show of his possessing the means so to do. No more, then. Since he will not quit me, I must quit him. I will change my offices; I will move elsewhere, and give him fair notice that if I find him on my new premises I will then proceed against him as a common trespasser.

Acting accordingly, next day I thus addressed him: "I find these chambers too far from the City Hall; the air is unwholesome. In a word, I propose to remove my offices next week, and shall no longer require your services. I tell you this now, in order that you may seek another place."

He made no reply, and nothing more was said.

On the appointed day I engaged carts and men, proceeded to my chambers, and, having but little furniture, everything was removed in a few hours. Throughout, the scrivener remained standing behind the screen, which I directed to be removed the last thing. It was withdrawn; and, being folded up like a huge folio, left him the motionless

Bartleby: A Story of Wall Street

occupant of a naked room. I stood in the entry watching him a moment, while something from within me upbraided me.

I reentered, with my hand in my pocket—and—and my heart in my mouth.

"Good-bye, Bartleby; I am going—good-bye, and God some way bless you; and take that," slipping something in his hand. But it dropped upon the floor, and then—strange to say—I tore myself from him whom I had so longed to be rid of.

Established in my new quarters, for a day or two I kept the door locked, and started at every footfall in the passages. When I returned to my rooms, after any little absence, I would pause at the threshold for an instant, and attentively listen, ere applying my key. But these fears were needless. Bartleby never came nigh me.

I thought all was going well, when a perturbed-looking stranger visited me, inquiring whether I was the person who had recently occupied rooms at No. — Wall Street.

Full of forebodings, I replied that I was.

"Then, sir," said the stranger, who proved a lawyer, "you are responsible for the man you left there. He refuses to do any copying; he refuses to do anything; he says he prefers not to; and he refuses to quit the premises."

"I am very sorry, sir," said I, with assumed tranquillity, but an inward tremor, "but, really, the man you allude to is nothing to me—he is no relation or apprentice of mine, that you should hold me responsible for him."

"In mercy's name, who is he?"

"I certainly cannot inform you. I know nothing about him. Formerly I employed him as a copyist; but he has done nothing for me now for some time past."

"I shall settle him, then—good morning, sir."

Several days passed, and I heard nothing more; and, though I often felt a charitable prompting to call at the place and see poor Bartleby, yet a certain squeamishness, of I know not what, withheld me.

All is over with him, by this time, thought I, at last, when, through another week, no further intelligence reached me. But, coming to my room the day after, I found several persons waiting at my door in a high state of nervous excitement.

"That's the man—here he comes," cried the foremost one, whom I recognized as the lawyer who had previously called upon me alone.

"You must take him away, sir, at once," cried a portly person among them, advancing upon me, and whom I knew to be the landlord of No. — Wall Street. "These gentlemen, my tenants, cannot stand it any longer; Mr. B——," pointing to the lawyer, "has turned him out of his room, and he now persists in haunting the building generally, sitting upon the banisters of the stairs by day, and sleeping in the entry by night. Everybody is concerned; clients are leaving the offices; some fears are entertained of a mob; something you must do, and that without delay."

Aghast at this torrent, I fell back before it, and would fain have locked myself in my new quarters. In vain I persisted that Bartleby was nothing to me—no more than to anyone else. In vain—I was the last person known to have anything to do with him, and they held me to the terrible account. Fearful, then, of being exposed in the papers (as one person present obscurely threatened), I considered the matter, and, at length, said that if the lawyer would give me a confidential interview with the scrivener, in his (the lawyer's) own room, I would, that afternoon, strive my best to rid them of the nuisance they complained of.

Going upstairs to my old haunt, there was Bartleby silently sitting upon the banister at the landing.

"What are you doing here, Bartleby?" said I.

"Sitting upon the banister," he mildly replied.

I motioned him into the lawyer's room, who then left us.

"Bartleby," said I, "are you aware that you are the cause of great tribulation to me, by persisting in occupying the entry after being dismissed from the office?"

No answer.

"Now one of two things must take place. Either you must do something, or something must be done to you. Now what sort of business would you like to engage in? Would you like to reengage in copying for someone?"

"No; I would prefer not to make any change."

"Would you like a clerkship in a dry-goods store?"

"There is too much confinement about that. No, I would not like a clerkship; but I am not particular."

"Too much confinement," I cried, "why, you keep yourself confined all the time!"

"I would prefer not to take a clerkship," he rejoined, as if to settle that little item at once.

"How would a bartender's business suit you? There is no trying of the eyesight in that."

"I would not like it at all; though, as I said before, I am not particular."

His unwonted wordiness inspirited me. I returned to the charge.

"Well, then, would you like to travel through the country collecting bills for the merchants? That would improve your health."

"No, I would prefer to be doing something else."

"How, then, would going as a companion to Europe, to entertain some young gentleman with your conversation—how would that suit you?"

"Not at all. It does not strike me that there is anything definite about that. I like to be stationary. But I am not particular."

"Stationary you shall be, then," I cried, now losing all patience, and, for the first time in all my exasperating connection with him, fairly flying into a passion. "If you do not go away from these premises before night, I shall feel bound—indeed, I *am* bound—to—to—to quit the premises myself!" I rather absurdly concluded, knowing not with what possible threat to try to frighten his immobility into compliance. Despairing of all further efforts, I was precipitately leaving him, when a final thought occurred to me—one which had not been wholly unindulged before.

"Bartleby," said I, in the kindest tone I could assume under such exciting circumstances, "will you go home with me now—not to my office, but my dwelling—and remain there till we can conclude upon some convenient arrangement for you at our leisure? Come, let us start now, right away."

"No: at present I would prefer not to make any change at all."

I answered nothing; but, effectually dodging everyone by the suddenness and rapidity of my flight, rushed from the building, ran up Wall Street towards Broadway, and, jumping into the first omnibus, was soon removed from pursuit. As soon as tranquillity returned, I distinctly perceived that I had now done all that I possibly could, both in respect to the demands of the landlord and his tenants, and with regard to my own desire and sense of duty, to benefit Bartleby, and shield him from rude persecution. I now strove to be entirely carefree and quiescent; and my conscience justified me in the attempt; though, indeed, it was not so successful as I could have wished. So fearful was I of being again hunted out by the incensed landlord and his exasperated tenants that, surrendering my business to Nippers, for a few days, I drove about the upper part of the town and through the suburbs, in my rockaway; crossed over to Jersey City and Hoboken, and paid fugitive visits to Manhattanville and Astoria. In fact, I almost lived in my rockaway for the time.

When again I entered my office, lo, a note from the landlord lay upon the desk. I opened it with trembling hands. It informed me that the writer had sent to the police, and had Bartleby removed to the Tombs as a vagrant. Moreover, since I knew more about him than anyone else, he wished me to appear at that place, and make a suitable statement of the facts. These tidings had a conflicting effect upon me. At first I was indignant; but, at last, almost approved. The landlord's energetic, summary disposition had led him to adopt a procedure which I do not think I would have decided upon myself; and yet, as a last resort, under such peculiar circumstances, it seemed the only plan.

As I afterwards learned, the poor scrivener, when told that he must be conducted to the Tombs, offered not the slightest obstacle, but, in his pale, unmoving way, silently acquiesced.

Some of the compassionate and curious bystanders joined the party; and headed by one of the constables arm in arm with Bartleby, the silent procession filed its way through all the noise, and heat, and joy of the roaring thoroughfares at noon.

The same day I received the note, I went to the Tombs, or, to speak more properly, the Halls of Justice. Seeking the right officer, I stated the purpose of my call, and was informed that the individual I described was, indeed, within. I then assured the functionary that Bartleby was a perfectly honest man, and greatly to be compassionated, however unaccountably eccentric. I narrated all I knew, and closed by suggesting the idea of letting him remain in as indulgent confinement as possible, till something less harsh might be done—though, indeed, I hardly knew what. At all events, if nothing else could be decided upon, the almshouse must receive him. I then begged to have an interview.

Being under no disgraceful charge, and quite serene and harmless in all his ways, they had permitted him freely to wander about the prison, and, especially, in the enclosed grass-platted yards thereof. And so I found him there, standing all alone in the quietest of the yards, his face towards a high wall, while all around, from the narrow slits of the jail windows, I thought I saw peering out upon him the eyes of murderers and thieves.

"Bartleby!"

"I know you," he said, without looking round—"and I want nothing to say to you."

"It was not I that brought you here, Bartleby," said I, keenly pained at his implied suspicion. "And to you, this should not be so vile a place. Nothing reproachful attaches to you by being here. And see, it is not so sad a place as one might think. Look, there is the sky, and here is the grass."

"I know where I am," he replied, but would say nothing more, and so I left him.

As I entered the corridor again, a broad meatlike man, in an apron, accosted me, and, jerking his thumb over his shoulder, said, "Is that your friend?"

"Yes."

"Does he want to starve? If he does, let him live on the prison fare, that's all."

"Who are you?" asked I, not knowing what to make of such an unofficially speaking person in such a place.

"I am the grub-man. Such gentlemen as have friends here hire me to provide them with something good to eat."

"Is this so?" said I, turning to the turnkey.

He said it was.

"Well, then," said I, slipping some silver into the grub-man's hands (for so they called him), "I want you to give particular attention to my friend there; let him have the best dinner you can get. And you must be as polite to him as possible."

"Introduce me, will you?" said the grub-man, looking at me with an expression which seemed to say he was all impatience for an opportunity to give a specimen of his breeding.

Thinking it would prove of benefit to the scrivener, I acquiesced; and, asking the grub-man his name, went up with him to Bartleby.

"Bartleby, this is a friend; you will find him very useful to you."

"Your sarvant, sir, your sarvant," said the grub-man, making a low salutation behind his apron. "Hope you find it pleasant here, sir; nice grounds—cool apartments—hope you'll stay with us some time—try to make it agreeable. What will you have for dinner today?"

"I prefer not to dine today," said Bartleby, turning away. "It would disagree with me; I am unused to dinners." So saying, he slowly moved to the other side of the enclosure, and took up a position fronting the dead wall.

"How's this?" said the grub-man, addressing me with a stare of astonishment. "He's odd, ain't he?"

"I think he is a little deranged," said I, sadly.

"Deranged? deranged is it? Well, now, upon my word, I thought that friend of yourn was a gentleman forger; they are always pale and genteellike, them forgers. I can't help pity 'em—can't help it, sir. Did you know Monroe Edwards?" he added, touchingly, and paused. Then, laying his hand piteously on my shoulder, sighed, "He died of consumption at Sing Sing. So you weren't acquainted with Monroe?"

"No, I was never socially acquainted with any forgers. But I cannot stop longer. Look to my friend yonder. You will not lose by it. I will see you again."

Some few days after this, I again obtained admission to the Tombs, and went through the corridors in quest of Bartleby; but without finding him.

"I saw him coming from his cell not long ago," said a turnkey; "may be he's gone to loiter in the yards."

So I went in that direction.

"Are you looking for the silent man?" said another turnkey, passing me. "Yonder he lies—sleeping in the yard there. 'Tis not twenty minutes since I saw him lie down."

The yard was entirely quiet. It was not accessible to the common prisoners. The surrounding walls, of amazing thickness, kept off all sounds behind them. The Egyptian character of the masonry weighed upon me with its gloom. But a soft imprisoned turf grew underfoot. The heart of the eternal pyramids, it seemed, wherein, by some strange magic, through the clefts, grass seed, dropped by birds, had sprung.

Strangely huddled at the base of the wall, his knees drawn up, and lying on his side, his head touching the cold stones, I saw the wasted Bartleby. But nothing stirred. I paused; then went close up to him; stooped over, and saw that his dim eyes were open; otherwise he seemed profoundly sleeping. Something prompted me to touch him. I felt his hand, when a tingling shiver ran up my arm and down my spine to my feet.

The round face of the grub-man peered upon me now. "His dinner is ready. Won't he dine today, either? Or does he live without dining?"

"Lives without dining," said I, and closed the eyes.

"Eh!—He's asleep, ain't he?"

"With kings and counselors," murmured I.

There would seem little need for proceeding further in this history. Imagination will readily supply the meager recital of poor Bartleby's interment. But, ere parting with the reader, let me say that if this little narrative has sufficiently interested him, to awaken curiosity as to who Bartleby was, and what manner of life he led prior to the present narrator's making his acquaintance, I can only reply that in such curiosity I fully share, but am wholly unable to gratify it. Yet here I hardly know whether I should divulge one little item of rumor, which came to my ear a few months after the scrivener's decease. Upon what basis it rested I could never ascertain; and hence, how true it is I cannot now tell. But, inasmuch as this vague report has not been without a certain suggestive interest to me, however sad, it may prove the same with some others; and so I will briefly mention it. The report was this: that Bartleby had been a subordinate clerk in the Dead Letter Office at Washington, from which he had been suddenly removed by a change in the administration. When I think over this rumor, hardly can I express the emotions which seize me. Dead letters! does it not sound like dead men? Conceive a man by nature and misfortune prone to a pallid hopelessness, can any business seem more fitted to heighten it than that of continually handling these dead letters, and assorting them for the flames? For by the cartload they are annually burned. Sometimes from out the folded paper the pale clerk takes a ring—the finger it was meant for, perhaps, moulders in the grave; a banknote sent in swiftest charity—he whom it would relieve nor eats nor hungers any more; pardon for those who died despairing; hope for those who died unhoping; good tidings for those who died stifled by unrelieved calamities. On errands of life, these letters speed to death.

Ah, Bartleby! Ah, humanity!

A Lover of Pumpkins

PEDRO ANTONIO DE ALARCÓN

Alarcón was esteemed as probably the best Spanish tale teller of the nineteenth century, because of his humor, imagination, quick action, portrayal of people, and local atmosphere.

Pedro Antonio de Alarcón (1833–1891) was born in Guadix in the southern province of Granada, of a family that may have had Moorish blood. His parents wanted him to be a priest, but he went to Madrid and turned to journalism and party politics, and even fought duels. He volunteered for the Spanish Army in the Morocco campaign of 1859–60 and was wounded. His book about the campaign marked him as the first modern war correspondent, and brought fame as well as money with which to travel and continue writing. His first collection of short stories appeared in 1859. Alarcón produced not only realistic stories but also novels, plays, poetry, essays, and books of travel. He is still the best-known Spanish story writer since Miguel Cervantes.

"The Stub Book," which might have grown from an anecdote about the farmers of Rota, sketches clearly the devotion and cunning of the peasant who must make a living while tilling barren soil.

PEDRO ANTONIO DE ALARCÓN

The Stub Book

*T*HE STORY BEGINS IN ROTA. Rota is the smallest of those charming towns that form the large semicircle around the Bay of Cádiz. But in spite of being the smallest, it was the favorite town of the Grand Duke of Osuna, who built there his castle, which I could describe stone by stone. However, we're not concerned here with castles or dukes, but rather with the fields that surround Rota and with a very humble farmer whom we'll call Old Beautyseeker, though this was not his real name.

From the fertile fields of Rota, especially the truck gardens, come the fruits and vegetables which furnish the markets of Huelva and Seville. The quality of its tomatoes and pumpkins is such that in Andalucía the people of Rota are always referred to as the Pumpkin-men or Tomato-men, nicknames of which they are very proud.

And, truly, they have reason to feel such pride, for it so happens that the soil around Rota which produces so well—that is to say, the truck-farm land, the earth that gives three or four harvests yearly—is not soil at all, but pure and clean sand blown up from the ocean by the violent west wind, and scattered over the whole Rota region.

But the callousness of nature there is more than compensated by the industriousness of man. I have never seen, nor do I believe that there is in the whole world, an agricultural worker who labors as hard as a Rota farmer. There isn't even a little stream running through those melancholy fields. What of it? The pumpkin raiser has dug many wells, from which he collects the precious liquid which is the lifeblood of his vegetables. The tomato grower spends half his life searching for substances which can be used as fertilizer. When he has both these elements, water and plant food, the Rota truck-gardener begins to fertilize tiny mounds of earth, and in each sows a tomato or pumpkin seed, which he then sprinkles by hand, as if he were giving a drink to a baby.

From then to harvesttime, he daily cares for the plants, one by one, as they spring up there, treating them with a love comparable only to that of parents for their children. One day he adds a little fertilizer to such-and-such a plant, throws a jar of water on another; today he kills insects which are eating the leaves; next day covers straw and dead leaves, those that can't stand too much sun or are too exposed to the winds from the sea. One day he counts the stems, the flowers, and even the fruits of the most precocious; another day he talks to them, caresses them, kisses them, blesses them, going so far as to give them affectionate names to distinguish and individualize them in his mind.

Without exaggeration, it is already proverbial (and I've heard it said many times in Rota) that the farmer in that place touches with his own hands, at least forty times a day, each tomato plant growing in his plot. This explains why the farmers of that region end up so bent over that their chins almost touch their knees.

Well, then, Old Beautyseeker was one of those farmers.

He began to be bent over at the time of the episode I am about to relate. He was now sixty years old—and had spent forty years caring for a garden near the beach.

That year he had raised some enormous pumpkins which were already turning golden, which is as much as to say it was the month of June. Old Beautyseeker was perfectly acquainted, by their form, color, and even by name, with the forty fattest and most golden, which were beckoning, "Cook me up!"

"Soon we'll have to part," he said tenderly, with a melancholy gaze.

Finally, one afternoon, he made up his mind to the sacrifice and pronounced the terrible sentence.

"Tomorrow," he said, "I'll cut these forty beauties and take them to the market in Cádiz. Happy the ones who eat them!"

He then strolled off slowly to his cottage and spent the night anguishing like a father who is about to marry off his daughter the following morning.

"My poor pumpkins!" he sighed from time to time, unable to sleep. Then he would reflect, and finally say to himself, "And what else should I do but sell them? That's why I raised them! They are worth at least fifteen duros."

The Stub Book

Imagine, then, his astonishment, his great fury, and his desperation the following morning when he went to his pumpkin patch and found someone had stolen the forty pumpkins! He started to calculate shrewdly and decided his pumpkins could not be in Rota, where it would be impossible to sell them without risk of his recognizing them.

"As I figure it, they're in Cádiz!" he said suddenly. "The thief who robbed me of them last night around nine or ten has escaped in the cargo boat.... I'll go to Cádiz this morning by the hour boat, and there I'll get the rascal and recover the daughters of my rearing!"

Thus mumbling, he hovered for twenty minutes more at the scene of the catastrophe, counting the pumpkins that were missing, until around eight o'clock he went off toward the wharf.

The hour boat was just about to take off. It was a little ferry that took passengers to Cádiz every morning at nine, just as the cargo boat left every night at midnight with the fruits and vegetables. The former was called the hour boat because in one hour, and even less sometimes, it made the three-league crossing between Rota and Cádiz.

It was, then, ten-thirty in the morning when Old Beautyseeker stopped in front of a vegetable stall in the Cádiz market, and said to the policeman he had along with him, "These are my pumpkins! Arrest this man!" He pointed at the seller.

"Arrest *me?*" replied the man, filled with amazement. "These are my pumpkins. I bought them—"

"Tell it to the judge!" answered Old Beautyseeker.

"Oh, no!"

"Oh, yes!"

"You thief!"

"You liar!"

"Speak more politely! You fellows shouldn't insult each other this way!" said the policeman calmly, giving each a good punch in the chest.

By now some people had gathered round, among them the official responsible for order in the public marketplace. When the official was informed of the whole incident, he asked the seller, in majestic tones, "From whom did you get these pumpkins?"

"From Mr. So-and-so, a man from Rota," said the vendor.

"He'd be the one!" yelled Old Beautyseeker. "Whenever his terrible garden doesn't produce, he steals from his neighbors!"

"But," said the official, "supposing you were robbed of forty pumpkins last night, how do you know these, and not some others, are yours?"

"Well," answered Old Beautyseeker, "it's because I know these as you would know your own daughters, if you had any! Don't you understand I raised them? Look, man! This one is Little Fatty; this, Plumpy Cheeks; this, Paunchy Baby; this, Blushy Face; and this one, Manuela, because she looks so much like my youngest daughter"; and the poor fellow began to weep like a child.

"All this sounds fine," said the official, "but the law isn't satisfied with your just recognizing your pumpkins. You have to identify them with absolute proof. You others there, this is no laughing matter. I'm a lawyer."

"Well, you'll see right now how I'll prove to the whole world, right here, that these pumpkins grew up in my truck patch," said Old Beautyseeker. And throwing down a sack which he carried, he knelt and calmly began to undo it. Everybody around him became most curious.

"What's he going to take out of there?" they all wondered.

At that moment, another person came up to look at what was going on in the crowd, and on seeing him, the vendor exclaimed: "I'm so happy you've arrived, Old So-and-so! This fellow says these pumpkins I bought from you last night are stolen. You answer him!"

The newcomer turned yellower than wax and tried to escape, but the other people stopped him, and the official himself ordered him to remain. As for Old Beautyseeker, he had already confronted the supposed thief, saying: "You're going to see something interesting now!"

Old So-and-so, regaining his composure, answered: "You're the one who's going to have to take care what you say; because if you can't prove it—and you can't—you're going to jail. These pumpkins are mine; I raised them in my plot like all the others I've brought to Cádiz this year, and nobody can prove I haven't."

"You'll see right now," repeated Old Beautyseeker as he finished opening his sack.

A big bunch of green stems tumbled to the ground, while the old farmer, squatting on his heels, addressed the crowd:

"Gentlemen, haven't you ever had to pay taxes? And haven't you noticed that green book from which the collector cuts out receipts, always leaving a piece in the book so he can find out later if some receipt is false or not?"

"What you're talking about is called the stub book," said the official solemnly.

"Well, that's what I've brought along here—my pumpkin-patch's stub book; in other words, the stems that were attached to these

The Stub Book

pumpkins before this robber stole them from me. This stem goes with this pumpkin—no one can deny it. This other—now you'll see—belongs to this one. This thicker one goes with that one over there—exactly—and this with this—that with that...."

And while he talked he kept matching the stems to the pumpkins one by one. The astonished spectators saw how each stem exactly matched each pumpkin, and they got so excited by such a clever proof that they all pitched in to help Old Beautyseeker, exclaiming: "Absolutely! Exactly! There's no doubt! Just look! This one goes here ... that there ... that other goes here, this over there ... "

The guffaws of the men mingled with the whistles of the boys, the women's curses, the triumphant sobs of the happy farmer, and the punches the police were giving the convicted thief.

It's hardly necessary to add that besides going off to jail, the thief had to return the fifteen duros to the seller, who delivered them over to Old Beautyseeker, who started back to Rota very satisfied, mumbling to himself on the way home:

"How beautiful they looked in the market! I should have brought back Manuela to eat tonight and save the seeds!"

Father and Son in Norway

BJÖRNSTJERNE BJÖRNSON

Björnson, who for sixty years was a leading writer and a patriot, was called "the uncrowned king of Norway" because of his literary and political powers.

Björnstjerne Martinius Björnson (1832–1910), son of a clergyman of peasant stock, enjoyed a happy childhood. After high school he left the University of Oslo and became the foremost journalist of his era. His first stories were published in 1856, aimed at uniting the ancient sagas of the North with the life of the common people of his own time. He wrote the words of the Norwegian national anthem. Along with Hendrik Ibsen he modernized the theater in Scandinavia. As a drama director and renowned lecturer, Björnson lived in a number of countries, including the United States. He was awarded the Nobel Prize in literature in 1903.

Björnson wanted his writing to serve ideas, to reveal the ultimate unity of life and literature. "The Father" was written in 1860. Beneath the terse lines of this apparently simple story lies a meaning that is more than a parable.

BJÖRNSTJERNE BJÖRNSON

The Father

THE MAN WHOSE STORY is here to be told was the wealthiest and most influential person in his parish; his name was Thord Overaas. He appeared in the priest's study one day, tall and earnest.

"I have got a son," said he, "and I wish to present him for baptism."

"What shall his name be?"

"Finn—after my father."

"And the sponsors?"

They were mentioned, and proved to be the best men and women of Thord's relations in the parish.

"Is there anything else?" inquired the priest, and looked up.

The peasant hesitated a little.

"I should like very much to have him baptized by himself," said he, finally.

"That is to say on a weekday?"

"Next Saturday, at twelve o'clock noon."

"Is there anything else?" inquired the priest.

"There is nothing else"; and the peasant twirled his cap, as though he were about to go.

Then the priest rose. "There is yet this, however," said he, and walking toward Thord, he took him by the hand and looked gravely into his eyes: "God grant that the child may become a blessing to you!"

One day sixteen years later, Thord stood once more in the priest's study.

"Really, you carry your age astonishingly well, Thord," said the priest; for he saw no change whatever in the man.

"That is because I have no troubles," replied Thord.

To this the priest said nothing, but after a while he asked: "What is your pleasure this evening?"

"I have come this evening about that son of mine who is to be confirmed tomorrow."

"He is a bright boy."

"I did not wish to pay the priest until I heard what number the boy would have when he takes his place in church tomorrow."

"He will stand number one."

"So I have heard; and here are ten dollars for the priest."

"Is there anything else I can do for you?" inquired the priest, fixing his eyes on Thord.

"There is nothing else."

Thord went out.

Eight years more rolled by, and then one day a noise was heard outside of the priest's study, for many men were approaching, and at their head was Thord, who entered first.

The priest looked up and recognized him.

"You come well attended this evening, Thord," said he.

"I am here to request that the banns may be published for my son; he is about to marry Karen Storliden, daughter of Gudmund, who stands here beside me."

"Why, that is the richest girl in the parish."

"So they say," replied the peasant, stroking back his hair with one hand.

The priest sat a while as if in deep thought, then entered the names in his book, without making any comments, and the men wrote their signatures underneath. Thord laid three dollars on the table.

"One is all I am to have," said the priest.

"I know that very well; but he is my only child. I want to do it handsomely."

The priest took the money.

"This is now the third time, Thord, that you have come here on your son's account."

"But now I am through with him," said Thord, and folding up his pocketbook he said farewell and walked away.

The men slowly followed him.

A fortnight later, the father and son were rowing across the lake, one calm, still day, to Storliden to make arrangements for the wedding.

"This thwart is not secure," said the son, and stood up to straighten the seat on which he was sitting.

At the same moment the board he was standing on slipped from under him; he threw out his arms, uttered a shriek, and fell overboard.

The Father

"Take hold of the oar!" shouted the father, springing to his feet and holding out the oar.

But when the son had made a couple of efforts he grew stiff.

"Wait a moment!" cried the father, and began to row toward his son.

Then the son rolled over on his back, gave his father one long look, and sank.

Thord could scarcely believe it; he held the boat still, and stared at the spot where his son had gone down, as though he must surely come to the surface again. There rose some bubbles, then some more, and finally one large one that burst; and the lake lay there as smooth and bright as a mirror again.

For three days and three nights people saw the father rowing round and round the spot, without taking either food or sleep; he was dragging the lake for the body of his son. And toward morning of the third day he found it, and carried it in his arms up over the hills to his gard.

It might have been about a year from that day, when the priest, late one autumn evening, heard someone in the passage outside of the door, carefully trying to find the latch. The priest opened the door, and in walked a tall, thin man, with bowed form and white hair. The priest looked long at him before he recognized him. It was Thord.

"Are you out walking so late?" said the priest, and stood still in front of him.

"Ah, yes! it is late," said Thord, and took a seat.

The priest sat down also, as though waiting. A long, long silence followed. At last Thord said:

"I have something with me that I should like to give to the poor; I want it to be invested as a legacy in my son's name."

He rose, laid some money on the table, and sat down again. The priest counted it.

"It is a great deal of money," said he.

"It is half the price of my gard. I sold it today."

The priest sat long in silence. At last he asked, but gently:

"What do you propose to do now, Thord?"

"Something better."

They sat there for a while, Thord with downcast eyes, the priest with his eyes fixed on Thord. Presently the priest said, slowly and softly:

"I think your son has at last brought you a true blessing."

"Yes, I think so myself," said Thord, looking up, while two big tears coursed slowly down his cheeks.

A Lion in the Path

GUY DE MAUPASSANT

One of the great nineteenth-century masters, De Maupassant not only perfected the European *conte* or compact story but, along with Chekhov, became a challenging model for dozens of later fiction writers.

Henri René Albert Guy de Maupassant (1850–1893) was brought up in the French province of Normandy by middle-class parents who frequently quarreled and who separated when he was fifteen. He graduated from the College of Rouen, served as a private in the Franco-Prussian war of 1870, and got a post as a civil servant.

He began writing as a poet, but at the age of twenty-three shifted to fiction. A seven-year period of training under his godfather, Gustav Flaubert, enabled him to attain an original style. By 1884 he was able to live by his pen. In ten amazing years he turned out thirty volumes of short stories, novels, plays, and travel sketches. At the same time he led a dissolute life which resulted, after an attempt at suicide, in his death at the age of forty-three.

De Maupassant practiced the use of the precisely correct word; perfect economy in narration and description; a simple, rhythmic style; strong visual imagery; and a sometimes cynical humor. He has been accused of a cruel attitude because of his objectivity, but much of his work condemns the sins of the world and shows pity for humanity's hard lot. As Joseph Conrad wrote in *Notes on Life and Letters,* "He refrains from setting his cleverness against the eloquence of the facts ... And yet it can be safely affirmed that this man wrote from the fullness of a compassionate heart." De Maupassant's mastery of the art of fiction caused Henry James to label him despairingly as "a lion in the path," because every writer who desired to develop a style of his own had first to face the almost overwhelming perfection of this French author.

De Maupassant grew up in the farming country of Normandy, and some of his best stories were based on yarns he heard from his mother or from hardworking peasants, such as the neighbors of Maître Hauchecorne in "A Piece of String." This story has become a world classic primarily because it shows in brief scope how a person falsely accused may destroy himself by guiltily protesting his innocence, but study may reveal deeper meanings.

GUY DE MAUPASSANT

A Piece of String

*I*T WAS MARKET DAY, and over all the roads round Goderville the peasants and their wives were coming towards the town. The men walked easily, lurching the whole body forward at every step. Their long legs were twisted and deformed by the slow, painful labors of the country: by bending over to plough, which is what also makes their left shoulders too high and their figures crooked; and by reaping corn, which obliges them for steadiness' sake to spread their knees too wide. Their starched blue blouses, shining as though varnished, ornamented at collar and cuffs with little patterns of white stitchwork, and blown up big around their bony bodies, seemed exactly like balloons about to soar, but putting forth a head, two arms, and two feet.

Some of these fellows dragged a cow or a calf at the end of a rope. And just behind the animal, beating it over the back with a leaf-covered branch to hasten its pace, went their wives, carrying large baskets from which came forth the heads of chickens or the heads of ducks. These women walked with steps far shorter and quicker than the men; their figures, withered and upright, were adorned with scanty little shawls pinned over their flat bosoms; and they enveloped their heads each in a white cloth, close fastened round the hair and surmounted by a cap.

Now a char-à-banc passed by, drawn by a jerky-paced nag. It shook up strangely the two men on the seat. And the woman at the bottom of the cart held fast to its sides to lessen the hard joltings.

In the marketplace at Goderville was a great crowd, a mingled multitude of men and beasts. The horns of cattle, the high and long napped hats of wealthy peasants, the headdresses of the women, came to the surface of that sea. And voices clamorous, sharp, shrill, made a continuous and savage din. Above it a huge burst of laughter from the sturdy lungs of a merry yokel would sometimes sound, and sometimes a long bellow from a cow tied fast to the wall of a house.

It all smelled of the stable, of milk, of hay, and of perspiration, giving off that half-human, half-animal odor which is peculiar to the men of the fields.

Maître Hauchecorne, of Bréauté, had just arrived at Goderville, and was taking his way towards the square, when he perceived on the ground a little piece of string. Maître Hauchecorne, economical, like all true Normans, reflected that everything was worth picking up which could be of any use; and he stooped down—but painfully, because he suffered from rheumatism. He took the bit of thin cord from the ground, and was carefully preparing to roll it up when he saw Maître Malandain, the harnessmaker, on his doorstep, looking at him. They had once had a quarrel about a halter, and they had remained angry, bearing malice on both sides. Maître Hauchecorne was overcome with a sort of shame at being seen by his enemy looking in the dirt so for a bit of string. He quickly hid his find beneath his blouse; then in the pocket of his breeches; then pretended to be still looking for something on the ground which he did not discover; and at last went off towards the marketplace, with his head bent forward, and a body almost doubled in two by rheumatic pains.

He lost himself immediately in the crowd, which was clamorous, slow, and agitated by interminable bargains. The peasants examined the cows, went off, came back, always in great perplexity and fear of being cheated, never quite daring to decide, spying at the eye of the seller, trying ceaselessly to discover the tricks of the man and the defect in the beast.

The women, having placed their great baskets at their feet, had pulled out the poultry, which lay upon the ground, tied by the legs, with eyes scared, with combs scarlet.

They listened to propositions, maintaining their prices, with a dry manner, with an impassible face; or, suddenly, perhaps, deciding to take the lower price which was offered, they cried out to the customer, who was departing slowly:

"All right, I'll let you have them, Maît' Anthime."

Then, little by little, the square became empty, and when the Angelus struck midday those who lived at a distance poured into the inns.

A Piece of String

At Jourdain's the great room was filled with eaters just as the vast court was filled with vehicles of every sort—wagons, gigs, char-à-bancs, tilburys, tilt-carts which have no name, yellow with mud, misshapen, pieced together, raising their shafts to heaven like two arms, or it may be with their nose in the dirt and their rear in the air.

Just opposite to where the diners were at table the huge fireplace, full of clear flame, threw a lively heat on the backs of those who sat along the right. Three spits were turning, loaded with chickens, with pigeons, and with joints of mutton, and a delectable odor of roast meat, and of gravy gushing over crisp brown skin, took wing from the hearth, kindled merriment, caused mouths to water.

All the aristocracy of the plough were eating there, at Maît' Jourdain's, the innkeeper's, a dealer in horses also, and a sharp fellow who had made a pretty penny in his day.

The dishes were passed round, were emptied, with jugs of yellow cider. Every one told of his affairs, of his purchases and his sales. They asked news about the crops. The weather was good for green stuffs, but a little wet for wheat.

All of a sudden the drum rolled in the court before the house. Every one, except some of the most indifferent, was on his feet at once, and ran to the door, to the windows, with his mouth still full and his napkin in his hand.

When the public crier had finished his tattoo he called forth in a jerky voice, making his pauses out of time:

"Be it known to the inhabitants of Goderville, and in general to all —persons present at the market, that there has been lost this morning, on the Beuzeville road, between—nine and ten o'clock, a pocketbook of black leather, containing five hundred francs and business papers. You are requested to return it—to the mayor's office, at once, or to Maître Fortune Houlbrèque, of Manneville. There will be twenty francs reward."

Then the man departed. They heard once more at a distance the dull beatings on the drum and the faint voice of the crier.

Then they began to talk of this event, reckoning up the chances which Maître Houlbrèque had of finding or of not finding his pocketbook again.

And the meal went on.

They were finishing their coffee when the corporal of gendarmes appeared on the threshold.

He asked:

"Is Maître Hauchecorne, of Bréauté, here?"

Maître Hauchecorne, seated at the other end of the table, answered: "Here I am."

And the corporal resumed:

"Maître Hauchecorne, will you have the kindness to come with me to the mayor's office? M. le Maire would like to speak to you."

The peasant, surprised and uneasy, gulped down his little glass of cognac, got up, and, even worse bent over than in the morning, since the first steps after a rest were always particularly difficult, started off, repeating:

"Here I am, here I am."

And he followed the corporal.

The mayor was waiting for him, seated in an armchair. He was the notary of the place, a tall, grave man of pompous speech.

"Maître Hauchecorne," said he, "this morning, on the Beuzeville road, you were seen to pick up the pocketbook lost by Maître Houlbrèque, of Manneville."

The countryman, speechless, regarded the mayor, frightened already by this suspicion which rested on him he knew not why.

"I, I picked up that pocketbook?"

"Yes, you."

"I swear I didn't even know nothing about it at all."

"You were seen."

"They saw me, me? Who is that who saw me?"

"M. Malandain, the harnessmaker."

Then the old man remembered, understood, and, reddening with anger:

"Ah! he saw me, did he, the rascal? He saw me picking up this string here, M'sieu' le Maire."

And, fumbling at the bottom of his pocket, he pulled out of it the little end of string.

But the mayor incredulously shook his head:

"You will not make me believe, Maître Hauchecorne, that M. Malandain, who is a man worthy of credit, has mistaken this string for a pocketbook."

The peasant, furious, raised his hand and spat as if to attest his good faith, repeating:

"For all that, it is the truth of the good God, the blessed truth, M'sieu' le Maire. There! on my soul and my salvation I repeat it."

The mayor continued:

A Piece of String

"After having picked up the thing in question, you even looked for some time in the mud to see if a piece of money had not dropped out of it."

The good man was suffocated with indignation and with fear:

"If they can say!—if they can say ... such lies as that to slander an honest man! If they can say!—"

He might protest, he was not believed.

He was confronted with M. Malandain, who repeated and sustained his testimony. They abused one another for an hour. At his own request Maître Hauchecorne was searched. Nothing was found upon him.

At last, the mayor, much perplexed, sent him away, warning him that he would inform the public prosecutor, and ask for orders.

The news had spread. When he left the mayor's office, the old man was surrounded, interrogated with a curiosity which was serious or mocking as the case might be, but into which no indignation entered. And he began to tell the story of the string. They did not believe him. They laughed.

He passed on, buttonholed by everyone, himself buttonholing his acquaintances, beginning over and over again his tale and his protestations, showing his pockets turned inside out to prove that he had nothing.

They said to him:

"You old rogue, *va!*"

And he grew angry, exasperated, feverish, in despair at not being believed, and always telling his story.

The night came. It was time to go home. He set out with three of his neighbors, to whom he pointed out the place where he had picked up the end of string; and all the way he talked of his adventure.

That evening he made the round in the village of Bréauté, so as to tell everyone. He met only unbelievers.

He was ill of it all night long.

The next day, about one in the afternoon, Marius Paumelle, a farm hand of Maître Breton, the market gardener at Ymauville, returned the pocketbook and its contents to Maître Houlbrèque, of Manneville.

This man said, indeed, that he had found it on the road; but not knowing how to read, he had carried it home and given it to his master.

The news spread to the environs. Maître Hauchecorne was informed. He put himself at once upon the go, and began to relate his story as completed by the denouement. He triumphed.

"What grieved me," said he, "was not the thing itself, do you understand; but it was the lies. There's nothing does you so much harm as being in disgrace for lying."

All day he talked of his adventure, he told it on the roads to the people who passed; at the cabaret to the people who drank; and the next Sunday, when they came out of church. He even stopped strangers to tell them about it. He was easy, now, and yet something worried him without his knowing exactly what it was. People had a joking manner while they listened. They did not seem convinced. He seemed to feel their tittle-tattle behind his back.

On Tuesday of the next week he went to market at Goderville, prompted entirely by the need of telling his story.

Malandain, standing on his doorstep, began to laugh as he saw him pass. Why?

He accosted a farmer of Criquetot, who did not let him finish, and, giving him a punch in the pit of his stomach, cried in his face:

"Oh you great rogue, *va!*" Then turned his heel upon him.

Maître Hauchecorne remained speechless, and grew more and more uneasy. Why had they called him "great rogue"?

When seated at table in Jourdain's tavern he began again to explain the whole affair.

A horse dealer of Montivilliers shouted at him:

"Get out, get out old scamp; I know all about your string!"

Hauchecorne stammered:

"But since they found it again, the pocketbook!"

But the other continued:

"Hold your tongue, daddy; there's one who finds it and there's another who returns it. And no one the wiser."

The peasant was choked. He understood at last. They accused him of having had the pocketbook brought back by an accomplice, by a confederate.

He tried to protest. The whole table began to laugh.

He could not finish his dinner, and went away amid a chorus of jeers.

He went home, ashamed and indignant, choked with rage, with confusion, the more castdown since from his Norman cunning, he was, perhaps, capable of having done what they accused him of, and even of boasting of it as a good trick. His innocence dimly seemed to him impossible to prove, his craftiness being so well known. And he felt himself struck to the heart by the injustice of the suspicion.

A Piece of String

Then he began anew to tell of his adventure, lengthening his recital every day, each time adding new proofs, more energetic protestations, and more solemn oaths which he thought of, which he prepared in his hours of solitude, his mind being entirely occupied by the story of the string. The more complicated his defense, the more artful his arguments, the less he was believed.

"Those are liars' proofs," they said behind his back.

He felt this; it preyed upon his heart. He exhausted himself in useless efforts.

He was visibly wasting away.

The jokers now made him tell the story of "A Piece of String" to amuse them, just as you make a soldier who has been on a campaign tell his story of the battle. His mind, struck at the root, grew weak.

About the end of December he took to his bed.

He died early in January, and, in the delirium of the death agony, he protested his innocence, repeating:

"A little bit of string—a little bit of string—see, here it is, M'sieu' le Maire."

A "Silken Jew" in the House

SHOLEM ALEICHEM

"Sholem Aleichem," the pen name of Solomon Rabinowitz, became known to the world as "the Jewish Mark Twain." Rabinowitz (1859–1916), poet, dramatist, fiction writer, and lecturer, was born in the Ukraine in Russia, and educated as a rabbi. His talent as a humorist was recognized even in boyhood. At the age of fourteen he wrote a story about a Jewish Robinson Crusoe. His reputation was recognized by the time he was twenty. His first story in Yiddish appeared in 1883, and he was the first person to write for children in that language. He inherited money from his wife's family but spent it on editing a Yiddish magazine and helping other writers. He left Russia in 1905 and lectured in many parts of Europe and the United States. He died in New York City in the middle of World War I. In later life he was poor and in bad health, but kept his gift for looking on the world cheerfully. Rabinowitz taught the Jews, a people with a tragic history, to find a grain of laughter in every trouble.

"The Passover Guest" is apparently merely a reminiscence of the boyhood of the author, son of a village rabbi; but the first pangs of youthful disillusion are shown with amusing pathos.

SHOLEM ALEICHEM

The Passover Guest

I HAVE A PASSOVER GUEST for you, Reb Yoneh, such a guest as you never had since you became a householder."

"What sort is he?"

"A real Oriental citron!"

"What does that mean?"

"It means a 'silken Jew,' a personage of distinction. The only thing against him is—he doesn't speak our language."

"What does he speak, then?"

"Hebrew."

"Is he from Jerusalem?"

"I don't know where he comes from, but his words are full of *a*'s."

Such was the conversation that took place between my father and the beadle, a day before Passover, and I was wild with curiosity to see the "guest" who didn't understand Yiddish, and who talked with *a*'s. I had already noticed, in synagogue, a strange-looking individual, in a fur cap, and a Turkish robe striped blue, red, and yellow. We boys crowded around him on all sides, and stared, and then caught it hot from the beadle, who said children had no business "to creep into a stranger's face" like that. Prayers over, everyone greeted the stranger, and wished him a happy Passover, and he, with a sweet smile on his red cheeks set in a round gray beard, replied to each one, "Shalom! Shalom!" instead of our Sholom. This "Shalom! Shalom!" of his sent us boys into fits of laughter. The beadle grew very angry, and pursued us with slaps. We eluded him, and stole deviously back to the stranger, listened to his "Shalom! Shalom!", exploded with laughter, and escaped anew from the hands of the beadle.

I am puffed up with pride as I follow my father and his guest to our house, and feel how all my comrades envy me. They stand looking after us, and every now and then I turn my head, and put out my tongue at them. The walk home is silent. When we arrive, my father greets my mother with "a happy Passover!" and the guest nods his head so that his fur cap shakes. "Shalom! Shalom!" he says. I think of my comrades, and hide my head under the table, not to burst out laughing. But I shoot continual glances at the guest, and his appearance pleases me; I like his Turkish robe, striped yellow, red, and blue, his fresh red cheeks set in a curly gray beard, his beautiful black eyes that look out so pleasantly from beneath his bushy eyebrows. And I see that my father is pleased with him too, that he is delighted with him. My mother looks at him as though he were something more than a man, and no one speaks to him but my father, who offers him the cushioned reclining-seat at table.

Mother is taken up with the preparations for the Passover meal, and Rikel the maid is helping her. It is only when the time comes for saying Kiddush that my father and the guest hold a Hebrew conversation. I am proud to find that I understand nearly every word of it. Here it is in full.

My father: "Nu?" (That means, "Won't you please say Kiddush?")
The guest: "Nu-nu!" (meaning, "Say it rather yourself!")
My father: "Nu-O?" ("Why not you?")
The guest: "O-nu?" ("Why should I?")
My father: "I-O!" ("You first!")
The guest: "O-ai!" ("*You* first!")
My father: "È-o-i!" ("I beg of you to say it!")
The guest: "Ai-o-ê!" ("I beg of you!")
My father: "Ai-e-o-nu?" ("Why should you refuse?")
The guest: "Oi-o-e-nu-nu!" ("If you insist, then I must!")

And the guest took the cup of wine from my father's hand, and recited a Kiddush. But what a Kiddush! A Kiddush such as we had never heard before, and shall never hear again. First, the Hebrew—all *a*'s. Secondly, the voice, which seemed to come, not out of his beard, but out of the striped Turkish robe. I thought of my comrades, how they would have laughed, what slaps would have rained down, had they been present at that Kiddush.

Being alone, I was able to contain myself. I asked my father the Four Questions, and we all recited the Haggadah together. And I was elated to think that such a guest was ours, and no one else's.

The Passover Guest

Our sage who wrote that one should not talk at meals (may he forgive me for saying so!) did not know Jewish life. When shall a Jew find time to talk, if not during a meal? Especially at Passover, when there is so much to say before the meal and after it. Rikel the maid handed the water, we washed our hands, repeated the benediction, mother helped us to fish, and my father turned up his sleeves and started a long Hebrew talk with the guest. He began with the first question one Jew asks another:

"What is your name?"

To which the guest replied all in *a*'s and all in one breath:

"Ayak Bakar Gashal Damas Hanoch Vassam Za'an Chafaf Tatzatz."

My father remained with his fork in the air, staring in amazement at the possessor of so long a name. I coughed and looked under the table, and my mother said, "Favele, you should be careful eating fish, or you might be choked with a bone," while she gazed at our guest with awe. She appeared overcome by his name, although unable to understand it. My father, who understood, thought it necessary to explain it to her.

"You see, Ayak Bakar, that is our Alef-Bes inverted. It is apparently their custom to name people after the alphabet."

"Alef-Bes! Alef-Bes!" repeated the guest with the sweet smile on his red cheeks, and his beautiful black eyes rested on us all, including Rikel the maid, in the most friendly fashion.

Having learned his name, my father was anxious to know whence, from what land, he came. I understood this from the names of countries and towns which I caught, and from what my father translated for my mother, giving her a Yiddish version of nearly every phrase. And my mother was quite overcome by every single thing she heard, and Rikel the maid was overcome likewise. And no wonder! It is not every day that a person comes from perhaps two thousand miles away, from a land only to be reached across seven seas and a desert, the desert journey alone requiring forty days and nights. And when you get near to the land, you have to climb a mountain of which the top reaches into the clouds, and this is covered with ice, and dreadful winds blow there, so that there is peril of death! But once the mountain is safely crossed, and the land is reached, one beholds a terrestrial Eden. Spices, cloves, herbs, and every kind of fruit—apples, pears, and oranges, grapes, dates, and olives, nuts and quantities of figs. And the houses there are all built of deal, and roofed with silver, the furniture is gold (here the guest cast a look at our silver cups, spoons, forks, and knives), and brilliants, pearls, and diamonds bestrew the roads, and no one cares to take the trouble of picking them up, they are of no value there. (He was looking at my mother's diamond earrings, and at the pearls round her white neck.)

"You hear that?" my father asked her, with a happy face.

"I hear," she answered, and added: "Why don't they bring some over here? They could make money by it. Ask him that, Yoneh!"

My father did so, and translated the answer for my mother's benefit:

"You see, when you arrive there, you may take what you like, but when you leave the country, you must leave everything in it behind, too, and if they shake out of you no matter what, you are done for."

"What do you mean?" questioned my mother, terrified.

"I mean, they either hang you on a tree, or they stone you with stones."

The more tales our guest told us, the more thrilling they became, and just as we were finishing the dumplings and taking another sip or two of wine, my father inquired to whom the country belonged. Was there a king there? And he was soon translating, with great delight, the following reply:

"The country belongs to the Jews who live there, and who are called Sephardim. And they have a king, also a Jew, and a very pious one, who wears a fur cap, and who is called Joseph ben Joseph. He is the high priest of the Sephardim, and drives out in a gilded carriage, drawn by six fiery horses. And when he enters the synagogue, the Levites meet him with songs."

"There are Levites who sing in your synagogue?" asked my father, wondering, and the answer caused his face to shine with joy.

"What do you think?" he said to my mother. "Our guest tells me that in this country there is a temple, with priests and Levites and an organ."

"Well, and an altar?" questioned my mother, and my father told her:

"He says they have an altar, and sacrifices, he says, and golden vessels—everything just as we used to have it in Jerusalem."

And with these words my father sighs deeply, and my mother, as she looks at him, sighs also, and I cannot understand the reason. Surely we should be proud and glad to think we have such a land, ruled over

The Passover Guest

by a Jewish king and high priest, a land with Levites and an organ, with an altar and sacrifices—and bright, sweet thoughts enfold me, and carry me away as on wings to that happy Jewish land where the houses are of pine wood and roofed with silver, where the furniture is gold, and diamonds and pearls lie scattered in the street. And I feel sure, were I really there, I should know what to do—I should know how to hide things—they would shake nothing out of *me*. I should certainly bring home a lovely present for my mother, diamond earrings and several pearl necklaces. I look at the one mother is wearing, at her earrings, and I feel a great desire to be in that country. And it occurs to me that after Passover I will travel there with our guest, secretly, no one shall know. I will only speak of it to our guest, open my heart to him, tell him the whole truth, and beg him to take me there, if only for a little while. He will certainly do so, he is a very kind and approachable man, he looks at everyone, even at Rikel the maid, in such a friendly, such a very friendly way!

So I think, and it seems to me, as I watch our guest, that he has read my thoughts, and that his beautiful black eyes say to me:

"Keep it dark, little friend, wait till after Passover, then we shall manage it!"

I dreamt all night long. I dreamt of a desert, a temple, a high priest, and a tall mountain. I climb the mountain. Diamonds and pearls grow on the trees, and my comrades sit on the boughs, and shake the jewels down onto the ground, whole showers of them, and I stand and gather them, and stuff them into my pockets, and, strange to say, however many I stuff in, there is still room! I stuff and stuff, and still there is room! I put my hand into my pocket and draw out—not pearls and brilliants, but fruits of all kinds—apples, pears, oranges, olives, dates, nuts, and figs. This makes me very unhappy, and I toss from side to side. Then I dream of the temple, I hear the priests chant, and the Levites sing, and the organ play. I want to go inside and I cannot—Rikel the maid has hold of me, and will not let me go. I beg of her, and scream and cry, and again I am very unhappy, and toss from side to side. I wake—and see my father and mother standing there, half dressed, both pale, my father hanging his head, and my mother wringing her hands, and with her soft eyes full of tears. I feel at once that something has gone very wrong, very wrong indeed, but my childish head is incapable of imagining the greatness of the disaster.

The fact is this: our guest from beyond the desert and the seven seas has disappeared, and a lot of things have disappeared with him:

all the silver wine cups, all the silver spoons, knives, and forks; all my mother's ornaments, all the money that happened to be in the house, and also Rikel the maid!

A pang goes through my heart. Not on account of the silver cups, the silver spoons, knives, and forks that have vanished; not on account of mother's ornaments or of the money, still less on account of Rikel the maid, good riddance! But because of the happy, happy land whose roads were strewn with brilliants, pearls, and diamonds; because of the temple with the priests, the Levites, and the organ; because of the altar and the sacrifices; because of all the other beautiful things that have been taken from me, taken, taken, taken!

I turn my face to the wall, and cry quietly to myself.

From India and Beyond

RUDYARD KIPLING

Stories and poems that began appearing in the 1880s in British India heralded the appearance of a magnificent, original talent.

Rudyard Kipling (1865–1936), poet, novelist, and short-story writer, was born in Bombay, India. His father, an artist, was curator for some years at the Lahore Museum. Rudyard went to school at the United Services College in north Devonshire in England. Returning to India, he became at the age of seventeen a subeditor of a Lahore newspaper. He published in 1886, his twenty-first year, a book of poems. His first collection of stories, *Plain Tales from the Hills,* appeared in 1887, and was soon followed by half a dozen other small volumes that recreated Indian life for a growing readership.

Kipling traveled around the world between 1887 and 1889 and returned to England to find himself famous. In 1892 he married an American lady. They lived in Vermont for four years and thereafter in England. Kipling later traveled to South Africa and the Caribbean, and especially enjoyed describing the work of soldiers, sailors, and civil servants who maintained the strength of the British Empire. He also wrote a number of well-known books for young people. Because of his remarks about "the Widow of Windsor," he was never honored by Queen Victoria with a title, but in 1907 he became the first Englishman to be given the high award of the Nobel Prize for literature. He lies buried in Westminster Abbey.

Kipling's energy, compassion, craftsmanship, and love of words made him an innovator in the progress of the short story. He might be called a romantic realist, seeking material in out-of-the-way places and even writing early science fiction. "His natural talent, which I feel was enormous . . . was for articulating, in brief compass, themes symbolically conceived; for articulating these themes formally, with infinite loving attention, into subtly significant brief structures," wrote critic Paul Fussell Jr. "It is to Kipling's short fictions, thus, that we must go if we are to do his striking talent justice. . . . Of all his short fictions, 'The Man Who Would Be King' seems to me the finest." A detailed analysis of this story will be found in Appendix B.

RUDYARD KIPLING

The Man Who Would Be King

"Brother to a Prince and fellow to a beggar if he be found worthy."

The Law, as quoted, lays down a fair conduct of life, and one not easy to follow. I have been fellow to a beggar again and again under circumstances which prevented either of us finding out whether the other was worthy. I have still to be brother to a Prince, though I once came near to kinship with what might have been a veritable King and was promised the reversion of a Kingdom—army, law courts, revenue, and policy all complete. But, today, I greatly fear that my King is dead, and if I want a crown I must go hunt it for myself.

THE BEGINNING OF EVERYTHING was in a railway train upon the road to Mhow from Ajmir. There had been a deficit in the budget, which necessitated traveling, not second-class, which is only half as dear as first-class, but by intermediate, which is very awful indeed. There are no cushions in the intermediate class, and the population are either intermediate, which is Eurasian, or native, which for a long night journey is nasty, or loafer, which is amusing though intoxicated. Intermediates do not buy from refreshment rooms. They carry their food in bundles and pots, and buy sweets from the native sweetmeat sellers, and drink the roadside water. That is why in hot weather intermediates are taken out of the carriages dead, and in all weathers are most properly looked down upon.

The Man Who Would Be King

My particular intermediate happened to be empty till I reached Nasirabad, when a big black-browed gentleman in shirt-sleeves entered, and, following the custom of intermediates, passed the time of day. He was a wanderer and a vagabond like myself, but with an educated taste for whisky. He told tales of things he had seen and done, of out-of-the-way corners of the Empire into which he had penetrated, and of adventures in which he risked his life for a few days' food.

"If India was filled with men like you and me, not knowing more than the crows where they'd get their next day's rations, it isn't seventy millions of revenue the land would be paying—it's seven hundred millions," said he; and as I looked at his mouth and chin I was disposed to agree with him.

We talked politics—the politics of Loaferdom that sees things from the underside where the lath and plaster is not smoothed off—and we talked postal arrangements because my friend wanted to send a telegram back from the next station to Ajmir, the turning-off place from the Bombay to the Mhow line as you travel westward. My friend had no money beyond eight annas which he wanted for dinner, and I had no money at all, owing to the hitch in the budget before mentioned. Further, I was going into a wilderness where, though I should resume touch with the treasury, there were no telegraph offices. I was, therefore, unable to help him in any way.

"We might threaten a station master, and make him send a wire on tick," said my friend, "but that'd mean inquiries for you and for me, and *I've* got my hands full these days. Did you say you were traveling back along this line, within any days?"

"Within ten," I said.

"Can't you make it eight?" said he. "Mine is rather urgent business."

"I can send your telegram within ten days if that will serve you," I said.

"I couldn't trust the wire to fetch him now I think of it. It's this way. He leaves Delhi on the twenty-third for Bombay. That means he'll be running through Ajmir about the night of the twenty-third."

"But I'm going into the Indian Desert," I explained.

"Well *and* good," said he. "You'll be changing at Marwar Junction to get into Jodhpore territory—you must do that—and he'll be coming through Marwar Junction in the early morning of the twenty-fourth by the Bombay Mail. Can you be at Marwar Junction on that time? I won't be inconveniencing you because I know that there's precious few pickings to be got out of these Central India States—even though you pretend to be correspondent of the *Backwoodsman.*"

"Have you ever tried that trick?" I asked.

"Again and again, but the residents find you out, and then you get escorted to the border before you've had time to get your knife into them. But about my friend here. I *must* give him a word o' mouth to tell him what's come to me or else he won't know where to go. I would take it more than kind of you if you was to come out of Central India in time to catch him at Marwar Junction, and say to him: 'He has gone South for the week.' He'll know what that means. He's a big man with a red beard, and a great swell he is. You'll find him sleeping like a gentleman with all his luggage round him in a second-class apartment. But don't you be afraid. Slip down the window and say: 'He has gone South for the week,' and he'll tumble. It's only cutting your time of stay in those parts by two days. I ask you as a stranger—going to the West," he said with emphasis.

"Where have *you* come from?" said I.

"From the East," said he, "and I am hoping that you will give him the message on the square—for the sake of my Mother as well as your own."

Englishmen are not usually softened by appeals to the memory of their mothers; but for certain reasons, which will be fully apparent, I saw fit to agree.

"It's more than a little matter," said he, "and that's why I asked you to do it—and now I know that I can depend on you doing it. A second-class carriage at Marwar Junction, and a red-haired man asleep in it. You'll be sure to remember. I get out at the next station, and I must hold on there till he comes or sends me what I want."

"I'll give the message if I catch him," I said, "and for the sake of your Mother as well as mine I'll give you a word of advice. Don't try to run the Central India States just now as the correspondent of the *Backwoodsman*. There's a real one knocking about here, and it might lead to trouble."

"Thank you," said he simply, "and when will the swine be gone? I can't starve because he's ruining my work. I wanted to get hold of the Degumber Rajah down here about his father's widow, and give him a jump."

"What did he do to his father's widow, then?"

"Filled her up with red pepper and slippered her to death as she hung from a beam. I found that out myself and I'm the only man that would dare going into the State to get hush money for it. They'll try

122

to poison me, same as they did in Chortumna when I went on the loot there. But you'll give the man at Marwar Junction my message?"

He got out at a little roadside station, and I reflected, I had heard, more than once, of men personating correspondents of newspapers and bleeding small native states with threats of exposure, but I had never met any of the caste before. They lead a hard life, and generally die with great suddenness. The native states have a wholesome horror of English newspapers, which may throw light on their peculiar methods of government, and do their best to choke correspondents with champagne, or drive them out of their mind with four-in-hand barouches. They do not understand that nobody cares a straw for the internal administration of native states so long as oppression and crime are kept within decent limits, and the ruler is not drugged, drunk, or diseased from one end of the year to the other. They are the dark places of the earth, full of unimaginable cruelty, touching the railway and the telegraph on one side, and, on the other, the days of Harun-al-Raschid. When I left the train I did business with divers kings, and in eight days passed through many changes of life. Sometimes I wore dress clothes and consorted with princes and politicals, drinking from crystal and eating from silver. Sometimes I lay out upon the ground and devoured what I could get, from a plate made of leaves, and drank the running water, and slept under the same rug as my servant. It was all in the day's work.

Then I headed for the Great Indian Desert upon the proper date, as I had promised, and the night mail set me down at Marwar Junction, where a funny little, happy-go-lucky, native-managed railway runs to Jodhpore. The Bombay Mail from Delhi makes a short halt at Marwar. She arrived as I got in, and I had just time to hurry to her platform and go down the carriages. There was only one second-class on the train. I slipped the window and looked down upon a flaming red beard, half covered by a railway rug. That was my man, fast asleep, and I dug him gently in the ribs. He woke with a grunt and I saw his face in the light of the lamps. It was a great and shining face.

"Tickets again?" said he.

"No," said I. "I am to tell you that he is gone South for the week. He has gone South for the week!"

The train had begun to move out. The red man rubbed his eyes. "He has gone South for the week," he repeated. "Now that's just like his impudence. Did he say that I was to give you anything? 'Cause I won't.'"

"He didn't," I said and dropped away, and watched the red lights die out in the dark. It was horribly cold because the wind was blowing off the sands. I climbed into my own train—not an intermediate carriage this time—and went to sleep.

If the man with the beard had given me a rupee I should have kept it as a memento of a rather curious affair. But the consciousness of having done my duty was my only reward.

Later on I reflected that two gentlemen like my friends could not do any good if they foregathered and personated correspondents of newspapers, and might, if they blackmailed one of the little rat-trap states of central India or southern Rajputana, get themselves into serious difficulties. I therefore took some trouble to describe them as accurately as I could remember to people who would be interested in deporting them; and succeeded, so I was later informed, in having them headed back from the Degumber borders.

Then I became respectable, and returned to an office where there were no kings and no incidents outside the daily manufacture of a newspaper. A newspaper office seems to attract every conceivable sort of person, to the prejudice of discipline. Zenana-mission ladies arrive, and beg that the editor will instantly abandon all his duties to describe a Christian prizegiving in a back slum of a perfectly inaccessible village; colonels who have been overpassed for command sit down and sketch the outline of a series of ten, twelve, or twenty-four leading articles on seniority *versus* selection; missionaries wish to know why they have not been permitted to escape from their regular vehicles of abuse and swear at a brother missionary under special patronage of the editorial We; stranded theatrical companies troop up to explain that they cannot pay for their advertisements, but on their return from New Zealand or Tahiti will do so with interest; inventors of patent punkah-pulling machines, carriage couplings, and unbreakable swords and axletrees call with specifications in their pockets and hours at their disposal; tea companies enter and elaborate their prospectuses with the office pens; secretaries of ball committees clamor to have the glories of their last dance more fully described; strange ladies rustle in and say: "I want a hundred lady's cards printed *at once,* please," which is manifestly part of an editor's duty; and every dissolute ruffian that ever tramped the Grand Trunk Road makes it his business to ask for employment as a proofreader. And, all the time, the telephone bell is ringing madly, and kings are being killed on the continent, and empires are saying, "You're another," and Mister Gladstone is calling down brimstone upon the British Dominions, and the little black copy boys are whining *"kaa-pi chay-ha-yeh"* (copy wanted) like tired bees, and most of the paper is as blank as Modred's shield.

But that is the amusing part of the year. There are six other months when none ever come to call, and the thermometer walks inch by inch up to the top of the glass, and the office is darkened to just above reading-light, and the press machines are red-hot to touch, and nobody writes anything but accounts of amusements in the Hill Stations or obituary notices. Then the telephone becomes a tinkling terror, because it tells you of the sudden deaths of men and women that you knew intimately, and the prickly heat covers you with a garment, and you sit down and write: "A slight increase of sickness is reported from the Khuda Santa Khan district. The outbreak is purely sporadic in its nature, and, thanks to the energetic efforts of the district authorities, is now almost at an end. It is, however, with deep regret we record the death," etc.

Then the sickness really breaks out, and the less recording and reporting the better for the peace of the subscribers. But the empires and the kings continue to divert themselves as selfishly as before, and the foreman thinks that a daily paper really ought to come out once in twenty-four hours, and all the people at the Hill Stations in the middle of their amusements say: "Good gracious! Why can't the paper be sparkling? I'm sure there's plenty going on up here."

That is the dark half of the moon, and, as the advertisements say, "must be experienced to be appreciated."

It was in that season, and a remarkably evil season, that the paper began running the last issue of the week on Saturday night, which is to say Sunday morning, after the custom of a London paper. This was a great convenience, for immediately after the paper was put to bed, the dawn would lower the thermometer from 96ö to almost 84ö for half an hour, and in that chill—you have no idea how cold is 84ö on the grass until you begin to pray for it—a very tired man could get off to sleep ere the heat roused him.

One Saturday night it was my pleasant duty to put the paper to bed alone. A king or courtier or a courtesan or a community was going to die or get a new constitution, or do something that was important on the other side of the world, and the paper was to be held open till the latest possible minute in order to catch the telegram.

It was a pitchy black night, as stifling as a June night can be, and the *loo*, the red-hot wind from the westward, was booming among the tinder-dry trees and pretending that the rain was on its heels. Now and again a spot of almost boiling water would fall on the dust with the flop of a frog, but all our weary world knew that was only pretense. It was a shade cooler in the pressroom than the office, so I sat there, while the type ticked and clicked, and the nightjars hooted at the windows, and the all but naked compositors wiped the sweat from their foreheads, and called for water. The thing that was keeping us back, whatever it was, would not come off, though the *loo* dropped and the last type was set, and the whole round earth stood still in the choking heat, with its finger on its lip, to wait the event. I drowsed, and wondered whether the telegraph was a blessing, and whether this dying man, or struggling people, might be aware of the inconvenience the delay was causing. There was no special reason beyond the heat and worry to make tension, but, as the clock hands crept up to three o'clock and the machines spun their flywheels two and three times to see that all was in order, before I said the word that would set them off, I could have shrieked aloud.

Then the roar and rattle of the wheels shivered the quiet into little bits. I rose to go away, but two men in white clothes stood in front of me. The first one said: "It's him!" The second said: "So it is!" And they both laughed almost as loudly as the machinery roared, and mopped their foreheads. "We seed there was a light burning across the road and we were sleeping in that ditch there for coolness, and I said to my friend here, the office is open. Let's come along and speak to him as turned us back from the Degumber State," said the smaller of the two. He was the man I had met in the Mhow train, and his fellow was the red-bearded man of Marwar Junction. There was no mistaking the eyebrows of the one or the beard of the other.

I was not pleased, because I wished to go to sleep, not to squabble with loafers. "What do you want?" I asked.

"Half an hour's talk with you, cool and comfortable, in the office," said the red-bearded man. "We'd like some drink—the Contrack doesn't begin yet, Peachey, so you needn't look—but what we really want is advice. We don't want money. We ask you as a favor, because we found out you did us a bad turn about Degumber State."

I led from the pressroom to the stifling office with the maps on the walls, and the red-haired man rubbed his hands. "That's something like," said he. "This was the proper shop to come to. Now, sir, let me introduce to you Brother Peachey Carnehan, that's him, and Brother Daniel Dravot, that is *me,* and the less said about our professions the better, for we have been most things in our time. Soldier, sailor, compositor, photographer, proofreader, street preacher, and correspondents of the *Backwoodsman* when we thought the paper wanted one. Carnehan is sober, and so am I. Look at us first, and see that's sure. It will save you cutting into my talk. We'll take one of your cigars apiece, and you shall see us light up."

I watched the test. The men were absolutely sober, so I gave them each a tepid whiskey and soda.

"Well *and* good," said Carnehan of the eyebrows, wiping the froth from his mustache. "Let me talk now, Dan. We have been all over India, mostly on foot. We have been boiler fitters, engine drivers, petty contractors, and all that, and we have decided that India isn't big enough for such as us."

They certainly were too big for the office. Dravot's beard seemed to fill half the room and Carnehan's shoulders the other half, as they sat on the big table. Carnehan continued: "The country isn't half worked out because they that governs it won't let you touch it. They spend all their blessed time in governing it, and you can't lift a spade, nor chip a rock, nor look for oil, nor anything like that without all the government saying—'Leave it alone, and let us govern.' Therefore, such *as* it is, we will let it alone, and go away to some other place where a man isn't crowded and can come to his own. We are not little men, and there is nothing that we are afraid of except drink, and we have signed a Contrack on that. *Therefore,* we are going away to be kings."

"Kings in our own right," muttered Dravot.

"Yes, of course," I said. "You've been tramping in the sun, and it's a very warm night, and hadn't you better sleep over the notion? Come tomorrow."

"Neither drunk nor sunstruck," said Dravot. "We have slept over the notion half a year, and require to see books and atlases, and we have decided that there is only one place now in the world that two strong men can Sar-a-*whack.* They call it Kafiristan. By my reckoning it's the top righthand corner of Afghanistan, not more than three hundred miles from Peshawar. They have two-and-thirty heathen idols there, and we'll be the thirty-third and fourth. It's a mountainous country, and the women of those parts are very beautiful."

"But that is provided against in the Contrack," said Carnehan. "Neither woman nor liquor, Daniel."

"And that's all we know, except that no one has gone there, and they fight, and in any place where they fight a man who knows how to drill men can always be a king. We shall go to those parts and say to any king we find—'D'you want to vanquish your foes?' and we will show him how to drill men; for that we know better than anything else. Then we will subvert that king and seize his throne and establish a dynasty."

"You'll be cut to pieces before you're fifty miles across the border," I said. "You have to travel through Afghanistan to get to that country.

RUDYARD KIPLING

It's one mass of mountains and peaks and glaciers, and no Englishman has been through it. The people are utter brutes, and even if you reached them you couldn't do anything."

"That's more like," said Carnehan. "If you could think us a little more mad we would be more pleased. We have come to you to know about this country, to read a book about it, and to be shown maps. We want you to tell us that we are fools and to show us your books." He turned to the bookcases.

"Are you at all in earnest?" I said.

"A little," said Dravot sweetly. "As big a map as you have got, even if it's all blank where Kafiristan is, and any books you've got. We can read, though we aren't very educated."

I uncased the big thirty-two-miles-to-the-inch map of India, and two smaller frontier maps, hauled down volume INF-KAN of the *Encyclopaedia Britannica,* and the men consulted them.

"See here!" said Dravot, his thumb on the map. "Up to Jagdallak, Peachey and me know the road. We was there with Roberts' army. We'll have to turn off to the right at Jagdallak through Laghmann territory. Then we get among the hills—fourteen thousand feet—fifteen thousand—it will be cold work there, but it don't look very far on the map."

I handed him Wood on the *Sources of the Oxus.* Carnehan was deep in the *Encyclopaedia.*

"They're a mixed lot," said Dravot reflectively; "and it won't help us to know the names of their tribes. The more tribes the more they'll fight, and the better for us. From Jagdallak to Ashang. H'mm!"

"But all the information about the country is as sketchy and inaccurate as can be," I protested. "No one knows anything about it really. Here's the file of the *United Services' Institute.* Read what Bellew says."

"Blow Bellew!" said Carnehan. "Dan, they're a stinkin' lot of heathens, but this book here says they think they're related to us English."

I smoked while the men pored over Raverty, Wood, the maps, and the *Encyclopaedia.*

"There is no use your waiting," said Dravot politely. "It's about four o'clock now. We'll go before six o'clock if you want to sleep, and we won't steal any of the papers. Don't you sit up. We're two harmless lunatics, and if you come tomorrow evening down to the Serai we'll say good-bye to you."

"You *are* two fools," I answered. "You'll be turned back at the frontier or cut up the minute you set foot in Afghanistan. Do you want any money or a recommendation down-country? I can help you to the chance of work next week."

"Next week we shall be hard at work ourselves, thank you," said Dravot. "It isn't so easy being a king as it looks. When we've got our kingdom in going order we'll let you know, and you can come up and help us to govern it."

"Would two lunatics make a Contrack like that?" said Carnehan, with subdued pride, showing me a greasy half-sheet of notepaper on which was written the following. I copied it, then and there, as a curiosity:

This contract between me and you persuing witnesseth in the name of God—Amen and soforth.

(One)   That me and you will settle this matter together; ie., to be Kings of Kafiristan.

(Two)   That you and me will not, while this matter is being settled, look at any Liquor, nor any Woman black, white, or brown, so as to get mixed up with one or the other harmful.

(Three)   That we conduct ourselves with Dignity and Discretion, and if one of us gets into trouble the other will stay by him.

Signed by you and me this day.
    Peachey Taliaferro Carnehan.
    Daniel Dravot.
    Both Gentlemen at Large.

"There was no need for the last article," said Carnehan, blushing modestly; "but it looks regular. Now you know the sort of men that loafers are—we are loafers, Dan, until we get out of India—and *do* you think that we would sign a Contrack like that unless we was in earnest? We have kept away from the two things that make life worth having."

"You won't enjoy your lives much longer if you are going to try this idiotic adventure. Don't set the office on fire," I said, "and go away before nine o'clock."

I left them still poring over the maps and making notes on the back of the "Contrack." "Be sure to come down to the Serai tomorrow," were their parting words.

The Kumharsen Serai is the great four-square sink of humanity where the strings of camels and horses from the North load and unload. All the nationalities of central Asia may be found there, and most of the folk of India proper. Balkh and Bokhara there meet Bengal and Bombay, and try to draw eyeteeth. You can buy ponies, turquoises, Persian pussycats, saddlebags, fat-tailed sheep, and musk in the Kumharsen Serai, and get many strange things for nothing. In the afternoon

I went down to see whether my friends intended to keep their word or were lying there drunk.

A priest attired in fragments of ribbons and rags stalked up to me, gravely twisting a child's paper whirligig. Behind him was his servant bending under the load of a crate of mud toys. The two were loading up two camels, and the inhabitants of the Serai watched them with shrieks of laughter.

"The priest is mad," said a horse dealer to me. "He is going up to Kabul to sell toys to the Amir. He will either be raised to honor or have his head cut off. He came in here this morning and has been behaving madly ever since."

"The witless are under the protection of God," stammered a flat-cheeked Usbeg in broken Hindi. "They foretell future events."

"Would they could have foretold that my caravan would have been cut up by the Shinwaris almost within shadow of the Pass!" grunted the Eusufzai agent of a Rajputana trading house whose goods had been diverted into the hands of other robbers just across the border, and whose misfortunes were the laughingstock of the bazaar. "Ohé, priest, whence come you and whither do you go?"

"From Roum have I come," shouted the priest, waving his whirligig; "from Roum, blown by the breath of a hundred devils across the sea! O thieves, robbers, liars, the blessing of Pir Khan on pigs, dogs, and perjurers! Who will take the Protected of God to the North to sell charms that are never still to the Amir? The camels shall not gall, the sons shall not fall sick, and the wives shall remain faithful while they are away, of the men who give me place in their caravan. Who will assist me to slipper the King of the Roos with a golden slipper with a silver heel? The protection of Pir Khan be upon his labors!" He spread out the skirts of his gaberdine and pirouetted between the lines of tethered horses.

"There starts a caravan from Peshawar to Kabul in twenty days, *Huzrut,*" said the Eusufzai trader. "My camels go therewith. Do thou also go and bring us good luck."

"I will go even now!" shouted the priest. "I will depart upon my winged camels, and be at Peshawar in a day! Ho! Hazar Mir Khan," he yelled to his servant, "drive out the camels, but let me first mount my own."

He leaped on the back of his beast as it knelt, and, turning round to me, cried: "Come thou also, Sahib, a little along the road, and I will sell thee a charm—an amulet that shall make thee King of Kafiristan."

Then the light broke upon me, and I followed the two camels out of the Serai till we reached open road and the priest halted.

"What d'you think o' that?" said he in English. "Carnehan can't talk their patter, so I've made him my servant. He makes a handsome servant. 'Tisn't for nothing that I've been knocking about the country for fourteen years. Didn't I do that talk neat? We'll hitch on to a caravan at Peshawar till we get to Jagdallak, and then we'll see if we can get donkeys for our camels, and strike into Kafiristan. Whirligigs for the Amir, O Lor! Put your hand under the camel bags and tell me what you feel."

I felt the butt of a Martini, and another and another.

"Twenty of 'em," said Dravot placidly. "Twenty of 'em and ammunition to correspond, under the whirligigs and the mud dolls."

"Heaven help you if you are caught with those things!" I said. "A Martini is worth her weight in silver among the Pathans."

"Fifteen hundred rupees of capital—every rupee we could beg, borrow, or steal—are invested on these two camels," said Dravot. "We won't get caught. We're going through the Khyber with a regular caravan. Who'd touch a poor mad priest?"

"Have you got everything you want?" I asked, overcome with astonishment.

"Not yet, but we shall soon. Give us a memento of your kindness, Brother; you did me a service, yesterday, and that time in Marwar. Half my Kingdom shall you have as the saying is." I slipped a small charm compass from my watch chain and handed it up to the priest.

"Good-bye," said Dravot, giving me his hand cautiously. "It's the last time we'll shake hands with an Englishman these many days. Shake hands with him, Carnehan," he cried, as the second camel passed me.

Carnehan leaned down and shook hands. Then the camels passed away along the dusty road, and I was left alone to wonder. My eye could detect no failure in the disguises. The scene in the Serai proved that they were complete to the native mind. There was just the chance, therefore, that Carnehan and Dravot would be able to wander through Afghanistan without detection. But, beyond, they would find death— certain and awful death.

Ten days later a native correspondent giving me the news of the day from Peshawar, wound up his letter with: "There has been much laughter here on account of a certain mad priest who is going in his estimation to sell petty gauds and insignificant trinkets, which he ascribes as great charms, to H. H. the Amir of Bokhara. He passed through Peshawar and associated himself to the second summer caravan that goes to Kabul. The merchants are pleased because through superstition they imagine that such mad fellows bring good fortune."

The two, then were beyond the border. I would have prayed for them, but, that night, a real king died in Europe, and demanded an obituary notice.

The wheel of the world swings through the same phases again and again. Summer passed and winter thereafter, and came and passed again. The daily paper continued and I with it, and upon the third summer there fell a hot night, a night issue, and a strained waiting for something to be telegraphed from the other side of the world, exactly as had happened before. A few great men had died in the past two years, the machines worked with more clatter, and some of the trees in the office garden were a few feet taller. But that was all the difference.

I passed over to the pressroom, and went through just such a scene as I have already described. The nervous tension was stronger than it had been two years before, and I felt the heat more acutely. At three o'clock I cried "Print off," and turned to go, when there crept to my chair what was left of a man. He was bent into a circle, his head was sunk between his shoulders, and he moved his feet one over the other like a bear. I could hardly see whether he walked or crawled—this rag-wrapped, whining cripple who addressed me by name, crying that he was come back. "Can you give me a drink?" he whimpered. "For the Lord's sake, give me a drink!"

I went back to the office, the man following with groans of pain, and I turned up the lamp.

"Don't you know me?" he gasped, dropping into a chair, and he turned his drawn face, surmounted by a shock of gray hair, to the light.

I looked at him intently. Once before had I seen eyebrows that met over the nose in an inch-broad black band, but for the life of me I could not tell where.

"I don't know you," I said, handing him the whisky. "What can I do for you?"

He took a gulp of the spirit raw, and shivered in spite of the suffocating heat.

"I've come back," he repeated; "and I was the King of Kafiristan—me and Dravot—crowned kings we was! In this office we settled it—you setting there and giving us the books. I am Peachey—Peachey

Taliaferro Carnehan, and you've been setting here ever since—O Lord!"

I was more than a little astonished, and expressed my feelings accordingly.

"It's true," said Carnehan, with a dry cackle, nursing his feet, which were wrapped in rags. "True as gospel. Kings we were, with crowns upon our heads—me and Dravot—poor Dan—oh, poor, poor Dan, that would never take advice, not though I begged of him!"

"Take the whisky," I said, "and take your own time. Tell me all you can recollect of everything from beginning to end. You got across the border on your camels, Dravot dressed as a mad priest and you his servant. Do you remember that?"

"I ain't mad—yet, but I shall be that way soon. Of course I remember. Keep looking at me, or maybe my words will go all to pieces. Keep looking at me in my eyes and don't say anything."

I leaned forward and looked into his face as steadily as I could. He dropped one hand upon the table and I grasped it by the wrist. It was twisted like a bird's claw, and upon the back was a ragged, red diamond-shaped scar.

"No, don't look there. Look at me," said Carnehan. "That comes afterwards, but for the Lord's sake don't distrack me. We left with that caravan, me and Dravot playing all sorts of antics to amuse the people we were with. Dravot used to make us laugh in the evenings when all the people was cooking their dinners—cooking their dinners, and ... what did they do then? They lit little fires with sparks that went into Dravot's beard, and we all laughed—fit to die. Little red fires they was, going into Dravot's big red beard—so funny." His eyes left mine and he smiled foolishly.

"You went as far as Jagdallak with that caravan," I said at a venture, "after you had lit those fires. To Jagdallak, where you turned off to try to get to Kafiristan."

"No, we didn't neither. What are you talking about? We turned off before Jagdallak, because we heard the roads was good. But they wasn't good enough for our two camels—mine and Dravot's. When we left the caravan, Dravot took off all his clothes and mine too, and said we would be heathen, because the Kafirs didn't allow Mohammedans to talk to them. So we dressed betwixt and between, and such a sight as Daniel Dravot I never saw yet nor expect to see again. He burned half his beard, and slung a sheepskin over his shoulder, and shaved his head into patterns. He shaved mine, too, and made me wear outrageous things to look like a heathen. That was in a most mountainous country, and our camels couldn't go along any more because of the mountains. They were tall and black, and coming home I saw them fight like wild goats—there are lots of goats in Kafiristan. And these mountains, they never keep still, no more than the goats. Always fighting they are, and don't let you sleep at night."

"Take some more whisky," I said very slowly. "What did you and Daniel Dravot do when the camels could go no further because of the rough roads that led into Kafiristan?"

"What did which do? There was a party called Peachey Taliaferro Carnehan that was with Dravot. Shall I tell you about him? He died out there in the cold. Slap from the bridge fell old Peachey, turning and twisting in the air like a penny whirligig that you can sell to the Amir. —No; they was two for three ha'pence, those whirligigs, or I am much mistaken and woeful sore . . . And then these camels were no use, and Peachey said to Dravot—'For the Lord's sake let's get out of this before our heads are chopped off,' and with that they killed the camels all among the mountains, not having anything in particular to eat, but first they took off the boxes with the guns and the ammunition, till two men came along driving four mules. Dravot up and dances in front of them, singing—'Sell me four mules.' Say the first man—'If you are rich enough to buy, you are rich enough to rob'; but before ever he could put his hand to his knife, Dravot breaks his neck over his knee, and the other party runs away. So Carnehan loaded the mules with the rifles that was taken off the camels, and together we starts forward into those bitter cold mountainous parts, and never a road broader than the back of your hand."

He paused for a moment, while I asked him if he could remember the nature of the country through which he had journeyed.

"I am telling you as straight as I can, but my head isn't as good as it might be. They drove nails through it to make me hear better how Dravot died. The country was mountainous and the mules were most contrary, and the inhabitants were dispersed and solitary. They went up and up, and down and down, and that other party, Carnehan, was imploring of Darvot not to sing and whistle so loud, for fear of bringing down the tremenjus avalanches. But Dravot says that if a king couldn't sing it wasn't worth being king, and whacked the mules over the rump, and never took no heed for ten cold days. We came to a big level valley all among the mountains, and the mules were near dead, so we killed them, not having anything in special for them or us to eat. We sat upon the boxes, and played odd and even with the cartridges that was jolted out.

"Then ten men with bows and arrows ran down that valley, chasing twenty men with bows and arrows, and the row was tremenjus. They was fair men—fairer than you or me—with yellow hair and remarkable well built. Says Dravot, unpacking the guns—'This is the beginning of the business. We'll fight for the ten men,' and with that he fires two rifles at the twenty men, and drops one of them at two hundred yards from the rock where he was sitting. The other men began to run, but Carnehan and Dravot sits on the boxes picking them off at all ranges, up and down the valley. Then we goes up to the ten men that had run across the snow too, and they fires a footy little arrow at us. Dravot he shoots above their heads and they all falls down flat. Then he walks over them and kicks them, and then he lifts them up and shakes hands all round to make them friendly like. He calls them and gives them the boxes to carry, and waves his hand for all the world as though he was king already. They takes the boxes and him across the valley and up the hill into a pine wood on the top, where there was half a dozen big stone idols. Dravot he goes to the biggest —a fellow they call Imbra—and lays a rifle and a cartridge at his feet, rubbing his nose respectful with his own nose, patting him on the head, and saluting in front of it. He turns round to the men and nods his head, and says—'That's all right. I'm in the know, too, and all these old jimjams are my friends.' Then he opens his mouth and points down it, and when the first man brings him food, he says—'No'; and when the second man brings him food he says—'No'; but when one of the old priests and the boss of the village brings him food, he says—'Yes'; very haughty, and eats it slow. That was how we came to our first village, without any trouble, just as though we had tumbled from the skies. But we tumbled from one of those damned rope bridges, you see and—you couldn't expect a man to laugh much after that?"

"Take some more whisky and go on," I said. "That was the first village you came into. How did you get to be king?"

"I wasn't king," said Carnehan. "Dravot he was the king, and a handsome man he looked with the gold crown on his head and all. Him and the other party stayed in that village, and every morning Dravot sat by the side of old Imbra, and the people came and worshipped. That was Dravot's order. Then a lot of men came into the valley, and Carnehan and Dravot picks them off with the rifles before they knew where they was, and runs down into the valley and up again the other side and finds another village, same as the first one, and the people all falls down flat on their faces, and Dravot says—'Now what is the trouble between you two villages?' and the people points to a woman, as fair as you or me, that was carried off, and Dravot takes her back to the first village and counts up the dead—eight there was. For each dead man Dravot pours a little milk on the ground and waves his arms like a whirligig and 'That's all right,' says he. Then he and Carnehan takes the big boss of each village by the arm and walks them down into the valley, and shows them how to scratch a line with a spear right down the valley, and gives each a sod of turf from both sides of the line. Then all the people comes down and shouts like the devil and all, and Dravot says— 'Go and dig the land, and be fruitful and multiply,' which they did, though they didn't understand. Then we asks the names of things in their lingo—bread and water and fire and idols and such, and Dravot leads the priest of each village up to the idol, and says he must sit there and judge the people, and if anything goes wrong he is to be shot.

"Next week they was all turning up the land in the valley as quiet as bees and much prettier, and the priests heard all the complaints and told Dravot in dumb show what it was about. 'That's just the beginning,' says Dravot. 'They think we're gods.' He and Carnehan picks out twenty good men and shows them how to click off a rifle, and form fours, and advance in line, and they was very pleased to do so and clever to see the hang of it. Then he takes out his pipe and his baccy pouch and leaves one at one village, and one at the other, and off we two goes to see what was to be done in the next valley. That was all rock, and there was a little village there, and Carnehan says—'Send 'em to the old valley to plant,' and takes 'em there and gives 'em some land that wasn't took before. They were a poor lot, and we blooded 'em with a kid before letting 'em into the new kingdom. That was to impress the people, and then they settled down quiet, and Carnehan went back to Dravot who had got into another valley, all snow and ice and most mountainous. There was no people there and the army got afraid, so Dravot shoots one of them, and goes on till he finds some people in a village, and the army explains that unless the people wants to be killed they had better not shoot their little matchlocks; for they had matchlocks. We makes friends with the priest and I stays there alone with two of the army, teaching the men how to drill, and a thundering big chief comes across the snow with kettledrums and horns twanging, because he heard there was a new god kicking about. Carnehan sights for the brown of the men half a mile across the snow and wings one of them. Then he sends a message to the chief that, unless he wished to be killed, he must come and shake hands with me and leave his arms behind. The chief comes alone first, and Carnehan shakes hands with him and whirls his arms about, same as Dravot used, and very much surprised that chief was, and strokes my eyebrows. Then Carnehan goes alone to the chief, and asks him in dumb show if he had an enemy he hated. 'I have,' says the chief. So Carnehan weeds out the pick of the men, and sets the two of the army to show them drill at the end of two weeks the men can maneuver about as well as volunteers. So he marches with the chief to a great big plain on the top of a mountain, and the chief's men rushes into a village and takes it; we three Martinis firing into the brown of the enemy. So we took that village too, and I gives the chief a rag from my coat and says 'Occupy till I come'; which was scriptural. By way of a reminder, when me and the army was eighteen hundred yards away, I drops a bullet near him standing on the snow, and all the people falls flat on their faces. Then I sends a letter to Dravot wherever he be by land or by sea."

At the risk of throwing the creature out of train I interrupted: "How could you write a letter up yonder?"

"The letter?—Oh!—The letter! Keep looking at me between the eyes, please. It was a string-talk letter, that we'd learned the way of it from a blind beggar in the Punjab."

I remember that there had once come to the office a blind man with a knotted twig and a piece of string which he wound round the twig according to some cipher of his own. He could, after the lapse of days or hours, repeat the sentence which he had reeled up. He had reduced the alphabet to eleven primitive sounds; and tried to teach me his method, but I could not understand.

"I sent that letter to Dravot," said Carnehan; "and told him to come back because this kingdom was growing too big for me to handle, and then I struck for the first valley, to see how the priests were working. They called the village we took along with the chief, Bashkai, and the first village we took, Er-Heb. The priests at Er-Heb was doing all right, but they had a lot of pending cases about land to show me, and some men from another village had been firing arrows at night. I went out and looked for that village, and fired four rounds at it from a thousand yards. That used all the cartridges I cared to spend, and I waited for Dravot, who had been away two or three months, and I kept my people quiet.

"One morning I heard the devil's own noise of drums and horns, and Dan Dravot marches down the hill with his army and a tail of hundreds of men, and, which was the most amazing, a great gold crown on his head. 'My Gord, Carnehan,' says Daniel, 'this is a tremenjus business, and we've got the whole country as far as it's worth having. I am the son of Alexander by Queen Semiramis, and you're my younger brother and a god too! It's the biggest thing we've ever seen. I've been marching and fighting for six weeks with the army, and every footy little village for fifty miles has come in rejoiceful; and more than that, I've got the key of the whole show, a place called Shu, where the gold lies in the rock like suet in mutton. Gold I've seen, and turquoise I've kicked out of the cliffs, and there's garnets in the sands of the river, and here's a chunk of amber that a man brought me. Call up all the priests and, here, take your crown.'

"One of the men opens a black hair bag, and I slips the crown on. It was too small and too heavy, but I wore it for the glory. Hammered gold it was—five pound weight, like a hoop of a barrel.

" 'Peachey,' says Dravot, 'we don't want to fight no more. The Craft's the trick, so help me!' and he brings forward that same chief that I left at Bashkai—Billy Fish we called him afterwards, because he was so like Billy Fish that drove the big tank-engine at Mach on the Bolan in the old days. 'Shake hands with him,' says Dravot, and I shook hands and nearly dropped, for Billy Fish gave me the Grip. I said nothing, but tried him with the Fellow Craft Grip. He answers, all right, and I tried the Master's Grip, but that was a slip. 'A Fellow Craft he is,' I says to Dan. 'Does he know the word?'—'He does,' says Dan, 'and all the priests know. It's a miracle. The chiefs and the priests can work a Fellow Craft Lodge in a way that's very like ours, and they've cut the marks on the rocks, but they don't know the Third Degree, and they've come to find out. It's Gord's Truth. I've known these long years that the Afghans knew up to the Fellow Craft Degree, but this is a miracle. A god and a Grand Master of the Craft am I, and a lodge in the Third Degree I will open, and we'll raise the head priests and the chiefs of the villages.'

" 'It's against all the law,' I say's, 'holding a lodge without warrant from any one; and you know we never held office in any lodge.'

" 'It's a master stroke o' policy,' says Dravot. 'It means running the country as easy as a four-wheeled bogie on a down grade. We can't stop to inquire now, or they'll turn against us. I've forty chiefs at my heel, and passed and raised according to their merit, they shall be. Billet these men on his villages, and see that we run up a lodge of some kind. The temple of Imbra will do for the lodge room. The women must make aprons as you show them. I'll hold a levee of chiefs tonight and lodge tomorrow.'

"I was fair run off my legs, but I wasn't such a fool as not to see what a pull this craft business gave us. I showed the priests' families how to make aprons of the degrees, but for Dravot's apron the blue border and marks was made of turquoise lumps on white hide, not cloth. We took a great square stone in the temple for the Master's chair, and little stones for the officers' chairs, and painted the black pavement with white squares, and did what we could to make things regular.

"At the levee which was held that night on the hillside with big bonfires, Dravot gives out that him and me were gods and sons of Alexander, and Past Grand Masters in the Craft, and was come to make Kafiristan a country where every man should eat in peace and drink in quiet, and specially obey us. Then the chiefs come round to shake hands, and they were so hairy and white and fair it was just shaking hands with old friends. We gave them names according as they was like men we had known in India—Billy Fish, Holly Dilworth, Pikky Kergan, that was bazaar-master when I was at Mhow, and so on, and so on.

"The most amazing miracles was at lodge next night. One of the old priests was watching us continuous, and I felt uneasy, for I knew we'd have to fudge the Ritual, and I didn't know what the men knew. The old priest was a stranger come in from beyond the village of Bashkai. The minute Dravot puts on the Master's apron that the girls had made for him, the priest fetches a whoop and a howl, and tries to overturn the stone that Dravot was sitting on. 'It's all up now,' I says. 'That comes of meddling with the Craft without warrant!' Dravot never winked an eye, not when ten priests took and tilted over the Grand Master's chair—which was to say the stone of Imbra. The priest begins rubbing the bottom end of it to clear away the black dirt, and presently he shows all the other priests the Master's Mark, same as was on Dravot's apron, cut into the stone. Not even the priests of the temple of Imbra knew it was there. The old chap falls flat on his face at Dravot's feet and kisses 'em. 'Luck again,' says Dravot, across the lodge to me, 'they say it's the missing mark that no one could understand the why of. We're more than safe now.' Then he bangs the butt of his gun for a gavel and says: 'By virtue of the authority vested in me by my own right hand and the help of Peachey, I declare myself Grand Master of all Freemasonry in Kafiristan in this the Mother

Lodge o' the country, and King of Kafiristan equally with Peachey!' At that he puts on his crown and I puts on mine—I was doing Senior Warden—and we opens the lodge in most ample form. It was a amazing miracle! The priests moved in lodge through the first two degrees almost without telling, as if the memory was coming back to them. After that, Peachey and Dravot raised such as was worthy—high priests and chiefs of far-off villages. Billy Fish was the first, and I can tell you we scared the soul out of him. It was not in any way according to Ritual, but it served our turn. We didn't raise more than ten of the biggest men, because we didn't want to make the degree common. And they was clamoring to be raised.

" 'In another six months,' says Dravot, 'We'll hold another Communication, and see how you are working.' Then he asks them about their villages, and learns that they was fighting one against the other, and were sick and tired of it. And when they wasn't doing that they was fighting with the Mohammedans. 'You can fight those when they come into our country,' says Dravot. 'Tell off every tenth man of your tribes for a frontier guard, and send two hundred at a time to this valley to be drilled. Nobody is going to be shot or speared any more so long as he does well, and I know that you won't cheat me, because you're white people—sons of Alexander—and not like common, black Mohammedans. You are *my* people, and by God,' says he, running off into English at the end—'I'll make a damned fine nation of you, or I'll die in the making!'

"I can't tell all we did for the next six months, because Dravot did a lot I couldn't see the hang of, and he learned their lingo in a way I never could. My work was to help the people plough, and now and again go out with some of the army and see what the other villages were doing, and make 'em throw rope bridges across the ravines which cut up the country horrid. Dravot was very kind to me, but when he walked up and down in the pine wood pulling that bloody red beard of his with both fists I knew he was thinking plans I could not advise about, and I just waited for orders.

"But Dravot never showed me disrespect before the people. They were afraid of me and the army, but they loved Dan. He was the best of friends with the priests and the chiefs; but any one could come across the hills with a complaint, and Dravot would hear him out fair, and call four priests together and say what was to be done. He used to call in Billy Fish from Bashkai, and Pikky Kergan from Shu, and an old chief we called Kafuzelum—it was like enough to his real name—and hold councils with 'em when there was any fighting to be done in small villages. That was his council of war, and the four priests of Bashkai, Shu, Khawak, and Madora was his privy council. Between the lot of 'em they sent me, with forty men and twenty rifles, and sixty men carrying turquoises, into the Ghorband country to buy those handmade Martini rifles, that come out of the Amir's workshops at Kabul, from one of the Amir's Herati regiments that would have sold the very teeth out of their mouths for turquoises.

"I stayed in Ghorband a month, and gave the governor there the pick of my baskets for hush money, and bribed the colonel of the regiment some more, and, between the two and the tribespeople, we got more than a hundred handmade Martinis, a hundred good Kohat Jezails that'll throw to six hundred yards, and forty manloads of very bad ammunition for the rifles. I came back with what I had, and distributed 'em among the men that the chiefs sent in to me to drill. Dravot was too busy to attend to those things, but the old army that we first made helped me, and we turned out five hundred men that could drill, and two hundred that knew how to hold arms pretty straight. Even those corkscrewed, handmade guns was a miracle to them. Dravot talked big about powdershops and factories, walking up and down in the pine wood when the winter was coming on.

" 'I won't make a nation,' says he. 'I'll make an empire! These men aren't niggers; they're English! Look at their eyes—look at their mouths. Look at the way they stand up. They sit on chairs in their own houses. They're the Lost Tribes, or something like it, and they've grown to be English. I'll take a census in the spring if the priests don't get frightened. There must be a fair two million of 'em in these hills. The villages are full o' little children. Two million people—two hundred and fifty thousand fighting men—and all English! They only want rifles and a little drilling. Two hundred and fifty thousand men, ready to cut in on Russia's right flank when she tries for India! Peachey, man,' he says, chewing his beard in great hunks, 'we shall be emperors —emperors of the earth! Rajah Brooke will be a suckling to us. I'll treat with the Viceroy on equal terms. I'll ask him to send me twelve picked English—twelve that I know of—to help us govern a bit. There's Mackray, sergeant-pensioner at Segowli—many's the good dinner he's given me, and his wife a pair of trousers. There's Donkin, the warder of Tounghoo Jail; there's hundreds that I could lay my hand on if I was in India. The Viceroy shall do it for me, I'll send a man through in the spring for those men, and I'll write for a dispensation from the Grand Lodge for what I've done as Grand Master. That—and all the Sniders that'll be thrown out when the native troops in India take up the

Martini. They'll be worn smooth, but they'll do for fighting in these hills. Twelve English, a hundred thousand Sniders run through the Amir's country in driblets—I'd be content with twenty thousand in one year—and we'd be an empire. When everything was ship-shape, I'd hand over the crown—this crown I'm wearing now—to Queen Victoria on my knees, and she'd say: "Rise up, Sir Daniel Dravot." Oh, it's big! It's big, I tell you! But there's so much to be done in every place—Bashkai, Khawak, Shu, and everywhere else.'

" 'What is it?' I says. 'There are no more men coming in to be drilled this autumn. Look at those fat, black clouds. They're bringing the snow.'

" 'It isn't that,' says Daniel, putting his hand very hard on my shoulder; 'and I don't wish to say anything that's against you, for no other living man would have followed me and made me what I am as you have done. You're a first-class commander-in-chief, and the people know you; but—it's a big country, and somehow you can't help me, Peachey, in the way I want to be helped.'

" 'Go to your blasted priests, then!' I said, and I was sorry when I made that remark, but it did hurt me sore to find Daniel talking so superior when I'd drilled all the men, and done all he told me.

" 'Don't let's quarrel, Peachey,' says Daniel without cursing. 'You're a king too, and the half of this kingdom is yours; but can't you see, Peachey, we want cleverer men than us now—three or four of 'em, that we can scatter about for our deputies. It's a hugeous great state, and I can't always tell the right thing to do, and I haven't time for all I want to do, and here's the winter coming on and all.' He put half his beard into his mouth, all red like the gold of his crown.

" 'I'm sorry, Daniel,' says I. 'I've done all I could. I've drilled the men and shown the people how to stack their oats better; and I've brought in those tinware rifles from Ghorband—but I know what you're driving at. I take it kings always feel oppressed that way.'

" 'There's another thing too,' says Dravot, walking up and down. 'The winter's coming and these people won't be giving much trouble, and if they do we can't move about. I want a wife.'

" 'For Gord's sake leave the women alone!' I says. 'We've both got all the work we can, though I *am* a fool. Remember the Contrack, and keep clear o' women.'

" 'The Contrack only lasted till such time as we was kings; and kings we have been these months past,' says Dravot, weighing his crown in his hand. 'You go get a wife too, Peachey—a nice, strappin', plump girl that'll keep you warm in the winter. They're prettier than

The Man Who Would Be King

English girls, and we can take the pick of 'em. Boil 'em once or twice in hot water, and they'll come out like chicken and ham.'

" 'Don't tempt me!' I says. 'I will not have any dealings with a woman not till we are a dam' side more settled than we are now. I've been doing the work o' two men, and you've been doing the work o' three. Let's lie off a bit, and see if we can get some better tobacco from Afghan country and run in some good liquor; but no women.'

" 'Who's talking o' *woman?*' says Dravot. 'I said *wife*—a queen to breed a king's son for the king. A queen out of the strongest tribe, that'll make them your blood brothers, and that'll lie by your side and tell you all the people thinks about you and their own affairs. That's what I want.'

" 'Do you remember that Bengali woman I kept at Mogul Serai when I was a platelayer?' says I. 'A fat lot o' good she was to me. She taught me the lingo and one or two other things; but what happened? She ran away with the stationmaster's servant and half my month's pay. Then she turned up at Dadur Junction in tow of a half-caste, and had the impidence to say I was her husband—all among the drivers in the running shed too!'

" 'We've done with that,' says Dravot, 'these women are whiter than you or me, and a queen I will have for the winter months.'

" 'For the last time o' asking, Dan, do *not*,' I says. 'It'll only bring us harm. The Bible says that kings ain't to waste their strength on women, 'specially when they've got a new raw kingdom to work over.'

" 'For the last time of answering I will,' said Dravot, and he went away through the pine trees looking like a big red devil, the sun being on his crown and beard and all.

"But getting a wife was not as easy as Dan thought. He put it before the council, and there was no answer till Billy Fish said he'd better ask the girls. Dravot damned them all round. 'What's wrong with me?' he shouts, standing by the idol Imbra. 'Am I a dog or am I not enough of a man for your wrenches? Haven't I put the shadow of my hand over this country? Who stopped the last Afghan raid?' It was me really, but Dravot was too angry to remember. 'Who bought your guns? Who repaired the bridges? Who's the Grand Master of the sign cut in the stone?' says he, and he thumped his hand on the block that he used to sit on in lodge, and at council, which opened like lodge always. Billy Fish said nothing and no more did the others. 'Keep your hair on, Dan,' said I; 'and ask the girls. That's how it's done at home, and these people are quite English.'

" 'The marriage of the king is a matter of state,' says Dan, in a white-hot rage, for he could feel, I hope, that he was going against his better mind. He walked out of the council room, and the others sat still, looking at the ground.

" 'Billy Fish,' says I to the Chief of Bashkai, 'what's the difficulty here? A straight answer to a true friend.'

" 'You know,' says Billy Fish. 'How should a man tell you who knows everything? How can daughters of men marry gods or devils? It's not proper.'

"I remembered something like that in the Bible; but if, after seeing us as long as they had, they still believed we were gods, it wasn't for me to undeceive them.

" 'A god can do anything,' says I. 'If the King is fond of a girl he'll not let her die.'—'She'll have to,' said Billy Fish. 'There are all sorts of gods and devils in these mountains, and now and again a girl marries one of them and isn't seen any more. Besides, you two know the mark cut in the stone. Only the gods know that. We thought you were men till you showed the sign of the Master.' "

"I wished then that we had explained about the loss of the genuine secrets of a Master Mason at the first go-off; but I said nothing. All that night there was a blowing of horns fit to die. One of the priests told us that she was being prepared to marry the King.

" 'I'll have no nonsense of that kind,' says Dan. 'I don't want to interfere with your customs, but I'll take my own wife.'—'The girl's a little bit afraid,' says the priest. 'She thinks she's going to die, and they are a-heartening of her up down in the temple.'

" 'Hearten her very tender, then,' says Dravot, 'or I'll hearten you with the butt of a gun so you'll never want to be heartened again.' He licked his lips, did Dan, and stayed up walking about more than half the night, thinking of the wife that he was going to get in the morning. I wasn't by any means comfortable, for I knew that dealings with a woman in foreign parts, though you was a crowned king twenty times over, could not but be risky. I got up very early in the morning while Dravot was asleep, and I saw the priests talking together in whispers, and the chiefs talking together too, and they looked at me out of the corners of their eyes.

" 'What is up, Fish?' I say to the Bashkai man, who was wrapped up in his furs and looking splendid to behold.

" 'I can't rightly say,' says he; 'but if you can make the King drop all this nonsense about marriage, you'll be doing him and me and yourself a great service.'

" 'That I do believe,' says I. 'But sure, you know, Billy, as well as me, having fought against and for us, that the King and me are nothing more than the finest men that God Almighty ever made. Nothing more I do assure you.'

"'That may be,' says Billy Fish, 'and yet I should be sorry if it was.' He sinks his head upon his great fur cloak for a minute and thinks. 'King,' says he, 'be you man or god or devil, I'll stick by you today. I have twenty of my men with me, and they will follow me. We'll go to Bashkai until the storm blows over.'

"A little snow had fallen in the night, and everything was white except the greasy fat clouds that blew down and down from the north. Dravot came out with his crown on his head, swinging his arms and stamping his feet, and looking more pleased than Punch.

"'For the last time, drop it, Dan,' says I in a whisper, 'Billy Fish here says that there will be a row.'

"'A row among my people!' says Dravot. 'Not much. Peachey, you're a fool not to get a wife too. Where's the girl?' says he with a voice as loud as the braying of a jackass. 'Call up all the chiefs and priests, and let the Emperor see if his wife suits him.'

"There was no need to call any one. They were all there leaning on their guns and spears round the clearing in the center of the pine wood. A lot of priests went down to the little temple to bring up the girl, and the horns blew fit to wake the dead. Billy Fish saunters round and gets as close to Daniel as he could, and behind him stood his twenty men with matchlocks. Not a man of them under six feet. I was next to Dravot, and behind me was twenty men of the regular army. Up comes the girl, and a strapping wench she was, covered with silver and turquoises but white as death, and looking back every minute at the priests.

"'She'll do,' said Dan, looking her over. 'What's to be afraid of, lass? Come and kiss me.' He puts his arm around her. She shuts her eyes, gives a bit of a squeak, and down goes her face in the side of Dan's flaming red beard.

"'The slut's bitten me!' says he, clapping his hand to his neck, and, sure enough, his hand was red with blood. Billy Fish and two of his matchlock men catches hold of Dan by the shoulders and drags him into the Bashkai lot, while the priests howl their lingo: 'Neither god nor devil but a man!' I was all taken aback, for a priest cut at me in front, and the army began firing into the Bashkai men.

"'God A'mighty!' says Dan. 'What is the meaning o' this?'

"'Come back! Come away!' says Billy Fish. 'Ruin and mutiny is the matter. We'll break for Bashkai if we can.'

"I tried to give some sort of orders to my men—the men o' the regular army—but it was no use, so I fired into the brown of 'em with an English Martini and drilled three beggars in a line. The valley was full of shouting, howling creatures, and every soul was shrieking, 'Not a god nor a devil but only a man!' The Bashkai troops stuck to Billy Fish all they were worth, but their matchlocks wasn't half as good as the Kabul breechloaders, and four of them dropped. Dan was bellowing like a bull, for he was very wrathy; and Billy Fish had a hard job to prevent him running out at the crowd.

" 'We can't stand,' says Billy Fish. 'Make a run for it down the valley! The whole place is against us.' The matchlockmen ran, and we went down the valley in spite of Dravot. He was swearing horrible and crying out he was a king. The priests rolled great stones on us, and the regular army fired hard, and there wasn't more than six men, not counting Dan, Billy Fish, and me, that came down to the bottom of the valley alive.

"Then they stopped firing and the horns in the temple blew again. 'Come away—for Gord's sake come away!' says Billy Fish. 'They'll send runners out to all the villages before ever we get to Bashkai. I can protect you there, but I can't do anything now.'

"My own notion is that Dan began to go mad in his head from that hour. He stared up and down like a stuck pig. Then he was all for walking back alone and killing the priests with his bare hands; which he could have done. 'An emperor am I,' says Daniel, 'and next year I shall be a knight of the queen.'

" 'All right, Dan,' says I; 'but come along now while there's time.'

" 'It's your fault,' says he, 'for not looking after your army better. There was a mutiny in the midst, and you didn't know—you damned engine-driving, plate-laying, missionary's-pass-hunting hound!' He sat upon a rock and called me every foul name he could lay tongue to. I was too heartsick to care, though it was all his foolishness that brought the smash.

" 'I'm sorry, Dan,' says I, 'but there's no accounting for natives. This business is our Fifty-seven. Maybe we'll make something out of it yet, when we've got to Bashkai.'

" 'Let's get to Bashkai, then,' says Dan, 'and, by God, when I come back here again I'll sweep the valley so there isn't a bug in a blanket left!'

"We walked all that day, and all that night Dan was stumping up and down on the snow, chewing his beard and muttering to himself.

" 'There's no hope o' getting clear,' said Billy Fish. 'The priests will have sent runners to the villages to say that you are only men. Why didn't you stick on as gods till things was more settled? I'm a dead man,' says Billy Fish, and he throws himself down on the snow and begins to pray to his gods.

"Next morning we was in a cruel bad country—all up and down, no level ground at all, and no food either. The six Bashkai men looked at Billy Fish hungry-way as if they wanted to ask something, but they said never a word. At noon we came to the top of a flat mountain all covered with snow, and when we climbed up into it, behold, there was an army in position waiting in the middle!

"'The runners have been very quick,' says Billy Fish, with a little bit of a laugh. 'They are waiting for us.'

"Three or four men began to fire from the enemy's side, and a chance shot took Daniel in the calf of the leg. That brought him to his senses. He looks across the snow at the army, and sees the rifles that we had brought into the country.

"'We're done for,' says he. 'They are Englishmen, these people—and it's my blasted nonsense that has brought you to this. Get back, Billy Fish, and take your men away; you've done what you could, and now cut for it. Carnehan,' says he, 'shake hands with me and go along with Billy. Maybe they won't kill you. I'll go and meet 'em alone. It's me that did it. Me, the King!'

"'Go!' says I. 'Go to hell, Dan. I'm with you here. Billy Fish, you clear out, and we two will meet those folk.'

"'I'm a chief,' says Billy Fish, quite quiet. 'I stay with you. My men can go.'

"The Bashkai fellows didn't wait for a second word but ran off, and Dan and me and Billy Fish walked across to where the drums were drumming and the horns were horning. It was cold—awful cold. I've got that cold in the back of my head now. There's a lump of it there."

The punkal coolies had gone to sleep. Two kerosene lamps were blazing in this office, and the perspiration poured down my face and splashed on the blotter as I leaned forward. Carnehan was shivering, and I feared that his mind might go. I wiped my face, took a fresh grip of the piteously mangled hands, and said, "What happened after that?"

The momentary shift of my eyes had broken the clear current.

"What was you pleased to say?" whined Carnehan. "They took them without any sound. Not a little whisper all along the snow, not though the King knocked down the first man that set hand on him—not though old Peachey fired his last cartridge into the brown of 'em

Not a single solitary sound did those swines make. They just closed up tight, and I tell you their furs stunk. There was a man called Billy Fish, a good friend of us all, and they cut his throat, sir, then and there, like a pig; and the King kicks up the bloody snow and says: 'We've had a dashed fine run for our money. What's coming next?' But Peachey, Peachey Taliaferro, I tell you, sir, in confidence as betwixt two friends, he lost his head, sir. No, he didn't neither. The King lost his head, so he did, all along o' one of those cunning rope bridges. Kindly let me have the paper cutter, sir. It tilted this way. They marched him a mile across that snow to a rope bridge over a ravine with a river at the bottom. You may have seen such. They prodded him behind like an ox. 'Damn your eyes!' says the King. 'D'you suppose I can't die like a gentleman?' He turns to Peachey—Peachey that was crying like a child. 'I've brought you to this, Peachey,' says he. 'Brought you out of your happy life to be killed in Kafiristan where you was late commander-in-chief of the Emperor's forces. Say you forgive me, Peachey.'—'I do,' says Peachey. 'Fully and freely do I forgive you, Dan.' —'Shake hands, Peachey,' says he. 'I'm going now.' Out he goes, looking neither right nor left, and when he was plumb in the middle of those dizzy dancing ropes: 'Cut, you beggars,' he shouts, and they cut, and old Dan fell, turning round and round and round, twenty thousand miles, for he took half an hour to fall till he struck the water, and I could see his body caught on a rock with the gold crown close beside.

"But do you know what they did to Peachey between two pine trees? They crucified him, sir, as Peachey's hands will show. They used wooden pegs for his hands and his feet; and he didn't die. He hung there and screamed, and they took him down next day, and said it was a miracle that he wasn't dead. They took him down—poor old Peachey that hadn't done them any harm—that hadn't done them any——"

He rocked to and fro and wept bitterly, wiping his eyes with the back of his scarred hands and moaning like a child for some ten minutes.

"They was cruel enough to feed him up in the temple, because they said he was more of a god than old Daniel that was a man. Then they turned him out on the snow, and told him to go home, and Peachey came home in about a year, begging along the roads quite safe; for Daniel Dravot he walked before and said: 'Come along, Peachey. It's a big thing we're doing.' The mountains they danced at night, and the mountains they tried to fall on Peachey's head, but Dan he held up his hand, and Peachey came along bent double. He never let go of Dan's hand, and he never let go of Dan's head. They gave it to him as a present in the temple, to remind him not to come again, and though the crown was pure gold, and Peachey was starving, never would Peachey sell the same. You knew Dravot, sir! You knew Right Worshipful Brother Dravot! Look at him now!"

He fumbled in the mass of rags round his bent waist; brought out a black horsehair bag embroidered with silver thread; and shook therefrom on to my table—the dried, whithered head of Daniel Dravot! The morning sun that had long been paling the lamps struck the red beard and blind sunken eyes; struck, too, a heavy circlet of gold studded with raw turquoises, that Carnehan placed tenderly on the battered temples.

"You be'old now," said Carnehan, "the Emperor in his 'abit as he lived—the King of Kafiristan with his crown upon his head. Poor old Daniel that was a monarch once!"

I shuddered, for, in spite of defacements manifold, I recognized the head of the man of Marwar Junction. Carnehan rose to go. I attempted to stop him. He was not fit to walk abroad. "Let me take away the whisky, and give me a little money," he gasped. "I was a king once. I'll go to the deputy commissioner and ask to set in the poorhouse till I get my health. No, thank you, I can't wait till you get a carriage for me. I've urgent private affairs—in the South—at Marwar."

He shambled out of the office and departed in the direction of the deputy commissioner's house. That day at noon I had occasion to go down the blinding hot mall, and I saw a crooked man crawling along the white dust of the roadside, his hat in his hand, quavering dolorously after the fashion of street singers at home. There was not a soul in sight, and he was out of all possible earshot of the houses. And he sang through his nose, turning his head from right to left:

> *"The Son of Man goes forth to war,*
> *A golden crown to gain;*
> *His blood-red banner streams afar—*
> *Who follows in his train?"*

I waited to hear no more, but put the poor wretch into my carriage and drove him off to the nearest missionary for eventual transfer to the asylum. He repeated the hymn twice while he was with me, whom he did not in the least recognize, and I left him singing it to the missionary.

Two days later I inquired after his welfare of the superintendent of the asylum.

"He was admitted suffering from sunstroke. He died early yesterday morning," said the superintendent. "Is it true that he was half an hour bareheaded in the sun at midday?"

"Yes," said I, "but do you happen to know if he had anything upon him by any chance when he died?"

"Not to my knowledge," said the superintendent.

And there the matter rests.

The Jamesian Touch

HENRY JAMES

One of the world's masters of fiction, Henry James wrote during half a century about twenty novels and a hundred stories, short and long, all of which show his intense interest in fiction as a form of art worthy to rank with other great achievements of mankind.

Henry James (1843–1916) was born in New York City. His father, Henry Sr., wrote a number of books, mainly on mystical theories, and gave his children an education through casual schooling, supplemented by wide travel as well as through cultural reading at home. Henry entered Harvard Law School at the age of nineteen but soon after dropped out and began earning his own living as a writer. Although he wrote sometimes about Americans in America, his adventures in Europe gave him much material to show the contrasts between the Old and the New Worlds, and thus he created "cosmopolitan fiction" in English. Part of the intense interest in James in the twentieth century reflects the fact that America has had to take up the role of world leadership and must be aware of such culture clashes as he continually portrays. Attracted by European life and the chance to make dozens of important friends abroad, James settled in England; thereafter, he spent most of his life in England, and in 1915 became a British subject.

"The Real Thing," first published in 1893, shows only slight traces of the involuted and subtle style of the later James, who plunged more and more deeply into psychological realism. It reveals, however, his conviction that, in the words of Professor Leon Edel, "the artist in fiction is a historian of that part of life never found in history books. . . . Literature for him was the great repository of life."

The life that Henry James knew best offered him many subjects. He was well acquainted with upper-class people but also with writers and other practitioners of the arts. As a young man he had briefly tried painting. Art and "aristocracy" come into conflict in "The Real Thing." The germ of this story, as stated in James' extensive notebooks, grew from a real event told to him by his friend George du Maurier, a popular illustrator, but James changed the facts to make significant fiction. "What I wish to represent," he wrote of the Major and his wife, "is the baffled, ineffectual, incompetent character of their attempt, and how it illustrates once again the everlasting English amateurishness—the way superficial, untrained, unprofessional effort goes to the wall when confronted with trained, competitive, intelligent, *qualified* art."

HENRY JAMES

The Real Thing

I

*W*HEN THE PORTER'S WIFE (she used to answer the house bell) announced "A gentleman—with a lady, sir," I had, as I often had in those days, for the wish was father to the thought, an immediate vision of sitters. Sitters my visitors in this case proved to be; but not in the sense I should have preferred. However, there was nothing at first to indicate that they might not have come for a portrait. The gentleman, a man of fifty, very high and very straight, with a mustache slightly grizzled and a dark grey walking-coat admirably fitted, both of which I noted professionally—I don't mean as a barber or yet as a tailor—would have struck me as a celebrity if celebrities often were striking. It was a truth of which I had for some time been conscious that a figure with a good deal of frontage was, as one might say, almost never a public institution. A glance at the lady helped to remind me of this paradoxical law: she also looked too distinguished to be a "personality." Moreover, one would scarcely come across two variations together.

Neither of the pair spoke immediately—they only prolonged the preliminary gaze which suggested that each wished to give the other a chance. They were visibly shy; they stood there letting me take them in—which, as I afterwards perceived, was the most practical thing they could have done. In this way their embarrassment served their cause. I had seen people painfully reluctant to mention that they desired anything so gross as to be represented on canvas, but the scruples of

The Real Thing

my new friends appeared almost insurmountable. Yet the gentleman might have said "I should like a portrait of my wife," and the lady might have said "I should like a portrait of my husband." Perhaps they were not husband and wife—this naturally would make the matter more delicate. Perhaps they wished to be done together—in which case they ought to have brought a third person to break the news.

"We come from Mr. Rivet," the lady said at last, with a dim smile which had the effect of a moist sponge passed over a "sunk" piece of painting, as well as of a vague allusion to vanished beauty. She was as tall and straight, in her degree, as her companion, and with ten years less to carry. She looked as sad as a woman could look whose face was not charged with expression; that is, her tinted oval mask showed friction as an exposed surface shows it. The hand of time had played over her freely, but only to simplify. She was slim and stiff, and so well-dressed, in dark blue cloth, with lappets and pockets and buttons, that it was clear she employed the same tailor as her husband. The couple had an indefinable air of prosperous thrift—they evidently got a good deal of luxury for their money. If I was to be one of their luxuries it would behoove me to consider my terms.

"Ah, Claude Rivet recommended me?" I inquired; and I added that it was very kind of him, though I could reflect that, as he only painted landscape, this was not a sacrifice.

The lady looked very hard at the gentleman, and the gentleman looked round the room. Then staring at the floor a moment and stroking his mustache, he rested his pleasant eyes on me with the remark: "He said you were the right one."

"I try to be, when people want to sit."

"Yes, we should like to," said the lady anxiously.

"Do you mean together?"

My visitors exchanged a glance. "If you could do anything with *me*, I suppose it would be double," the gentleman stammered.

"Oh yes, there's naturally a higher charge for two figures than for one."

"We should like to make it pay," the husband confessed.

"That's very good of you," I returned, appreciating so unwonted a sympathy—for I supposed he meant pay the artist.

A sense of strangeness seemed to dawn on the lady. "We mean for the illustrations—Mr. Rivet said you might put one in."

"Put one in—an illustration?" I was equally confused.

"Sketch her off, you know," said the gentleman, coloring.

It was only then that I understood the service Claude Rivet had rendered me; he had told them that I worked in black-and-white, for magazines, for storybooks, for sketches of contemporary life, and consequently had frequent employment for models. These things were true, but it was not less true (I may confess it now—whether because the aspiration was to lead to everything or to nothing I leave the reader to guess), that I couldn't get the honors, to say nothing of the emoluments, of a great painter of portraits out of my head. My "illustrations" were my potboilers; I looked to a different branch of art (far and away the most interesting it had always seemed to me) to perpetuate my fame. There was no shame in looking to it also to make my fortune; but that fortune was by so much further from being made from the moment my visitors wished to be "done" for nothing. I was disappointed; for in the pictorial sense I had immediately *seen* them. I had seized their type—I had already settled what I would do with it. Something that wouldn't absolutely have pleased them, I afterwards reflected.

"Ah you're—you're—a—?" I began as soon as I had mastered my surprise. I couldn't bring out the dingy word "models": it seemed to fit the case so little.

"We haven't had much practice," said the lady.

"We've got to *do* something, and we've thought that an artist in your line might perhaps make something of us," her husband threw off. He further mentioned that they didn't know many artists and that they had gone first, on the off-chance (he painted views of course, but sometimes put in figures—perhaps I remembered), to Mr. Rivet, whom they had met a few years before at a place in Norfolk where he was sketching.

"We used to sketch a little ourselves," the lady hinted.

"It's very awkward, but we absolutely *must* do something," her husband went on.

"Of course, we're not so *very* young," she admitted, with a wan smile.

With the remark that I might as well know something more about them, the husband had handed me a card extracted from a neat new pocketbook (their appurtenances were all of the freshest) and inscribed with the words "Major Monarch." Impressive as these words were they didn't carry my knowledge much further; but my visitor presently added: "I've left the army, and we've had the misfortune to lose our money. In fact our means are dreadfully small."

"It's an awful bore," said Mrs. Monarch.

The Real Thing

They evidently wished to be discreet—to take care not to swagger because they were gentlefolks. I perceived they would have been willing to recognize this as something of a drawback, at the same time that I guessed at an underlying sense—their consolation in adversity —that they *had* their points. They certainly had; but these advantages struck me as preponderantly social; such for instance as would help to make a drawing-room look well. However, a drawing-room was always, or ought to be, a picture.

In consequence of his wife's allusion to their age Major Monarch observed: "Naturally, it's more for the figure that we thought of going in. We can still hold ourselves up." On the instant I saw that the figure was indeed their strong point. His "naturally" didn't sound vain, but it lighted up the question. *"She* has got the best," he continued, nodding at his **wife,** with a pleasant after-dinner absence of circumlocution. I could only reply, as if we were in fact sitting over our wine, that this didn't prevent his own from being very good; which led him in turn to rejoin: "We thought that if you ever have to do people like us, we might be something like it. *She* particularly—for a lady in a book, you know."

I was so amused by them that, to get more of it, I did my best to take their point of view; and though it was an embarrassment to find myself appraising physically, as if they were animals on hire or useful blacks, a pair whom I should have expected to meet only in one of the relations in which criticism is tacit, I looked at Mrs. Monarch judicially enough to be able to exclaim, after a moment, with conviction: "Oh yes, a lady in a book!" She was singularly like a bad illustration.

"We'll stand up, if you like," said the Major; and he raised himself before me with a really grand air.

I could take his measure at a glance—he was six feet two and a perfect gentleman. It would have paid any club in process of formation and in want of a stamp to engage him at a salary to stand in the principal window. What struck me immediately was that in coming to me they had rather missed their vocation; they could surely have been turned to better account for advertising purposes. I couldn't of course see the thing in detail, but I could see them make someone's fortune —I don't mean their own. There was something in them for a waistcoat-maker, an hotelkeeper or a soap vendor. I could imagine "We always use it" pinned on their bosoms with the greatest effect; I had a vision of the promptitude with which they would launch a table d'hôte.

Mrs. Monarch sat still, not from pride but from shyness, and presently her husband said to her: "Get up, my dear, and show how smart you are." She obeyed, but she had no need to get up to show it. She walked to the end of the studio, and then she came back blushing, her fluttered eyes on her husband. I was reminded of an incident I had accidentally had a glimpse of in Paris—being with a friend there, a dramatist about to produce a play—when an actress came to him to ask to be entrusted with a part. She went through her paces before him, walked up and down as Mrs. Monarch was doing. Mrs. Monarch did it quite as well, but I abstained from applauding. It was very odd to see such people apply for such poor pay. She looked as if she had ten thousand a year. Her husband had used the word that described her: she was, in the London current jargon, essentially and typically "smart." Her figure was, in the same order of ideas, conspicuously and irreproachably "good." For a woman of her age her waist was surprisingly small; her elbow, moreover, had the orthodox crook. She held her head at the conventional angle; but why did she come to *me?* She ought to have tried on jackets at a big shop. I feared my visitors were not only destitute, but "artistic"—which would be a great complication. When she sat down again I thanked her, observing that what a draughtsman most valued in his model was the faculty of keeping quiet.

"Oh, *she* can keep quiet," said Major Monarch. Then he added, jocosely: "I've always kept her quiet."

"I'm not a nasty fidget, am I?" Mrs. Monarch appealed to her husband.

He addressed his answer to me. "Perhaps it isn't out of place to mention—because we ought to be quite businesslike, oughtn't we?—that when I married her she was known as the Beautiful Statue."

"Oh, dear!" said Mrs. Monarch, ruefully.

"Of course I should want a certain amount of expression," I rejoined.

"Of *course!*" they both exclaimed.

"And then I suppose you know that you'll get awfully tired."

"Oh, we *never* get tired!" they eagerly cried.

"Have you had any kind of practice?"

They hesitated—they looked at each other. "We've been photographed, *immensely,*" said Mrs. Monarch.

"She means the fellows have asked us," added the Major.

"I see—because you're so good-looking."

"I don't know what they thought, but they were always after us."

The Real Thing

"We always got our photographs for nothing," smiled Mrs. Monarch.

"We might have brought some, my dear," her husband remarked.

"I'm not sure we have any left. We've given quantities away," she explained to me.

"With our autographs and that sort of thing," said the Major.

"Are they to be got in the shops?" I inquired, as a harmless pleasantry.

"Oh yes, *hers*—they used to be."

"Not now," said Mrs. Monarch, with her eyes on the floor.

II

I could fancy the "sort of thing" they put on the presentation copies of their photographs, and I was sure they wrote a beautiful hand. It was odd how quickly I was sure of everything that concerned them. If they were now so poor as to have to earn shillings and pence, they never had had much of a margin. Their good looks had been their capital, and they had good-humoredly made the most of the career that this resource marked out for them. It was in their faces, the blankness, the deep intellectual repose of the twenty years of country-house visiting which had given them pleasant intonations. I could see the sunny drawing-rooms, sprinkled with periodicals she didn't read, in which Mrs. Monarch had continuously sat; I could see the wet shrubberies in which she had walked, equipped to admiration for either exercise. I could see the rich covers the Major had helped to shoot and the wonderful garments in which, late at night, he repaired to the smoking-room to talk about them. I could imagine their leggings and waterproofs, their knowing tweeds and rugs, their rolls of sticks and cases of tackle and neat umbrellas; and I could evoke the exact appearance of their servants and the compact variety of their luggage on the platforms of country stations.

They gave small tips, but they were liked; they didn't do anything themselves, but they were welcome. They looked so well everywhere; they gratified the general relish for stature, complexion, and "form." They knew it without fatuity or vulgarity, and they respected themselves in consequence. They were not superficial; they were thorough and kept themselves up—it had been their line. People with such a taste for activity had to have some line. I could feel how even in a dull house, they could have been counted upon for cheerfulness. At present something had happened—it didn't matter what, their little income had grown less, it had grown least—and they had to do something for pocket money. Their friends liked them, but didn't like to support them. There was something about them that represented credit—their clothes, their manners, their type; but if credit is a large empty pocket in which an occasional chink reverberates, the chink at least must be audible. What they wanted of me was to help to make it so. Fortunately they had no children—I soon divined that. They would also perhaps wish our relations to be kept secret: this was why it was "for the figure"—the reproduction of the face would betray them.

I liked them—they were so simple; and I had no objection to them if they would suit. But, somehow, with all their perfections I didn't easily believe in them. After all they were amateurs, and the ruling passion of my life was the detestation of the amateur. Combined with this was another perversity—an innate preference for the represented subject over the real one: the defect of the real one was so apt to be a lack of representation. I like things that appeared; then one was sure. Whether they *were* or not was a subordinate and almost always a profitless question. There were other considerations, the first of which was that I already had two or three people in use, notably a young person with big feet, in alpaca, from Kilburn, who for a couple of years had come to me regularly for my illustrations and with whom I was still—perhaps ignobly—satisfied. I frankly explained to my visitors how the case stood; but they had taken more precautions than I supposed. They had reasoned out their opportunity, for Claude Rivet had told them of the projected *édition de luxe* of one of the writers of our day—the rarest of the novelists—who, long neglected by the multitudinous vulgar and dearly prized by the attentive (need I mention Philip Vincent?) had had the happy fortune of seeing, late in life, the dawn and then the full light of a higher criticism—an estimate in which, on the part of the public, there was something really of expiation. The edition in question, planned by a publisher of taste, was practically an act of high reparation; the woodcuts with which it was to be enriched were the homage of English art to one of the most independent representatives of English letters. Major and Mrs. Monarch confessed to me they had hoped I might be able to work *them* into my share of the enterprise. They knew I was to do the first of the books, *Rutland Ramsay*, but I had to make clear to them that my participation in the rest of the affair—this first book was to be a test —was to depend on the satisfaction I should give. If this should be

The Real Thing

limited my employers would drop me without a scruple. It was therefore a crisis for me, and naturally I was making special preparations, looking about for new people, if they should be necessary, and securing the best types. I admitted, however, that I should like to settle down to two or three good models who would do for everything.

"Should we have often to—a—put on special clothes?" Mrs. Monarch timidly demanded.

"Dear, yes—that's half the business."

"And should we be expected to supply our own costumes?"

"Oh, no; I've got a lot of things. A painter's models put on—or put off—anything he likes."

"And do you mean—a—the same?"

"The same?"

Mrs. Monarch looked at her husband again.

"Oh, she was just wondering," he explained, "if the costumes are in *general* use." I had to confess that they were, and I mentioned further that some of them (I had a lot of genuine, greasy last-century things), had served their time, a hundred years ago, on living, world-stained men and women. "We'll put on anything that *fits*," said the Major.

"Oh, I arrange that—they fit in the pictures."

"I'm afraid I should do better for the modern books. I would come as you like," said Mrs. Monarch.

"She has got a lot of clothes at home: they might do for contemporary life," her husband continued.

"Oh, I can fancy scenes in which you'd be quite natural." And indeed I could see the slipshod rearrangements of stale properties—the stories I tried to produce pictures for without the exasperation of reading them—whose sandy tracts the good lady might help to people. But I had to return to the fact for this sort of work—the daily mechanical grind—I was already equipped: the people I was working with were fully adequate.

"We only thought we might be more like *some* characters," said Mrs. Monarch mildly, getting up.

Her husband also rose; he stood looking at me with a dim wistfulness that was touching in so fine a man. "Wouldn't it be rather a pull sometimes to have—a—to have—?" He hung fire; he wanted me to help him by phrasing what he meant. But I couldn't—I didn't know. So he brought it out, awkwardly: "The *real* thing; a gentleman, you know, or a lady." I was quite ready to give a general assent—I admitted that there was a great deal in that. This encouraged Major Monarch to say, following up his appeal with an unacted gulp: "It's awfully hard—we've tried everything." The gulp was communicative; it proved too much for his wife. Before I knew it Mrs. Monarch had dropped again upon a divan and burst into tears. Her husband sat down beside her, holding one of her hands; whereupon she quickly dried her eyes with the other, while I felt embarrassed as she looked up at me. "There isn't a confounded job I haven't applied for—waited for—prayed for. You can fancy we'd be pretty bad first. Secretaryships and that sort of thing? You might as well ask for a peerage. I'd be *anything*—I'm strong; a messenger or a coalheaver. I'd put on a gold-laced cap and open carriage doors in front of the haberdasher's; I'd hang about a station, to carry portmanteaux; I'd be a postman. But they won't *look* at you; there are thousands, as good as yourself, already on the ground. Gentlemen, poor beggars, who have drunk their wine, who have kept their hunters!"

I was as reassuring as I knew how to be, and my visitors were presently on their feet again while, for the experiment, we agreed on an hour. We were discussing it when the door opened and Miss Churm came in with a wet umbrella. Miss Churm had to take the omnibus to Maida Vale and then walk half a mile. She looked a trifle blowsy and slightly splashed. I scarcely ever saw her come in without thinking afresh how odd it was that, being so little in herself, she should yet be so much in others. She was a meager little Miss Churm, but she was an ample heroine of romance. She was only a freckled cockney, but she could represent everything, from a fine lady to a shepherdess; she had the faculty, as she might have had a fine voice or long hair. She couldn't spell, and she loved beer, but she had two or three "points," and practice, and a knack, and mother wit, and a whimsical sensibility, and a love of the theater, and seven sisters, and not an ounce of respect, especially for the *h.* The first thing my visitors saw was that her umbrella was wet, and in their spotless perfection they visibly winced at it. The rain had come on since their arrival.

"I'm all in a soak; there *was* a mess of people in the bus. I wish you lived near a styion," said Miss Churm. I requested her to get ready as quickly as possible, and she passed into the room in which she always changed her dress. But before going out she asked me what she was to get into this time.

"It's the Russian princess, don't you know?" I answered; "the one with the 'golden eyes,' in black velvet, for the long thing in the *Cheapside.*"

"Golden eyes? I *say!*" cried Miss Churm, while my companions watched her with intensity as she withdrew. She always arranged

The Real Thing

herself, when she was late, before I could turn around; and I kept my visitors a little on purpose, so that they might get an idea, from seeing her, what would be expected of themselves. I mentioned that she was quite my notion of an excellent model—she was really very clever.

"Do you think she looks like a Russian princess?" Major Monarch asked with lurking alarm.

"When I make her, yes."

"Oh, if you have to *make* her—!" he reasoned, acutely.

"That's the most you can ask. There are so many that are not makeable."

"Well now, *here's* a lady"—and with a persuasive smile he passed his arm into his wife's—"who's already made!"

"Oh, I'm not a Russian princess," Mrs. Monarch protested, a little coldly. I could see that she had known some and didn't like them. There, immediately, was a complication of a kind I never had to fear with Miss Churm.

This young lady came back in black velvet—the gown was rather rusty and very low on her lean shoulders—and with a Japanese fan in her red hands. I reminded her that in the scene I was doing she had to look over someone's head. "I forgot whose it is; but it doesn't matter. Just look over a head."

"I'd rather look over a stove," said Miss Churm; and she took her station near the fire. She fell into position, settled herself into a tall attitude, gave a certain backward inclination to her head and a certain forward droop to her fan, and looked, at least to my prejudiced sense, distinguished and charming, foreign and dangerous. We left her looking so, while I went downstairs with Major and Mrs. Monarch.

"I think I could come about as near it as that," said Mrs. Monarch.

"Oh, you think she's shabby, but you must allow for the alchemy of art."

However, they went off with an evident increase of comfort, founded on their demonstrable advantage in being the real thing. I could fancy them shuddering over Miss Churm. She was very droll about them when I went back, for I told her what they wanted.

"Well, if *she* can sit I'll tyke to bookkeeping," said my model.

"She's very ladylike," I replied, as an innocent form of aggravation.

"So much the worse for *you*. That means she can't turn round."

"She'll do for the fashionable novels."

"Oh, yes, she'll *do* for them!" my model humorously declared. "Ain't they bad enough without her?" I had often sociably denounced them to Miss Churm.

161

III

It was for the elucidation of a mystery in one of these works that I first tried Mrs. Monarch. Her husband came with her, to be useful if necessary—it was sufficiently clear that as a general thing he would prefer to come with her. At first I wondered if this were for "propriety's" sake —if he were going to be jealous and meddling. The idea was too tiresome, and if it had been confirmed it would speedily have brought our acquaintance to a close. But I soon saw there was nothing in it and that if he accompanied Mrs. Monarch it was (in addition to the chance of being wanted) simply because he had nothing else to do. When she was away from him his occupation was gone—she never *had* been away from him. I judged, rightly, that in their awkward situation their close union was their main comfort and that this union had no weak spot. It was a real marriage, an encouragement to the hesitating, a nut for pessimists to crack. Their address was humble (I remember afterwards thinking it had been the only thing about them that was really professional), and I could fancy the lamentable lodgings in which the Major would have been left alone. He could bear them with his wife —he couldn't bear them without her.

He had too much tact to try and make himself agreeable when he couldn't be useful; so he simply sat and waited, when I was too absorbed in my work to talk. But I liked to make him talk—it made my work, when it didn't interrupt it, less sordid, less special. To listen to him was to combine the excitement of going out with the economy of staying at home. There was only one hindrance: that I seemed not to know any of the people he and his wife had known. I think he wondered extremely, during the term of our intercourse, whom the deuce I *did* know. He hadn't a stray sixpence of an idea to fumble for, so we didn't spin it very fine—we confined ourselves to questions of leather and even of liquor (saddlers and breeches-makers and how to get good claret cheap), and matters like "good trains" and the habits of small game. His lore on these last subjects was astonishing—he managed to interweave the stationmaster with the ornithologist. When he couldn't talk about greater things he could talk cheerfully about smaller, and since I couldn't accompany him into reminiscences of the fashionable world he could lower the conversation without a visible effort to my level.

So earnest a desire to please was touching in a man who could so easily have knocked one down. He looked after the fire and had an opinion on the draught of the stove without my asking him, and I

The Real Thing

could see that he thought many of my arrangements not half clever enough. I remember telling him that if I were only rich I'd offer him a salary to come and teach me how to live. Sometimes he gave a random sigh of which the essence was: "Give me even such a bare old barrack as *this,* and I'd do something with it!" When I wanted to use him he came alone; which was an illustration of the superior courage of women. His wife could bear her solitary second floor, and she was in general more discreet; showing by various small reserves that she was alive to the propriety of keeping our relations markedly professional—not letting them slide into sociability. She wished it to remain clear that she and the Major were employed, not cultivated, and if she approved of me as a superior, who could be kept in his place, she never thought me quite good enough for an equal.

She sat with great intensity, giving the whole of her mind to it, and was capable of remaining for an hour almost as motionless as if she were before a photographer's lens. I could see she had been photographed often, but somehow the very habit that made her good for that purpose unfitted her for mine. At first I was extremely pleased with her ladylike air, and it was a satisfaction, on coming to follow her lines, to see how good they were and how far they could lead the pencil. But after a few times I began to find her too insurmountably stiff; do what I would with it my drawing looked like a photograph or a copy of a photograph. Her figure had no variety of expression— she herself had no sense of variety. You may say that this was my business and was only a question of placing her. I placed her in every conceivable position but she managed to obliterate their differences. She was always a lady certainly, and into the bargain was always the same lady. She was the real thing, but always the same thing. There were moments when I was oppressed by the serenity of her confidence that she *was* the real thing. All her dealings with me and all her husband's were an implication that this was lucky for *me.* Meanwhile I found myself trying to invent types that approached her own, instead of making her own transform itself—in the clever way that was not impossible, for instance, to poor Miss Churm. Arrange as I would and take the precautions I would, she always, in my pictures, came out too tall—landing me in the dilemma of having represented a fascinating woman as seven feet high, which, out of respect perhaps to my own very much scantier inches, was far from my idea of such a personage.

The case was worse with the Major—nothing I could do would keep *him* down, so that he became useful only for the representation of brawny giants. I adored variety and range, I cherished human accidents, the illustrative note; I wanted to characterize closely, and the thing in the world I most hated was the danger of being ridden by a type. I had quarrelled with some of my friends about it; I had parted company with them for maintaining that one *had* to be, and that if the type was beautiful (witness Raphael and Leonardo), the servitude was only a gain. I was neither Leonardo nor Raphael; I might only be a presumptuous young modern searcher, but I held that everything was to be sacrificed sooner than character. When they averred that the haunting type in question could easily *be* character, I retorted, perhaps superficially, "Whose?" It couldn't be everybody's—it might end in being nobody's.

After I had drawn Mrs. Monarch a dozen times I perceived more clearly than before that the value of such a model as Miss Churm resided precisely in the fact that she had no positive stamp, combined of course with the other fact that what she did have was a curious and inexplicable talent for imitation. Her usual appearance was like a curtain which she could draw up at request for a capital performance. This performance was simply suggestive; but it was a word to the wise—it was vivid and pretty. Sometimes, even, I thought it, though she was plain herself, too insipidly pretty; I made it a reproach to her that the figures drawn from her were monotonously (*bêtement*, as we used to say) graceful. Nothing made her more angry; it was so much her pride to feel she could sit for characters that had nothing in common with each other. She would accuse me at such moments of taking away her "reputytion."

It suffered a certain shrinkage, this queer quantity, from the repeated visits of my new friends. Miss Churm was greatly in demand, never in want of employment, so I had no scruple in putting her off occasionally, to try them more at my ease. It was certainly amusing at first to do the real thing—it was amusing to do Major Monarch's trousers. They *were* the real thing, even if he did come out colossal. It was amusing to do his wife's back hair (it was so mathematically neat), and the particular "smart" tension of her tight stays. She lent herself especially to positions in which the face was somewhat averted or blurred; she abounded in ladylike back views and *profils perdus*. When she stood erect she took naturally one of the attitudes in which court painters represent queens and princesses; so that I found myself wondering whether, to draw out this accomplishment, I couldn't get the editor of the *Cheapside* to publish a really royal romance, "A Tale of Buckingham Palace." Sometimes, however, the real thing and the make-believe came into contact; by which I mean that Miss Churm, keeping an appointment or coming to make one on days when I had much work in hand, encountered her invidious rivals. The encounter was not on their part, for they noticed her no more than if she had been the housemaid; not from intentional loftiness, but simply because as yet, professionally, they didn't know how to fraternize, as I could guess they would have liked—or at least that the Major would. They couldn't talk about the omnibus—they always walked; and they didn't know what else to try—she wasn't interested in good trains or cheap claret. Besides, they must have felt—in the air—that she was amused at them, secretly derisive of their ever knowing how. She wasn't a person to conceal her skepticism if she had had a chance to show it. On the other hand Mrs. Monarch didn't think her tidy; for why else did she take pains to say to me (it was going out of the way, for Mrs. Monarch), that she didn't like dirty women?

One day when my young lady happened to be present with my other sitters (she even dropped in, when it was convenient, for a chat), I asked her to be so good as to lend a hand in getting tea—a service with which she was familiar and which was one of a class that, living as I did in a small way, with slender domestic resources, I often appealed to my models to render. They liked to lay hands on my property, to break the sitting, and sometimes the china—I made them feel Bohemian. The next time I saw Miss Churm after this incident she surprised me greatly by making a scene about it—she accused me of having wished to humiliate her. She hadn't resented the outrage at the time, but had seemed obliging and amused, enjoying the comedy of asking Mrs. Monarch, who sat vague and silent, whether she would have cream and sugar, and putting an exaggerated simper into the question. She had tried intonations—as if she too wished to pass for the real thing; till I was afraid my other visitors would take offense.

Oh, they were determined not to do this, and their touching patience was the measure of their great need. They would sit by the hour, uncomplaining, till I was ready to use them; they would come back on the chance of being wanted and would walk away cheerfully if they were not. I used to go to the door with them to see in what magnificent order they retreated. I tried to find other employment for them—I introduced them to several artists. But they didn't "take," for reasons I could appreciate, and I became conscious, rather anxiously, that after such disappointments they fell back upon me with a heavier weight. They did me the honor to think that it was I who was most *their* form. They were not picturesque enough for the painters, and in those days there were not so many serious workers in black-and-white. Besides, they had an eye to the great job I had mentioned to them—they had secretly set their hearts on supplying the right essence for my pictorial vindication of our fine novelist. They knew that for this undertaking I should want no costume effects, none of the frippery of past ages—that it was a case in which everything would be contemporary and satirical and presumably genteel. If I could work them into it their future would be assured, for the labor would of course be long and the occupation steady.

One day Mrs. Monarch came without her husband—she explained his absence by his having had to go to the City. While she sat there in her usual anxious stiffness, there came at the door a knock which I immediately recognized as the subdued appeal of a model out of work. It was followed by the entrance of a young man whom I easily perceived to be a foreigner and who proved in fact an Italian acquainted with no English word but my name, which he uttered in a way that made it seem to include all others. I had not then visited his country, nor was I proficient in his tongue; but as he was not so meanly constituted—what Italian is?—as to depend only on that member for expression he conveyed to me, in familiar but graceful mimicry, that he was in search of exactly the employment in which the lady before me was engaged. I was not struck with him at first, and while I continued to draw I emitted rough sounds of discouragement or dismissal. He stood his ground however—not importunately, but with a dumb, doglike fidelity in his eyes which amounted to innocent impudence, the manner of a devoted servant (he might have been in the house for years), unjustly suspected. Suddenly I saw that this very attitude and expression made a picture; whereupon I told him to sit down and wait till I should be free. There was another picture in the way he obeyed me, and I observed as I worked that there were others still in the way he looked wonderingly, with his head thrown back, about the high studio. He might have been crossing himself in Saint Peter's. Before I finished I said to myself "The fellow's a bankrupt orange monger, but he's a treasure."

When Mrs. Monarch withdrew he passed across the room like a flash to open the door for her, standing there with the rapt, pure gaze of the young Dante spellbound by the young Beatrice. As I never insisted, in such situations, on the blankness of the British domestic, I reflected that he had the making of a servant (and I needed one, but couldn't pay him to be only that), as well as of a model; in short I made up my mind to adopt my bright adventurer if he would agree to officiate in the double capacity. He jumped at my offer, and in the event my rashness (for I had known nothing about him), was not brought home to me. He proved a sympathetic though a desultory ministrant, and had in a wonderful degree the *sentiment de la pose*. It was uncultivated, instinctive, a part of the happy instinct which had guided him to my door and helped him to spell out my name on the card nailed to it. He had had no other introduction to me than a guess, from the shape of my high north window, seen outside, that my place was a studio and that as a studio it would contain an artist. He had wandered to England in search of fortune, like other itinerants, and had embarked, with a partner and a small green handcart, on the sale of penny ices. The ices had melted away and the partner had dissolved in their train. My young man wore tight yellow trousers with reddish stripes and his name was Oronte. He was sallow but fair, and when I put him into some old clothes of my own he looked like an Englishman. He was as good as Miss Churm, who could look, when required, like an Italian.

IV

I thought Mrs. Monarch's face slightly convulsed when, on her coming back with her husband, she found Oronte installed. It was strange to have to recognize in a scrap of a lazzarone a competitor to her magnificent Major. It was she who scented danger first, for the Major was anecdotically unconscious. But Oronte gave us tea, with a hundred eager confusions (he had never seen such a queer process), and I think she thought better of me for having at last an "establishment." They saw a couple of drawings that I had made of the establishment, and Mrs. Monarch hinted that it never would have struck her that he had sat for them. "Now the drawings you make from *us*, they look exactly like us," she reminded me, smiling in triumph; and I recognized that this was indeed just their defect. When I drew the Monarchs I couldn't somehow get away from them—get into the character I wanted to represent; and I had not the least desire my model should be discoverable in my picture. Miss Churm never was, and Mrs. Monarch thought I hid her, very properly, because she was vulgar; whereas if she was lost it was only as the dead who go to heaven are lost—in the gain of an angel the more.

By this time I had got a certain start with *Rutland Ramsay,* the first novel in the great projected series; that is, I had produced a dozen drawings, several with the help of the Major and his wife, and I had sent them in for approval. My understanding with the publishers, as I have already hinted, had been that I was to be left to do my work, in this particular case, as I liked, with the whole book committed to me; but my connection with the rest of the series was only contingent. There were moments when, frankly, it *was* a comfort to have the real thing under one's hand; for there were characters in *Rutland Ramsay* that were very much like it. There were people presumably as straight as the Major and women of as good a fashion as Mrs. Monarch. There was a great deal of country-house life—treated, it is true, in a fine, fanciful, ironical, generalized way—and there was a considerable implication of knickerbockers and kilts. There were certain things I had to settle at the outset; such things for instance as the exact appearance of the hero, the particular bloom of the heroine. The author of course gave me a lead, but there was a margin for interpretation. I took the Monarchs into my confidence. I told them frankly what I was about, I mentioned my embarrassments and alternatives. "Oh, take *him!*" Mrs. Monarch murmured sweetly, looking at her husband; and "What could you want better than my wife?" the Major inquired, with the comfortable candor that now prevailed between us.

I was not obliged to answer these remarks—I was only obliged to place my sitters. I was not easy in mind, and I postponed, a little timidly perhaps, the solution of the question. The book was a large canvas, the other figures were numerous, and I worked off at first some of the episodes in which the hero and the heroine were not concerned. When once I had set *them* up I should have to stick to them—I couldn't make my young man seven feet high in one place and five feet nine in another. I inclined on the whole to the latter measurement, though the Major more than once reminded me that *he* looked about as young as anyone. It was indeed quite possible to arrange him, for the figure, so that it would have been difficult to detect his age. After the spontaneous Oronte had been with me a month, and after I had given him to understand several different times that his native exuberance would presently constitute an insurmountable barrier to our further intercourse, I waked to a sense of his heroic capacity. He was only five feet seven, but the remaining inches were latent. I tried him almost secretly at first, for I was really rather afraid of the judgment my other models would pass on such a choice. If they regarded Miss Churm as little better than a snare, what would they think of the representation by a person so little the real thing as an Italian street vendor of a protagonist formed by a public school?

If I went a little in fear of them it was not because they bullied me, because they had got an oppressive foothold, but because in their really pathetic decorum and mysteriously permanent newness they

The Real Thing

counted on me so intensely. I was therefore very glad when Jack Hawley came home: he was always of such good counsel. He painted badly himself, but there was no one like him for putting his finger on the place. He had been absent from England for a year; he had been somewhere—I don't remember where—to get a fresh eye. I was in a good deal of dread of any such organ, but we were old friends; he had been away for months and a sense of emptiness was creeping into my life. I hadn't dodged a missile for a year.

He came back with a fresh eye, but with the same old black velvet blouse, and the first evening he spent in my studio we smoked cigarettes till the small hours. He had done no work himself, he had only got the eye; so the field was clear for the production of my little things. He wanted to see what I had done for the *Cheapside,* but he was disappointed in the exhibition. That at least seemed the meaning of two or three comprehensive groans which, as he lounged on my big divan, on a folded leg, looking at my latest drawings, issued from his lips with the smoke of the cigarette.

"What's the matter with you?" I asked.

"What's the matter with *you?"*

"Nothing save that I'm mystified."

"You are indeed. You're quite off the hinge. What's the meaning of this new fad?" And he tossed me, with visible irreverence, a drawing in which I happened to have depicted both my majestic models. I asked if he didn't think it good, and he replied that it struck him as execrable, given the sort of thing I had always represented myself to him as wishing to arrive at; but I let that pass—I was so anxious to see exactly what he meant. The two figures in the picture looked colossal, but I supposed this was *not* what he meant, inasmuch as, for aught he knew to the contrary, I might have been trying for that. I maintained that I was working exactly in the same way as when he last had done me the honor to commend me. "Well, there's a big hole somewhere," he answered; "wait a bit and I'll discover it." I depended upon him to do so: where else was the fresh eye? But he produced at last nothing more luminous than "I don't know—I don't like your types." This was lame for a critic who had never consented to discuss with me anything but the question of execution, the direction of strokes, and the mystery of values.

"In the drawings you've been looking at I think my types are very handsome."

"Oh, they won't do!"

"I've had a couple of new models."

"I see you have. *They* won't do."

"Are you very sure of that?"

"Absolutely—they're stupid."

"You mean *I* am—for I ought to get round that."

"You *can't*—with such people. Who are they?"

I told him, as far as was necessary, and he declared, heartlessly: *"Ce sont des gens qu'il faut mettre à la porte."*

"You've never seen them; they're awfully good," I compassionately objected.

"Not seen them? Why, all this recent work of yours drops to pieces with them. It's all I want to see of them."

"No one else has said anything against it—the *Cheapside* people are pleased."

"Everyone else is an ass, and the *Cheapside* people the biggest asses of all. Come, don't pretend at this time of day to have pretty illusions about the public, especially about publishers and editors. It's not for *such* animals you work—it's for those who know, *coloro che sanno;* so keep straight for *me* if you can't keep straight for yourself. There's a certain sort of thing you've tried for from the first—and a very good thing it is. But this twaddle isn't *in* it." When I talked with Hawley later about *Rutland Ramsay* and its possible successors he declared that I must get back into my boat again or I should go to the bottom. His voice in short was the voice of warning.

I noted the warning, but I didn't turn my friends out of doors. They bored me a good deal; but the very fact that they bored me admonished me not to sacrifice them—if there was anything to be done with them—simply to irritation. As I look back at this phase they seem to me to have pervaded my life not a little. I have a vision of them as most of the time in my studio, seated against the wall on an old velvet bench to be out of the way, and looking like a pair of patient courtiers in a royal antechamber. I'm convinced that during the coldest weeks of the winter they held their ground because it saved them fire. Their newness was losing its gloss, and it was impossible not to feel that they were objects of charity. Whenever Miss Churm arrived they went away, and after I was fairly launched in *Rutland Ramsay* Miss Churm arrived pretty often. They managed to express to me tacitly that they supposed I wanted her for the low life of the book, and I let them suppose it, since they had attempted to study the work—it was lying about the studio—without discovering that it dealt only with the highest circles. They had dipped into the most brilliant of our novelists without deciphering many passages. I still took an hour from them,

The Real Thing

now and again, in spite of Jack Hawley's warning: it would be time enough to dismiss them, if dismissal should be necessary, when the rigor of the season was over. Hawley had made their acquaintance—he had met them at my fireside—and thought them a ridiculous pair. Learning that he was a painter they tried to approach him, to show him too that they were the real thing; but he looked at them, across the big room, as if they were miles away: they were a compendium of everything he most objected to in the social system of his country. Such people as that, all convention and patent leather, with ejaculations that stopped conversation, had no business in a studio. A studio was a place to learn to see, and how could you see through a pair of featherbeds?

The main inconvenience I suffered at their hands was that at first I was shy of letting them discover how my artful little servant had begun to sit for me for *Rutland Ramsay*. They knew I had been odd enough (they were prepared by this time to allow oddity to artists) to pick a foreign vagabond out of the streets when I might have had a person with whiskers and credentials; but it was some time before they learned how high I rated his accomplishments. They found him in an attitude more than once, but they never doubted I was doing him as an organ-grinder. There were several things they never guessed, and one of them was that for a striking scene in the novel, in which a footman briefly figured, it occurred to me to make use of Major Monarch as the menial. I kept putting this off, I didn't like to ask him to don the livery—besides the difficulty of finding a livery to fit him. At last, one day late in the winter, when I was at work on the despised Oronte (he caught one's idea in an instant), and was in the glow of feeling that I was going very straight, they came in, the Major and his wife, with their society laugh about nothing (there was less and less to laugh at), like country callers—they always reminded me of that—who have walked across the park after church and are presently persuaded to stay to luncheon. Luncheon was over, but they could stay to tea—I knew they wanted it. The fit was on me, however, and I couldn't let my ardor cool and my work wait, with the fading daylight, while my model prepared it. So I asked Mrs. Monarch if she would mind laying it out—a request which for an instant brought all the blood to her face. Her eyes were on her husband's for a second, and some mute telegraphy passed between them. Their folly was over the next instant; his cheerful shrewdness put an end to it. So far from pitying their wounded pride, I must add, I was moved to give it as complete a lesson as I could. They bustled about together and got out the cups and saucers and made the kettle boil. I know they felt as if they were waiting on my servant, and when the tea was prepared I said: "He'll have a cup, please—he's tired." Mrs. Monarch brought him one where he stood, and he took it from her as if he had been a gentleman at a party squeezing a crush-hat with an elbow.

Then it came over me that she had made a great effort for me— made it with a kind of nobleness—and that I owed her a compensation. Each time I saw her after this I wondered what the compensation could be. I couldn't go on doing the wrong thing to oblige them. Oh, it *was* the wrong thing, the stamp of the work for which they sat—Hawley was not the only person to say it now. I sent in a large number of the drawings I had made for *Rutland Ramsay,* and I received a warning that was more to the point than Hawley's. The artistic adviser of the house for which I was working was of opinion that many of my illustrations were not what had been looked for. Most of these illustrations were the subjects in which the Monarchs had figured. Without going into the question of what *had* been looked for, I saw at this rate I shouldn't get the other books to do. I hurled myself in despair upon Miss Churm —I put her through all her paces. I not only adopted Oronte publicly as my hero, but one morning when the Major looked in to see if I didn't require him to finish a figure for the *Cheapside* for which he had begun to sit the week before, I told him that I had changed my mind—I would do the drawing from my man. At this my visitor turned pale and stood looking at me. "Is *he* your idea of an English gentleman?" he asked.

I was disappointed, I was nervous, I wanted to get on with my work; so I replied with irritation: "Oh, my dear Major—I can't be ruined for *you!*"

He stood another moment; then, without a word, he quitted the studio. I drew a long breath when he was gone, for I said to myself that I shouldn't see him again. I had not told him definitely that I was in danger of having my work rejected, but I was vexed at his not having felt the catastrophe in the air, read with me the moral of our fruitless collaboration, the lesson that in the deceptive atmosphere of art even the highest respectability may fail of being plastic.

I didn't owe my friends money, but I did see them again. They reappeared together three days later, and under the circumstances, there was something tragic in the fact. It was a proof to me that they could find nothing else in life to do. They had threshed the matter out in a dismal conference—they had digested the bad news that they were not in for the series. If they were not useful to me even for the *Cheapside* their function seemed difficult to determine, and I could only judge at first that they had come, forgivingly, decorously, to take a last

The Real Thing

leave. This made me rejoice in secret that I had little leisure for a scene; for I had placed both my other models in position together and I was pegging away at a drawing from which I hoped to derive glory. It had been suggested by the passage in which Rutland Ramsay, drawing up a chair to Artemisia's piano stool, says extraordinary things to her while she ostensibly fingers out a difficult piece of music. I had done Miss Churm at the piano before—it was an attitude in which she knew how to take on an absolutely poetic grace. I wished the two figures to "compose" together, intensely, and my little Italian had entered perfectly into my conception. The pair were vividly before me, the piano had been pulled out; it was a charming picture of blended youth and murmured love, which I had only to catch and keep. My visitors stood and looked at it, and I was friendly to them over my shoulder.

They made no response, but I was used to silent company and went on with my work, only a little disconcerted (even though exhilarated by the sense that *this* was at least the ideal thing), at not having got rid of them after all. Presently I heard Mrs. Monarch's sweet voice beside or rather above me: "I wish her hair was a little better done." I looked up and she was staring with a strange fixedness at Miss Churm, whose back was turned to her. "Do you mind my just touching it?" she went on—a question which made me spring up for an instant as with the instinctive fear that she might do the young lady a harm. But she quieted me with a glance I shall never forget—I confess I should like to have been able to paint *that*—and went for a moment to my model. She spoke to her softly, laying a hand upon her shoulder and bending over her; and as the girl, understanding, gratefully assented, she disposed her rough curls, with a few quick passes, in such a way as to make Miss Churm's head twice as charming. It was one of the most heroic personal services I've ever seen rendered. Then Mrs. Monarch turned away with a low sigh and, looking about her as if for something to do, stooped to the floor with a noble humility and picked up a dirty rag that had dropped out of my paint box.

The Major meanwhile had also been looking for something to do, and, wandering to the other end of the studio, saw before him my breakfast things neglected, unremoved. "I say, can't I be useful *here?"* he called out to me with an irrepressible quaver. I assented with a laugh that I fear was awkward, and for the next ten minutes, while I worked, I heard the light clatter of china and the tinkle of spoons and glass. Mrs. Monarch assisted her husband—they washed up my crockery, they put it away. They wandered off into my little scullery, and I afterwards found that they had cleaned my knives and that my slender stock of plate had an unprecedented surface. When it came over me, the latent eloquence of what they were doing, I confess that my drawing was blurred for a moment—the picture swam. They had accepted their failure, but they couldn't accept their fate. They had bowed their heads in bewilderment to the perverse and cruel law in virtue of which the real thing could be so much less precious than the unreal; but they didn't want to starve. If my servants were my models, my models might be my servants. They would reverse the parts—the others would sit for the ladies and gentlemen and *they* would do the work. They would still be in the studio—it was an intense dumb appeal to me not to turn them out. "Take us on," they wanted to say—we'll do *anything.*"

When all this hung before me, the *afflatus* vanished—my pencil dropped from my hand. My sitting was spoiled and I got rid of my sitters, who were also evidently rather mystified and awestruck. Then, alone with the Major and his wife, I had a most uncomfortable moment. He put their prayer into a single sentence: "I say, you know—just let *us* do for you, can't you?" I couldn't—it was dreadful to see them emptying my slops; but I pretended I could, to oblige them, for about a week. Then I gave them a sum of money to go away, and I never saw them again. I obtained the remaining books, but my friend Hawley repeats that Major and Mrs. Monarch did me a permanent harm, got me into a second-rate trick. If it be true I'm content to have paid the price—for the memory.

Why Did You Tell Me of the Just God?

SELMA LAGERLÖF

Sweden's finest storyteller, Miss Lagerlöf was the first woman to win the Nobel Prize for literature.

Selma Ottiliana Lovisa Lagerlöf (1858–1940) was born on a farm and enjoyed a happy childhood. She became a schoolteacher, but published an excellent first novel in 1891, and thereafter her writing was considered to play a leading part in the Swedish romantic revival of the 1890s. Her first collection of short stories appeared in 1894. Best known of her works among young Americans is *The Wonderful Adventures of Nils* (1907) and its sequel; both these fantasies were written to acquaint Swedish schoolchildren with various parts of their homeland. Miss Lagerlöf used the money from her Nobel Prize to buy back the farm where she was born, and during her long life produced many volumes of fiction rooted in the legends of her country.

"The Outlaws," written before 1894, deals with Miss Lagerlöf's favorite theme, the problem of combining happiness with goodness. The irony of having a Christian outlaw convert a pagan outlaw, who then must betray his companion to justice, is obvious. The richness of language and the power of description, however, almost overshadow the plot.

SELMA LAGERLÖF

The Outlaws

A PEASANT WHO HAD murdered a monk took to the woods and was made an outlaw. He found there before him in the wilderness another outlaw, a fisherman from the outermost islands, who had been accused of stealing a herring net. They joined together, lived in a cave, set snares, sharpened darts, baked bread on a granite rock, and guarded one another's lives. The peasant never left the woods, but the fisherman, who had not committed such an abominable crime, sometimes loaded game on his shoulders and stole down among men. There he got in exchange for blackcocks, for long-eared hares and fine-limbed red deer, milk and butter, arrowheads and clothes. These helped the outlaws to sustain life.

The cave where they lived was dug in the side of a hill. Broad stones and thorny sloe bushes hid the entrance. Above it stood a thick growing pine tree. At its roots was the venthole of the cave. The rising smoke filtered through the tree's thick branches and vanished into space. The men used to go to and from their dwelling place, wading in the mountain stream, which ran down the hill. No one looked for their tracks under the merry, bubbling water.

At first they were hunted like wild beasts. The peasants gathered as if for a chase of bear or wolf. The wood was surrounded by men with bows and arrows. Men with spears went through it and left no dark crevice, no bushy thicket unexplored. While the noisy battue hunted through the wood, the outlaws lay in their dark hole, listening breathlessly, panting with terror. The fisherman held out a whole day, but he who had murdered was driven by unbearable fear out into the open, where he could see his enemy. He was seen and hunted, but it

The Outlaws

seemed to him seven times better than to lie still in helpless inactivity. He fled from his pursuers, slid down precipices, sprang over streams, climbed up perpendicular mountain walls. All latent strength and dexterity in him was called forth by the excitement of danger. His body became elastic like a steel spring, his foot made no false step, his hand never lost its hold, eye and ear were twice as sharp as usual. He understood what the leaves whispered and the rocks warned. When he had climbed up a precipice, he turned toward his pursuers, sending them gibes in biting rhyme. When the whistling darts whizzed by him, he caught them, swift as lightning, and hurled them down on his enemies. As he forced his way through whipping branches, something within him sang a song of triumph.

The bald mountain ridge ran through the wood and alone on its summit stood a lofty fir. The red-brown trunk was bare, but in the branching top rocked an eagle's nest. The fugitive was now so audaciously bold that he climbed up there, while his pursuers looked for him on the wooded slopes. There he sat twisting the young eaglets' necks, while the hunt passed by far below him. The male and female eagle, longing for revenge, swooped on the ravisher. They fluttered before his face, they struck with their beaks at his eyes, they beat him with their wings and tore with their claws bleeding weals in his weatherbeaten skin. Laughing, he fought with them. Standing upright in the shaking nest, he cut at them with his sharp knife and forgot in the pleasure of the play his danger and his pursuers. When he found time to look for them, they had gone by to some other part of the forest. No one had thought to look for their prey on the bald mountain ridge. No one had raised his eyes to the clouds to see him practicing boyish tricks and sleepwalking feats while his life was in the greatest danger.

The man trembled when he found that he was saved. With shaking hands he caught at a support; giddy he measured the height to which he had climbed. And moaning with the fear of falling, afraid of the birds, afraid of being seen, afraid of everything, he slid down the trunk. He laid himself down on the ground, so as not to be seen, and dragged himself over the rocks until the underbrush covered him. There he hid himself under the young pine tree's tangled branches. Weak and powerless, he sank down on the moss. A single man could have captured him.

Tord was the fisherman's name. He was not more than sixteen years old, but strong and bold. He had already lived a year in the woods.

The peasant's name was Berg, with the surname Rese. He was the tallest and strongest man in the whole district, and moreover handsome and well built. He was broad in the shoulders and slender in the waist. His hands were well shaped as if he had never done any hard work. His hair was brown and his skin fair. After he had been some time in the woods he acquired in all ways a more formidable appearance. His eyes became piercing, his eyebrows grew bushy, and the muscles which knitted them lay finger-thick above his nose. It showed now more plainly than before how the upper part of his athlete's brow projected over the lower. His lips closed more firmly than of old, his whole face was thinner, the hollows at the temples grew very deep, and his powerful jaw was much more prominent. His body was less well filled out but his muscles were as hard as steel. His hair grew suddenly gray.

Young Tord could never weary of looking at this man. He had never before seen anything so beautiful and powerful. In his imagination he stood high as the forest, strong as the sea. He served him as a master and worshiped him as a god. It was a matter of course that Tord should carry the hunting spears, drag home the game, fetch the water, and build the fire. Berg Rese accepted all his services, but almost never gave him a friendly word. He despised him because he was a thief.

The outlaws did not lead a robber's or brigand's life; they supported themselves by hunting and fishing. If Berg Rese had not murdered a holy man, the peasants would soon have ceased to pursue him and have left him in peace in the mountains. But they feared great disaster to the district, because he who had raised his hand against the servant of God was still unpunished. When Tord came down to the valley with game, they offered him riches and pardon for his own crime if he would show them the way to Berg Rese's hole, so that they might take him while he slept. But the boy always refused; and if anyone tried to sneak after him up to the wood, he led him so cleverly astray that he gave up the pursuit.

Once Berg asked him if the peasants had not tried to tempt him to betray him, and when he heard what they had offered him as a reward, he said scornfully that Tord had been foolish not to accept such a proposal.

Then Tord looked at him with a glance, the like of which Berg Rese had never before seen. Never had any beautiful woman in his youth, never had his wife or child looked so at him. "You are my lord, my elected master," said the glance. "Know that you may strike and abuse me as you will, I am faithful notwithstanding."

The Outlaws

After that Berg Rese paid more attention to the boy and noticed that he was bold to act but timid to speak. He had no fear of death. When the ponds were first frozen, or when the bogs were most dangerous in the spring, when the quagmires were hidden under richly flowering grasses and cloudberry, he took his way over them by choice. He seemed to feel the need of exposing himself to danger as a compensation for the storms and terrors of the ocean, which he had no longer to meet. At night he was afraid in the woods, and even in the middle of the day the darkest thickets or the wide-stretching roots of a fallen pine could frighten him. But when Berg Rese asked him about it, he was too shy to even answer.

Tord did not sleep near the fire, far in the cave, on the bed which was made soft with moss and warm with skins, but every night, when Berg had fallen asleep, he crept out to the entrance and lay there on a rock. Berg discovered this, and although he well understood the reason, he asked what it meant. Tord would not explain. To escape any more questions, he did not lie at the door for two nights, but then he returned to his post.

One night, when the drifting snow whirled about the forest tops and drove into the thickest underbrush, the driving snowflakes found their way into the outlaws' cave. Tord, who lay just inside the entrance, was, when he waked in the morning, covered by a melting snowdrift. A few days later he fell ill. His lungs wheezed, and when they were expanded to take in air, he felt excruciating pain. He kept up as long as his strength held out, but when one evening he leaned down to blow the fire, he fell over and remained lying.

Berg Rese came to him and told him to go to his bed. Tord moaned with pain and could not raise himself. Berg then thrust his arms under him and carried him there. But he felt as if he had got hold of a slimy snake; he had a taste in the mouth as if he had eaten the unholy horseflesh, it was so odious to him to touch the miserable thief.

He laid his own big bearskin over him and gave him water; more he could not do. Nor was it anything dangerous. Tord was soon well again. But through Berg's being obliged to do his tasks and to be his servant, they had come nearer to one another. Tord dared to talk to him when he sat in the cave in the evening and cut arrow shafts.

"You are of a good race, Berg," said Tord. "Your kinsmen are the richest in the valley. Your ancestors have served with kings and fought in their castles."

"They have oftener fought with bands of rebels and done the kings great injury," replied Berg Rese.

"Your ancestors gave great feasts at Christmas, and so did you, when you were at home. Hundreds of men and women could find a place to sit in your big house, which was already built before Sant Olof first gave the baptism here in Viken. You owned old silver vessels and great drinking horns, which passed from man to man, filled with mead."

Again Berg Rese had to look at the boy. He sat up with his legs hanging out of the bed and his head resting on his hands, with which he at the same time held back the wild masses of hair which would fall over his eyes. His face had become pale and delicate from the ravages of sickness. In his eyes fever still burned. He smiled at the pictures he conjured up: at the adorned house, at the silver vessels, at the guests in gala array, and at Berg Rese, sitting in the seat of honor in the hall of his ancestors. The peasant thought that no one had ever looked at him with such shining, admiring eyes, or thought him so magnificent, arrayed in his festival clothes, as that boy thought him in the torn skin dress.

He was both touched and provoked. That miserable thief had no right to admire him.

"Were there no feasts in your house?" he asked.

Tord laughed. "Out there on the rocks with father and mother! Father is a wrecker and mother is a witch. No one will come to us."

"Is your mother a witch?"

"She is," answered Tord, quite untroubled. "In stormy weather she rides out on a seal to meet the ships over which the waves are washing, and those who are carried overboard are hers."

"What does she do with them?" asked Berg.

"Oh, a witch always needs corpses. She makes ointments out of them, or perhaps she eats them. On moonlight nights she sits in the surf, where it is whitest, and the spray dashes over her. They say that she sits and searches for shipwrecked children's fingers and eyes."

"That is awful," said Berg.

The boy answered with infinite assurance: "That would be awful in others, but not in witches. They have to do so."

Berg Rese found that he had here come upon a new way of regarding the world and things.

"Do thieves have to steal, as witches have to use witchcraft?" he asked sharply.

"Yes, of course," answered the boy; "everyone has to do what he is destined to do." But then he added, with a cautious smile: "There are thieves also who have never stolen."

"Say out what you mean," said Berg.

The Outlaws

The boy continued with his mysterious smile, proud at being an unsolvable riddle: "It is like speaking of birds who do not fly, to talk of thieves who do not steal."

Berg Rese pretended to be stupid in order to find out what he wanted. "No one can be called a thief without having stolen," he said.

"No; but," said the boy, and pressed his lips together as if to keep in the words, "but if someone had a father who stole," he hinted after a while.

"One inherits money and lands," replied Berg Rese, "but no one bears the name of thief if he has not himself earned it."

Tord laughed quietly. "But if somebody has a mother who begs and prays him to take his father's crime on him. But if such a one cheats the hangman and escapes to the woods. But if someone is made an outlaw for a fishnet which he has never seen."

Berg Rese struck the stone table with his clenched fist. He was angry. This fair young man had thrown away his whole life. He could never win love, nor riches, nor esteem after that. The wretched striving for food and clothes was all which was left him. And the fool had let him, Berg Rese, go on despising one who was innocent. He rebuked him with stern words, but Tord was not even as afraid as a sick child is of its mother, when she chides it because it has caught cold by wading in the spring brooks.

On one of the broad, wooded mountains lay a dark tarn. It was square, with as straight shores and as sharp corners as if it had been cut by the hand of man. On three sides it was surrounded by steep cliffs, on which pines clung with roots as thick as a man's arm. Down by the pool, where the earth had been gradually washed away, their roots stood up out of the water, bare and crooked and wonderfully twisted about one another. It was like an infinite number of serpents which had wanted all at the same time to crawl up out of the pool but had got entangled in one another and been held fast. Or it was like a mass of blackened skeletons of drowned giants which the pool wanted to throw up on the land. Arms and legs writhed about one another, the long fingers dug deep into the very cliff to get a hold, the mighty ribs formed arches, which held up primeval trees. It had happened, however, that the iron arms, the steellike fingers with which the pines held themselves fast, had given way, and a pine had been borne by a mighty north wind from the top of the cliff down into the pool. It had burrowed deep down into the muddy bottom with its top and now stood there. The smaller fish had a good place of refuge among its branches, but the roots stuck up above the water like a many-armed monster and contributed to make the pool awful and terrifying.

On the tarn's fourth side the cliff sank down. There a little foaming stream carried away its waters. Before this stream could find the only possible way, it had tried to get out between stones and tufts, and had by so doing made a little world of islands, some no bigger than a little hillock, others covered with trees.

Here where the encircling cliffs did not shut out all the sun, leafy trees flourished. Here stood thirsty, gray-green alders and smooth-leaved willows. The birch tree grew there as it does everywhere where it is trying to crowd out the pine woods, and the wild cherry and the mountain ash, those two which edge the forest pastures, filling them with fragrance and adorning them with beauty.

Here at the outlet there was a forest of reeds as high as a man, which made the sunlight fall green on the water just as it falls on the moss in the real forest. Among the reeds there were open places; small, round pools, and water lilies were floating there. The tall stalks looked down with mild seriousness on those sensitive beauties, who discontentedly shut their white petals and yellow stamens in a hard, leather-like sheath as soon as the sun ceased to show itself.

One sunshiny day the outlaws came to this tarn to fish. They waded out to a couple of big stones in the midst of the reed forest and sat there and threw out bait for the big, green-striped pickerel that lay and slept near the surface of the water.

These men, who were always wandering in the woods and the mountains, had, without their knowing it themselves, come under nature's rule as much as the plants and the animals. When the sun shone, they were openhearted and brave, but in the evening, as soon as the sun had disappeared, they became silent; and the night, which seemed to them much greater and more powerful than the day, made them anxious and helpless. Now the green light, which slanted in between the rushes and colored the water with brown and dark-green streaked with gold, affected their mood until they were ready for any miracle. Every outlook was shut off. Sometimes the reeds rocked in an imperceptible wind, their stalks rustled, and the long, ribbonlike leaves fluttered against their faces. They sat in gray skins on the gray stones. The shadows in the skins repeated the shadows of the weather-beaten, mossy stone. Each saw his companion in his silence and immovability change into a stone image. But in among the rushes swam mighty fishes with rainbow-colored backs. When the men threw out their hooks and saw the circles spreading among the reeds, it seemed as if the motion grew stronger and stronger, until they perceived that it was not caused only by their cast. A sea nymph, half human, half a shining fish, lay and slept on the surface of the water. She lay on her back with her whole body under water. The waves so nearly covered her that they had not noticed her before. It was her breathing that caused the motion of the waves. But there was nothing strange in her lying there, and when the next instant she was gone, they were not sure that she had been only an illusion.

The green light entered through the eyes into the brain like a gentle intoxication. The men sat and stared with dulled thoughts, seeing visions among the reeds, of which they did not dare to tell one another. Their catch was poor. The day was devoted to dreams and apparitions.

The stroke of oars was heard among the rushes, and they started up as from sleep. The next moment, a flat-bottomed boat appeared, heavy, hollowed out with no skill and with oars as small as sticks. A young girl, who had been picking water lilies, rowed it. She had dark-brown hair, gathered in great braids, and big dark eyes; otherwise she was strangely pale. But her paleness toned to pink and not to gray. Her cheeks had no higher color than the rest of her face, the lips had hardly enough. She wore a white linen shirt and a leather belt with a gold buckle. Her skirt was blue with a red hem. She rowed by the outlaws without seeing them. They kept breathlessly still, but not for fear of being seen, but only to be able to really see her. As soon as she had gone they were as if changed from stone images to living beings. Smiling, they looked at one another.

"She was white like the water lilies," said one. "Her eyes were as dark as the water there under the pine roots."

They were so excited that they wanted to laugh, really laugh as no one had ever laughed by that pool, till the cliffs thundered with echoes and the roots of the pines loosened with fright.

"Did you think she was pretty?" asked Berg Rese.

"Oh, I do not know, I saw her for such a short time. Perhaps she was."

"I do not believe you dared to look at her. You thought that it was a mermaid."

And they were again shaken by the same extravagant merriment.

Tord had once as a child seen a drowned man. He had found the body on the shore on a summer day and had not been at all afraid, but at night he had dreamed terrible dreams. He saw a sea, where every wave rolled a dead man to his feet. He saw, too, that all the islands were covered with drowned men, who were dead and belonged to the sea, but who still could speak and move and threaten him with withered white hands.

It was so with him now. The girl whom he had seen among the rushes came back in his dreams. He met her out in the open pool, where the sunlight fell even greener than among the rushes, and he had time to see that she was beautiful. He dreamed that he had crept up on the big pine root in the middle of the dark tarn, but the pine swayed and rocked so that sometimes he was quite under water. Then she came forward on the little islands. She stood under the red mountain ashes and laughed at him. In the last dream-vision he had come so far that she kissed him. It was already morning, and he heard that Berg Rese had got up, but he obstinately shut his eyes to be able to go on with his dream. When he awoke, he was as though dizzy and stunned by what had happened to him in the night. He thought much more now of the girl than he had done the day before.

Toward night he happened to ask Berg Rese if he knew her name.

Berg looked at him inquiringly. "Perhaps it is best for you to hear it," he said. "She is Unn. We are cousins."

Tord then knew it was for that pale girl's sake Berg Rese wandered an outlaw in forest and mountain. Tord tried to remember what he knew of her. Unn was the daughter of a rich peasant. Her mother was dead, so that she managed her father's house. This she liked, for she was fond of her own way and she had no wish to be married.

Unn and Berg Rese were the children of brothers, and it had long been said that Berg preferred to sit with Unn and her maids and jest with them than to work on his own lands. When the great Christmas feast was celebrated at his house, his wife had invited a monk from Draksmark, for she wanted him to remonstrate with Berg, because he was forgetting her for another woman. This monk was hateful to Berg and to many on account of his appearance. He was very fat and quite white. The ring of hair about his bald head, the eyebrows above his watery eyes, his face, his hands and his whole cloak, everything was white. Many found it hard to endure his looks.

At this banquet table, in the hearing of all the guests, this monk now said, for he was fearless and thought that his words would have more effect if they were heard by many, "People are in the habit of saying that the cuckoo is the worst of birds because he does not rear his young in his own nest, but here sits a man who does not provide for his home and his children, but seeks his pleasure with a strange woman. Him will I call the worst of men." Unn then rose up. "That, Berg, is said to you and me," she said. "Never have I been so insulted, and my father is not here either." She had wished to go, but Berg sprang after her. "Do not move!" she said. "I will never see you again." He caught up with her in the hall and asked her what he should do to make her stay. She answered with flashing eyes that he must know that best for himself. Then Berg went in and killed the monk.

Berg and Tord were busy with the same thoughts, for after a while Berg said: "You should have seen her, Unn, when the white monk fell. The mistress of the house gathered the small children about her and cursed her. She turned their faces toward her, that they might forever remember her who had made their father a murderer. But Unn stood calm and so beautiful that the men trembled. She thanked me for the deed and told me to fly to the woods. She bade me not to be robber, and not to use the knife until I could do it for an equally just cause."

"Your deed had been to her honor," said Tord.

Berg Rese noticed again what had astonished him before in the boy. He was like a heathen, worse than a heathen; he never condemned what was wrong. He felt no responsibility. That which must be, was. He knew of God and Christ and the saints, but only by name, as one knows the gods of foreign lands. The ghosts of the rocks were his gods. His mother, wise in witchcraft, had taught him to believe in the spirits of the dead.

Then Berg Rese undertook a task which was as foolish as to twist a rope about his own neck. He set before those ignorant eyes the great God, the Lord of justice, the Avenger of misdeeds, who casts the wicked into places of everlasting torment. And he taught him to love Christ and His mother and the holy men and women, who with lifted hands kneeled before God's throne to avert the wrath of the great Avenger from the hosts of sinners. He taught him all that men do to appease God's wrath. He showed him the crowds of pilgrims making pilgrimages to holy places, the flight of self-torturing penitents and monks from a worldly life.

As he spoke, the boy became more eager and more pale, his eyes grew large as if for terrible visions. Berg Rese wished to stop, but thoughts streamed to him, and he went on speaking. The night sank down over them, the black forest night, when the owls hoot. God came so near to them that they saw His throne darken the stars, and the chastizing angels sank down to the tops of the trees. And under them the fires of Hell flamed up to the earth's crust, eagerly licking that shaking place of refuge for the sorrowing races of men.

The autumn had come with a heavy storm. Tord went alone in the woods to see after the snares and traps. Berg Rese sat at home to mend his clothes. Tord's way led in a broad path up a wooded height.

Every gust carried the dry leaves in a rustling whirl up the path. Time after time, Tord thought that someone went behind him. He often looked round. Sometimes he stopped to listen, but he understood that it was the leaves and the wind, and went on. As soon as he started again, he heard someone come dancing on silken foot up the slope. Small feet came tripping. Elves and fairies played behind him. When he turned round, there was no one, always no one. He shook his fists at the rustling leaves and went on.

They did not grow silent for that, but they took another tone. They began to hiss and to pant behind him. A big viper came gliding. Its tongue dripping venom hung far out of its mouth, and its bright body shone against the withered leaves. Beside the snake pattered a wolf, a big, gaunt monster, who was ready to seize fast in his throat when the snake had twisted about his feet and bitten him in the heel. Sometimes they were both silent, as if to approach him unperceived, but they soon betrayed themselves by hissing and panting, sometimes the wolf's claws rung against a stone. Involuntarily Tord walked quicker and quicker, but the creature hastened after him. When he felt that they were only two steps distant and were preparing to strike, he turned. There was nothing there, and he had known it the whole time.

He sat down on a stone to rest. Then the dry leaves played about his feet as if to amuse him. All the leaves of the forest were there: small, light yellow birch leaves, red-speckled mountain ash, the elm's dry, dark-brown leaves, the aspen's tough light red, and the willow's yellow-green. Transformed and withered, scarred and torn were they, and much unlike the downy, light-green, delicately shaped leaves, which a few months ago had rolled out of their buds.

"Sinners," said the boy, "sinners, nothing is pure in God's eyes. The flame of his wrath has already reached you."

When he resumed his wandering, he saw the forest under him bend before the storm like a heaving sea, but in the path it was calm. But he heard what he did not feel. The woods were full of voices.

He heard whisperings, wailing songs, coarse threats, thundering oaths. There was laughter and laments, there was the noise of many people. That which hounded and pursued, which rustled and hissed, which seemed to be something and still was nothing, gave him wild thoughts. He felt again the anguish of death, as when he lay on the floor in his den and the peasants hunted him through the wood. He heard again the crashing of branches, the people's heavy tread, the ring of weapons, the resounding cries, the wild, bloodthirsty noise, which followed the crowd.

But it was not only that which he heard in the storm. There was something else, something still more terrible, voices which he could not interpret, a confusion of voices, which seemed to him to speak in foreign tongues. He had heard mightier storms than this whistle through the rigging, but never before had he heard the wind play on such a many-voiced harp. Each tree had its own voice; the pine did not murmur like the aspen nor the poplar like the mountain ash. Every hole had its note, every cliff's sounding echo its own ring. And the noise of the brooks and the cry of foxes mingled with the marvelous forest storm. But all that he could interpret; there were other strange sounds. It was those which made him begin to scream and scoff and groan in emulation with the storm.

He had always been afraid when he was alone in the darkness of the forest. He liked the open sea and the bare rocks. Spirits and phantoms crept about among the trees.

Suddenly he heard who it was who spoke in the storm. It was God, the great Avenger, the God of justice. He was hunting him for the sake of his comrade. He demanded that he should deliver up the murderer to His vengeance.

Then Tord began to speak in the midst of the storm. He told God what he had wished to do, but had not been able. He had wished to speak to Berg Rese and to beg him to make his peace with God, but he had been too shy. Bashfulness had made him dumb. "When I heard that the earth was ruled by a just God," he cried, "I understood that he was a lost man. I have lain and wept for my friend many long nights. I knew that God would find him out, wherever he might hide. But I could not speak, nor teach him to understand. I was speechless, because I loved him so much. Ask not that I shall speak to him, ask not that the sea shall rise up against the mountain."

He was silent, and in the storm the deep voice, which had been the voice of God for him, ceased. It was suddenly calm, with a sharp sun and a splashing as of oars and a gentle rustle as of stiff rushes. These sounds brought Unn's image before him.—The outlaw cannot have anything, not riches, nor women, nor the esteem of men.—If he should betray Berg, he would be taken under the protection of the law.—But Unn must love Berg, after what he had done for her. There was no way out of it all.

When the storm increased, he heard again steps behind him and sometimes a breathless panting. Now he did not dare to look back, for he knew that the white monk went behind him. He came from the feast at Berg Rese's house, drenched with blood, with a gaping axe wound in his forehead. And he whispered: "Denounce him, betray him, save his soul. Leave his body to the pyre, that his soul may be spared. Leave him to the slow torture of the rack, that his soul may have time to repent."

Tord ran. All this fright of what was nothing in itself grew, when it so continually played on the soul, to an unspeakable terror. He wished to escape from it all. As he began to run, again thundered that deep, terrible voice, which was God's. God himself hunted him with alarms, that he should give up the murderer. Berg Rese's crime seemed more detestable than ever to him. An unarmed man had been murdered, a man of God pierced with shining steel. It was like a defiance of the Lord of the world. And the murderer dared to live! He rejoiced in the sun's light and in the fruits of the earth as if the Almighty's arms were too short to reach him.

He stopped, clenched his fists, and howled out a threat. Then he ran like a madman from the wood down to the valley.

Tord hardly needed to tell his errand; instantly ten peasants were ready to follow him. It was decided that Tord should go alone up to the cave, so that Berg's suspicions should not be aroused. But where he should scatter peas, so that the peasants could find the way.

When Tord came to the cave, the outlaw sat on the stone bench and sewed. The fire gave hardly any light, and the work seemed to go badly. The boy's heart swelled up with pity. The splendid Berg Rese seemed to him poor and unhappy. And the only thing he possessed, his life, should be taken from him. Tord began to weep.

"What is it?" asked Berg. "Are you ill? Have you been frightened?"

Then for the first time Tord spoke of his fear. "It was terrible in the wood. I heard ghosts and saw specters. I saw white monks."

" 'Sdeath, boy!"

"They crowded round me all the way up Broad Mountain. I ran, but they followed after and sang. Can I never be rid of the sound?

The Outlaws

What have I to do with them? I think that they could go to one who needed it more."

"Are you mad tonight, Tord?"

Tord talked, hardly knowing what words he used. He was free from all shyness. The words streamed from his lips.

"They are all white monks, white, pale as death. They all have blood on their cloaks. They drag their hoods down over the brows, but still the wound shines from under; the big, red, gaping wound from the blow of the axe."

"The big, red, gaping wound from the blow of the axe?"

"Is it I who perhaps have struck it? Why shall I see it?"

"The saints only know, Tord," said Berg Rese, pale and with terrible earnestness, "what it means that you see a wound from an axe. I killed the monk with a couple of knife thrusts."

Tord stood trembling before Berg and wrung his hands. "They demand you of me! They want to force me to betray you!"

"Who? The monks?"

"They, yes, the monks. They show me visions. They show me her, Unn. They show me the shining, sunny sea. They show me the fishermen's camping ground, where there is dancing and merrymaking. I close my eyes, but still I see. 'Leave me in peace,' I say. 'My friend has murdered, but he is not bad. Let me be, and I will talk to him, so that he repents and atones. He shall confess his sin and go to Christ's grave. We will both go together to the places which are so holy that all sin is taken away from him who draws near them."

"What do the monks answer?" asked Berg. "They want to have me saved. They want to have me on the rack and wheel."

"Shall I betray my dearest friend, I ask them," continued Tord. "He is my world. He has saved me from the bear that had his paw on my throat. We have been cold together and suffered every want together. He has spread his bearskin over me when I was sick. I have carried wood and water for him; I have watched over him while he slept; I have fooled his enemies. Why do they think that I am one who will betray a friend? My friend will soon of his own accord go to the priest and confess, then we will go together to the land of atonement."

Berg listened earnestly, his eyes sharply searching Tord's face. "You shall go to the priest and tell him the truth," he said. "You need to be among people."

"Does that help me if I go alone? For your sin, Death and all his specters follow me. Do you not see how I shudder at you? You have lifted your hand against God himself. No crime is like yours. I think that I must rejoice when I see you on rack and wheel. It is well for him who can receive his punishment in this world and escapes the wrath to come. Why did you tell me of the just God? You compel me to betray you. Save me from that sin. Go to the priest." And he fell on his knees before Berg.

The murderer laid his hand on his head and looked at him. He was measuring his sin against his friend's anguish, and it grew big and terrible before his soul. He saw himself at variance with the Will which rules the world. Repentance entered his heart.

"Woe to me that I have done what I have done," he said. "That which awaits me is too hard to meet voluntarily. If I give myself up to the priests, they will torture me for hours; they will roast me with slow fires. And is not this life of misery, which we lead in fear and want, penance enough? Have I not lost lands and home? Do I not live parted from friends and everything which makes a man's happiness? What more is required?"

When he spoke so, Tord sprang up wild with terror. "Can you repent?" he cried. "Can my words move your heart? Then come instantly! How could I believe that! Let us escape! There is still time."

Berg Rese sprang up, he too. "You have done it, then—"

"Yes, yes, yes! I have betrayed you! But come quickly! Come, as you can repent! They will let us go. We shall escape them!"

The murderer bent down to the floor, where the battle-axe of his ancestors lay at his feet. "You son of a thief!" he said, hissing out the words, "I have trusted you and loved you."

But when Tord saw him bend for the axe, he knew that it was now a question of his own life. He snatched his own axe from his own belt and struck at Berg before he had time to raise himself. The edge cut through the whistling air and sank in the bent head. Berg Rese fell head foremost to the floor, his body rolled after. Blood and brains spouted out, the axe fell from the wound. In the matted hair Tord saw a big, red, gaping hole from the blow of an axe.

The peasants came rushing in. They rejoiced and praised the deed.

"You will win by this," they said to Tord.

Tord looked down at his hands as if he saw there the fetters with which he had been dragged forward to kill him he loved. They were forged from nothing. Of the rushes' green light, of the play of the shadows, of the song of the storm, of the rustling of the leaves, of dreams were they created. And he said aloud: "God is great."

The Outlaws

But again the old thought came to him. He fell on his knees beside the body and put his arm under his head.

"Do him no harm," he said. "He repents; he is going to the Holy Sepulcher. He is not dead, he is not a prisoner. We were just ready to go when he fell. The white monk did not want him to repent, but God, the God of justice, loves repentance."

He lay beside the body, talked to it, wept and begged the dead man to awake. The peasants arranged a bier. They wished to carry the peasant's body down to his house. They had respect for the dead and spoke softly in his presence. When they lifted him up on the bier, Tord rose, shook the hair back from his face, and said with a voice which shook with sobs:

"Say to Unn, who made Berg Rese a murderer, that he was killed by Tord the fisherman, whose father is a wrecker and whose mother is a witch, because he taught him that the foundation of the world is justice."

Voyage to the Gorgeous East

JOSEPH CONRAD

Conrad, one of the greatest authors in English, was born in Poland and taught himself painfully to master a new language and forge a new art of storytelling.

Josef Teodor Konrad Nalecz Korzeniowski (1857–1924), who later shortened his name to Joseph Conrad, was born of parents who were political idealists in revolt against Russia, of which Poland was then a part. The father was exiled before 1863 to a place near the Ural Mountains, where he was joined by his wife and little son. Josef's mother died when he was eight. His father died four years later, and he went to live with his mother's brother. Josef enrolled in the high school at Cracow, Poland, and later was tutored by a young university student. He became fluent in French and could well have written his fiction in that language. His delight in reading English and American sea stories impelled him at the age of sixteen to leave for Marseilles, France, to become a sailor.

Eventually, having served as a seaman and an officer in merchant ships, Conrad became in 1886 a qualified master mariner and a naturalized British subject. Voyages to many foreign ports gave him material for stories, especially about the Asian coasts and the western Pacific. A voyage up the Congo River in 1890 resulted in a famous story, "Heart of Darkness," but Conrad caught malarial fever which affected his health. He had begun writing before 1886, and in 1898 finally abandoned the idea of remaining a sailor and began the more difficult task of trying to support a wife and children by his pen. He wrote a number of fine novels and stories without much financial return until his work was recognized around 1914 as that of a genius. Thereafter his great contribution to fiction and criticism in English was the subject of many books and essays.

"Youth," first published in 1898, is one of his earliest stories, recollecting some of his seafaring adventures. For two years, 1881–1883, Conrad had served intermittently on a vessel called the *Palestine*, which became the *Judea* of "Youth." His story, however, is a work of imagination, put together in an artistic frame. Of it he wrote: " 'Youth' is a feat of memory. It is a record of experience; but that experience, in its facts, in its inwardness and in its outward coloring, begins and ends in myself."

JOSEPH CONRAD

Youth

THIS COULD HAVE OCCURRED nowhere but in England, where men and sea interpenetrate, so to speak—the sea entering into the life of most men, and the men knowing something or everything about the sea, in the way of amusement, of travel, or of breadwinning.

We were sitting round a mahogany table that reflected the bottle, the claret glasses, and our faces as we leaned on our elbows. There was a director of companies, an accountant, a lawyer, Marlow, and myself. The director had been a *Conway* boy, the accountant had served four years at sea, the lawyer—a fine crusted Tory, High Churchman, the best of old fellows, the soul of honor—had been chief officer in the P. & O. service in the good old days when mail boats were square-rigged at least on two masts, and used to come down the China Sea before a fair monsoon with stun sails set alow and aloft. We all began life in the merchant service. Between the five of us there was the strong bond of the sea, and also the fellowship of the craft, which no amount of enthusiasm for yachting, cruising, and so on can give, since one is only the amusement of life and the other is life itself.

Marlow (at least I think that is how he spelled his name) told the story, or rather the chronicle, of a voyage:

"Yes, I have seen a little of the Eastern seas; but what I remember best is my first voyage there. You fellows know there are those voyages that seem ordered for the illustration of life, that might stand for a symbol of existence. You fight, work, sweat, nearly kill yourself, sometimes do kill yourself, trying to accomplish something—and you can't. Not from any fault of yours. You simply can do nothing, neither great nor little—not a thing in the world—not even marry an old maid, or get a wretched 600-ton cargo of coal to its port of destination.

"It was altogether a memorable affair. It was my first voyage to the East, and my first voyage as second mate; it was also my skipper's first command. You'll admit it was time. He was sixty if a day; a little man, with a broad, not very straight back, with bowed shoulders and one leg more bandy than the other, he had that queer twisted-about appearance you see so often in men who work in the fields. He had a nutcracker face—chin and nose trying to come together over a sunken mouth—and it was framed in iron-gray, fluffy hair, that looked like a chin strap of cotton wool sprinkled with coal dust. And he had blue eyes in that old face of his, which were amazingly like a boy's, with that candid expression some quite common men preserve to the end of their days by a rare internal gift of simplicity of heart and rectitude of soul. What induced him to accept me was a wonder. I had come out of a crack Australian clipper, where I had been third officer, and he seemed to have a prejudice against crack clippers as aristocratic and high-toned. He said to me, 'You know, in this ship you will have to work.' I said I had to work in every ship I had ever been in. 'Ah, but this is different, and you gentlemen out of them big ships; . . . but there! I dare say you will do. Join tomorrow.'

"I joined tomorrow. It was twenty-two years ago; and I was just twenty. How time passes! It was one of the happiest days of my life. Fancy! Second mate for the first time—a really responsible officer! I wouldn't have thrown up my new billet for a fortune. The mate looked me over carefully. He was also an old chap, but of another stamp. He had a Roman nose, a snow-white, long beard, and his name was Mahon, but he insisted that it should be pronounced Mann. He was well connected; yet there was something wrong with his luck, and he had never got on.

"As to the captain, he had been for years in coasters, then in the Mediterranean, and last in the West Indian trade. He had never been round the Capes. He could just write a kind of sketchy hand, and didn't care for writing at all. Both were thorough good seamen of course, and between those two old chaps I felt like a small boy between two grandfathers.

"The ship also was old. Her name was the *Judea*. Queer name, isn't it? She belonged to a man Wilmer, Wilcox—some name like that; but he has been bankrupt and dead these twenty years or more, and his name don't matter. She had been laid up in Shadwell basin for ever so long. You may imagine her state. She was all rust, dust, grime—soot aloft, dirt on deck. To me it was like coming out of a palace into a ruined cottage. She was four-hundred tons, had a primitive windlass,

Youth

wooden latches to the doors, not a bit of brass about her, and a big square stern. There was on it, below her name in big letters, a lot of scrollwork, with the gilt off, and some sort of a coat of arms, with the motto 'Do or Die' underneath. I remember it took my fancy immensely. There was a touch of romance in it, something that made me love the old thing—something that appealed to my youth!

"We left London in ballast—sand ballast—to load a cargo of coal in a northern port of Bangkok. Bangkok! I thrilled. I had been six years at sea, but had only seen Melbourne and Sydney, very good places, charming places in their way—but Bangkok!

"We worked out of the Thames under canvas, with a North Sea pilot on board. His name was Jermyn, and he dodged all day long about the galley drying his handkerchief before the stove. Apparently he never slept. He was a dismal man, with a perpetual tear sparkling at the end of his nose, who either had been in trouble, or was in trouble, or expected to be in trouble—couldn't be happy unless something went wrong. He mistrusted my youth, my common sense, and my seamanship, and made a point of showing it in a hundred little ways. I dare say he was right. It seems to me I knew very little then, and I know not much more now; but I cherish a hate for that Jermyn to this day.

"We were a week working up as far as Yarmouth Roads, and then we got into a gale—the famous October gale of twenty-two years ago. It was wind, lightning, sleet, snow, and a terrific sea. We were flying light, and you may imagine how bad it was when I tell you we had smashed bulwarks and a flooded deck. On the second night she shifted her ballast into the lee bow, and by that time we had been blown off somewhere on the Dogger Bank. There was nothing for it but go below with shovels and try to right her, and there we were in that vast hold, gloomy like a cavern, the tallow dips stuck and flickering on the beams, the gale howling above, the ship tossing about like mad on her side; there we all were, Jermyn, the captain, everyone, hardly able to keep our feet, engaged on that gravedigger's work, and trying to toss shovelfuls of wet sand up to windward. At every tumble of the ship you could see vaguely in the dim light men falling down with a great flourish of shovels. One of the ship's boys (we had two), impressed by the weirdness of the scene, wept as if his heart would break. We could hear him blubbering somewhere in the shadows.

"On the third day the gale died out, and by and by a north-country tug picked us up. We took sixteen days in all to get from London to the Tyne! When we got into dock we had lost our turn for loading, and they hauled us off to a tier where we remained for a month. Mrs. Beard (the captain's name was Beard) came from Colchester to see the old man. She lived on board. The crew of runners had left, and there remained only the officers, one boy, and the steward, a mulatto who answered to the name of Abraham. Mrs. Beard was an old woman, with a face all wrinkled and ruddy like a winter apple, and the figure of a young girl. She caught sight of me once, sewing on a button, and insisted on having my shirts to repair. This was something different from the captains' wives I had known on board crack clippers. When I brought her the shirts, she said: 'And the socks? They want mending, I am sure, and John's—Captain Beard's—things are all in order now. I would be glad of something to do.' Bless the old woman. She overhauled my outfit for me, and meantime I read for the first time *Sartor Resartus* and Burnaby's *Ride to Khiva*. I didn't understand much of the first then; but I remember I preferred the soldier to the philosopher at the time; a preference which life has only confirmed. One was a man, and the other was either more—or less. However, they are both dead and Mrs. Beard is dead, and youth, strength, genius, thoughts, achievements, simple hearts—all die. . . . No matter.

"They loaded us at last. We shipped a crew. Eight able seamen and two boys. We hauled off one evening to the buoys at the dock gates, ready to go out, and with a fair prospect of beginning the voyage next day. Mrs. Beard was to start for home by a late train. When the ship was fast we went to tea. We sat rather silent through the meal—Mahon, the old couple, and I. I finished first, and slipped away for a smoke, my cabin being in a deckhouse just against the poop. It was high water, blowing fresh with a drizzle; the double dock gates were opened, and the steam colliers were going in and out in the darkness with their lights burning bright, a great plashing of propellers, rattling of winches, and a lot of hailing on the pier heads. I watched the procession of headlights gliding high and of green lights gliding low in the night, when suddenly a red gleam flashed at me, vanished, came into view again, and remained. The fore end of a steamer loomed up close. I shouted down the cabin, 'Come up, quick!' and then heard a startled voice saying afar in the dark, 'Stop her, sir.' A bell jingled. Another voice cried warningly, 'We are going right into that barque, sir.' The answer to this was a gruff 'All right,' and the next thing was a heavy crash as the steamer struck a glancing blow with the bluff of her bow about our fore rigging. There was a moment of confusion, yelling, and running about. Steam roared. Then somebody was heard saying, 'All clear, sir.' . . . 'Are you all right?' asked the gruff voice. I had jumped forward to see the damage, and hailed back, 'I think so.' 'Easy astern,' said the gruff voice. A bell jingled. 'What steamer is that?' screamed Mahon. By that time she was no more to us than a bulky shadow maneuvering a little way off. They shouted at us some name—a woman's name, Miranda or Melissa—or some such thing. 'This means another month in this beastly hole,' said Mahon to me, as we peered with lamps about the splintered bulwarks and broken braces. 'But where's the captain?'

"We had not heard or seen anything of him all that time. We went aft to look. A doleful voice arose hailing somewhere in the middle of the dock, *Judea* ahoy!' . . . How the devil did he get there? . . . 'Hallo!' we shouted. 'I am adrift in our boat without oars,' he cried. A belated waterman offered his services, and Mahon struck a bargain with him for half-a-crown to tow our skipper alongside; but it was Mrs. Beard that came up the ladder first. They had been floating about the dock in that mizzly cold rain for nearly an hour. I was never so surprised in my life.

"It appears that when he heard my shout 'Come up' he understood at once what was the matter, caught up his wife, ran on deck, and across, and down into our boat, which was fast to the ladder. Not bad for a sixty-year-old. Just imagine that old fellow saving heroically in his arms that old woman—the woman of his life. He set her down on a thwart, and was ready to climb back on board when the painter came adrift somehow, and away they went together. Of course in the confusion we did not hear him shouting. He looked abashed. She said cheerfully, 'I suppose it does not matter my losing the train now?' 'No, Jenny—you go below and get warm,' he growled. Then to us: 'A sailor has no business with a wife—I say. There I was, out of the ship. Well, no harm done this time. Let's go and look at what that fool of a steamer smashed.'

"It wasn't much, but it delayed us three weeks. At the end of that time, the captain being engaged with his agents, I carried Mrs. Beard's bag to the railway station and put her all comfy into a third-class carriage. She lowered the window to say, 'You are a good young man. If you see John—Captain Beard—without his muffler at night, just remind him from me to keep his throat well wrapped up.' 'Certainly, Mrs. Beard,' I said. 'You are a good young man; I noticed how attentive you are to John—to Captain——' The train pulled out suddenly; I took my cap off to the old woman: I never saw her again. . . . Pass the bottle.

"We went to sea next day. When we made that start for Bangkok we had been already three months out of London. We had expected to be a fortnight or so—at the outside.

"It was January, and the weather was beautiful—the beautiful sunny winter weather that has more charm than in the summertime, because it is unexpected, and crisp, and you know it won't, it can't, last long. It's like a windfall, like a godsend, like an unexpected piece of luck.

"It lasted all down the North Sea, all down the Channel; and it lasted till we were three hundred miles or so to the westward of the Lizards: then the wind went round to the sou'west and began to pipe up. In two days it blew a gale. The *Judea,* hove to, wallowed on the Atlantic like an old candle box. It blew day after day: it blew with spite, without interval, without mercy, without rest. The world was nothing but an immensity of great foaming waves rushing at us, under a sky low enough to touch with the hand and dirty like a smoked ceiling. In the stormy space surrounding us there was as much flying spray as air. Day after day and night after night there was nothing round the ship but the howl of the wind, the tumult of the sea, the noise of water pouring over her deck. There was no rest for her and no rest for us. She tossed, she pitched, she stood on her head, she sat on her tail, she rolled, she groaned, and we had to hold on while on deck and cling to our bunks when below, in a constant effort of body and worry of mind.

"One night Mahon spoke through the small window of my berth. It opened right into my very bed, and I was lying there sleepless, in my boots, feeling as though I had not slept for years, and could not if I tried. He said excitedly—

" 'You got the sounding rod in here, Marlow? I can't get the pumps to suck. By God! it's no child's play.'

"I gave him the sounding rod and lay down again, trying to think of various things—but I thought only of the pumps. When I came on deck they were still at it, and my watch relieved at the pumps. By the light of the lantern brought on deck to examine the sounding rod I caught a glimpse of their weary, serious faces. We pumped all the four hours. We pumped all night, all day, all the week—watch and watch. She was working herself loose, and leaked badly—not enough to drown us at once, but enough to kill us with the work at the pumps. And while we pumped the ship was going from us piecemeal: the bulwarks went, the stanchions were torn out, the ventilators smashed, the cabin door burst in. There was not a dry spot in the ship. She was being gutted bit by bit. The longboat changed, as if by magic, into matchwood where she stood in her gripes. I had lashed her myself, and was rather proud of my handiwork, which had withstood so long the malice of the sea. And we pumped. And there was no break in the weather. The sea was white like a sheet of foam, like a caldron of boiling milk; there was not a break in the clouds, no—not the size of a man's hand—no, not for so much as ten seconds. There was for us no sky, there were for us no stars, no sun, no universe—nothing but angry clouds and an infuriated sea. We pumped watch and watch, for dear life; and it seemed to last for months, for years, for all eternity, as though we had been dead and gone to a hell for sailors. We forgot the day of the week, the name of the month, what year it was, and whether we had ever been ashore. The sails blew away, she lay broadside on under a weather-cloth, the ocean poured over her, and we did not care. We turned those handles, and had the eyes of idiots. As soon as we had crawled on deck I used to take a round turn with a rope about the men, the pumps, and the mainmast, and we turned, we turned incessantly, with the water to our waists, to our necks, over our heads. It was all one. We had forgotten how it felt to be dry.

"And there was somewhere in me the thought: By Jove! this is the deuce of an adventure—something you read about; and it is my first voyage as second mate—and I am only twenty—and here I am lasting it out as well as any of these men, and keeping my chaps up to the mark. I was pleased. I would not have given up the experience for worlds. I had moments of exultation. Whenever the old dismantled craft pitched heavily with her counter high in the air, she seemed to me to throw up, like an appeal, like a defiance, like a cry to the clouds without mercy, the words written on her stern: *Judea,* London. Do or Die.'

"O youth! The strength of it, the faith of it, the imagination of it! To me she was not an old rattletrap carting about the world a lot of coal for a freight—to me she was the endeavor, the test, the trial of life. I think of her with pleasure, with affection, with regret—as you would think of someone dead you have loved. I shall never forget her. . . . Pass the bottle.

"One night when tied to the mast, as I explained, we were pumping on, deafened with the wind, and without spirit enough in us to wish ourselves dead, a heavy sea crashed aboard and swept clean over us. As soon as I got my breath I shouted, as in duty bound, 'Keep on, boys!' when suddenly I felt something hard floating on deck strike the calf of my leg. I made a grab at it and missed. It was so dark we could not see each other's faces within a foot—you understand.

"After that thump the ship kept quiet for a while, and the thing, whatever it was, struck my leg again. This time I caught it—and it was a saucepan. At first, being stupid with fatigue and thinking of nothing but the pumps, I did not understand what I had in my hand. Suddenly it dawned upon me, and I shouted, 'Boys, the house on deck is gone. Leave this, and let's look for the cook.'

"There was a deckhouse forward, which contained the galley, the cook's berth, and the quarters of the crew. As we had expected for days to see it swept away, the hands had been ordered to sleep in the cabin —the only safe place in the ship. The steward, Abraham, however, persisted in clinging to his berth, stupidly, like a mule—from sheer fright I believe, like an animal that won't leave a stable falling in an earthquake. So we went to look for him. It was chancing death, since once out of our lashings we were exposed as if on a raft. But we went. The house was shattered as if a shell had exploded inside. Most of it had gone overboard—stove, men's quarters, and their property, all was gone; but two posts, holding a portion of the bulkhead to which Abraham's bunk was attached, remained as if by a miracle. We groped in the ruins and came upon this, and there he was, sitting in his bunk, surrounded by foam and wreckage, jabbering cheerfully to himself. He was out of his mind; completely and forever mad, with this sudden shock coming upon the fag-end of his endurance. We snatched him up, lugged him aft, and pitched him head-first down the cabin companion. You understand there was no time to carry him down with infinite precautions and wait to see how he got on. Those below would pick him up at the bottom of the stairs all right. We were in a hurry to go back to the pumps. That business could not wait. A bad leak is an inhuman thing.

"One would think that the sole purpose of that fiendish gale had been to make a lunatic of that poor devil of a mulatto. It eased before morning, and the next day the sky cleared, and as the sea went down the leak took up. When it came to bending a fresh set of sails the crew demanded to put back—and really there was nothing else to do. Boats gone, decks swept clean, cabin gutted, men without a stitch but what they stood in, stores spoiled, ship strained. We put her head for home, and—would you believe it? The wind came east right in our teeth. It blew fresh, it blew continuously. We had to beat up every inch of the

Youth

way, but she did not leak so badly, the water keeping comparatively smooth. Two hours' pumping in every four is no joke—but it kept her afloat as far as Falmouth.

"The good people there live on casualties of the sea, and no doubt were glad to see us. A hungry crowd of shipwrights sharpened their chisels at the sight of that carcass of a ship. And, by Jove! they had pretty pickings off us before they were done. I fancy the owner was already in a tight place. There were delays. Then it was decided to take part of the cargo out and caulk her topsides. This was done, the repairs finished, cargo reshipped; a new crew came on board, and we went out —for Bangkok. At the end of a week we were back again. The crew said they weren't going to Bangkok—a hundred and fifty days' passage—in a something hooker that wanted pumping eight hours out of the twenty-four; and the nautical papers inserted again the little paragraph: '*Judea.* Barque. Tyne to Bangkok; coals; put back to Falmouth leaky and with crew refusing duty.'

"There were more delays—more tinkering. The owner came down for a day, and said she was as right as a little fiddle. Poor old Captain Beard looked like the ghost of a Geordie skipper—through the worry and humiliation of it. Remember he was sixty, and it was his first command. Mahon said it was a foolish business, and would end badly. I loved the ship more than ever, and wanted awfully to get to Bangkok. To Bangkok! Magic name, blessed name. Mesopotamia wasn't a patch on it. Remember I was twenty, and it was my first second mate's billet, and the East was waiting for me.

"We went out and anchored in the outer roads with a fresh crew —the third. She leaked worse than ever. It was as if those confounded shipwrights had actually made a hole in her. This time we did not even go outside. The crew simply refused to man the windlass.

"They towed us back to the inner harbor, and we became a fixture, a feature, an institution of the place. People pointed us out to visitors as 'That 'ere barque that's going to Bangkok—has been here six months—put back three times.' On holidays the small boys pulling about in boats would hail, '*Judea,* ahoy!' and if a head showed above the rail shouted, 'Where you bound to?—Bangkok?' and jeered. We were only three on board. The poor old skipper mooned in the cabin. Mahon undertook the cooking, and unexpectedly developed all a Frenchman's genius for preparing nice little messes. I looked languidly after the rigging. We became citizens of Falmouth. Every shopkeeper knew us. At the barber's or tobacconist's they asked familiarly, 'Do you think you will ever get to Bangkok?' Meanwhile the owner, the underwriters, and the charterers squabbled amongst themselves in London, and our pay went on. . . . Pass the bottle.

"It was horrid. Morally it was worse than pumping for life. It seemed as though we had been forgotten by the world, belonged to nobody, would get nowhere; it seemed that, as if bewitched, we would have to live forever and ever in that inner harbor, a derision and a byword to generations of longshore loafers and dishonest boatmen. I obtained three months' pay and a five days' leave, and made a rush for London. It took me a day to get there and pretty well another to come back—but three months' pay went all the same. I don't know what I did with it. I went to a music hall, I believe, lunched, dined, and supped in a swell place in Regent Street, and was back to time, with nothing but a complete set of Byron's works and a new railway rug to show for three months' work. The boatman who pulled me off to the ship said: 'Hallo! I thought you had left the old thing. *She* will never get to Bangkok.' 'That's all *you* know about it,' I said scornfully—but I didn't like that prophecy at all.

"Suddenly a man, some kind of agent to somebody, appeared with full powers. He had grog-blossoms all over his face, an indomitable energy, and was a jolly soul. We leaped into life again. A hulk came alongside, took our cargo, and then we went into dry dock to get our copper stripped. No wonder she leaked. The poor thing, strained beyond endurance by the gale, had, as if in disgust, spat out all the oakum of her lower seams. She was recaulked, new coppered, and made as tight as a bottle. We went back to the hulk and reshipped our cargo.

"Then, on a fine moonlight night, all the rats left the ship.

"We had been infested with them. They had destroyed our sails, consumed more stores than the crew, affably shared our beds and our dangers, and now, when the ship was made seaworthy, concluded to clear out. I called Mahon to enjoy the spectacle. Rat after rat appeared on our rail, took a last look over his shoulder, and leaped with a hollow thud into the empty hulk. We tried to count them, but soon lost the tale. Mahon said: 'Well, well! don't talk to me about the intelligence of rats. They ought to have left before, when we had that narrow squeak from foundering. There you have the proof how silly is the superstition about them. They leave a good ship for an old rotten hulk, where there is nothing to eat, too, the fools! . . . I don't believe they know what is safe or what is good for them, any more than you or I.'

"And after some more talk we agreed that the wisdom of rats had been grossly overrated, being in fact no greater than that of men.

Youth

"The story of the ship was known, by this, all up the Channel from Land's End to the Forelands, and we could get no crew on the south coast. They sent us one all complete from Liverpool, and we left once more—for Bangkok.

"We had fair breezes, smooth water right into the tropics, and the old *Judea* lumbered along in the sunshine. When she went eight knots everything cracked aloft, and we tied our caps to our heads; but mostly she strolled on at the rate of three miles an hour. What could you expect? She was tired—that old ship. Her youth was where mine is—where yours is—you fellows who listen to this yarn; and what friend would throw your years and your weariness in your face? We didn't grumble at her. To us aft, at least, it seemed as though we had been born in her, reared in her, had lived in her for ages, had never known any other ship. I would just as soon have abused the old village church at home for not being a cathedral.

"And for me there was also my youth to make me patient. There was all the East before me, and all life, and the thought that I had been tried in that ship and had come out pretty well. And I thought of men of old who, centuries ago, went that road in ships that sailed no better, to the land of palms, and spices, and yellow sands, and of brown nations ruled by kings more cruel than Nero the Roman, and more splendid than Solomon the Jew. The old bark lumbered on, heavy with her age and the burden of her cargo, while I lived the life of youth in ignorance and hope. She lumbered on through an interminable procession of days; and the fresh gilding flashed back at the setting sun, seemed to cry out over the darkening sea the words painted on her stern, '*Judea,* London. Do or Die.'

"Then we entered the Indian Ocean and steered northerly for Java Head. The winds were light. Weeks slipped by. She crawled on, do or die, and people at home began to think of posting us as overdue.

"One Saturday evening, I being off duty, the men asked me to give them an extra bucket of water or so—for washing clothes. As I did not wish to screw on the fresh-water pump so late, I went forward whistling, and with a key in my hand to unlock the forepeak scuttle, intending to serve the water out of a spare tank we kept there.

"The smell down below was as unexpected as it was frightful. One would have thought hundreds of paraffin lamps had been flaring and smoking in that hole for days. I was glad to get out. The man with me coughed and said, 'Funny smell, sir.' I answered negligently, 'It's good for the health they say,' and walked aft.

"The first thing I did was to put my head down the square of the midship ventilator. As I lifted the lid a visible breath, something like a thin fog, a puff of faint haze, rose from the opening. The ascending air was hot, and had a heavy, sooty, paraffiny smell. I gave one sniff, and put down the lid gently. It was no use choking myself. The cargo was on fire.

"Next day she began to smoke in earnest. You see it was to be expected, for though the coal was of a safe kind, that cargo had been so handled, so broken up with handling, that it looked more like smithy coal than anything else. Then it had been wetted—more than once. It rained all the time we were taking it back from the hulk, and now with this long passage it got heated, and there was another case of spontaneous combustion.

"The captain called us into the cabin. He had a chart spread on the table, and looked unhappy. He said, 'The coast of West Australia is near, but I mean to proceed to our destination. It is the hurricane month, too; but we will just keep her head for Bangkok, and fight the fire. No more putting back anywhere, if we all get roasted. We will try first to stifle this 'ere damned combustion by want of air.'

"We tried. We battened down everything, and still she smoked. The smoke kept coming out through imperceptible crevices; it forced itself through bulkheads and covers; it oozed here and there and everywhere in slender threads, in an invisible film, in an incomprehensible manner. It made its way into the cabin, into the forecastle; it poisoned the sheltered places on the deck, it could be sniffed as high as the main yard. It was clear that if the smoke came out the air came in. This was disheartening. This combustion refused to be stifled.

"We resolved to try water, and took the hatches off. Enormous volumes of smoke, whitish, yellowish, thick, greasy, misty, choking, ascended as high as the trucks. All hands cleared out aft. Then the poisonous cloud blew away, and we went back to work in a smoke that was no thicker now than that of an ordinary factory chimney.

"We rigged the force pump, got the hose along, and by and by it burst. Well, it was as old as the ship—a prehistoric hose, and past repair. Then we pumped with the feeble head pump, drew water with buckets, and in this way managed in time to pour lots of Indian Ocean into the main hatch. The bright stream flashed in sunshine, fell into a layer of white crawling smoke, and vanished on the black surface of coal. Steam ascended mingling with the smoke. We poured salt water as into a barrel without a bottom. It was our fate to pump in that ship, to pump out of her, to pump into her; and after keeping water out of her to save ourselves from being drowned, we frantically poured water into her to save ourselves from being burnt.

"And she crawled on, do or die, in the serene weather. The sky was a miracle of purity, a miracle of azure. The sea was polished, was blue, was pellucid, was sparkling like a precious stone, extending on all sides, all round to the horizon—as if the whole terrestrial globe had been one jewel, one colossal sapphire, a single gem fashioned into a planet. And on the lustre of the great calm waters the *Judea* glided imperceptibly, enveloped in languid and unclean vapors, in a lazy cloud that drifted to leeward, light and slow; a pestiferous cloud defiling the splendor of sea and sky.

"All this time of course we saw no fire. The cargo smouldered at the bottom somewhere. Once Mahon, as we were working side by side, said to me with a queer smile: 'Now, if she only would spring a tidy leak—like that time when we first left the Channel—it would put a stopper on this fire. Wouldn't it?' I remarked irrelevantly, 'Do you remember the rats?'

"We fought the fire and sailed the ship too as carefully as though nothing had been the matter. The steward cooked and attended on us. Of the other twelve men, eight worked while four rested. Everyone took his turn, captain included. There was equality, and if not exactly fraternity, then a deal of good feeling. Sometimes a man, as he dashed a bucketful of water down the hatchway, would yell out, 'Hurrah for Bangkok!' and the rest laughed. But generally we were taciturn and serious—and thirsty. Oh! how thirsty! And we had to be careful with the water. Strict allowance. The ship smoked, the sun blazed. . . . Pass the bottle.

"We tried everything. We even made an attempt to dig down to the fire. No good, of course. No man could remain more than a minute below. Mahon, who went first, fainted there, and the man who went to fetch him out did likewise. We lugged them out on deck. Then I leaped down to show how easily it could be done. They had learned wisdom by that time, and contented themselves by fishing for me with a chain hook tied to a broom handle, I believe. I did not offer to go and fetch up my shovel, which was left down below.

"Things began to look bad. We put the longboat into the water. The second boat was ready to swing out. We had also another, a fourteen-foot thing, on davits aft, where it was quite safe.

"Then, behold, the smoke suddenly decreased. We redoubled our efforts to flood the bottom of the ship. In two days there was no smoke at all. Everybody was on the broad grin. This was on a Friday. On Saturday no work, but sailing the ship, of course, was done. The men washed their clothes and their faces for the first time in a fortnight, and had a special dinner given them. They spoke of spontaneous combustion with contempt, and they implied *they* were the boys to put out combustions. Somehow we all felt as though we each had inherited a large fortune. But a beastly smell of burning hung about the ship. Captain Beard had hollow eyes and sunken cheeks. I had never noticed so much before how twisted and bowed he was. He and Mahon prowled soberly about hatches and ventilators, sniffing. It struck me suddenly poor Mahon was a very, very old chap. As to me, I was as pleased and proud as though I had helped to win a great naval battle. Oh youth!

"The night was fine. In the morning a homeward-bound ship passed us hull down—the first we had seen for months; but we were nearing the land at last, Java Head being about one hundred and ninety miles off, and nearly due north.

"Next day it was my watch on deck from eight to twelve. At breakfast the captain observed, 'It's wonderful how that smell hangs about the cabin.' About ten, the mate being on the poop, I stepped down on the main deck for a moment. The carpenter's bench stood abaft the mainmast: I leaned against it sucking at my pipe, and the carpenter, a young chap, came to talk to me. He remarked, 'I think we have done very well, haven't we?' and then I perceived with annoyance the fool was trying to tilt the bench. I said curtly, 'Don't, Chips,' and immediately became aware of a queer sensation, of an absurd delusion,—I seemed somehow to be in the air. I heard all round me like a pent-up breath released—as if a thousand giants simultaneously had said Phoo!—and felt a dull concussion which made my ribs ache suddenly. No doubt about it—I was in the air and my body was describing a short parabola. But short as it was, I had the time to think several thoughts in, as far as I can remember, the following order: 'This can't be the carpenter—What is it?—Some accident—Submarine volcano? —Coals, gas!—By Jove! we are being blown up—Everybody's dead— I am falling into the after hatch—I see fire in it.'

"The coal dust suspended in the air of the hold had glowed dull-red at the moment of the explosion. In the twinkling of an eye, in an infinitesimal fraction of a second since the first tilt of the bench, I was sprawling full length on the cargo. I picked myself up and scrambled out. It was quick like a rebound. The deck was a wilderness of smashed timber, lying crosswise like trees in a wood after a hurricane; an immense curtain of soiled rags waved gently before me—it was the mainsail blown to strips. I thought, 'The masts will be toppling over directly'; and to get out of the way bolted on all fours toward the poop ladder. The first person I saw was Mahon, with eyes like saucers, his mouth open, and the long white hair standing straight on end round his head like a silver halo. He was just about to go down when the sight of the main deck stirring, heaving up, and changing into splinters before his eyes, petrified him on the top step. I stared at him in unbelief, and he stared at me with a queer kind of shocked curiosity. I did not know that I had no hair, no eyebrows, no eyelashes, that my young moustache was burnt off, that my face was black, one cheek laid open, my nose cut, and my chin bleeding. I had lost my cap, one of my slippers, and my shirt was torn to rags. Of all this I was not aware. I was amazed to see the ship still afloat, the poop deck whole—and, most of all, to see anybody alive. Also the peace of the sky and the serenity of the sea were distinctly surprising. I suppose I expected to see them convulsed with horror. . . . Pass the bottle.

"There was a voice hailing the ship from somewhere—in the air, in the sky—I couldn't tell. Presently I saw the captain—and he was mad. He asked me eagerly, 'Where's the cabin table?' and to hear such a question was a frightful shock. I had just been blown up, you understand, and vibrated with that experience,—I wasn't quite sure whether I was alive. Mahon began to stamp with both feet and yelled at him, 'Good God! don't you see the deck's blown out of her?' I found my voice, and stammered out as if conscious of some gross neglect of duty, 'I don't know where the cabin table is.' It was like an absurd dream.

"Do you know what he wanted next? Well, he wanted to trim the yards. Very placidly, and as if lost in thought, he insisted on having the foreyard squared. 'I don't know if there's anybody alive,' said Mahon, almost tearfully. 'Surely,' he said, gently, 'there will be enough left to square the foreyard.'

"The old chap, it seems, was in his own berth winding up the chronometers, when the shock sent him spinning. Immediately it occurred to him—as he said afterwards—that the ship had struck something, and he ran out into the cabin. There, he saw, the cabin table had vanished somewhere. The deck being blown up, it had fallen down into the lazarette, of course. Where we had our breakfast that morning he saw only a great hole in the floor. This appeared to him so awfully mysterious, and impressed him so immensely, that what he saw and heard after he got on deck were mere trifles in comparison. And, mark, he noticed directly the wheel deserted and his barque off her course —and his only thought was to get that miserable, stripped, undecked, smouldering shell of a ship back again with her head pointing at her port of destination. Bangkok! That's what he was after. I tell you this quiet, bowed, bandy-legged, almost deformed little man was immense in the singleness of his idea and in his placid ignorance of our agitation. He motioned us forward with a commanding gesture, and went to take the wheel himself.

"Yes; that was the first thing we did—trim the yards of that wreck! No one was killed, or even disabled, but everyone was more or less hurt. You should have seen them! Some were in rags, with black faces, like coal heavers, like sweeps, and had bullet heads that seemed closely cropped, but were in fact singed to the skin. Others, of the watch below, awakened by being shot out from their collapsing bunks, shivered incessantly, and kept on groaning even as we went about our work. But they all worked. That crew of Liverpool hard cases had in them the right stuff. It's my experience they always have. It is the sea that gives in—the vastness, the loneliness surrounding their dark stolid souls. Ah! Well! We stumbled, we crept, we fell, we barked our shins on the wreckage, we hauled. The masts stood, but we did not know how much they might be charred down below. It was nearly calm but a long swell ran from the west and made her roll. They might go at any moment. We looked at them with apprehension. One could not foresee which way they would fall.

"Then we retreated aft and looked about us. The deck was a tangle of planks on edge, of planks on end, of splinters, of ruined woodwork. The masts rose from that chaos like big trees above a matted undergrowth. The interstices of that mass of wreckage were full of something whitish, sluggish, stirring—of something that was like a greasy fog. The smoke of the invisible fire was coming up again, was trailing, like a poisonous thick mist in some valley choked with dead wood. Already lazy wisps were beginning to curl upwards amongst the mass of splinters. Here and there a piece of timber, stuck upright, resembled a post. Half of a fife rail had been shot through the foresail, and the sky made a patch of glorious blue in the ignobly soiled canvas. A portion of several boards holding together had fallen across the rail, and one end protruded overboard, like a gangway leading upon nothing, like a gangway leading over the deep sea, leading to death—as if inviting us to walk the plank at once and be done with our ridiculous troubles. And still the air, the sky—a ghost, something invisible was hailing the ship.

"Someone had the sense to look over, and there was the helmsman, who had impulsively jumped overboard, anxious to come back. He yelled and swam lustily like a merman, keeping up with the ship. We threw him a rope, and presently he stood amongst us streaming with

Youth

water and very crestfallen. The captain had surrendered the wheel, and apart, elbow on rail and chin in hand, gazed at the sea wistfully. We asked ourselves, What next? I thought, Now, this is something like it. This is great. I wonder what will happen. O youth!

"Suddenly Mahon sighted a steamer far astern. Captain Beard said, 'We may do something with her yet.' We hoisted two flags, which said in the international language of the sea, 'On fire. Want immediate assistance.' The steamer grew bigger rapidly, and by and by spoke with two flags on her foremast, 'I am coming to your assistance.'

"In half an hour she was abreast, to windward, within hail, and rolling slightly, with her engines stopped. We lost our composure, and yelled all together with excitement, 'We've been blown up.' A man in a white helmet, on the bridge, cried, 'Yes! All right! all right!' and he nodded his head, and smiled, and made soothing motions with his hand as though at a lot of frightened children. One of the boats dropped in the water, and walked towards us upon the sea with her long oars. Four Calashes pulled a swinging stroke. This was my first sight of Malay seamen. I've known them since, but what struck me then was their unconcern: they came alongside, and even the bowman standing up and holding to our main chains with the boathook did not deign to lift his head for a glance. I thought people who had been blown up deserved more attention.

"A little man, dry like a chip and agile like a monkey, clambered up. It was the mate of the steamer. He gave one look, and cried, 'O boys—you had better quit.'

"We were silent. He talked apart with the captain for a time,—seemed to argue with him. Then they went away together to the steamer.

"When our skipper came back we learned that the steamer was the *Somerville,* Captain Nash, from West Australia to Singapore via Batavia with mails, and that the agreement was she should tow us to Anjer or Batavia, if possible, where we could extinguish the fire by scuttling, and then proceed on our voyage—to Bangkok! The old man seemed excited. 'We will do it yet,' he said to Mahon, fiercely. He shook his fist at the sky. Nobody else said a word.

"At noon the steamer began to tow. She went ahead slim and high, and what was left of the *Judea* followed at the end of seventy fathom of towrope—followed her swiftly like a cloud of smoke with mastheads protruding above. We went aloft to furl the sails. We coughed on the yards, and were careful about the bunts. Do you see the lot of us there, putting a neat furl on the sails of that ship doomed to arrive nowhere? There was not a man who didn't think that at any moment the masts would topple over. From aloft we could not see the ship for smoke, and they worked carefully, passing the gaskets with even turns. 'Harbor furl—aloft there!' cried Mahon from below.

"You understand this? I don't think one of those chaps expected to get down in the usual way. When we did I heard them saying to each other, 'Well, I thought we would come down overboard, in a lump—sticks and all—blame me if I didn't.' 'That's what I was thinking to myself,' would answer wearily another battered and bandaged scarecrow. And, mind, these were men without the drilled-in habit of obedience. To an onlooker they would be a lot of profane scallywags without a redeeming point. What made them do it—what made them obey me when I, thinking consciously how fine it was, made them drop the bunt of the foresail twice to try and do it better? What? They had no professional reputation—no examples, no praise. It wasn't a sense of duty; they all knew well enough how to shirk, and laze, and dodge—when they had a mind to it—and mostly they had. Was it the two pounds ten a month that sent them there? They didn't think their pay half good enough. No; it was something in them, something inborn and subtle and everlasting. I don't say positively that the crew of a French or German merchantman wouldn't have done it, but I doubt whether it would have been done in the same way. There was a completeness in it, something solid like a principle, and masterful like an instinct—a disclosure of something secret—of that hidden something, that gift of good or evil that makes racial difference, that shapes the fate of nations.

"It was that night at ten that, for the first time since we had been fighting it, we saw the fire. The speed of the towing had fanned the smouldering destruction. A blue gleam appeared forward, shining below the wreck of the deck. It wavered in patches, it seemed to stir and creep like the light of a glowworm. I saw it first, and told Mahon. 'Then the game's up,' he said. 'We had better stop this towing, or she will burst out suddenly fore and aft before we can clear out.' We set up a yell; rang bells to attract their attention; they towed on. At last Mahon and I had to crawl forward and cut the rope with an axe. There was no time to cast off the lashings. Red tongues could be seen licking the wilderness of splinters under our feet as we made our way back to the poop.

"Of course they very soon found out in the steamer that the rope was gone. She gave a loud blast of her whistle, her lights were seen sweeping in a wide circle, she came up ranging close alongside, and stopped. We were all in a tight group on the poop looking at her. Every man had saved a little bundle or a bag. Suddenly a conical flame with a twisted top shot up forward and threw upon the black sea a circle of light, with the two vessels side by side and heaving gently in its center. Captain Beard had been sitting on the gratings still and mute for hours, but now he rose slowly and advanced in front of us, to the mizzen shrouds. Captain Nash hailed: 'Come along! Look sharp. I have mailbags on board. I will take you and your boats to Singapore.'

" 'Thank you! No!' said our skipper. 'We must see the last of the ship.'

" 'I can't stand by any longer,' shouted the other. 'Mails—you know.'

" 'Ay, ay! We are all right.'

" 'Very well! I'll report you in Singapore. . . . Good-bye!'

"He waved his hand. Our men dropped their bundles quietly. The steamer moved ahead, and passing out of the circle of light, vanished at once from our sight, dazzled by the fire which burned fiercely. And then I knew that I would see the East first as commander of a small boat. I thought it fine; and the fidelity to the old ship was fine. We should see the last of her. Oh, the glamor of youth! Oh, the fire of it, more dazzling than the flames of the burning ship, throwing a magic light on the wide earth, leaping audaciously to the sky, presently to be quenched by time, more cruel, more pitiless, more bitter than the sea—and like the flames of the burning ship surrounded by an impenetrable night.

"The old man warned us in his gentle and inflexible way that it was part of our duty to save for the underwriters as much as we could of the ship's gear. Accordingly we went to work aft, while she blazed forward to give us plenty of light. We lugged out a lot of rubbish. What didn't we save? An old barometer fixed with an absurd quantity of screws nearly cost me my life: a sudden rush of smoke came upon me, and I just got away in time. There were various stores, bolts of canvas, coils of rope; the poop looked like a marine bazaar, and the boats were lumbered to the gunwales. One would have thought the old man wanted to take as much as he could of his first command with him. He was very, very quiet, but off his balance evidently. Would you believe it? He wanted to take a length of old stream cable and a kedge anchor with him in the longboat. We said, 'Ay, ay, sir,' deferentially, and on the quiet let the things slip overboard. The heavy medicine chest went that way, two bags of green coffee, tins of paint—fancy, paint!—a whole lot of things. Then I was ordered with two hands into the boats to make a stowage and get them ready against the time it would be proper for us to leave the ship.

"We put everything straight, stepped the longboat's mast for our skipper, who was to take charge of her, and I was not sorry to sit down for a moment. My face felt raw, every limb ached as if broken, I was aware of all my ribs, and would have sworn to a twist in the backbone. The boats, fast astern, lay in a deep shadow, and all around I could see the circle of the sea lighted by the fire. A gigantic flame arose forward straight and clear. It flared fierce, with noises like the whirr of wings, with rumbles as of thunder. There were cracks, detonations, and from the cone of flame the sparks flew upwards, as man is born to trouble, to leaky ships, and to ships that burn.

"What bothered me was that the ship, lying broadside to the swell and to such wind as there was—a mere breath—the boats would not keep astern where they were safe, but persisted, in a pigheaded way boats have, in getting under the counter and then swinging alongside. They were knocking about dangerously and coming near the flame, while the ship rolled on them, and, of course, there was always the danger of the masts going over the side at any moment. I and my two boat keepers kept them off as best we could, with oars and boathooks; but to be constantly at it became exasperating, since there was no reason why we should not leave at once. We could not see those on board, nor could we imagine what caused the delay. The boat keepers were swearing feebly, and I had not only my share of the work but also had to keep at it two men who showed a constant inclination to lay themselves down and let things slide.

"At last I hailed, 'On deck there,' and someone looked over. 'We're ready here,' I said. The head disappeared, and very soon popped up again. 'The captain says, All right, sir, and to keep the boats well clear of the ship.'

"Half an hour passed. Suddenly there was a frightful racket, rattle, clanking of chain, hiss of water, and millions of sparks flew up into the shivering column of smoke that stood leaning slightly above the ship. The catheads had burned away, and the two red-hot anchors had gone to the bottom, tearing out after them two hundred fathom of red-hot chain. The ship trembled, the mass of flame swayed as if ready to collapse, and the fore topgallant mast fell. It darted down like an arrow of fire, shot under, and instantly leaping up within an oar's length of the boats, floated quietly, very black on the luminous sea. I hailed the deck again. After some time a man in an unexpectedly cheerful but also muffled tone, as though he had been trying to speak

Youth

with his mouth shut, informed me, 'Coming directly, sir,' and vanished. For a long time I heard nothing but the whirr and roar of the fire. There were also whistling sounds. The boats jumped, tugged at the painters, ran at each other playfully, knocked their sides together, or, do what we would, swung in a bunch against the ship's side. I couldn't stand it any longer, and swarming up a rope, clambered aboard over the stern.

"It was as bright as day. Coming up like this, the sheet of fire facing me was a terrifying sight, and the heat seemed hardly bearable at first. On a settee cushion dragged out of the cabin Captain Beard, his legs drawn up and one arm under his head, slept with the light playing on him. Do you know what the rest were busy about? They were sitting on deck right aft, round an open case, eating bread and cheese and drinking bottled stout.

"On the background of flames twisting in fierce tongues above their heads they seemed at home like salamanders, and looked like a band of desperate pirates. The fire sparkled in the whites of their eyes, gleamed on patches of white skin seen through the torn shirts. Each had the marks as of a battle about him—bandaged heads, tied-up arms, a strip of dirty rag round a knee—and each man had a bottle between his legs and a chunk of cheese in his hand. Mahon got up. With his handsome and disreputable head, his hooked profile, his long white beard, and with an uncorked bottle in his hand, he resembled one of those reckless sea robbers of old making merry amidst violence and disaster. 'The last meal on board,' he explained solemnly. 'We had nothing to eat all day, and it was no use leaving all this.' He flourished the bottle and indicated the sleeping skipper. 'He said he couldn't swallow anything, so I got him to lie down,' he went on; and as I stared, 'I don't know whether you are aware, young fellow, the man had no sleep to speak of for days—and there will be dam' little sleep in the boats.' 'There will be no boats by-and-by if you fool about much longer,' I said, indignantly. I walked up to the skipper and shook him by the shoulder. At last he opened his eyes, but did not move. 'Time to leave her, sir,' I said quietly.

"He got up painfully, looked at the flames, at the sea sparkling round the ship, and black, black as ink farther away; he looked at the stars shining dim through a thin veil of smoke in a sky black, black as Erebus.

" 'Youngest first,' he said.

"And the ordinary seaman, wiping his mouth with the back of his hand, got up, clambered over the taffrail, and vanished. Others followed. One, on the point of going over, stopped short to drain his bottle, and with a great swing of his arm flung it at the fire. 'Take this!' he cried.

"The skipper lingered disconsolately, and we left him to commune alone for awhile with his first command. Then I went up again and brought him away at last. It was time. The ironwork on the poop was hot to the touch.

"Then the painter of the longboat was cut, and the three boats, tied together, drifted clear of the ship. It was just sixteen hours after the explosion when we abandoned her. Mahon had charge of the second boat, and I had the smallest—the fourteen-foot thing. The longboat would have taken the lot of us; but the skipper said we must save as much property as we could—for the underwriters—and so I got my first command. I had two men with me, a bag of biscuits, a few tins of meat, and a breaker of water. I was ordered to keep close to the longboat, that in case of bad weather we might be taken into her.

"And do you know what I thought? I thought I would part company as soon as I could. I wanted to have my first command all to myself. I wasn't going to sail in a squadron if there were a chance for independent cruising. I would make land by myself. I would beat the other boats. Youth! All youth! The silly, charming, beautiful youth.

"But we did not make a start at once. We must see the last of the ship. And so the boats drifted about that night, heaving and setting on the swell. The men dozed, waked, sighed, groaned. I looked at the burning ship.

"Between the darkness of earth and heaven she was burning fiercely upon a disc of purple sea shot by the blood-red play of gleams; upon a disc of water glittering and sinister. A high, clear flame, an immense and lonely flame, ascended from the ocean, and from its summit the black smoke poured continuously at the sky. She burned furiously; mournful and imposing like a funeral pile kindled in the night, surrounded by the sea, watched over by the stars. A magnificent death had come like a grace, like a gift, like a reward to that old ship at the end of her laborious days. The surrender of her weary ghost to the keeping of stars and sea was stirring like the sight of a glorious triumph. The masts fell just before daybreak, and for a moment there was a burst and turmoil of sparks that seemed to fill with flying fire the night patient and watchful, the vast night lying silent upon the sea. At daylight she was only a charred shell, floating still under a cloud of smoke and bearing a glowing mass of coal within.

"Then the oars were got out, and the boats forming in a line moved round her remains as if in procession—the longboat leading. As we pulled across her stern a slim dart of fire shot out viciously at us, and suddenly she went down, head first, in a great hiss of steam. The unconsumed stern was the last to sink; but the paint had gone, had cracked, had peeled off, and there were no letters, there was no word, no stubborn device that was like her soul, to flash at the rising sun her creed and her name.

"We made our way north. A breeze sprang up, and about noon all the boats came together for the last time. I had no mast or sail in mine, but I made a mast out of a spare oar and hoisted a boat awning for a sail, with a boathook for a yard. She was certainly overmasted, but I had the satisfaction of knowing that with the wind aft I could beat the other two. I had to wait for them. Then we all had a look at the captain's chart, and, after a sociable meal of hard bread and water, got our last instructions. These were simple: steer north, and keep together as much as possible. 'Be careful with that jury rig, Marlow,' said the captain; and Mahon, as I sailed proudly past his boat, wrinkled his curved nose and hailed, 'You will sail that ship of yours under water, if you don't look out, young fellow.' He was a malicious old man—and may the deep sea where he sleeps now rock him gently, rock him tenderly to the end of time!

"Before sunset a thick rain squall passed over the two boats, which were far astern, and that was the last I saw of them for a time. Next day I sat steering my cockleshell—my first command—with nothing but water and sky around me. I did sight in the afternoon the upper sails of a ship far away, but said nothing, and my men did not notice her. You see I was afraid she might be homeward bound, and I had no mind to turn back from the portals of the East. I was steering for Java —another blessed name—like Bangkok, you know. I steered many days.

"I need not tell you what it is to be knocking about in an open boat. I remember nights and days of calm, and we pulled, we pulled, and the boat seem to stand still, as if bewitched within the circle of the sea horizon. I remember the heat, the deluge of rain squalls that kept us baling for dear life (but filled our water cask), and I remember sixteen hours on end with a mouth dry as a cinder and a steering oar over the stern to keep my first command head on to a breaking sea. I did not know how good a man I was till then. I remember the drawn faces, the dejected figures of my two men, and I remember my youth and the feeling that will never come back any more—the feeling that I could last forever, outlast the sea, the earth, and all men; the deceitful feeling that lures us on to joys, to perils, to love, to vain effort—to death; the triumphant conviction of strength, the heat of life in the handful of dust, the glow in the heart that with every year grows dim, grows cold, grows small, and expires—and expires, too soon, too soon—before life itself.

"And this is how I see the East. I have seen its secret places and have looked into its very soul; but now I see it always from a small boat, a high outline of mountains, blue and afar in the morning; like faint mist at noon; a jagged wall of purple at sunset. I have the feel of the oar in my hand, the vision of a scorching blue sea in my eyes. And I see a bay, a wide bay, smooth as glass and polished like ice, shimmering in the dark. A red light burns far off upon the gloom of the land, and the night is soft and warm. We drag at the oars with aching arms, and suddenly a puff of wind, a puff faint and tepid and laden with strange odors of blossoms, of aromatic wood, comes out of the still night—the first sigh of the East on my face. That I can never forget. It was impalpable and enslaving, like a charm, like a whispered promise of mysterious delight.

"We had been pulling this finishing spell for eleven hours. Two pulled, and he whose turn it was to rest sat at the tiller. We had made out the red light in that bay and steered for it, guessing it must mark some small coasting port. We passed two vessels, outlandish and high-sterned, sleeping at anchor, and, approaching the light, now very dim, ran the boat's nose against the end of a jutting wharf. We were blind with fatigue. My men dropped the oars and fell off the thwarts as if dead. I made fast to a pile. A current rippled softly. The scented obscurity of the shore was grouped into vast masses, a density of colossal clumps of vegetation, probably—mute and fantastic shapes. And at their foot the semicircle of a beach gleamed faintly, like an illusion. There was not a light, not a stir, not a sound. The mysterious East faced me, perfumed like a flower, silent like death, dark like a grave.

"And I sat weary beyond expression, exulting like a conqueror, sleepless and entranced as if before a profound, a fateful enigma.

"A splashing of oars, a measured dip reverberating on the level of water, intensified by the silence of the shore into loud claps, made me jump up. A boat, a European boat, was coming in. I invoked the name of the dead; I hailed: *Judea* ahoy! A thin shout answered.

"It was the captain. I had beaten the flagship by three hours, and I was glad to hear the old man's voice again, tremulous and tired. 'Is it you, Marlow?' 'Mind the end of that jetty, sir,' I cried.

"He approached cautiously, and brought up with the deep-sea lead line which we had saved—for the underwriters. I eased my painter and

Youth

fell alongside. He sat, a broken figure at the stern, wet with dew, his hands clasped in his lap. His men were asleep already. 'I had a terrible time of it,' he murmured. 'Mahon is behind—not very far.' We conversed in whispers, in low whispers, as if afraid to wake up the land. Guns, thunder, earthquakes would not have awakened the men just then.

"Looking round as we talked, I saw away at sea a bright light traveling in the night. 'There's a steamer passing the bay,' I said. She was not passing, she was entering, and she even came close and anchored. 'I wish,' said the old man, 'you would find out whether she is English. Perhaps they could give us a passage somewhere.' He seemed nervously anxious. So by dint of punching and kicking I started one of my men into a state of somnambulism, and giving him an oar, took another and pulled towards the lights of the steamer.

"There was a murmur of voices in her, metallic hollow clangs of the engine room, footsteps on the deck. Her ports shone, round like dilated eyes. Shapes moved about, and there was a shadowy man high up on the bridge. He heard my oars.

"And then, before I could open my lips, the East spoke to me, but it was in a Western voice. A torrent of words was poured into the enigmatical, the fateful silence; outlandish, angry words, mixed with words and even whole sentences of good English, less strange but even more surprising. The voice swore and cursed violently; it riddled the solemn peace of the bay by a volley of abuse. It began by calling me Pig, and from that went crescendo into unmentionable adjectives—in English. The man up there raged aloud in two languages, and with a sincerity in his fury that almost convinced me I had, in some way, sinned against the harmony of the universe. I could hardly see him, but began to think he would work himself into a fit.

"Suddenly he ceased, and I could hear him snorting and blowing like a porpoise. I said—

" 'What steamer is this, pray?'

" 'Eh? What's this? And who are you?'

" 'Castaway crew of an English barque burnt at sea. We came here tonight. I am the second mate. The captain is in the longboat, and wishes to know if you would give us a passage somewhere.'

" 'Oh, my goodness! I say.... This is the *Celestial* from Singapore on her return trip. I'll arrange with your captain in the morning, ... and, ... I say, ... did you hear me just now?"

" 'I should think the whole bay heard you.'

" 'I thought you were a shore boat. Now, look here—this infernal lazy scoundrel of a caretaker has gone to sleep again—curse him. The light is out, and I nearly ran foul to the end of this damned jetty. This is the third time he plays me this trick. Now, I ask you, can anybody stand this kind of thing? It's enough to drive a man out of his mind. I'll report him.... I'll get the Assistant Resident to give him the sack, by ...! See—there's no light. It's out, isn't it! I take you to witness the light's out. There should be a light, you know. A red light on the——'

" 'There was a light,' I said, mildly.

" 'But it's out, man! What's the use of talking like this? You can see for yourself it's out—don't you? If you had to take a valuable steamer along this God-forsaken coast you would want a light, too. I'll kick him from end to end of his miserable wharf. You'll see if I don't. I will——'

" 'So I may tell my captain you'll take us?' I broke in.

" 'Yes, I'll take you. Good-night,' he said, brusquely.

"I pulled back, made fast again to the jetty, and then went to sleep at last. I had faced the silence of the East. I had heard some of its language. But when I opened my eyes again the silence was as complete as though it had never been broken. I was lying in a flood of light, and the sky had never looked so far, so high, before. I opened my eyes and lay without moving.

"And then I saw the men of the East—they were looking at me. The whole length of the jetty was full of people. I saw brown, bronze, yellow faces, the black eyes, the glitter, the color of an Eastern crowd. And all these beings stared without a murmur, without a sigh, without a movement. They stared down at the boats, at the sleeping men who at night had come to them from the sea. Nothing moved. The fronds of palms stood still against the sky. Not a branch stirred along the shore, and the brown roofs of hidden houses peeped through the green foliage, through the big leaves that hung shining and still like leaves forged of heavy metal. This was the East of the ancient navigators, so old, so mysterious, resplendent and sombre, living and unchanged, full of danger and promise. And these were the men. I sat up suddenly. A wave of movement passed through the crowd from end to end, passed along the heads, swayed the bodies, ran along the jetty like a ripple on the water, like a breath of wind on a field—and all was still again. I see it now—the wide sweep of the bay, the glittering sands, the wealth of green infinite and varied, the sea blue like the sea of a dream the crowd of attentive faces, the blaze of vivid color—the water reflecting it all, the curve of the shore, the jetty, the high-sterned outlandish craft floating still, and the three boats with the tired men from the West sleeping, unconscious of the land and the people and of the violence of sunshine. They slept thrown across the thwarts, curled on bottom boards, in the careless attitudes of death. The head of the old skipper, leaning back in the stern of the longboat, had fallen on his breast, and he looked as though he would never wake. Farther out old Mahon's face was upturned to the sky, with the long white beard spread out on his breast as though he had been shot where he sat at the tiller; and a man, all in a heap in the bows of the boat, slept with both arms embracing the stem head and with his cheek laid on the gunwale. The East looked at them without a sound.

"I have known its fascination since; I have seen the mysterious shores, the still water, the lands of brown nations, where a stealthy Nemesis lies in wait, pursues, overtakes so many of the conquering race, who are proud of their wisdom, of their knowledge, of their strength. But for me all the East is contained in that vision of my youth. It is all in that moment when I opened my young eyes on it. I came upon it from a tussle with the sea—and I was young—and I saw it looking at me. And this is all that is left of it! Only a moment; a moment of strength, of romance, of glamor—of youth! ... A flick of sunshine upon a strange shore, the time to remember, the time for a sigh, and—good-bye!—Night—Goodbye ... !"

He drank.

"Ah! The good old time—the good old time. Youth and the sea. Glamor and the sea! The good, strong sea, the salt, bitter sea, that could whisper to you and roar at you and knock your breath out of you."

He drank again.

"By all that's wonderful it is the sea, I believe, the sea itself—or is it youth alone? Who can tell? But you here—you all had something out of life: money, love—whatever one gets on shore—and, tell me, wasn't that the best time, that time when we were young at sea; young and had nothing, on the sea that gives nothing, except hard knocks—and sometimes a chance to feel your strength—that only—what you all regret?"

And we all nodded at him: the man of finance, the man of accounts, the man of law, we all nodded at him over the polished table that like a still sheet of brown water reflected our faces, lined, wrinkled; our faces marked by toil, by deceptions, by success, by love; our weary eyes looking still, looking always, looking anxiously for something out of life, that while it is expected is already gone—has passed unseen, in a sigh, in a flash—together with the youth, with the strength, with the romance of illusions.

A Talent for Humanity

ANTON CHEKHOV

After Chekhov's first collection of short stories appeared in 1884, the idea of what fiction should be was never again the same. The Chekhov kind of story is perhaps more widely written today in many countries than any other type.

Anton Pavlovich Chekhov (1860–1904) was born at Taganrog, in southern Russia. In 1879 he earned a scholarship to study medicine at Moscow University and there began supporting himself and his family by writing humorous stories. He gained a doctor's degree in 1884 and continued to practice medicine, but the writer's life claimed him more and more. He had published more than three hundred short stories by 1885.

In later years, Chekhov lived on a small farm outside Moscow and in 1901 married an actress of the Moscow Art Theater. He has been recognized as one of the world's great dramatists as well as a great innovator in the art of the short story. He contracted tuberculosis in his twenties, and died at a German health resort at the age of forty-four, having achieved a reputation that has caused his stories and plays to be translated into many languages.

"The aim of fiction is absolute and honest truth," Chekhov declared. His early stories were written merely to entertain, but as time went by, he concentrated upon bringing out, by impressionistic detail, the traits of ordinary people in a tragicomic world. His main contribution to the art might be called "character suspense," for he concentrates upon the peak events in the life of a person and briefly shows his nature, just as a surgeon with his scalpel reveals a body's tissues.

Chekhov was a doctor of souls. As the critic Virginia Woolf wrote in *The Common Reader:* "These stories are always showing us some affectation, pose, insincerity.... The soul is ill; the soul is cured; the soul is not cured." What, we ask, will happen to this particular soul? We watch the process with an interest more profound than that of observing the usual hero of adventure achieve victory or a victim suffer from a clever reversal. Chekhov's objectivity seems cruel, but he believed in progress and had what one of his characters termed "a talent for humanity." The influence of his method on many later writers has been profound.

"The Darling," written in 1899, was greatly admired by Chekhov's mentor, Leo Tolstoy, who said: "The soul of 'Darling,' with her capacity for devoting herself with her whole being to the one she loves, is not ridiculous, but wonderful and holy."

ANTON CHEKHOV

The Darling

*O*LENKA, THE DAUGHTER of the retired collegiate assessor Plemiannikov, was sitting on the back steps of her father's house. She was only thinking that the weather was hot and the flies were annoying, and that she was glad the sun would soon be setting and that every now and then a breath of moisture blew down from the dark rain clouds in the east.

A certain Kukin who had a room in the house was standing in the garden, and he was looking up at the sky because he was manager of an open-air theater called the Tivoli.

"Again," he said, despairingly, "rain again. Rain every day just to spite me. I might as well hang myself and have it over. The rain is ruining me. I lose money every evening." He threw up his hands, and then went on. "What a life, Olga Semyonova! I could weep when I think of it. I work as hard as I can and I lie awake at night to think up new plans. And then what happens? I give the public the best light operas, charming ballets, excellent artists. But do you suppose they appreciate what I give them? They don't understand it. They want common clowns and common circuses. And then think of the weather. The rain began on the tenth of May and we've hardly had a fair evening in June. The theater is empty, but I have to pay the rent and the artists just as if it were full."

The clouds gathered again the next afternoon and Kukin laughed hysterically.

"All right, go on raining. Wash the garden away, and wash me away with it. Ruin my chances in this world and in the next. Let the artists sue me for their salaries. Let me go to Siberia—let me go to the gallows. Ha, ha, ha!"

And the same thing again on the third day.

Olenka listened to Kukin silently and solemnly, and sometimes she even cried. She was so sorry for him that she ended by falling in love with him. He was short and thin and his curly hair covered his yellow forehead. He always looked miserable and his mouth twisted to one side when he talked in his high tenor voice. And nevertheless Olenka fell deeply in love with him.

She had never been able to live without adoring someone, and she had loved her father before he began gasping all day in his big chair in his dark room. Then she loved her French master until her aunt began coming from Briansk every year. She was gentle and tenderhearted and sympathetic, and her eyes were also gentle and tender. She was always strong and well and when men saw her plump rosy cheeks and her soft white neck with a little brown mole on it and her simple amiable smile, they smiled too, and they always thought to themselves, "Not so bad." And the women who came to the house took her hand in the middle of a conversation and exclaimed "You darling!" in a burst of delight.

She had been born in the house and it would be her own when her father died. The house was in the Gipsy Road, on the edge of the town, and it was not far from the Tivoli. From early evening until late at night she could hear the music in the theater and the explosion of the fireworks, and they seemed to her the explosion of Kukin's guns storming the battlements of the indifferent public. She loved him so much that she did not even want to sleep, and when he came home at daybreak she tapped on her window and he saw her face and her smile and one shoulder between the curtains.

He proposed to her and they were married. And when he had a husband's look at her white neck and her plump shoulders he threw up his arms.

"You darling!" he cried.

He was really happy, but he still looked miserable because the rain never once stopped on the afternoon and evening of their wedding day.

They got on extremely well together. She stayed in his office at the Tivoli and kept the accounts and paid the actors and the workmen. Sometimes her rosy cheeks and her simple radiant smile beamed through the ticket window and sometimes from behind the bar and sometimes back of the scenes. She had already begun telling people that the theater was the most important thing in the world, and the only thing which could divert people and teach them everything they needed to know at the same time.

The Darling

"But do you suppose the public realizes that?" she was always saying. "The public loves circuses. Vanichka and I gave the parody of Faust yesterday and nearly all the boxes were empty. But if we had been giving some vulgar thing, of course the theater would have been crowded. Vanichka and I are giving Orpheus in Hades tomorrow. Do come."

And she was always repeating what Kukin said about the theater and the actors. She abused the public for its ignorance of art and for its indifference. She meddled with the actors and the musicians at rehearsals and she cried and went to see the editor whenever the paper printed a disparaging review.

The actors were fond of her, and they were always calling her "Vanichka and I" or "the darling." She sympathized with them, and sometimes she lent them a little money. She cried when they cheated her out of it, but she never complained to her husband.

And they got on well in the winter. They took a theater inside the town for the whole season, and leased it first to a company from Little Russia, and then to a conjuror, and to a company that was formed in the town.

Olenka became plumper and plumper and she went on beaming with happiness. Kukin became thinner and yellower and he went on complaining of their terrible losses although he had done rather well the whole season. He coughed badly at night and she gave him hot raspberry shrub and lime water and then rubbed him with eau de Cologne and wrapped him in warm shawls.

"You're a sweet lamb," she said, "you're a perfect dear." And she really meant what she said.

About the beginning of Lent he went to get his company together in Moscow. Olenka could not sleep, and she sat at her window every night and looked at the stars and thought that she was like the hens who are restless all night when the cock is not in the henhouse. Kukin did not come back as soon as he had intended to come and he finally wrote her that he would be back for Easter and gave her some directions about the Tivoli. But on Palm Sunday night there was an alarming knock at the gate that sounded like thumping on an empty barrel. The cook was barely awake when she ran through the puddles to open it.

"Please open the gate," a voice outside it said. "I have a telegram for you."

Olenka's husband had sent her telegrams now and then, but this was the first time she had felt numb with terror. Her hands shook as she opened the telegram and read it.

"Ivan Petrovich died suddenly today. Awaiting innediate commands for huneral Tuesday."

That was the way the telegram was written—"huneral" and "innediate." It was signed by the stage manager of Kukin's company.

"My dearest," Olenka sobbed. "Vanichka, my sweetheart, my dearest. Why did I get to know you and love you? Why did I ever see you? Who will comfort your poor heartbroken Olenka?"

Kukin was buried in Moscow on Tuesday. Olenka went home on Wednesday and she threw herself on her bed and sobbed so loudly that the people in the next house and the people in the street were distressed.

"Poor darling," her neighbors said, crossing themselves. "Poor darling Olga Semyonova! She does take it hard!"

Olenka was going home from church about three months after Kukin died, and she was a melancholy sight in her deep mourning. A neighbor of hers called Vassili Andreich Pustalov happened to walk along with her. He was manager for Babakiev the timber merchant, but his straw hat and his white waistcoat and gold watchchain made him look more like a landowner than a businessman.

"Everything happens as it has been ordained, Olga Semyonova," he said solemnly and sympathetically, "and when those we love die, we should be brave and not rebel against God's will."

He walked to her gate with Olenka and then he said good-bye and went on. She heard his solemn dignified voice all day, and whenever she shut her eyes she saw his dark beard. She liked him. And apparently he took an interest in her. Not very long after he walked home with her, an older woman whom she barely knew came in to drink coffee with her, and as soon as she sat down she began to talk of what an excellent reliable man Pustalov was and how glad any woman should be to get him for a husband. And Pustalov himself came three days later. He did not stay more than ten minutes and he said very little, but Olenka fell so much in love with him that she did not sleep at all, and the next morning she sent for the matchmaking lady. The marriage was arranged at once, and the wedding followed.

Pustalov and Olenka got on very well together.

He was usually in his office until he came to dinner. After dinner he went out on business and Olenka went into the office and kept the accounts and looked after the orders until evening.

"Timber is twenty percent dearer than it was last year," she told everyone. "Do you know that Vassichka used to buy wood from the

The Darling

forests in this district, but now he has to go as far as the government of Mogilev every year. And what he pays to get it here!" she exclaimed, covering her eyes in horror.

She felt that she had been selling timber for years and that it was the most important thing in the world. There was something affectionate and touching in the very way she spoke of beams and posts and planks and laths and all the other forms of timber. She dreamed of whole mountains of planks and of endless streams of wagons dragging them far away. And she dreamed that a whole regiment of beams five vershoks wide and twelve arshins long stood up and marched against the timber yard and that logs and beams and boards crashed against each other and that they were all falling down and getting up and piling themselves on top of each other. She cried out in her sleep, and Pustalov spoke to her tenderly.

"What's the matter, Olenka darling? Cross yourself."

Her husband's opinions were her opinions. She thought a room was too hot when he thought it was too hot and she thought business was dull when he thought it was dull. Pustalov did not like theaters and parties and when he stayed at home on holidays Olenka stayed with him.

"You are always either at home or in the office," her friends told her. "Why don't you ever go to the theater and the circus, darling?"

"Vassichka and I have no time for the theater," she always answered. "We have no time for nonsense. What do you get out of going to a play?"

Olenka and Pustalov went to church on Saturday evening and on holidays they went early in the morning. They walked home side by side with pious faces and with an agreeable fragrance of soap and an agreeable rustle of silk. They drank tea with elaborate breads and jams and afterwards they had pastries. An appetizing odor floated out into the street from their kitchen every day at twelve o'clock, and they dined on cabbage soup and mutton or duck, or on fish if it were a fastday. No one could pass their house without feeling hungry. The samovar was always boiling in the office and the customers were cheered up with tea and biscuits. Once a week they went to the baths and walked home together with red faces.

"We are getting on very well, thank God," Olenka said to her friends. "I wish every one were as comfortable as Vassichka and I."

She was dreadfully lonely when Pustalov went to buy his wood in the government of Mogilev and she cried all day and all night. They had let their lodgings to a veterinary surgeon called Smirnin, and sometimes he came to see her in the evenings and played cards with her. She liked talking to him while she was lonely and she was particularly interested in what he told her about his own life. He was married and he had a son, but he was separated from his wife because she had taken a lover and now he detested her and only sent her forty roubles a month because of their son. Olenka sighed and shook her head. She was sorry for him.

"Well, God help you," she said, as she lighted him out with a candle. "Thank you for coming in to cheer me up. May the Mother of God keep you."

She always spoke in her husband's solemn and dignified and judicious manner. And she always called out to the veterinary surgeon just as he was disappearing behind the door.

"You ought to forgive your wife for the sake of your son, Vladimir Platonich. You may be sure he understands all about it."

When Pustalov came back, she whispered to him about the veterinary surgeon and how unhappy he was with his wife, and both of them sighed and shook their heads and said that the boy must miss his father, and then they knelt before the holy ikons and prayed that God would send them children.

And so the Pustalovs passed six whole years in perfect love and harmony, and in peace and quiet. And then Vassili Andreich drank some very hot tea and went into the yard without his hat. He caught a cold and although he had the best doctors he died four months later and Olenka was a widow again.

"Who will comfort me since you have left me, my dearest?" she sobbed after the funeral. "How can I live on without you? Pity my wretchedness and misery, good people, pity me, fatherless and motherless and all alone in the world!"

She hardly went out of her house except to church and to her husband's grave, and when she did go out she was dressed in the deepest mourning and covered with long veils. She lived like a nun for six months before she opened her shutters and left off her veils. She went to the market with her cook now and then, but people could only guess what was going on in her house when they saw her drinking tea with the veterinary surgeon in her garden while he read the newspaper to her and from a remark she made to one of her acquaintances in the postoffice.

"The cattle are not properly inspected in our town, and that's why people are always catching diseases from the milk or from the cows

The Darling

and horses. Domestic animals should be looked after as carefully as human beings."

She said whatever the veterinary surgeon said, and people began to realize that she could never get through a year without being in love with some one, and that she had found an object in her own house. They would have been shocked if anyone else had done such a thing, but Olenka did everything so much as a matter of course that no one could ever be shocked by what she did. She and the veterinary surgeon never spoke of the change in their relations, but they could not conceal it. Olenka was quite unable to keep a secret, and when he had the men in his regiment to supper, she poured tea for them and talked all the time of cattle plagues and foot and mouth disease and municipal slaughterhouses. The veterinary surgeon was very much embarrassed, and when his guests were gone he always seized her hand and spoke to her furiously.

"Haven't I told you not to talk about matters you don't understand? When we doctors are discussing scientific matters among ourselves, please don't make a nuisance of yourself."

She was always surprised and dismayed.

"But, Volodichka," she asked, "what shall I talk about?"

And then she cried and put her arms around his neck and begged him not to be angry and they were both happy again.

But her happiness did not last. The veterinary surgeon went away with his regiment to some place as remote as Siberia and Olenka was left alone.

And this time she was quite alone. Her father had been dead so long that his old armchair stood in the attic on three legs and covered with dust. She became thinner and plainer, and when people met her in the street they did not smile at her as they did when she had some one to love. Her happy days were evidently over, and the new days were too painful to think about. She sat on her porch in the evening and heard the music in the Tivoli and the explosion of the fireworks, but she was not interested in them. She looked at her garden listlessly and she did not think of anything or want anything and when she went to bed she dreamed of her empty garden. And she seemed to eat and drink against her wishes.

And worse than all that, she had no opinions of any kind. She saw objects and the actions about her, but she could not form any opinions about them, and she never had anything to talk about. She saw bottles and rain and peasants driving their carts, but for a thousand roubles she could not have said why bottles and rain should exist, or why peasants should drive their carts. Olenka had opinions about everything when she had Kukin and Pustalov and the veterinary surgeon, but now her heart and her brain were as empty as her garden, and the emptiness was as bitter to her as wormwood in her mouth.

The town gradually grew in every direction. The Gipsy Road became a street and there were new streets and new houses where the timberyard and the Tivoli had been. Time passes quickly. Olenka's house became shabby and the roof rusted and the shed sagged and docks and thistles overran the garden. Olenka was older and plainer and her soul was empty and dreary and bitter. She still sat on her back steps in summer and looked, at the garden, and in winter she sat at her window and looked at the snow. When she felt a breath of spring or heard the sound of the cathedral bells her heart was warmed for a moment and she cried a little, and then the emptiness and the dreariness of life came over her again. Her black kitten rubbed against her and purred softly, but feline caresses were not what Olenka needed. She wanted a love that would absorb her whole being and that would give her ideas and a reason for living, and that would warm her aging blood. She shook the black kitten off her skirt.

"Go away! I don't want you here," she said angrily.

Day in and day out, year in and year out, she had no happiness and no ideas. She accepted whatever her cook happened to say.

One hot afternoon, just when the returning cows were filling the street and the garden with dust, someone knocked on her gate. Olenka opened it herself, and she was overcome when she saw the veterinary surgeon. His hair was grey, and he was in civilian clothes. She remembered everything when she saw him and she threw her arms around his neck and laid her head on his shoulder and burst into tears. She was so overcome that she was unconscious all the time they were walking into the house and sitting down to tea.

"My dearest Vladimir Platonich," she murmured, trembling with joy, "how did God send you here?"

"I want to settle here, Olga Semyonova," he told her. "I have resigned from the army, and I want to try my luck on my own. And besides, my son is a big boy now, and he must go to school. My wife and I are living together again, you know."

"Where is she?" Olenka asked.

"She and the boy are at the hotel, and I am looking for lodgings."

"Good heavens, my dear. Why don't you take my house? I won't want any rent." Olenka cried in happy excitement, and wept again.

The Darling

"You can live here, and your old lodgings will do for me. Heavens, how delightful!"

The roof was painted the next day and all the walls were whitewashed and Olenka walked about the garden with her hands on her hips and gave directions. Her face was beaming with her old smile, and she looked as fresh as if she had just waked from a very long sleep. The veterinary surgeon's wife and son came in. His wife was thin and plain, and her hair was short and she looked bad-tempered. Little Sasha was ten years old and short for his age, but he was a plump boy with blue eyes and dimples. He ran after the cat as soon as he came into the garden, and he laughed happily as he ran.

"Is this your cat, auntie?" he asked Olenka. "When she has kittens, do give us one. Mama is awfully afraid of mice."

Olenka talked to him and gave him tea, and her heart was as heavy and as happy as if he had been her own child.

And when he sat studying his lessons in the dining room that evening, Olenka sat and looked at him tenderly and pityingly.

"What a pretty precious you are," she murmured to herself. "So pretty, and so clever."

"An island is a body of land entirely surrounded by water," he recited.

"An island is a body of land," she repeated. That was the first opinion she stated positively after all those years when she had no ideas and nothing to say.

She had plenty of opinions now, and at supper she talked to Sasha's father and mother about how difficult the studies were at high school nowadays, but how much better the high school was than a commercial education, because you could choose any profession you liked after you had been through the high school, and you could be a doctor or an engineer or anything you liked.

Sasha began going to the high school. His mother went to stay with her sister in Kharkov and never came back and his father was away all day inspecting cattle and sometimes he did not come home for three days. Olenka felt that Sasha was quite abandoned, and that he was starving. So she took him to live with her and gave him a little room next to hers.

He had been living with her for six months, and every morning she went into his room and found him sleeping quietly with one hand under his cheek. She could hardly bear to wake him.

"Sashenka," she said sadly, "you must get up and dress for school."

He dressed and said his prayers and then sat down and drank three glasses of tea and ate two large biscuits and half of a buttered roll. All this time he was so sleepy that he was rather cross.

"You don't quite know your fable, Sashenka," Olenka said, looking at him as if he were setting off on a long journey. "I have so much trouble with you. Try hard to learn, dearest, and obey your teachers."

"Please leave me alone," Sasha said.

Olenka followed him when he put on his big cap and took his satchel and walked down the street towards his school.

"Sashenka," she called.

He stopped, and she slipped a date or a caramel into his hand. When they came to the street where his school was he began to feel ashamed of being followed by a tall fat woman.

"You'd better go home, auntie," he said. "I can go the rest of the way by myself."

She stopped and gazed at him until he disappeared into the door of the school.

How she did love him! None of her other attachments had been so strong, and she had never given herself so happily or so unselfishly as she had done since her maternal instinct was roused. She would have given her life for this little boy with the dimples and the big cap, and she would have cried joyfully while she was giving it. Why? Who knows why?

When she had seen Sasha into his school she walked home serenely and happily, radiating love. Her face had become young again in the last six months. She smiled and beamed and when people met her they looked at her with pleasure.

"Good morning, Olga Semyonova, darling. How are you getting on, darling?"

"The lessons at the high school are too difficult nowadays," she told the women at the market. "They have too much to do. Yesterday the first class had a fable to memorize and a Latin translation and a problem. You know that is too much for a little boy."

And she went on talking about the masters and the lessons and the books and she said just what Sasha said.

They had dinner together at three o'clock, and in the evening they studied the lessons together and Olenka and Sasha both cried over them. When she had put him to bed, she knelt by him a long time making the sign of the cross over him and whispering prayers. And when she went to bed herself she thought about what would happen after Sasha had finished his studies, after he had become a doctor or an engineer and had a house of his own and a carriage and a wife and

The Darling

children. She fell asleep thinking of him, and tears rolled down her cheeks from her closed eyes, and the black cat purred beside her.

And then sometimes there was a loud knock on the gate. Olenka always waked up breathless from fright and from the violent beating of her heart. Half a minute later there was another knock.

"His mother has sent a telegram from Kharkov," she thought. "She wants Sasha sent to Kharkov. Oh God, have mercy!"

She was in despair. Her head and her hands and her feet turned cold, and she knew that she was the most unhappy creature in the world. But she heard voices after another minute and the veterinary surgeon came in from his club.

"Thank God!" she said.

And gradually the heaviness left her heart and she was happy again. She went back to bed thinking of Sasha, who was fast asleep in the room next to hers.

Sometimes he called out in his sleep. "I'll give it to you! Go away! Stop talking to me!"

Revelation of Another Love

JAMES JOYCE

One of the greatest stylists in English, Joyce joined his own life with the experience of all mankind in all times and places.

James Augustine Aloysius Joyce (1882–1941) was born in Dublin, Ireland, eldest of a family on the edge of poverty. His mother wanted him to be a priest, and he got a good Jesuit education at several schools before entering University College. James lost his faith at an early age, but by then he was imbued with a Catholic background. He was an arrogant young man with a gift for modern languages and music. He left Dublin in 1904 with Nora Barnacle, a girl from western Ireland whom he later married; they had two children.

For the next dozen years Joyce earned a bare living as a language teacher in Europe. During World War I the family went to neutral Switzerland; later they moved to Paris, where critics slowly began to recognize Joyce as probably the most powerful twentieth-century author in English. He had begun in Dublin as a poet, but turned to short stories around 1905. He also wrote one play, *Exiles* (1914). A complex novel, *Ulysses* (1922), growing out of his autobiographical *Portrait of the Artist as a Young Man* (1916), took seven years to finish and used many new narrative devices that heavily influenced later writers. Joyce's final years, marred by worries and almost total blindness, were devoted to the completion of *Finnegans Wake* (1939), an endless dream put down in what might seem a private language, full of complicated humor and based on world myths.

"The Dead," written in 1905 or 1906, when Joyce was still in his mid-twenties, was part of a volume, *Dubliners* (1914), which the publisher held up for eight years. The book is a linked collection of stories about Joyce's townspeople, and the climaxes usually center upon a moment of spiritual revelation for which Joyce coined the term "epiphany." These narratives marked a new turn of modern short-story technique, by which the psychology of a person is suddenly "shown forth" as a result of the reader's realization that an apparently trivial action sums up a lifetime. Many scholars have discovered profound symbolism and significance in "The Dead," but it can be read as a realistic story of a self-centered husband who discovers with a shock at Christmastime that he has never understood his wife's deepest feelings.

JAMES JOYCE

The Dead

*L*ILY, THE CARETAKER'S DAUGHTER, was literally run off her feet. Hardly had she brought one gentleman into the little pantry behind the office on the ground floor and helped him off with his overcoat than the wheezy hall-door bell clanged again and she had to scamper along the bare hallway to let in another guest. It was well for her she had not to attend to the ladies also. But Miss Kate and Miss Julia had thought of that and had converted the bathroom upstairs into a ladies' dressing room. Miss Kate and Miss Julia were there, gossiping and laughing and fussing, walking after each other to the head of the stairs, peering down over the banisters and calling down to Lily to ask her who had come.

It was always a great affair, the Misses Morkan's annual dance. Everybody who knew them came to it, members of the family, old friends of the family, the members of Julia's choir, any of Kate's pupils that were grown up enough, and even some of Mary Jane's pupils too. Never once had it fallen flat. For years and years it had gone off in splendid style, as long as anyone could remember; ever since Kate and Julia, after the death of their brother Pat, had left the house in Stoney Batter and taken Mary Jane, their only niece, to live with them in the dark, gaunt house on Usher's Island, the upper part of which they had rented from Mr. Fulham, the corn factor on the ground floor. That was a good thirty years ago if it was a day. Mary Jane, who was then a little girl in short clothes, was now the main prop of the household, for she had the organ in Haddington Road. She had been through the Academy and gave a pupils' concert every year in the upper room of the Antient Concert Rooms. Many of her pupils belonged to the better-class families on the Kingstown and Dalkey line. Old as they were, her aunts also did their share. Julia, though she was quite grey, was still the leading soprano in Adam and Eve's, and Kate, being too feeble to go about much, gave music lessons to beginners on the old square piano in the back room. Lily, the caretaker's daughter, did housemaid's work for them. Though their life was modest, they believed in eating well; the best of everything: diamond-bone sirloins, three-shilling tea, and the best bottled stout. But Lily seldom made a mistake in the orders, so that she got on well with her three mistresses. They were fussy, that was all. But the only thing they would not stand was back answers.

Of course, they had good reason to be fussy on such a night. And then it was long after ten o'clock and yet there was no sign of Gabriel and his wife. Besides they were dreadfully afraid that Freddy Malins might turn up screwed. They would not wish for worlds that any of Mary Jane's pupils should see him under the influence; and when he was like that it was sometimes very hard to manage him. Freddy Malins always came late, but they wondered what could be keeping Gabriel: and that was what brought them every two minutes to the banisters to ask Lily had Gabriel or Freddy come.

"Oh, Mr. Conroy," said Lily to Gabriel when she opened the door for him, "Miss Kate and Miss Julia thought you were never coming. Good-night, Mrs. Conroy."

"I'll engage they did," said Gabriel, "but they forget that my wife here takes three mortal hours to dress herself."

He stood on the mat, scraping the snow from his galoshes, while Lily led his wife to the foot of the stairs and called out:

"Miss Kate, here's Mrs. Conroy."

Kate and Julia came toddling down the dark stairs at once. Both of them kissed Gabriel's wife, said she must be perished alive, and asked was Gabriel with her.

"Here I am as right as the mail, Aunt Kate! Go on up. I'll follow," called out Gabriel from the dark.

He continued scraping his feet vigorously while the three women went upstairs, laughing, to the ladies' dressing room. A light fringe of snow lay like a cape on the shoulders of his overcoat and like toe caps on the toes of his galoshes; and, as the buttons of his overcoat slipped with a squeaking noise through the snow-stiffened frieze, a cold, fragrant air from out-of-doors escaped from crevices and folds.

"Is it snowing again, Mr. Conroy?" asked Lily.

She had preceded him into the pantry to help him off with his

The Dead

overcoat. Gabriel smiled at the three syllables she had given his surname and glanced at her. She was a slim, growing girl, pale in complexion and with hay-colored hair. The gas in the pantry made her look still paler. Gabriel had known her when she was a child and used to sit on the lowest step nursing a rag doll.

"Yes, Lily," he answered, "and I think we're in for a night of it."

He looked up at the pantry ceiling, which was shaking with the stamping and shuffling of feet on the floor above, listened for a moment to the piano, and then glanced at the girl, who was folding his overcoat carefully at the end of a shelf.

"Tell me, Lily," he said in a friendly tone, "do you still go to school?"

"Oh, no, sir," she answered. "I'm done schooling this year and more."

"Oh, then," said Gabriel gaily, "I suppose we'll be going to your wedding one of these fine days with your young man, eh?"

The girl glanced back at him over her shoulder and said with great bitterness:

"The men that is now is only all palaver and what they can get out of you."

Gabriel colored, as if he felt he had made a mistake and, without looking at her, kicked off his galoshes and flicked actively with his muffler at his patent-leather shoes.

He was a stout, tallish young man. The high color of his cheeks pushed upwards even to his forehead, where it scattered itself in a few formless patches of pale red; and on his hairless face there scintillated restlessly the polished lenses and the bright gilt rims of the glasses which screened his delicate and restless eyes. His glossy black hair was parted in the middle and brushed in a long curve behind his ears, where it curled slightly beneath the groove left by his hat.

When he had flicked luster into his shoes he stood up and pulled his waistcoat down more tightly on his plump body. Then he took a coin rapidly from his pocket.

"Oh, Lily," he said, thrusting it into her hands, "it's Christmastime, isn't it? Just ... here's a little. ... "

He walked rapidly towards the door.

"Oh, no, sir!" cried the girl, following him. "Really, sir, I wouldn't take it."

"Christmastime! Christmastime!" said Gabriel, almost trotting to the stairs and waving his hand to her in deprecation.

The girl, seeing that he had gained the stairs, called out after him:

"Well, thank you, sir."

He waited outside the drawing-room door until the waltz should finish, listening to the skirts that swept against it and to the shuffling of feet. He was still discomposed by the girl's bitter and sudden retort. It had cast a gloom over him which he tried to dispel by arranging his cuffs and the bows of his tie. He then took from his waistcoat pocket a little paper and glanced at the headings he had made for his speech. He was undecided about the lines from Robert Browning, for he feared they would be above the heads of his hearers. Some quotation that they would recognize from Shakespeare or from the Melodies would be better. The indelicate clacking of the men's heels and the shuffling of their soles reminded him that their grade of culture differed from his. He would only make himself ridiculous by quoting poetry to them which they could not understand. They would think that he was airing his superior education. He would fail with them just as he had failed with the girl in the pantry. He had taken up a wrong tone. His whole speech was a mistake from first to last, an utter failure.

Just then his aunts and his wife came out of the ladies' dressing-room. His aunts were two small, plainly dressed old women. Aunt Julia was an inch or so the taller. Her hair, drawn low over the tops of her ears, was grey; and grey also, with darker shadows, was her large flaccid face. Though she was stout in build and stood erect, her slow eyes and parted lips gave her the appearance of a woman who did not know where she was or where she was going. Aunt Kate was more vivacious. Her face, healthier than her sister's, was all puckers and creases, like a shriveled red apple, and her hair, braided in the same old-fashioned way, had not lost its ripe nut color.

They both kissed Gabriel frankly. He was their favorite nephew, the son of their dead elder sister, Ellen, who had married T. J. Conroy of the Port and Docks.

"Gretta tells me you're not going to take a cab back to Monkstown tonight, Gabriel," said Aunt Kate.

"No," said Gabriel, turning to his wife, "we had quite enough of that last year, hadn't we? Don't you remember, Aunt Kate, what a cold Gretta got out of it? Cab windows rattling all the way, and the east wind blowing in after we passed Merrion. Very jolly it was. Gretta caught a dreadful cold."

Aunt Kate frowned severely and nodded her head at every word.

"Quite right, Gabriel, quite right," she said. "You can't be too careful."

The Dead

"But as for Gretta there," said Gabriel, "she'd walk home in the snow if she were let."

Mrs. Conroy laughed.

"Don't mind him, Aunt Kate," she said. "He's really an awful bother, what with green shades for Tom's eyes at night and making him do the dumbbells, and forcing Eva to eat the stirabout. The poor child! And she simply hates the sight of it! ... Oh, but you'll never guess what he makes me wear now!"

She broke out into a peal of laughter and glanced at her husband, whose admiring and happy eyes had been wandering from her dress to her face and hair. The two aunts laughed heartily, too, for Gabriel's solicitude was a standing joke with them.

"Galoshes!" said Mrs. Conroy. "That's the latest. Whenever it's wet underfoot I must put on my galoshes. Tonight even, he wanted me to put them on, but I wouldn't. The next thing he'll buy me will be a diving suit."

Gabriel laughed nervously and patted his tie reassuringly, while Aunt Kate nearly doubled herself, so heartily did she enjoy the joke. The smile soon faded from Aunt Julia's face and her mirthless eyes were directed towards her nephew's face. After a pause she asked:

"And what are galoshes, Gabriel?"

"Galoshes, Julia!" exclaimed her sister. "Goodness me, don't you know what galoshes are? You wear them over your ... over your boots, Gretta, isn't it?"

"Yes," said Mrs. Conroy. "Gutta-percha things. We both have a pair now. Gabriel says everyone wears them on the Continent."

"Oh, on the Continent," murmured Aunt Julia, nodding her head slowly.

Gabriel knitted his brows and said, as if he were slightly angered:

"It's nothing very wonderful, but Gretta thinks it very funny because she says the word reminds her of Christy Minstrels."

"But tell me, Gabriel," said Aunt Kate, with brisk tact. "Of course, you've seen about the room. Gretta was saying ... "

"Oh, the room is all right," replied Gabriel. "I've taken one in the Gresham."

"To be sure," said Aunt Kate, "by far the best thing to do. And the children, Gretta, you're not anxious about them?"

"Oh, for one night," said Mrs. Conroy. "Besides, Bessie will look after them."

"To be sure," said Aunt Kate again. "What a comfort it is to have a girl like that, one you can depend on! There's that Lily, I'm sure I don't know what has come over her lately. She's not the girl she was at all."

Gabriel was about to ask his aunt some questions on this point, but she broke off suddenly to gaze after her sister, who had wandered down the stairs and was craning her neck over the banisters.

"Now, I ask you," she said almost testily, "where is Julia going? Julia! Julia! Where are you going?"

Julia, who had gone half-way down one flight, came back and announced blandly: "Here's Freddy."

At the same moment a clapping of hands and a final flourish of the pianist told that the waltz had ended. The drawing-room door was opened from within and some couples came out. Aunt Kate drew Gabriel aside hurriedly and whispered into his ear:

"Slip down, Gabriel, like a good fellow and see if he's all right, and don't let him up if he's screwed. I'm sure he's screwed. I'm sure he is."

Gabriel went to the stairs and listened over the banisters. He could hear two persons talking in the pantry. Then he recognized Freddy Malins' laugh. He went down the stairs noisily.

"It's such a relief," said Aunt Kate to Mrs. Conroy, "that Gabriel is here. I always feel easier in my mind when he's here.... Julia, there's Miss Daly and Miss Power will take some refreshment. Thanks for your beautiful waltz, Miss Daly. It made lovely time."

A tall wizen-faced man, with a stiff grizzled moustache and swarthy skin, who was passing out with his partner, said:

"And may we have some refreshment, too, Miss Morkan?"

"Julia," said Aunt Kate summarily, "and here's Mr. Browne and Miss Furlong. Take them in, Julia, with Miss Daly and Miss Power."

"I'm the man for the ladies," said Mr. Browne, pursing his lips until his moustache bristled and smiling in all his wrinkles. "You know, Miss Morkan, the reason they are so fond of me is——"

He did not finish his sentence, but, seeing that Aunt Kate was out of earshot, at once led the three young ladies into the back room. The middle of the room was occupied by two square tables placed end to end, and on these Aunt Julia and the caretaker were straightening and smoothing a large cloth. On the sideboard were arrayed dishes and plates, and glasses and bundles of knives and forks and spoons. The top of the closed square piano served also as a sideboard for viands and sweets. At a smaller sideboard in one corner two young men were standing, drinking hop bitters.

Mr. Browne led his charges thither and invited them all, in jest, to

The Dead

some ladies' punch, hot, strong and sweet. As they said they never took anything strong, he opened three bottles of lemonade for them. Then he asked one of the young men to move aside, and, taking hold of the decanter, filled out for himself a goodly measure of whisky. The young men eyed him respectfully while he took a trial sip.

"God help me," he said, smiling, "it's the doctor's orders."

His wizened face broke into a broader smile, and the three young ladies laughed in musical echo to his pleasantry, swaying their bodies to and fro, with nervous jerks of their shoulders. The boldest said:

"Oh, now, Mr. Browne, I'm sure the doctor never ordered anything of the kind."

Mr. Browne took another sip of his whisky and said, with sidling mimicry:

"Well, you see, I'm like the famous Mrs. Cassidy, who is reported to have said: 'Now, Mary Grimes, if I don't take it, make me take it, for I feel I want it.'"

His hot face had leaned forward a little too confidentially and he had assumed a very low Dublin accent so that the young ladies, with one instinct, received his speech in silence. Miss Furlong, who was one of Mary Jane's pupils, asked Miss Daly what was the name of the pretty waltz she had played; and Mr. Browne, seeing that he was ignored, turned promptly to the two young men who were more appreciative.

A red-faced young woman, dressed in pansy, came into the room, excitedly clapping her hands and crying:

"Quadrilles! Quadrilles!"

Close on her heels came Aunt Kate, crying:

"Two gentlemen and three ladies, Mary Jane!"

"Oh, here's Mr. Bergin and Mr. Kerrigan," said Mary Jane. "Mr. Kerrigan, will you take Miss Power? Miss Furlong, may I get you a partner, Mr. Bergin. Oh, that'll just do now."

"Three ladies, Mary Jane," said Aunt Kate.

The two young gentlemen asked the ladies if they might have the pleasure, and Mary Jane turned to Miss Daly.

"Oh, Miss Daly, you're really awfully good, after playing for the last two dances, but really we're so short of ladies tonight."

"I don't mind in the least, Miss Morkan."

"But I've a nice partner for you, Mr. Bartell D'Arcy, the tenor. I'll get him to sing later on. All Dublin is raving about him."

"Lovely voice, lovely voice!" said Aunt Kate.

As the piano had twice begun the prelude to the first figure Mary

Jane led her recruits quickly from the room. They had hardly gone when Aunt Julia wandered slowly into the room, looking behind her at something.

"What is the matter, Julia?" asked Aunt Kate anxiously. "Who is it?"

Julia, who was carrying in a column of table napkins, turned to her sister and said, simply, as if the question had surprised her:

"It's only Freddy, Kate, and Gabriel with him."

In fact right behind her Gabriel could be seen piloting Freddy Malins across the landing. The latter, a young man of about forty, was of Gabriel's size and build, with very round shoulders. His face was fleshy and pallid, touched with color only at the thick hanging lobes of his ears and at the wide wings of his nose. He had coarse features, a blunt nose, a convex and receding brow, tumid and protruded lips. His heavy-lidded eyes and the disorder of his scanty hair made him look sleepy. He was laughing heartily in a high key at a story which he had been telling Gabriel on the stairs and at the same time rubbing the knuckles of his left fist backwards and forwards into his left eye.

"Good evening, Freddy," said Aunt Julia.

Freddy Malins bade the Misses Morkan good evening in what seemed an offhand fashion by reason of the habitual catch in his voice and then, seeing that Mr. Browne was grinning at him from the sideboard, crossed the room on rather shaky legs and began to repeat in an undertone the story he had just told to Gabriel.

"He's not so bad, is he?" said Aunt Kate to Gabriel.

Gabriel's brows were dark but he raised them quickly and answered:

"Oh, no, hardly noticeable."

"Now, isn't he a terrible fellow!" she said. "And his poor mother made him take the pledge on New Year's Eve. But come on, Gabriel, into the drawing room."

Before leaving the room with Gabriel she signaled to Mr. Browne by frowning and shaking her forefinger in warning to and fro. Mr. Browne nodded in answer and, when she had gone, said to Freddy Malins:

"Now, then, Teddy, I'm going to fill you out a good glass of lemonade just to buck you up."

Freddy Malins, who was nearing the climax of his story, waved the offer aside impatiently, but Mr. Browne, having first called Freddy Malins' attention to a disarray in his dress, filled out and handed him a full glass of lemonade. Freddy Malins' left hand accepted the glass

The Dead

mechanically, his right hand being engaged in the mechanical readjustment of his dress. Mr. Browne, whose face was once more wrinkling with mirth, poured out for himself a glass of whisky while Freddy Malins exploded, before he had well reached the climax of his story, in a kink of high-pitched bronchitic laughter and, setting down his untasted and overflowing glass, began to rub the knuckles of his left fist backwards and forwards into his left eye, repeating words of his last phrase as well as his fit of laughter would allow him.

Gabriel could not listen while Mary Jane was playing her Academy piece, full of runs and difficult passages, to the hushed drawing room. He liked music, but the piece she was playing had no melody for him and he doubted whether it had any melody for the other listeners, though they had begged Mary Jane to play something. Four young men, who had come from the refreshment room to stand in the doorway at the sound of the piano, had gone away quietly in couples after a few minutes. The only persons who seemed to follow the music were Mary Jane herself, her hands racing along the keyboard or lifted from it at the pauses like those of a priestess in momentary imprecation, and Aunt Kate standing at her elbow to turn the page.

Gabriel's eyes, irritated by the floor, which glittered with beeswax under the heavy chandelier, wandered to the wall above the piano. A picture of the balcony scene in *Romeo and Juliet* hung there and beside it was a picture of the two murdered princes in the Tower which Aunt Julia had worked in red, blue, and brown wools when she was a girl. Probably in the school they had gone to as girls that kind of work had been taught for one year. His mother had worked for him as a birthday present a waistcoat of purple tabinet, with little foxes' heads upon it, lined with brown satin and having round mulberry buttons. It was strange that his mother had had no musical talent, though Aunt Kate used to call her the brains carrier of the Morkan family. Both she and Julia had always seemed a little proud of their serious and matronly sister. Her photograph stood before the pier glass. She held an open book on her knees and was pointing out something in it to Constantine who, dressed in a man-o'-war suit, lay at her feet. It was she who had chosen the names of her sons, for she was very sensible of the dignity of family life. Thanks to her, Constantine was now senior curate in Balbriggan and, thanks to her, Gabriel himself had taken his degree in the Royal University. A shadow passed over his face as he remembered her sullen opposition to his marriage. Some slighting phrases she had used still rankled in his memory; she had once spoken of Gretta as being country cute and that was not true of Gretta at all. It was Gretta who had nursed her during all her last long illness in their house at Monkstown.

He knew that Mary Jane must be near the end of her piece, for she was playing again the opening melody with runs of scales after every bar and while he waited for the end the resentment died down in his heart. The piece ended with a trill of octaves in the treble and a final deep octave in the bass. Great applause greeted Mary Jane as, blushing and rolling up her music nervously, she escaped from the room. The most vigorous clapping came from the four young men in the doorway who had gone away to the refreshment room at the beginning of the piece but had come back when the piano had stopped.

Lancers were arranged. Gabriel found himself partnered with Miss Ivors. She was a frank-mannered, talkative young lady, with a freckled face and prominent eyes. She did not wear a low-cut bodice and the large brooch which was fixed in the front of her collar bore on it an Irish device and motto.

When they had taken their places she said abruptly:

"I have a crow to pluck with you."

"With me?" said Gabriel.

She nodded her head gravely.

"What is it?" asked Gabriel, smiling at her solemn manner.

"Who is G. C.?" answered Miss Ivors, turning her eyes upon him.

Gabriel colored and was about to knit his brows, as if he did not understand, when she said bluntly:

"Oh, innocent Amy! I have found out that you write for *The Daily Express.* Now, aren't you ashamed of yourself?"

"Why should I be ashamed of myself?" asked Gabriel, blinking his eyes and trying to smile.

"Well, I'm ashamed of you," said Miss Ivors frankly. "To say you'd write for a paper like that. I didn't think you were a West Briton."

A look of perplexity appeared on Gabriel's face. It was true that he wrote a literary column every Wednesday in *The Daily Express,* for which he was paid fifteen shillings. But that did not make him a West Briton surely. The books he received for review were almost more welcome than the paltry check. He loved to feel the covers and turn over the pages of newly printed books. Nearly every day when his teaching in the college was ended he used to wander down the quays to the second-hand booksellers, to Hickey's on Bachelor's Walk, to Webb's or Massey's on Aston's Quay, or to O'Clohissey's in the bystreet. He did not know how to meet her charge. He wanted to say that literature was above politics. But they were friends of many years'

The Dead

standing and their careers had been parallel, first at the University and then as teachers: he could not risk a grandiose phrase with her. He continued blinking his eyes and trying to smile and murmured lamely that he saw nothing political in writing reviews of books.

When their turn to cross had come he was still perplexed and inattentive. Miss Ivors promptly took his hand in a warm grasp and said in a soft friendly tone:

"Of course, I was only joking. Come, we cross now."

When they were together again she spoke of the University question and Gabriel felt more at ease. A friend of hers had shown her his review of Browning's poems. That was how she had found out the secret: but she liked the review immensely. Then she said suddenly:

"Oh, Mr. Conroy, will you come for an excursion to the Aran Isles this summer? We're going to stay there a whole month. It will be splendid out in the Atlantic. You ought to come. Mr. Clancy is coming, and Mr. Kilkelly and Kathleen Kearney. It would be splendid for Gretta too if she'd come. She's from Connacht, isn't she?"

"Her people are," said Gabriel shortly.

"But you will come, won't you?" said Miss Ivors, laying her warm hand eagerly on his arm.

"The fact is," said Gabriel, "I have just arranged to go——"

"Go where?" asked Miss Ivors.

"Well, you know, every year I go for a cycling tour with some fellows and so——"

"But where?" asked Miss Ivors.

"Well, we usually go to France or Belgium or perhaps Germany," said Gabriel awkwardly.

"And why do you go to France and Belgium," said Miss Ivors, "instead of visiting your own land?"

"Well," said Gabriel, "it's partly to keep in touch with the languages and partly for a change."

"And haven't you your own language to keep in touch with—Irish?" asked Miss Ivors.

"Well," said Gabriel, "if it comes to that, you know, Irish is not my language."

Their neighbors had turned to listen to the cross-examination. Gabriel glanced right and left nervously and tried to keep his good humor under the ordeal which was making a blush invade his forehead.

"And haven't you your own land to visit," continued Miss Ivors, "that you know nothing of, your own people, and your own country?"

"Oh, to tell you the truth," retorted Gabriel suddenly, "I'm sick of my own country, sick of it!"

"Why?" asked Miss Ivors.

Gabriel did not answer, for his retort had heated him.

"Why?" repeated Miss Ivors.

They had to go visiting together and, as he had not answered her, Miss Ivors said warmly:

"Of course, you've no answer."

Gabriel tried to cover his agitation by taking part in the dance with great energy. He avoided her eyes, for he had seen a sour expression on her face. But when they met in the long chain he was surprised to feel his hand firmly pressed. She looked at him from under her brows for a moment quizzically until he smiled. Then, just as the chain was about to start again, she stood on tiptoe and whispered into his ear:

"West Briton!"

When the lancers were over Gabriel went away to a remote corner of the room where Freddy Malins' mother was sitting. She was a stout, feeble old woman with white hair. Her voice had a catch in it like her son's and she stuttered slightly. She had been told that Freddy had come and that he was nearly all right. Gabriel asked her whether she had had a good crossing. She lived with her married daughter in Glasgow and came to Dublin on a visit once a year. She answered placidly that she had had a beautiful crossing and that the captain had been most attentive to her. She spoke also of the beautiful house her daughter kept in Glasgow, and of all the friends they had there. While her tongue rambled on Gabriel tried to banish from his mind all memory of the unpleasant incident with Miss Ivors. Of course the girl or woman, or whatever she was, was an enthusiast, but there was a time for all things. Perhaps he ought not to have answered her like that. But she had no right to call him a West Briton before people, even in joke. She had tried to make him ridiculous before people, heckling him and staring at him with her rabbit's eyes.

He saw his wife making her way towards him through the waltzing couples. When she reached him she said into his ear:

"Gabriel, Aunt Kate wants to know won't you carve the goose as usual. Miss Daly will carve the ham and I'll do the pudding."

"All right," said Gabriel.

"She's sending in the younger ones first as soon as this waltz is over so that we'll have the table to ourselves."

"Were you dancing?" asked Gabriel.

"Of course I was. Didn't you see me? What row had you with Molly Ivors?"

The Dead

"No row. Why? Did she say so?"

"Something like that. I'm trying to get that Mr. D'Arcy to sing. He's full of conceit, I think."

"There was no row," said Gabriel moodily, "only she wanted me to go for a trip to the west of Ireland and I said I wouldn't."

His wife clasped her hands excitedly and gave a little jump.

"Oh, do go, Gabriel," she cried. "I'd love to see Galway again."

"You can go if you like," said Gabriel coldly.

She looked at him for a moment, then turned to Mrs. Malins and said:

"There's a nice husband for you, Mrs. Malins."

While she was threading her way back across the room Mrs. Malins, without adverting to the interruption, went on to tell Gabriel what beautiful places there were in Scotland and beautiful scenery. Her son-in-law brought them every year to the lakes and they used to go fishing. Her son-in-law was a splendid fisher. One day he caught a beautiful fish and the man in the hotel cooked it for their dinner.

Gabriel hardly heard what she said. Now that supper was coming near he began to think again about his speech and about the quotation. When he saw Freddy Malins coming across the room to visit his mother Gabriel left the chair free for him and retired into the embrasure of the window. The room had already cleared and from the back room came the clatter of plates and knives. Those who still remained in the drawing room seemed tired of dancing and were conversing quietly in little groups. Gabriel's warm trembling fingers tapped the cold pane of the window. How cool it must be outside! How pleasant it would be to walk out alone, first along by the river and then through the park! The snow would be lying on the branches of the trees and forming a bright cap on the top of the Wellington Monument. How much more pleasant it would be there than at the supper table!

He ran over the headings of his speech: Irish hospitality, sad memories, the Three Graces, Paris, the quotation from Browning. He repeated to himself a phrase he had written in his review: "One feels that one is listening to a thought-tormented music." Miss Ivors had praised the review. Was she sincere? Had she really any life of her own behind all her propagandism? There had never been any ill feeling between them until that night. It unnerved him to think that she would be at the supper table, looking up at him while he spoke with her critical, quizzing eyes. Perhaps she would not be sorry to see him fail in his speech. An idea came into his mind and gave him courage. He would say, alluding to Aunt Kate and Aunt Julia: "Ladies and Gentlemen, the generation which is now on the wane among us may have had its faults, but for my part I think it had certain qualities of hospitality, of humor, of humanity, which the new and very serious and hypereducated generation that is growing up around us seems to me to lack." Very good: that was one for Miss Ivors. What did he care that his aunts were only two ignorant old women?

A murmur in the room attracted his attention. Mr. Browne was advancing from the door, gallantly escorting Aunt Julia, who leaned upon his arm, smiling and hanging her head. An irregular musketry of applause escorted her also as far as the piano and then, as Mary Jane seated herself on the stool, and Aunt Julia, no longer smiling, half turned so as to pitch her voice fairly into the room, gradually ceased. Gabriel recognized the prelude. It was that of an old song of Aunt Julia's—*Arrayed for the Bridal.* Her voice, strong and clear in tone, attacked with great spirit the runs which embellish the air and though she sang very rapidly she did not miss even the smallest of the grace notes. To follow the voice, without looking at the singer's face, was to feel and share the excitement of swift and secure flight. Gabriel applauded loudly with all the others at the close of the song and loud applause was borne in from the invisible supper table. It sounded so genuine that a little color struggled into Aunt Julia's face as she bent to replace in the music stand the old leather-bound songbook that had her initials on the cover. Freddy Malins, who had listened with his head perched sideways to hear her better, was still applauding when everyone else had ceased and talking animatedly to his mother, who nodded her head gravely and slowly in acquiescence. At last, when he could clap no more, he stood up suddenly and hurried across the room to Aunt Julia, whose hand he seized and held in both his hands, shaking it when words failed him or the catch in his voice proved too much for him.

"I was just telling my mother," he said, "I never heard you sing so well, never. No, I never heard your voice so good as it is tonight. Now! Would you believe that now? That's the truth. Upon my word and honor that's the truth. I never heard your voice sound so fresh and so ... so clear and fresh, never."

Aunt Julia smiled broadly and murmured something about compliments as she released her hand from his grasp. Mr. Browne extended his open hand towards her and said to those who were near him in the manner of a showman introducing a prodigy to an audience:

"Miss Julia Morkan, my latest discovery!"

He was laughing very heartily at this himself when Freddy Malins turned to him and said:

The Dead

"Well, Browne, if you're serious you might make a worse discovery. All I can say is I never heard her sing half so well as long as I am coming here. And that's the honest truth."

"Neither did I," said Mr. Browne. "I think her voice has greatly improved."

Aunt Julia shrugged her shoulders and said with meek pride:

"Thirty years ago I hadn't a bad voice as voices go."

"I often told Julia," said Aunt Kate emphatically, "that she was simply thrown away in that choir. But she never would be said by me."

She turned as if to appeal to the good sense of the others against a refractory child while Aunt Julia gazed in front of her, a vague smile of reminiscence playing on her face.

"No," continued Aunt Kate, "she wouldn't be said or led by anyone, slaving there in that choir night and day, night and day. Six o'clock on Christmas morning! And all for what?"

"Well, isn't it for the honor of God, Aunt Kate?" asked Mary Jane, twisting round on the piano stool and smiling.

Aunt Kate turned fiercely on her niece and said:

"I know all about the honor of God, Mary Jane, but I think it's not at all honorable for the pope to turn out the women out of the choirs that have slaved there all their lives and put little whippersnappers of boys over their heads. I suppose it is for the good of the Church if the pope does it. But it's not just, Mary Jane, and it's not right."

She had worked herself into a passion and would have continued in defense of her sister, for it was a sore subject with her, but Mary Jane, seeing that all the dancers had come back, intervened pacifically:

"Now, Aunt Kate, you're giving scandal to Mr. Browne, who is of the other persuasion."

Aunt Kate turned to Mr. Browne, who was grinning at this allusion to his religion, and said hastily:

"Oh, I don't question the pope's being right. I'm only a stupid old woman and I wouldn't presume to do such a thing. But there's such a thing as common everyday politeness and gratitude. And if I were in Julia's place I'd tell that Father Healey straight up to his face ... "

"And besides, Aunt Kate," said Mary Jane, "we really are all hungry and when we are hungry we are all very quarrelsome."

"And when we are thirsty we are also quarrelsome," added Mr. Browne.

"So that we had better go to supper," said Mary Jane, "and finish the discussion afterwards."

On the landing outside the drawing room Gabriel found his wife and Mary Jane trying to persuade Miss Ivors to stay for supper. But Miss Ivors, who had put on her hat and was buttoning her cloak, would not stay. She did not feel in the least hungry and she had already overstayed her time.

"But only for ten minutes, Molly," said Mrs. Conroy. "That won't delay you."

"To take a pick itself," said Mary Jane, "after all your dancing."

"I really couldn't," said Miss Ivors.

"I am afraid you didn't enjoy yourself at all," said Mary Jane hopelessly.

"Ever so much, I assure you," said Miss Ivors, "but you really must let me run off now."

"But how can you get home?" asked Mrs. Conroy.

"Oh, it's only two steps up the quay."

Gabriel hesitated a moment and said:

"If you will allow me, Miss Ivors, I'll see you home if you are really obliged to go."

But Miss Ivors broke away from them.

"I won't hear of it," she cried. "For goodness' sake go in to your suppers and don't mind me. I'm quite well able to take care of myself."

"Well, you're the comical girl, Molly," said Mrs. Conroy frankly.

"Beannacht libh," cried Miss Ivors, with a laugh, as she ran down the staircase.

Mary Jane gazed after her, a moody, puzzled expression on her face, while Mrs. Conroy leaned over the banisters to listen for the hall door. Gabriel asked himself was he the cause of her abrupt departure. But she did not seem to be in ill humor: she had gone away laughing. He stared blankly down the staircase.

At the moment Aunt Kate came toddling out of the supper room, almost wringing her hands in despair.

"Where is Gabriel?" she cried. "Where on earth is Gabriel? There's everyone waiting in there, stage to let, and nobody to carve the goose!"

"Here I am, Aunt Kate!" cried Gabriel, with sudden animation, "ready to carve a flock of geese, if necessary."

A fat brown goose lay at one end of the table and at the other end, on a bed of creased paper strewn with springs of parsley, lay a great ham, stripped of its outer skin and peppered over with crust crumbs, a neat paper frill round its shin, and beside this was a round of spiced beef. Between these rival ends ran parallel lines of side dishes: two little minsters of jelly, red and yellow; a shallow dish full of blocks of

The Dead

blancmange and red jam, a large green leaf-shaped dish with a stalk-shaped handle, on which lay bunches of purple raisins and peeled almonds, a companion dish on which lay a solid rectangle of Smyrna figs, a dish of custard topped with grated nutmeg, a small bowl full of chocolates and sweets wrapped in gold and silver papers, and a glass vase in which stood some tall celery stalks. In the center of the table there stood, as sentries to a fruit stand which upheld a pyramid of oranges and American apples, two squat old-fashioned decanters of cut glass, one containing port and the other dark sherry. On the closed square piano a pudding in a huge yellow dish lay in waiting, and behind it were three squads of bottles of stout and ale and minerals, drawn up according to the colors of their uniforms, the first two black, with brown and red labels, the third and smallest squad white, with transverse green sashes.

Gabriel took his seat boldly at the head of the table and, having looked to the edge of the carver, plunged his fork firmly into the goose. He felt quite at ease now, for he was an expert carver and liked nothing better than to find himself at the head of a well-laden table.

"Miss Furlong, what shall I send you?" he asked. "A wing or a slice of the breast?"

"Just a small slice of the breast."

"Miss Higgins, what for you?"

"Oh, anything at all, Mr. Conroy."

While Gabriel and Miss Daly exchanged plates of goose and plates of ham and spiced beef, Lily went from guest to guest with a dish of hot floury potatoes wrapped in a white napkin. This was Mary Jane's idea, and she had also suggested applesauce for the goose, but Aunt Kate had said that plain roast goose without any applesauce had always been good enough for her and she hoped she might never eat worse. Mary Jane waited on her pupils and saw that they got the best slices and Aunt Kate and Aunt Julia opened and carried across from the piano bottles of stout and ale for the gentlemen and bottles of minerals for the ladies. There was a great deal of confusion and laughter and noise, the noise of orders and counterorders, of knives and forks, or corks and glass-stoppers. Gabriel began to carve second helpings as soon as he had finished the first round, without serving himself. Everyone protested loudly, so that he compromised by taking a long draught of stout, for he had found the carving hot work. Mary Jane settled down quietly to her supper, but Aunt Kate and Aunt Julia were still toddling round the table, walking on each other's heels, getting in each other's way and giving each other unheeded orders. Mr. Browne begged of them to sit down and eat their suppers and so did Gabriel, but they said there was time enough, so that, at last, Freddy Malins stood up and, capturing Aunt Kate, plumped her down on her chair amid general laughter.

When everyone had been well served Gabriel said, smiling:

"Now, if anyone wants a little more of what vulgar people call stuffing let him or her speak."

A chorus of voices invited him to begin his own supper and Lily came forward with three potatoes which she had reserved for him.

"Very well," said Gabriel amiably, as he took another preparatory draught, "kindly forget my existence, ladies and gentlemen, for a few minutes."

He set to his supper and took no part in the conversation with which the table covered Lily's removal of the plates. The subject of talk was the opera company, which was then at the Theatre Royal. Mr. Bartell D'Arcy, the tenor, a dark-complexioned young man with a smart moustache, praised very highly the leading contralto of the company, but Miss Furlong thought she had a rather vulgar style of production. Freddy Malins said there was a Negro chieftain singing in the second part of the Gaiety pantomime who had one of the finest tenor voices he had ever heard.

"Have you heard him?" he asked Mr. Bartell D'Arcy across the table.

"No," answered Mr. Bartell D'Arcy carelessly.

"Because," Freddy Malins explained, "now I'd be curious to hear your opinion of him. I think he has a grand voice."

"It takes Teddy to find out the really good things," said Mr. Browne familiarly to the table.

"And why couldn't he have a voice too?" asked Freddy Malins sharply. "Is it because he's only a black?"

Nobody answered this question and Mary Jane led the table back to the legitimate opera. One of her pupils had given her a pass for *Mignon*. Of course it was very fine, she said, but it made her think of poor Georgina Burns. Mr. Browne could go back farther still, to the old Italian companies that used to come to Dublin—Tietjens, Ilma de Murzka, Campanini, the great Trebelli, Giuglini, Ravelli, Aramburo. Those were the days, he said, when there was something like singing to be heard in Dublin. He told too of how the top gallery of the old Royal used to be packed night after night, of how one night an Italian tenor had sung five encores to "Let me like a soldier fall," introducing a high C every time, and how the gallery boys would sometimes in their enthusiasm unyoke the horses from the carriage of some great prima donna and pull her themselves through the streets to her hotel. Why did they never play the grand old operas now, he asked, Dinorah, Lucrezia Borgia? Because they could not get the voices to sing them: that was why.

"Oh, well," said Mr. Bartell D'Arcy, "I presume there are as good singers today as there were then."

"Where are they?" asked Mr. Browne defiantly.

"In London, Paris, Milan," said Mr. Bartell D'Arcy warmly. "I suppose Caruso, for example, is quite as good, if not better than any of the men you have mentioned."

"Maybe so," said Mr. Browne. "But I may tell you I doubt it strongly."

"Oh, I'd give anything to hear Caruso sing," said Mary Jane.

"For me," said Aunt Kate, who had been picking a bone, "there was only one tenor. To please me, I mean. But I suppose none of you ever heard of him."

"Who was he, Miss Morkan?" asked Mr. Bartell D'Arcy politely.

"His name," said Aunt Kate, "was Parkinson. I heard him when he was in his prime and I think he had then the purest tenor voice that was ever put into a man's throat."

"Strange," said Mr. Bartell D'Arcy. "I never even heard of him."

"Yes, yes, Miss Morkan is right," said Mr. Browne. "I remember hearing of old Parkinson but he's too far back for me."

"A beautiful, pure, sweet, mellow English tenor," said Aunt Kate with enthusiasm.

Gabriel having finished, the huge pudding was transferred to the table. The clatter of forks and spoons began again. Gabriel's wife served out spoonfuls of the pudding and passed the plates down the table. Midway down they were held up by Mary Jane, who replenished them with raspberry or orange jelly or with blancmange and jam. The pudding was of Aunt Julia's making and she received praises for it from all quarters. She herself said that it was not quite brown enough.

"Well, I hope, Miss Morkan," said Mr. Browne, "that I'm brown enough for you because, you know, I'm all brown."

All the gentlemen, except Gabriel, ate some of the pudding out of compliment to Aunt Julia. As Gabriel never ate sweets, the celery had been left for him. Freddy Malins also took a stalk of celery and ate it with his pudding. He had been told that celery was a capital thing for the blood and he was just then under doctor's care. Mrs. Malins, who had been silent all through the supper, said that her son was going down to Mount Melleray in a week or so. The table then spoke of Mount Melleray, how bracing the air was down there, how hospitable the monks were and how they never asked for a penny-piece from their guests.

"And do you mean to say," asked Mr. Browne incredulously, "that a chap can go down there and put up there as if it were a hotel and live on the fat of the land and then come away without paying anything?"

"Oh, most people give some donation to the monastery when they leave," said Mary Jane.

"I wish we had an institution like that in our Church," said Mr. Browne candidly.

He was astonished to hear that the monks never spoke, got up at two in the morning and slept in their coffins. He asked what they did it for.

"That's the rule of the order," said Aunt Kate firmly.

"Yes, but why?" asked Mr. Browne.

Aunt Kate repeated that it was the rule, that was all. Mr. Browne still seemed not to understand. Freddy Malins explained to him, as best he could, that the monks were trying to make up for the sins committed by all the sinners in the outside world. The explanation was not very clear, for Mr. Browne grinned and said:

"I like that idea very much, but wouldn't a comfortable spring bed do them as well as a coffin?"

"The coffin," said Mary Jane, "is to remind them of their last end."

As the subject had grown lugubrious it was buried in a silence of the table, during which Mrs. Malins could be heard saying to her neighbor in an indistinct undertone:

"They are very good men, the monks, very pious men."

The raisins and almonds and figs and apples and oranges and chocolates and sweets were now passed about the table and Aunt Julia invited all the guests to have either port or sherry. At first Mr. Bartell D'Arcy refused to take either, but one of his neighbors nudged him and whispered something to him, upon which he allowed his glass to be filled. Gradually as the last glasses were being filled the conversation ceased. A pause followed, broken only by the noise of the wine

The Dead

and by unsettlings of chairs. The Misses Morkan, all three, looked down at the tablecloth. Someone coughed once or twice and then a few gentlemen patted the table gently as a signal for silence. The silence came and Gabriel pushed back his chair and stood up.

The patting at once grew louder in encouragement and then ceased altogether. Gabriel leaned his ten trembling fingers on the tablecloth and smiled nervously at the company. Meeting a row of upturned faces, he raised his eyes to the chandelier. The piano was playing a waltz tune and he could hear the skirts sweeping against the drawing-room door. People, perhaps, were standing in the snow on the quay outside, gazing up at the lighted windows and listening to the waltz music. The air was pure there. In the distance lay the park where the trees were weighted with snow. The Wellington Monument wore a gleaming cap of snow that flashed westward over the white field of Fifteen Acres.

He began:

"Ladies and Gentlemen,

"It has fallen to my lot this evening, as in years past, to perform a very pleasing task, but a task for which I am afraid my poor powers as a speaker are all too inadequate."

"No, no!" said Mr. Browne.

"But, however that may be, I can only ask you tonight to take the will for the deed and to lend me your attention for a few moments while I endeavor to express to you in words what my feelings are on this occasion.

"Ladies and Gentlemen, it is not the first time that we have gathered together under this hospitable roof, around this hospitable board. It is not the first time that we have been the recipients—or perhaps, I had better say, the victims—of the hospitality of certain good ladies."

He made a circle in the air with his arm and paused. Everyone laughed or smiled at Aunt Kate and Aunt Julia and Mary Jane, who all turned crimson with pleasure. Gabriel went on more boldly:

"I feel more strongly with every recurring year that our country has no tradition which does it so much honor and which it should guard so jealously as that of its hospitality. It is a tradition that is unique as far as my experience goes (and I have visited not a few places abroad) among the modern nations. Some would say, perhaps, that with us it is rather a failing than anything to be boasted of. But granted even that, it is, to my mind, a princely failing, and one that I trust will long be cultivated among us. Of one thing, at least, I am sure. As long as this one roof shelters the good ladies aforesaid—and I wish from my heart it may do so for many and many a long year to come—the tradition of genuine warm-hearted courteous Irish hospitality, which our forefathers have handed down to us and which we in turn must hand down to our descendants, is still alive among us."

A hearty murmur of assent ran round the table. It shot through Gabriel's mind that Miss Ivors was not there and that she had gone away discourteously: and he said with confidence in himself:

"Ladies and Gentlemen,

"A new generation is growing up in our midst, a generation actuated by new ideas and new principles. It is serious and enthusiastic, for these new ideas and its enthusiasm, even when it is misdirected, is, I believe, in the main sincere. But we are living in a sceptical and, if I may use the phrase, a thought-tormented age: and sometimes I fear that this new generation, educated or hypereducated as it is, will lack those qualities of humanity, of hospitality, of kindly humor which belonged to an older day. Listening tonight to the names of all those great singers of the past it seemed to me, I must confess, that we were living in a less spacious age. Those days might, without exaggeration, be called spacious days: and if they are gone beyond recall let us hope, at least, that in gatherings such as this we shall still speak of them with pride and affection, still cherish in our hearts the memory of those dead and gone great ones whose fame the world will not willingly let die."

"Hear, hear!" said Mr. Browne loudly.

"But yet," continued Gabriel, his voice falling into a softer inflection, "there are always in gatherings such as this sadder thoughts that will recur to our minds: thoughts of the past, of youth, of changes, of absent faces that we miss here tonight. Our path through life is strewn with many such sad memories: and were we to brood upon them always we could not find the heart to go on bravely with our work among the living. We have all of us living duties and living affections which claim, and rightly claim, our strenuous endeavors.

"Therefore, I will not linger on the past. I will not let any gloomy moralizing intrude upon us here tonight. Here we are gathered together for a brief moment from the bustle and rush of our everyday routine. We are met here as friends, in the spirit of good-fellowship, as colleagues, also to a certain extent, in the true spirit of *camaraderie,* and as the guests of—what shall I call them?—the Three Graces of the Dublin musical world."

The Dead

The table burst into applanse and laughter at this allusion. Aunt Julia vainly asked each of her neighbors in turn to tell her what Gabriel had said.

"He says we are the Three Graces, Aunt Julia," said Mary Jane.

Aunt Julia did not understand but she looked up, smiling, at Gabriel, who continued in the same vein:

"Ladies and Gentlemen,

"I will not attempt to play tonight the part that Paris played on another occasion. I will not attempt to choose between them. The task would be an invidious one and one beyond my poor powers. For when I view them in turn, whether it be our chief hostess herself, whose good heart, whose too good heart, has become a byword with all who know her, or her sister, who seems to be gifted with perennial youth and whose singing must have been a surprise and a revelation to us all tonight, or, last but not least, when I consider our youngest hostess, talented, cheerful, hardworking and the best of nieces, I confess, Ladies and Gentlemen, that I do not know to which of them I should award the prize."

Gabriel glanced down at his aunts and, seeing the large smile on Aunt Julia's face and the tears which had risen to Aunt Kate's eyes, hastened to his close. He raised his glass of port gallantly, while every member of the company fingered a glass expectantly, and said loudly:

"Let us toast them all three together. Let us drink to their health, wealth, long life, happiness, and prosperity, and may they long continue to hold the proud and self-won position which they hold in their profession and the position of honor and affection which they hold in our hearts."

All the guests stood up, glass in hand, and turning towards the three seated ladies, sang in unison, with Mr. Browne as leader:

> *For they are jolly gay fellows,*
> *For they are jolly gay fellows,*
> *For they are jolly gay fellows,*
> *Which nobody can deny.*

Aunt Kate was making frank use of her handkerchief and even Aunt Julia seemed moved. Freddy Malins beat time with his pudding fork and the singers turned towards one another, as if in melodious conference, while they sang with emphasis:

> *Unless he tells a lie,*
> *Unless he tells a lie,*

Then, turning once more towards their hostesses, they sang:

For they are jolly gay fellows,
For they are jolly gay fellows,
For they are jolly gay fellows,
Which nobody can deny.

The acclamation which followed was taken up beyond the door of the supper room by many of the other guests and renewed time after time, Freddy Malins acting as officer with his fork on high.

The piercing morning air came into the hall where they were standing so that Aunt Kate said:

"Close the door, somebody. Mrs. Malins will get her death of cold."

"Browne is out there, Aunt Kate," said Mary Jane.

"Browne is everywhere," said Aunt Kate, lowering her voice.

Mary Jane laughed at her tone.

"Really," she said archly, "he is very attentive."

"He has been laid on here like the gas," said Aunt Kate in the same tone, "all during the Christmas."

She laughed herself this time good-humoredly and then added quickly:

"But tell him to come in, Mary Jane, and close the door. I hope to goodness he didn't hear me."

At that moment the hall door was opened and Mr. Browne came in from the doorstep, laughing as if his heart would break. He was dressed in a long green overcoat with mock astrakhan cuffs and collar, and wore on his head an oval fur cap. He pointed down the snow-covered quay from where the sound of shrill prolonged whistling was borne in.

"Teddy will have all the cabs in Dublin out," he said.

Gabriel advanced from the little pantry behind the office, struggling into his overcoat and, looking round the hall, said:

"Gretta not down yet?"

"She's getting on her things, Gabriel," said Aunt Kate.

"Who's playing up there?" asked Gabriel.

"Nobody. They're all gone."

"Oh, no, Aunt Kate," said Mary Jane. "Bartell D'Arcy and Miss O'Callaghan aren't gone yet."

"Someone is fooling at the piano anyhow," said Gabriel.

The Dead

Mary Jane glanced at Gabriel and Mr. Browne and said with a shiver:

"It makes me feel cold to look at you two gentlemen muffled up like that. I wouldn't like to face your journey home at this hour."

"I'd like nothing better this minute," said Mr. Browne stoutly, "than a rattling fine walk in the country or a fast drive with a good spanking goer between the shafts."

"We used to have a very good horse and trap at home," said Aunt Julia sadly.

"The never-to-be-forgotten Johnny," said Mary Jane, laughing.

Aunt Kate and Gabriel laughed too.

"Why, what was wonderful about Johnny?" asked Mr. Browne.

"The late lamented Patrick Morkan, our grandfather, that is," explained Gabriel, "commonly known in his later years as the old gentleman, was a glue-boiler."

"Oh, now, Gabriel," said Aunt Kate, laughing, "he had a starch mill."

"Well, glue or starch," said Gabriel, "the old gentleman had a horse by the name of Johnny. And Johnny used to work in the old gentleman's mill, walking round and round in order to drive the mill. That was all very well; but now comes the tragic part about Johnny. One fine day the old gentleman thought he'd like to drive out with the quality to a military review in the park."

"The Lord have mercy on his soul," said Aunt Kate compassionately.

"Amen," said Gabriel. "So the old gentleman, as I said, harnessed Johnny and put on his very best tall hat and his very best stock collar and drove out in grand style from his ancestral mansion somewhere near Back Lane, I think."

Everyone laughed, even Mrs. Malins, at Gabriel's manner and Aunt Kate said:

"Oh, now, Gabriel, he didn't live in Back Lane, really. Only the mill was there."

"Out from the mansion of his forefathers," continued Gabriel, "he drove with Johnny. And everything went on beautifully until Johnny came in sight of King Billy's statue: and whether he fell in love with the horse King Billy sits on or whether he thought he was back again in the mill, anyhow he began to walk round the statue."

Gabriel paced in a circle round the hall in his galoshes amid the laughter of the others.

"Round and round he went," said Gabriel, "and the old gentleman, who was a very pompous old gentleman, was highly indignant. 'Go on, sir! What do you mean, sir? Johnny! Johnny! Most extraordinary conduct! Can't understand the horse!' "

The peal of laughter which followed Gabriel's imitation of the incident was interrupted by a resounding knock at the hall door. Mary Jane ran to open it and let in Freddy Malins. Freddy Malins, with his hat well back on his head and his shoulders humped with cold, was puffing and steaming after his exertions.

"I could only get one cab," he said.

"Oh, we'll find another along the quay," said Gabriel.

"Yes," said Aunt Kate. "Better not keep Mrs. Malins standing in the draught."

Mrs. Malins was helped down the front steps by her son and Mr. Browne and, after many maneuvers, hoisted into the cab. Freddy Malins clambered in after her and spent a long time settling her on the seat, Mr. Browne helping him with advice. At last she was settled comfortably and Freddy Malins invited Mr. Browne into the cab. There was a good deal of confused talk, and then Mr. Browne got into the cab. The cabman settled his rug over his knees, and bent down for the address. The confusion grew greater and the cabman was directed differently by Freddy Malins and Mr. Browne, each of whom had his head out through a window of the cab. The difficulty was to know where to drop Mr. Browne along the route, and Aunt Kate, Aunt Julia, and Mary Jane helped the discussion from the doorstep with cross-directions and contradictions and abundance of laughter. As for Freddy Malins, he was speechless with laughter. He popped his head in and out of the window every moment to the great danger of his hat, and told his mother how the discussion was progressing, till at last Mr. Browne shouted to the bewildered cabman above the din of everybody's laughter:

"Do you know Trinity College?"

"Yes, sir," said the cabman.

"Well, drive bang up against Trinity College gates," said Mr. Browne, "and then we'll tell you where to go. You understand now?"

"Yes, sir," said the cabman.

"Make like a bird for Trinity College."

"Right, sir," said the cabman.

The horse was whipped up and the cab rattled off along the quay amid a chorus of laughter and adieus.

The Dead

Gabriel had not gone to the door with the others. He was in a dark part of the hall gazing up the staircase. A woman was standing near the top of the first flight, in the shadow also. He could not see her face, but he could see the terra-cotta and salmon-pink panels of her skirt which the shadow made appear black and white. It was his wife. She was leaning on the banisters, listening to something. Gabriel was surprised at her stillness and strained his ear to listen also. But he could hear little save the noise of laughter and dispute on the front steps, a few chords struck on the piano and a few notes of a man's voice singing.

He stood still in the gloom of the hall, trying to catch the air that the voice was singing and gazing up at his wife. There was grace and mystery in her attitude, as if she were a symbol of something. He asked himself what is a woman standing on the stairs in the shadow, listening to distant music, a symbol of. If he were a painter he would paint her in that attitude. Her blue felt hat would show off the bronze of her hair against the darkness and the dark panels of her skirt would show off the light ones. *Distant Music* he would call the picture if he were a painter.

The hall door was closed; and Aunt Kate, Aunt Julia and Mary Jane came down the hall, still laughing.

"Well, isn't Freddy terrible?" said Mary Jane. "He's really terrible."

Gabriel said nothing but pointed up the stairs towards where his wife was standing. Now that the hall door was closed, the voice and the piano could be heard more clearly. Gabriel held up his hand for them to be silent. The song seemed to be in the old Irish tonality and the singer seemed uncertain both of his words and of his voice. The voice, made plaintive by distance and by the singer's hoarseness, faintly illuminated the cadence of the air with words expressing grief:

> *O, the rain falls on my heavy locks*
> *And the dew wets my skin,*
> *My babe lies cold . . .*

"Oh," exclaimed Mary Jane. "It's Bartell D'Arcy singing and he wouldn't sing all the night. Oh, I'll get him to sing a song before he goes."

"Oh, do, Mary Jane," said Aunt Kate.

Mary Jane brushed past the others and ran to the staircase, but before she reached it the singing stopped and the piano was closed abruptly.

"Oh, what a pity!" she cried. "Is he coming down, Gretta?"

Gabriel heard his wife answer yes and saw her come down towards them. A few steps behind her were Mr. Bartell D'Arcy and Miss O'Callaghan.

"Oh, Mr. D'Arcy," cried Mary Jane, "it's downright mean of you to break off like that when we were all in raptures listening to you."

"I have been at him all the evening," said Miss O'Callaghan, "and Mrs. Conroy, too, and he told us he had a dreadful cold and couldn't sing."

"Oh, Mr. D'Arcy," said Aunt Kate, "now that was a great fib to tell."

"Can't you see that I'm as hoarse as a crow?" said Mr. D'Arcy roughly.

He went into the pantry hastily and put on his overcoat. The others, taken aback by his rude speech, could find nothing to say. Aunt Kate wrinkled her brows and made signs to the others to drop the subject. Mr. D'Arcy stood swathing his neck carefully and frowning.

"It's the weather," said Aunt Julia, after a pause.

"Yes, everybody has colds," said Aunt Kate readily, "everybody."

"They say," said Mary Jame, "we haven't had snow like it for thirty years; and I read this morning in the newspapers that the snow is general all over Ireland."

"I love the look of snow," said Aunt Julia sadly.

"So do I," said Miss O'Callaghan. "I think Christmas is never really Christmas unless we have the snow on the ground."

"But poor Mr. D'Arcy doesn't like the snow," said Aunt Kate, smiling.

Mr. D'Arcy came from the pantry, fully swathed and buttoned, and in a repentant tone told them the history of his cold. Everyone gave him advice and said it was a great pity and urged him to be very careful of his throat in the night air. Gabriel watched his wife, who did not join in the conversation. She was standing right under the dusty fanlight and the flame of the gas lit up the rich bronze of her hair, which he had seen her drying at the fire a few days before. She was in the same attitude and seemed unaware of the talk about her. At last she turned towards them and Gabriel saw that there was color on her cheeks and that her eyes were shining. A sudden tide of joy went leaping out of his heart.

"Mr. D'Arcy," she said, "what is the name of that song you were singing?"

The Dead

"It's called *The Lass of Aughrim,*" said Mr. D'Arcy, "but I couldn't remember it properly. Why? Do you know it?"

"The Lass of Aughrim," she repeated. "I couldn't think of the name."

"It's a very nice air," said Mary Jane. "I'm sorry you were not in voice tonight."

"Now, Mary Jane," said Aunt Kate, "don't annoy Mr. D'Arcy. I won't have him annoyed."

Seeing that all were ready to start, she shepherded them to the door, where good-night was said:

"Well, good-night, Aunt Kate, and thanks for the pleasant evening."

"Good-night, Gabriel. Good-night, Gretta!"

"Good-night, Aunt Kate, and thanks ever so much. Good-night, Aunt Julia."

"Oh, good-night, Gretta. I didn't see you."

"Good-night, Mr. D'Arcy. Good-night, Miss O'Callaghan."

"Good-night, Miss Morkan."

"Good-night, again."

"Good-night, all. Safe home."

"Good-night. Good-night."

The morning was still dark. A dull, yellow light brooded over the houses and the river; and the sky seemed to be descending. It was slushy underfoot; and only streaks and patches of snow lay on the roofs, on the parapets of the quay, and on the area railings. The lamps were still burning redly in the murky air and, across the river, the palace of the Four Courts stood out menacingly against the heavy sky.

She was walking on before him with Mr. Bartell D'Arcy, her shoes in a brown parcel tucked under one arm and her hands holding her skirt up from the slush. She had no longer any grace of attitude, but Gabriel's eyes were still bright with happiness. The blood went bounding along his veins; and the thoughts went rioting through his brain, proud, joyful, tender, valorous.

She was walking on before him so lightly and so erect that he longed to run after her noiselessly, catch her by the shoulders and say something foolish and affectionate into her ear. She seemed to him so frail that he longed to defend her against something and then to be alone with her. Moments of their secret life together burst like stars upon his memory. A heliotrope envelope was lying beside his breakfast cup and he was caressing it with his hand. Birds were twittering in the ivy and the sunny web of the curtain was shimmering along the floor: he could not eat for happiness. They were standing on the crowded platform and he was placing a ticket inside the warm palm of her glove. He was standing with her in the cold, looking in through a grated window at a man making bottles in a roaring furnace. It was very cold. Her face, fragrant in the cold air, was quite close to his; and suddenly he called out to the man at the furnace:

"Is the fire hot, sir?"

But the man could not hear with the noise of the furnace. It was just as well. He might have answered rudely.

A wave of yet more tender joy escaped from his heart and went coursing in warm flood along his arteries. Like the tender fire of stars, moments of their life together, that no one knew of or would ever know of, broke upon and illumined his memory. He longed to recall to her those moments, to make her forget the years of their dull existence together and remember only their moments of ecstasy. For the years, he felt, had not quenched his soul or hers. Their children, his writing, her household cares had not quenched all their souls' tender fire. In one letter that he had written to her then he had said: "Why is it that words like these seem to me so dull and cold? Is it because there is no word tender enough to be your name?"

Like distant music these words that he had written years before were borne towards him from the past. He longed to be alone with her. When the others had gone away, when he and she were in the room in the hotel, then they would be alone together. He would call her softly:

"Gretta!"

Perhaps she would not hear at once: she would be undressing. Then something in his voice would strike her. She would turn and look at him....

At the corner of Winetavern Street they met a cab. He was glad of its rattling noise, as it saved him from conversation. She was looking out of the window and seemed tired. The others spoke only a few words, pointing out some building or street. The horse galloped along wearily under the murky morning sky, dragging his old rattling box after his heels, and Gabriel was again in a cab with her, galloping to catch the boat, galloping to their honeymoon.

As the cab drove across O'Connell Bridge Miss O'Callaghan said:

"They say you never cross O'Connell Bridge without seeing a white horse."

"I see a white man this time," said Gabriel.

The Dead

"Where?" asked Mr. Bartell D'Arcy.

Gabriel pointed to the statue, on which lay patches of snow. Then he nodded familiarly to it and waved his hand.

"Good-night, Dan," he said gaily.

When the cab drew up before the hotel, Gabriel jumped out and, in spite of Mr. Bartell D'Arcy's protest, paid the driver. He gave the man a shilling over his fare. The man saluted and said:

"A prosperous New Year to you, sir."

"The same to you," said Gabriel cordially.

She leaned for a moment on his arm in getting out of the cab and while standing at the curbstone, bidding the others good-night. She leaned lightly on his arm, as lightly as when she had danced with him a few hours before. He had felt proud and happy then, happy that she was his, proud of her grace and wifely carriage. But now, after the kindling again of so many memories, the first touch of her body, musical and strange and perfumed, sent through him a keen pang of lust. Under cover of her silence he pressed her arm closely to his side; and, as they stood at the hotel door, he felt that they had escaped from their lives and duties, escaped from home and friends and run away together with wild and radiant hearts to a new adventure.

An old man was dozing in a great hooded chair in the hall. He lit a candle in the office and went before them to the stairs. They followed him in silence, their feet falling in soft thuds on the thickly carpeted stairs. She mounted the stairs behind the porter, her head bowed in the ascent, her frail shoulders curved as with a burden, her skirt girt tightly about her. He could have flung his arms about her hips and held her still, for his arms were trembling with desire to seize her and only the stress of his nails against the palms of his hands held the wild impulse of his body in check. The porter halted on the stairs to settle his guttering candle. They halted, too, on the steps below him. In the silence Gabriel could hear the falling of the molten wax into the tray and the thumping of his own heart against his ribs.

The porter led them along a corridor and opened a door. Then he set his unstable candle down on a toilet table and asked at what hour they were to be called in the morning.

"Eight," said Gabriel.

The porter pointed to the tap of the electric light and began a muttered apology, but Gabriel cut him short.

"We don't want any light. We have light enough from the street. And I say," he added, pointing to the candle, "you might remove that handsome article, like a good man."

The porter took up his candle again, but slowly, for he was surprised by such a novel idea. Then he mumbled good-night and went out. Gabriel shot the lock to.

A ghastly light from the street lamp lay in a long shaft from one window to the door. Gabriel threw his overcoat and hat on a couch and crossed the room towards the window. He looked down into the street in order that his emotion might calm a little. Then he turned and leaned against a chest of drawers with his back to the light. She had taken off her hat and cloak and was standing before a large swinging mirror, unhooking her waist. Gabriel paused for a few moments, watching her, and then said:

"Gretta!"

She turned away from the mirror slowly and walked along the shaft of light towards him. Her face looked so serious and weary that the words would not pass Gabriel's lips. No, it was not the moment yet.

"You look tired," he said.

"I am a little," she answered.

"You don't feel ill or weak?"

"No, tired: that's all."

She went on to the window and stood there, looking out. Gabriel waited again and then, fearing that diffidence was about to conquer him, he said abruptly:

"By the way, Gretta!"

"What is it?"

"You know that poor fellow Malins?" he said quickly.

"Yes. What about him?"

"Well, poor fellow, he's a decent sort of chap, after all," continued Gabriel in a false voice. "He gave me back that sovereign I lent him, and I didn't expect it, really. It's a pity he wouldn't keep away from that Browne, because he's not a bad fellow, really."

He was trembling now with annoyance. Why did she seem so abstracted? He did not know how he could begin. Was she annoyed, too, about something? If she would only turn to him or come to him of her own accord! To take her as she was would be brutal. No, he must see some ardor in her eyes first. He longed to be master of her strange mood.

"When did you lend him the pound?" she asked, after a pause.

Gabriel strove to restrain himself from breaking out into brutal language about the sottish Malins and his pound. He longed to cry to

The Dead

her from his soul, to crush her body against his, to overmaster her. But he said:

"Oh, at Christmas, when he opened that little Christmas-card shop in Henry Street."

He was in such a fever of rage and desire that he did not hear her come from the window. She stood before him for an instant, looking at him strangely. Then, suddenly raising herself on tiptoe and resting her hands lightly on his shoulders, she kissed him.

"You are a very generous person, Gabriel," she said.

Gabriel, trembling with delight at her sudden kiss and at the quaintness of her phrase, put his hands on her hair and began smoothing it back, scarcely touching it with his fingers. The washing had made it fine and brilliant. His heart was brimming over with happiness. Just when he was wishing for it, she had come to him of her own accord. Perhaps her thoughts had been running with his. Perhaps she had felt the impetuous desire that was in him, and then the yielding mood had come upon her. Now that she had fallen to him so easily, he wondered why he had been so diffident.

He stood, holding her head between his hands. Then, slipping one arm swiftly about her body and drawing her towards him, he said softly:

"Gretta, dear, what are you thinking about?"

She did not answer nor yield wholly to his arm. He said again, softly:

"Tell me what it is, Gretta. I think I know what is the matter. Do I know?"

She did not answer at once. Then she said in an outburst of tears:

"Oh, I am thinking about that song, *The Lass of Aughrim.*"

She broke loose from him and ran to the bed and, throwing her arms across the bed rail, hid her face. Gabriel stood stock—still for a moment in astonishment and then followed her. As he passed in the way of the cheval glass he caught sight of himself in full length, his broad, well-filled shirtfront, the face whose expression always puzzled him when he saw it in a mirror, and his glimmering gilt-rimmed eyeglasses. He halted a few paces from her and said:

"What about the song? Why does that make you cry?"

She raised her head from her arms and dried her eyes with the back of her hand like a child. A kinder note than he had intended went into his voice.

"Why, Gretta?" he asked.

"I am thinking about a person long ago who used to sing that song."

"And who was the person long ago?" asked Gabriel, smiling.

"It was a person I used to know in Galway when I was living with my grandmother," she said.

The smile passed away from Gabriel's face. A dull anger began to gather again at the back of his mind and the dull fires of his lust began to glow angrily in his veins.

"Someone you were in love with?" he asked ironically.

"It was a young boy I used to know," she answered, "named Michael Furey. He used to sing that song, *The Lass of Aughrim*. He was very delicate."

Gabriel was silent. He did not wish her to think that he was interested in this delicate boy.

"I can see him so plainly," she said, after a moment. "Such eyes as he had: big, dark eyes! And such an expression in them—an expression!"

"Oh, then, you are in love with him?" said Gabriel.

"I used to go out walking with him," she said, "when I was in Galway."

A thought flew across Gabriel's mind.

"Perhaps that was why you wanted to go to Galway with that Ivors girl?" he said coldly.

She looked at him and asked in surprise:

"What for?"

Her eyes made Gabriel feel awkward. He shrugged his shoulders and said:

"How do I know? To see him, perhaps."

She looked away from him along the shaft of light towards the window in silence.

"He is dead," she said at length. "He died when he was only seventeen. Isn't it a terrible thing to die so young as that?"

"What was he?" asked Gabriel, still ironically.

"He was in the gasworks," she said.

Gabriel felt humiliated by the failure of his irony and by the evocation of this figure from the dead, a boy in the gasworks. While he had been full of memories of their secret life together, full of tenderness and joy and desire, she had been comparing him in her mind with another. A shameful consciousness of his own person assailed him. He saw himself as a ludicrous figure, acting as a pennyboy

The Dead

for his aunts, a nervous, well-meaning sentimentalist, orating to vulgarians and idealizing his own clownish lusts, the pitiable fatuous fellow he had caught a glimpse of in the mirror. Instinctively he turned his back more to the light lest she might see the shame that burned upon his forehead.

He tried to keep up his tone of cold interrogation, but his voice when he spoke was humble and indifferent.

"I suppose you were in love with this Michael Furey, Gretta," he said.

"I was great with him at that time," she said.

Her voice was veiled and sad. Gabriel, feeling now how vain it would be to try to lead her whither he had purposed, caressed one of her hands and said, also sadly:

"And what did he die of so young, Gretta? Consumption, was it?"

"I think he died for me," she answered.

A vague terror seized Gabriel at this answer, as if, at that hour when he had hoped to triumph, some impalpable and vindictive being was coming against him, gathering forces against him in its vague world. But he shook himself free of it with an effort of reason and continued to caress her hand. He did not question her again, for he felt that she would tell him of herself. Her hand was warm and moist; it did not respond to his touch, but he continued to caress it just as he had caressed her first letter to him that spring morning.

"It was in the winter," she said, "about the beginning of the winter when I was going to leave my grandmother's and come up here to the convent. And he was ill at the time in his lodgings in Galway and wouldn't be let out, and his people in Oughterard were written to. He was in decline, they said, or something like that. I never knew rightly."

She paused for a moment and sighed.

"Poor fellow," she said. "He was very fond of me and he was such a gentle boy. We used to go out together, walking, you know, Gabriel, like the way they do in the country. He was going to study singing only for his health. He had a very good voice, poor Michael Furey."

"Well; and then?" asked Gabriel.

"And then when it came to the time for me to leave Galway and come up to the convent he was much worse and I wouldn't be let see him, so I wrote him a letter saying I was going up to Dublin and would be back in the summer, and hoping he would be better then."

She paused for a moment to get her voice under control, and then went on:

"Then the night before I left, I was in my grandmother's house in Nuns' Island, packing up, and I heard gravel thrown up against the window. The window was so wet I couldn't see, so I ran downstairs as I was and slipped out the back into the garden and there was the poor fellow at the end of the garden, shivering."

"And did you not tell him to go back?" asked Gabriel.

"I implored of him to go home at once and told him he would get his death in the rain. But he said he did not want to live. I can see his eyes as well as well! He was standing at the end of the wall where there was a tree."

"And did he go home?" asked Gabriel.

"Yes, he went home. And when I was only a week in the convent he died and he was buried in Oughterard, where his people came from. Oh, the day I heard that, that he was dead!"

She stopped, choking with sobs, and, overcome by emotion, flung herself face downward on the bed, sobbing in the quilt. Gabriel held her hand for a moment longer, irresolutely, and then, shy of intruding on her grief, let it fall gently and walked quietly to the window.

She was fast asleep.

Gabriel, leaning on his elbow, looked for a few moments unresentfully on her tangled hair and half-open mouth, listening to her deep-drawn breath. So she had had that romance in her life: a man had died for her sake. It hardly pained him now to think how poor a part he, her husband, had played in her life. He watched her while she slept, as though he and she had never lived together as man and wife. His curious eyes rested long upon her face and on her hair: and, as he thought of what she must have been then, in that time of her first girlish beauty, a strange, friendly pity for her entered his soul. He did not like to say even to himself that her face was no longer beautiful, but he knew that it was no longer the face for which Michael Furey had braved death.

Perhaps she had not told him all the story. His eyes moved to the chair over which she had thrown some of her clothes. A petticoat string dangled to the floor. One boot stood upright, its limp upper fallen down; the fellow of it lay upon its side. He wondered at his riot of emotions of an hour before. From what had it proceeded? From his aunt's supper, from his own foolish speech, from the wine and dancing, the merrymaking when saying good-night in the hall, the pleasure of the walk along the river in the snow. Poor Aunt Julia! She, too, would soon be a shade with the shade of Patrick Morkan and his horse. He had caught that haggard look upon her face for a moment when she was singing *Arrayed for the Bridal*. Soon, perhaps, he would be sitting in that same drawing room, dressed in black, his silk hat on his knees. The blinds would be drawn down and Aunt Kate would be sitting beside him, crying and blowing her nose and telling him how Julia had died. He would cast about in his mind for some words that might console her, and would find only lame and useless ones. Yes, yes: that would happen very soon.

The air of the room chilled his shoulders. He stretched himself cautiously along under the sheets and lay down beside his wife. One by one, they were all becoming shades. Better pass boldly into that other world, in the full glory of some passion, than fade and wither dismally with age. He thought of how she who lay beside him had locked in her heart for so many years that image of her lover's eyes when he had told her that he did not wish to live.

Generous tears filled Gabriel's eyes. He had never felt like that himself towards any woman, but he knew that such a feeling must be love. The tears gathered more thickly in his eyes, and in the partial darkness he imagined he saw the form of a young man standing under a dripping tree. Other forms were near. His soul had approached that region where dwell the vast hosts of the dead. He was conscious of, but could not apprehend, their wayward and flickering existence. His own identity was fading out into a grey impalpable world; the solid world itself, which these dead had one time reared and lived in, was dissolving and dwindling.

A few light taps upon the pane made him turn to the window. It had begun to snow again. He watched sleepily the flakes, silver and dark, falling obliquely against the lamplight. The time had come for him to set out on his journey westward. Yes, the newspapers were right: snow was general all over Ireland. It was falling on every part of the dark central plain, on the treeless hills, falling softly upon the Bog of Allen and, farther westward, softly falling into the dark mutinous Shannon waves. It was falling, too, upon every part of the lonely churchyard on the hill where Michael Furey lay buried. It lay thickly drifted on the crooked crosses and headstones, on the spears of the little gate, on the barren thorns. His soul swooned slowly as he heard the snow falling faintly through the universe and faintly falling, like the descent of their last end, upon all the living and the dead.

A Boy's Trip to "Heaven"

ries for young people. The incidents are apparently more suitable for a fairy tale than for a realistic story of modern boyhood, but show a "truth beyond truth" that many fact-minded people miss. The story also shows Forster's quick characterization, subtle humor, irony, flexibility of style, and the use of allusions which flatter the attentive reader who from a few hints can recognize the appearance of characters drawn from the world's great stories.

E. M. FORSTER

Known more widely as a craftsman in the novel, Forster wrote some outstanding short stories, many of which deal with apparently fantastic adventures.

Edward Morgan Forster, an English writer with some Welsh ancestry, was born in 1879. After the usual British schooling, he went to King's College, Cambridge, famed for producing authors. After graduation he began writing stories and novels, the earliest of which resulted from a residence in Italy. Two trips to India brought forth his masterpiece in the novel, *A Passage to India* (1924), showing the defects of British colonialism. As a professional literary man, he also wrote reviews and magazine articles. His critical volume, *Aspects of the Novel,* based on a series of lectures at King's College, is a light but penetrating study of a form in which he was an expert. He also took an active part in protecting the rights of authors and fighting outworn censorship of literature. Forster wrote comparatively little during his lifetime, and sometimes took years to meditate upon a story before writing it down. He died in 1970.

"The Celestial Omnibus," first published in 1908, is a story about the proper appreciation of literature, and thus is especially suitable for a collection of sto-

E. M. FORSTER

The Celestial Omnibus

I

The boy who resided at Agathox Lodge, 28, Buckingham Park Road, Surbiton, had often been puzzled by the old signpost that stood almost opposite. He asked his mother about it, and she replied that it was a joke, and not a very nice one, which had been made many years back by some naughty young men, and that the police ought to remove it. For there were two strange things about this signpost: firstly, it pointed up a blank alley, and, secondly, it had painted on it, in faded characters, the words, "To Heaven."

"What kind of young men were they?" he asked.

"I think your father told me that one of them wrote verses, and was expelled from the university and came to grief in other ways. Still, it was a long time ago. You must ask your father about it. He will say the same as I do, that it was put up as a joke."

"So it doesn't mean anything at all?"

She sent him upstairs to put on his best things, for the Bonses were coming to tea, and he was to hand the cake stand.

It struck him, as he wrenched on his tightening trousers, that he might do worse than ask Mr. Bons about the signpost. His father, though very kind, always laughed at him—shrieked with laughter whenever he or any other child asked a question or spoke. But Mr. Bons was serious as well as kind. He had a beautiful house and lent one books, he was a church warden, and a candidate for the County

Council; he had donated to the Free Library enormously, he presided over the Literary Society, and had Members of Parliament to stop with him—in short, he was probably the wisest person alive.

Yet even Mr. Bons could only say that the signpost was a joke—the joke of a person named Shelley.

"Of course!" cried the mother; "I told you so, dear. That was the name."

"Had you never heard of Shelley?" asked Mr. Bons.

"No," said the boy, and hung his head.

"But is there no Shelley in the house?"

"Why, yes!" exclaimed the lady, in much agitation. "Dear Mr. Bons, we aren't such Philistines as that. Two at the least. One a wedding present, and the other, smaller print, in one of the spare rooms."

"I believe we have seven Shelleys," said Mr. Bons, with a slow smile. Then he brushed the cake crumbs off his stomach and, together with his daughter, rose to go.

The boy, obeying a wink from his mother, saw them all the way to the garden gate, and when they had gone he did not at once return to the house, but gazed for a little up and down Buckingham Park Road.

His parents lived at the right end of it. After No. 39 the quality of the houses dropped very suddenly, and 64 had not even a separate servants' entrance. But at the present moment the whole road looked rather pretty, for the sun had just set in splendor, and the inequalities of rent were drowned in a saffron afterglow. Small birds twittered, and the breadwinners' train shrieked musically down through the cutting —that wonderful cutting which has drawn to itself the whole beauty out of Surbiton, and clad itself, like any Alpine valley, with the glory of the fir and the silver birch and the primrose. It was this cutting that had first stirred desires within the boy—desires for something just a little different, he knew not what, desires that would return whenever things were sunlit, as they were this evening, running up and down inside him, up and down, up and down, till he would feel quite unusual all over, and as likely as not would want to cry. This evening he was even sillier, for he slipped across the road towards the signpost and began to run up the blank alley.

The alley runs between high walls—the walls of the gardens of "Ivanhoe" and "Belle Vista" respectively. It smells a little all the way, and is scarcely twenty yards long, including the turn at the end. So not unnaturally the boy soon came to a standstill. "I'd like to kick that Shelley," he exclaimed, and glanced idly at a piece of paper which was

The Celestial Omnibus

pasted on the wall. Rather an odd piece of paper, and he read it carefully before he turned back. This is what he read:

S. AND C. R. C. C.

Alteration in Service

Owing to lack of patronage the Company are regretfully compelled to suspend the hourly service, and to retain only the

Sunrise and Sunset Omnibuses,

which will run as usual. It is to be hoped that the public will patronize an arrangement which is intended for their convenience. As an extra inducement, the Company will, for the first time, now issue

Return Tickets!

(available one day only), which may be obtained of the driver. Passengers are again reminded that *no tickets are issued at the other end*, and that no complaints in this connection will receive consideration from the Company. Nor will the Company be responsible for any negligence or stupidity on the part of Passengers, nor for Hailstorms, Lightning, Loss of Tickets, nor for any Act of God.

For the Direction.

Now he had never seen this notice before, nor could he imagine where the omnibus went to. S. of course was for Surbiton, and R.C.C. meant Road Car Company. But what was the meaning of the other C? Coombe and Malden, perhaps, or possibly "City." Yet it could not hope to compete with the South-Western. The whole thing, the boy reflected, was run on hopelessly unbusinesslike lines. Why no tickets from the other end? And what an hour to start! Then he realized that unless the notice was a hoax, an omnibus must have been starting just as he was wishing the Bonses good-bye. He peered at the ground through the gathering dusk, and there he saw what might or might not be the marks of wheels. Yet nothing had come out of the alley. And he had never seen an omnibus at any time in the Buckingham Park Road. No: it must be a hoax, like the signposts, like the fairy tales, like the dreams upon which he would wake suddenly in the night. And with a sigh he stepped from the alley—right into the arms of his father.

Oh, how his father laughed! "Poor, poor Popsey!" he cried. "Diddums! Diddums! Diddums think he'd walky-palky up to Evvink!" And his mother, also convulsed with laughter, appeared on the steps of Agathox Lodge. "Don't, Bob!" she gasped. "Don't be so naughty! Oh, you'll kill me! Oh, leave the boy alone!"

But all that evening the joke was kept up. The father implored to be taken too. Was it a very tiring walk? Need one wipe one's shoes on the doormat? And the boy went to bed feeling faint and sore, and thankful for only one thing—that he had not said a word about the omnibus. It was a hoax, yet through his dreams it grew more and more real, and the streets of Surbiton, through which he saw it driving, seemed instead to become hoaxes and shadows. And very early in the morning he woke with a cry, for he had had a glimpse of its destination.

He struck a match, and its light fell not only on his watch but also on his calendar, so that he knew it to be half an hour to sunrise. It was pitch dark, for the fog had come down from London in the night, and all Surbiton was wrapped in its embraces. Yet he sprang out and dressed himself, for he was determined to settle once for all which was real: the omnibus or the streets. "I shall be a fool one way or the other," he thought, "until I know." Soon he was shivering in the road under the gas lamp that guarded the entrance to the alley.

To enter the alley itself required some courage. Not only was it horribly dark, but he now realized that it was an impossible terminus for an omnibus. If it had not been for a policeman, whom he heard approaching through the fog, he would never have made the attempt. The next moment he had made the attempt and failed. Nothing. Nothing but a blank alley and a very silly boy gaping at its dirty floor. It *was* a hoax. "I'll tell papa and mamma," he decided. "I deserve it. I deserve that they should know. I am too silly to be alive." And he went back to the gate of Agathox Lodge.

There he remembered that this watch was fast. The sun was not risen; it would not rise for two minutes. "Give the bus every chance," he thought cynically, and returned into the alley.

But the omnibus was there.

II

It had two horses, whose sides were still smoking from their journey and its two great lamps shone through the fog against the alley's walls, changing their cobwebs and moss into tissues of fairyland. The driver was huddled up in a cape. He faced the blank wall, and how he had managed to drive in so neatly and so silently was one of the many things that the boy never discovered. Nor could he imagine however he would drive out.

The Celestial Omnibus

"Please," his voice quavered through the foul brown air. "Please, is that an omnibus?"

"Omnibus est," said the driver, without turning round. There was a moment's silence. The policeman passed, coughing, by the entrance of the alley. The boy crouched in the shadow, for he did not want to be found out. He was pretty sure, too, that it was a pirate; nothing else, he reasoned, would go from such odd places and at such odd hours.

"About when do you start?" He tried to sound nonchalant.

"At sunrise."

"How far do you go?"

"The whole way."

"And can I have a return ticket which will bring me all the way back?"

"You can."

"Do you know, I half think I'll come." The driver made no answer. The sun must have risen, for he unhitched the brake. And scarcely had the boy jumped in before the omnibus was off.

How? Did it turn? There was no room. Did it go forward? There was a blank wall. Yet it was moving—moving at a stately pace through the fog, which had turned from brown to yellow. The thought of warm bed and warmer breakfast made the boy feel faint. He wished he had not come. His parents would not have approved. He would have gone back to them if the weather had not made it impossible. The solitude was terrible; he was the only passenger. And the omnibus, though well-built, was cold and somewhat musty. He drew his coat round him, and in so doing chanced to feel his pocket. It was empty. He had forgotten his purse.

"Stop!" he shouted. "Stop!" And then, being of a polite disposition, he glanced up at the painted notice board so that he might call the driver by name. "Mr. Browne! stop; Oh, do please stop!"

Mr. Browne did not stop, but he opened a little window and looked in at the boy. His face was a surprise, so kind it was and modest.

"Mr. Browne, I've left my purse behind. I've not got a penny. I can't pay for the ticket. Will you take my watch, please? I am in the most awful hole."

"Tickets on this line," said the driver "whether single or return, can be purchased by coinage from no terrene mint. And a chronometer, though it had solaced the vigils of Charlemagne, or measured the slumbers of Laura, can acquire by no mutation the double cake that charms the fangless Cerberus of Heaven!" So saying, he handed in the necessary ticket, and, while the boy said "Thank you," continued: "Titular pretensions, I know it well, are vanity. Yet they merit no censure when uttered on a laughing lip, and in an homonymous world are in some sort useful, since they do serve to distinguish one Jack from his fellow. Remember me, therefore, as Sir Thomas Browne."

"Are you a Sir? Oh, sorry!" He had heard of these gentlemen drivers. "It *is* good of you about the ticket. But if you go on at this rate, however does your bus pay?"

"It does not pay. It was not intended to pay. Many are the faults of my equipage; it is compounded too curiously of foreign woods; its cushions tickle erudition rather than promote repose; and my horses are nourished not on the evergreen pastures of the moment, but on the dried bents and clovers of Latinity. But that it pays!—that error at all events was never intended and never attained."

"Sorry again," said the boy rather hopelessly. Sir Thomas looked sad, fearing that, even for a moment, he had been the cause of sadness. He invited the boy to come up and sit beside him on the box, and together they journeyed on through the fog, which was now changing from yellow to white. There were no houses by the road; so it must be either Putney Heath or Wimbledon Common.

"Have you been a driver always?"

"I was a physician once."

"But why did you stop? Weren't you good?"

"As a healer of bodies I had scant success, and several of my patients preceded me. But as a healer of the spirit I have succeeded beyond my hopes and my deserts. For though my draughts were not better nor subtler than those of other men, yet, by reason of the cunning goblets wherein I offered them, the queasy soul was ofttimes tempted to sip and be refreshed."

"The queasy soul," he murmured; "if the sun sets with trees in front of it, and you suddenly come strange all over, is that a queasy soul?"

"Have you felt that?"

"Why yes."

After a pause he told the boy a little, a very little about the journey's end. But they did not chatter much, for the boy, when he liked a person, would as soon sit silent in his company as speak, and this, he discovered, was also the mind of Sir Thomas Browne and of many others with whom he was to be acquainted. He heard, however, about the young man Shelley, who was now quite a famous person, with a carriage of his own, and about some of the other drivers who are in the service of the Company. Meanwhile the light grew stronger, though the fog did not disperse. It was now more like mist than fog, and at times would travel quickly across them, as if it was part of a cloud. They had been ascending, too, in a most puzzling way; for over two hours the horses had been pulling against the collar, and even if it were Richmond Hill they ought to have been at the top long ago. Perhaps it was Epsom, or even the North Downs; yet the air seemed keener than that which blows on either. And as to the name of their destination, Sir Thomas Browne was silent.

Crash!

"Thunder, by Jove!" said the boy, "and not so far off either. Listen to the echoes! It's more like mountains."

He thought, not very vividly, of his father and mother. He saw them sitting down to sausages and listening to the storm. He saw his own empty place. Then there would be questions, alarms, theories, jokes, consolations. They would expect him back at lunch. To lunch he would not come, nor to tea, but he would be in for dinner, and so his day's truancy would be over. If he had had his purse he would have bought them presents—not that he should have known what to get them.

Crash!

The peal and the lightning came together. The cloud quivered as if it were alive, and torn streamers of mist rushed past. "Are you afraid?" asked Sir Thomas Browne.

"What is there to be afraid of? Is it much farther?"

The horses of the omnibus stopped just as a ball of fire burst up and exploded with a ringing noise that was deafening but clear, like the noise of a blacksmith's forge. All the cloud was shattered.

"Oh, listen, Sir Thomas Browne! No, I mean look; we shall get a view at last. No, I mean listen; that sounds like a rainbow!"

The noise had died into the faintest murmur, beneath which another murmur grew, spreading stealthily, steadily, in a curve that widened but did not vary. And in widening curves a rainbow was spreading from the horses' feet into the dissolving mists.

"But how beautiful! What colors! Where will it stop? It is more like the rainbows you can tread on. More like dreams."

The color and the sound grew together. The rainbow spanned an enormous gulf. Clouds rushed under it and were pierced by it, and still it grew, reaching forward, conquering the darkness, until it touched something that seemed more solid than a cloud.

The boy stood up. "What is that out there?" he called. "What does it rest on, out at that other end?"

In the morning sunshine a precipice shone forth beyond the gulf. A precipice—or was it a castle? The horses moved. They set their feet upon the rainbow.

"Oh, look!" the boy shouted. "Oh, listen! Those caves—or are they gateways? Oh, look between those cliffs at those ledges. I see people! I see trees!"

"Look also below," whispered Sir Thomas. "Neglect not the diviner Acheron."

The boy looked below, past the flames of the rainbow that licked against their wheels. The gulf also had cleared, and in its depths there flowed an everlasting river. One sunbeam entered and struck a green pool, and as they passed over he saw three maidens rise to the surface of the pool, singing, and playing with something that glistened like a ring.

"You down in the water——" he called.

They answered, "You up on the bridge——" There was a burst of music. "You up on the bridge, good luck to you. Truth in the depth, truth on the height."

"You down in the water, what are you doing?"

Sir Thomas Browne replied: "They sport in the mancipiary possession of their gold"; and the omnibus arrived.

III

The boy was in disgrace. He sat locked up in the nursery of Agathox Lodge, learning poetry for a punishment. His father had said, "My boy! I can pardon anything but untruthfulness," and had caned him, saying at each stroke, "There is *no* omnibus, *no* driver, *no* bridge, *no* mountain; you are a *truant,* a *guttersnipe,* a *liar."* His father could be very stern at times. His mother had begged him to say he was sorry. But he could not say that. It was the greatest day of his life, in spite of the caning and the poetry at the end of it.

He had returned punctually at sunset—driven not by Sir Thomas Browne, but by a maiden lady who was full of quiet fun. They had talked of omnibuses and also of barouche landaus. How far away her gentle voice seemed now! Yet it was scarcely three hours since he had left her up the alley.

His mother called through the door. "Dear, you are to come down and to bring your poetry with you."

He came down, and found that Mr. Bons was in the smokingroom with his father. It had been a dinner party.

"Here is the great traveler!" said his father grimly. "Here is the young gentleman who drives in an omnibus over rainbows, while young ladies sing to him." Pleased with his wit, he laughed.

The Celestial Omnibus

"After all," said Mr. Bons, smiling, "there is something a little like it in Wagner. It is odd how, in quite illiterate minds, you will find glimmers of artistic truth. The case interests me. Let me plead for the culprit. We have all romanced in our time, haven't we?"

"Hear how kind Mr. Bons is," said his mother, while his father said, "Very well. Let him say his poem, and that will do. He is going away to my sister on Tuesday, and *she* will cure him of this alley-slopering." (Laughter.) "Say your poem."

The boy began, " 'Standing aloof in giant ignorance.' "

His father laughed again—roared. "One for you, my son! 'Standing aloof in giant ignorance!' I never knew these poets talked sense. Just describes you. Here, Bons, you go in for poetry. Put him through it, will you, while I fetch up the whisky?"

"Yes, give me the Keats," said Mr. Bons. "Let him say his Keats to me."

So for a few moments the wise man and the ignorant boy were left alone in the smokingroom.

" 'Standing aloof in giant ignorance, of thee I dream and of the Cyclades, as one who sits ashore and longs perchance to visit—' "

"Quite right. To visit what?"

" 'To visit dolphin coral in deep seas,' " said the boy, and burst into tears.

"Come, come! why do you cry?"

"Because—because all these words that only rhymed before, now that I've come back they're me."

Mr. Bons laid the Keats down. The case was more interesting than he had expected. *"You?"* he exclaimed. "This sonnet, *you?"*

"Yes—and look further on: 'Aye, on the shores of darkness there is light, and precipices show untrodden green.' It *is* so, sir. All these things are true."

"I never doubted it," said Mr. Bons, with closed eyes.

"You—then you believe me? You believe in the omnibus and the driver and the storm and that return ticket I got for nothing and——"

"Tut, tut! No more of your yarns, my boy. I meant that I never doubted the essential truth of poetry. Some day, when you have read more, you will understand what I mean."

"But Mr. Bons, it *is* so. There *is* light upon the shores of darkness I have seen it coming. Light and a wind."

"Nonsense," said Mr. Bons.

"If I had stopped! They tempted me. They told me to give up my ticket—for you cannot come back if you lose your ticket. They called from the river for it, and indeed I was tempted, for I have never been so happy as among those precipices. But I thought of my mother and father, and that I must fetch them. Yet they will not come, though the road starts opposite our house. It has all happened as the people up there warned me, and Mr. Bons has disbelieved me like everyone else. I have been caned. I shall never see that mountain again."

"What's that about me?" said Mr. Bons, sitting up in his chair very suddenly.

"I told them about you, and how clever you were, and how many books you had, and they said, 'Mr. Bons will certainly disbelieve you.'"

"Stuff and nonsense, my young friend. You grow impertinent. I—well—I will settle the matter. Not a word to your father. I will cure you. Tomorrow evening I will myself call here to take you for a walk, and at sunset we will go up this alley opposite and hunt for your omnibus, you silly little boy."

His face grew serious, for the boy was not disconcerted, but leapt about the room singing, "Joy! joy! I told them you would believe me. We will drive together over the rainbow. I told them that you would come." After all, could there be anything in the story? Wagner? Keats? Shelley? Sir Thomas Browne? Certainly the case was interesting.

And on the morrow evening, though it was pouring with rain, Mr. Bons did not omit to call at Agathox Lodge.

The boy was ready, bubbling with excitement, and skipping about in a way that rather vexed the President of the Literary Society. They took a turn down Buckingham Park Road, and then—having seen that no one was watching them—slipped up the alley. Naturally enough (for the sun was setting) they ran straight against the omnibus.

"Good heavens!" exclaimed Mr. Bons. "Good gracious heavens!"

It was not the omnibus in which the boy had driven first, nor yet that in which he had returned. There were three horses—black, gray, and white, the gray being the finest. The driver, who turned round at the mention of goodness and of heaven, was a sallow man with terrifying jaws and sunken eyes. Mr. Bons, on seeing him, gave a cry as if of recognition, and began to tremble violently.

The boy jumped in.

"Is it possible?" cried Mr. Bons. "Is the impossible possible?"

"Sir; come in, sir. It is such a fine omnibus. Oh, here is his name —Dan some one."

The Celestial Omnibus

Mr. Bons sprang in too. A blast of wind immediately slammed the omnibus door, and the shock jerked down all the omnibus blinds, which were very weak on their springs.

"Dan . . . Show me. Good gracious heavens! we're moving."

"Hooray!" said the boy.

Mr. Bons became flustered. He had not intended to be kidnapped. He could not find the door handle, nor push up the blinds. The omnibus was quite dark, and by the time he had struck a match, night had come on outside also. They were moving rapidly.

"A strange, a memorable adventure," he said, surveying the interior of the omnibus, which was large, roomy, and constructed with extreme regularity, every part exactly answering to every other part. Over the door (the handle of which was outside) was written, *"Lasciate ogni baldanza voi che entrate"*—at least, that was what was written, but Mr. Bons said that it was Lashy arty something, and that *baldanza* was a mistake for *speranza*. His voice sounded as if he was in church. Meanwhile, the boy called to the cadaverous driver for two return tickets. They were handed in without a word. Mr. Bons covered his face with his hand and again trembled. "Do you know who that is?" he whispered, when the little window had shut upon them. "It is the impossible."

"Well, I don't like him as much as Sir Thomas Browne, though I shouldn't be surprised if he had even more in him."

"More in him?" He stamped irritably. "By accident you have made the greatest discovery of the century, and all you can say is that there is more in this man. Do you remember those vellum books in my library, stamped with red lilies? This—sit still, I bring you stupendous news!—*this is the man who wrote them."*

The boy sat quite still. "I wonder if we shall see Mrs. Gamp?" he asked, after a civil pause.

"Mrs.———?"

"Mrs. Gamp and Mrs. Harris. I like Mrs. Harris. I came upon them quite suddenly. Mrs. Gamp's bandboxes have moved over the rainbow so badly. All the bottoms have fallen out, and two of the pippins off her bedstead tumbled into the stream."

"Out there sits the man who wrote my vellum books!" thundered Mr. Bons, "and you talk to me of Dickens and of Mrs. Gamp?"

"I know Mrs. Gamp so well," he apologized. "I could not help being glad to see her. I recognized her voice. She was telling Mrs. Harris about Mrs. Prig."

"Did you spend the whole day in her elevating company?"

"Oh, no. I raced. I met a man who took me out beyond to a racecourse. You run, and there are dolphins out at sea."

"Indeed. Do you remember the man's name?"

"Achilles. No; he was later. Tom Jones."

Mr. Bons sighed heavily. "Well, my lad, you have made a miserable mess of it. Think of a cultured person with your opportunities! A cultured person would have known all these characters and known what to have said to each. He would not have wasted his time with a Mrs. Gamp or a Tom Jones. The creations of Homer, of Shakespeare, and of Him who drives us now, would alone have contented him. He would not have raced. He would have asked intelligent questions."

"But, Mr. Bons," said the boy humbly, "you will be a cultured person. I told them so."

"True, true, and I beg you not to disgrace me when we arrive. No gossiping. No running. Keep close to my side, and never speak to these Immortals unless they speak to you. Yes, and give me the return tickets. You will be losing them."

The boy surrendered the tickets, but felt a little sore. After all, he had found the way to this place. It was hard first to be disbelieved and then to be lectured. Meanwhile, the rain had stopped, and moonlight crept into the omnibus through the cracks in the blinds.

"But how is there to be a rainbow?" cried the boy.

"You distract me," snapped Mr. Bons. "I wish to meditate on beauty. I wish to goodness I was with a reverent and sympathetic person."

The lad bit his lip. He made a hundred good resolutions. He would imitate Mr. Bons all the visit. He would not laugh, or run, or sing, or do any of the vulgar things that must have disgusted his new friends last time. He would be very careful to pronounce their names properly, and to remember who knew whom. Achilles did not know Tom Jones —at least, so Mr. Bons said. The Duchess of Malfi was older than Mrs. Gamp—at least, so Mr. Bons said. He would be self-conscious, reticent, and prim. He would never say he liked anyone. Yet, when the blinds flew up at a chance touch of his head, all these good resolutions went to the winds, for the omnibus had reached the summit of a moonlit hill, and there was the chasm, and there, across it, stood the old precipices, dreaming, with their feet in the everlasting river. He exclaimed, "The mountain! Listen to the new tune in the water! Look at the camp fires in the ravines," and Mr. Bons, after a hasty glance,

The Celestial Omnibus

retorted, "Water? Camp fires? Ridiculous rubbish. Hold your tongue. There is nothing at all."

Yet, under his eyes, a rainbow formed, compounded not of sunlight and storm, but of moonlight and the spray of the river. The three horses put their feet upon it. He thought it the finest rainbow he had seen, but did not dare to say so, since Mr. Bons said that nothing was there. He leant out—the window had opened—and sang the tune that rose from the sleeping waters.

"The prelude to Rhinegold?" said Mr. Bons suddenly. "Who taught you these leit motifs?" He, too, looked out the window. Then he behaved very oddly. He gave a choking cry, and fell back onto the omnibus floor. He writhed and kicked. His face was green.

"Does the bridge make you dizzy?" the boy asked.

"Dizzy!" gasped Mr. Bons. "I want to go back. Tell the driver."

But the driver shook his head.

"We are nearly there," said the boy. "They are asleep. Shall I call? They will be so pleased to see you, for I have prepared them."

Mr. Bons moaned. They moved over the lunar rainbow, which ever and ever broke away behind their wheels. How still the night was! Who would be sentry at the Gate?

"I am coming," he shouted, again forgetting the hundred resolutions. "I am returning—I, the boy."

"The boy is returning," cried a voice to other voices, who repeated, "The boy is returning."

"I am bringing Mr. Bons with me."

Silence.

"I should have said Mr. Bons is bringing me with him."

Profound silence.

"Who stands sentry?"

"Achilles."

And on the rocky causeway, close to the springing of the rainbow bridge he saw a young man who carried a wonderful shield.

"Mr. Bons, it is Achilles, armed."

"I want to go back," said Mr. Bons.

The last fragment of the rainbow melted, the wheels sang upon the living rock, the door of the omnibus burst open. Out leapt the boy—he could not resist—and sprang to meet the warrior, who, stooping suddenly, caught him on his shield.

"Achilles!" he cried, "let me down, for I am ignorant and vulgar, and I must wait for Mr. Bons of whom I told you yesterday."

But Achilles raised him aloft. He crouched on the wonderful shield, on heroes and burning cities, on vineyards graven in gold, on every dear passion, every joy, on the entire image of the Mountain that he had discovered, encircled, like it, with an everlasting stream. "No, no." he protested, "I am not worthy. It is Mr. Bons who must be up here."

But Mr. Bons was whimpering, and Achilles trumpeted and cried, "Stand upright upon my shield!"

"Sir, I did not mean to stand! something made me stand. Sir, why do you delay? Here is only the great Achilles, whom you knew."

Mr. Bons screamed, "I see no one. I see nothing. I want to go back." Then he cried to the driver, "Save me! Let me stop in your chariot. I have honored you. I have quoted you. I have bound you in vellum. Take me back to my world."

The driver replied, "I am the means and not the end. I am the food and not the life. Stand by yourself, as that boy has stood. I cannot save you. For poetry is a spirit; and they that would worship it must worship in spirit and in truth."

Mr. Bons—he could not resist—crawled out of the beautiful omnibus. His face appeared, gaping horribly. His hands followed, one gripping the step, the other beating the air. Now his shoulders emerged, his chest, his stomach. With a shriek of "I see London," he fell—fell against the hard, moonlit rock, fell into it as if were water, fell through it, vanished, and was seen by the boy no more.

"Where have you fallen to, Mr. Bons? Here is a procession arriving to honor you with music and torches. Here come the men and women whose names you know. The mountain is awake, the river is awake, over the race course the sea is awaking those dolphins, and it is all for you. They want you——"

There was the touch of fresh leaves on his forehead. Some one had crowned him.

ΤΕΛΟΣ

• • • • • • •

From the *Kingston Gazette, Surbiton Times* and *Raynes Park Observer*

The body of Mr. Septimus Bons has been found in a shockingly mutilated condition in the vicinity of the Bermondsey gasworks. The deceased's pockets contained a sovereign purse, a silver cigar case, a bijou pronouncing dictionary, and a couple of omnibus tickets. The unfortunate gentleman had apparently been hurled from a considerable height. Foul play is suspected, and a thorough investigation is pending by the authorities.

The Cat Who Told the Truth

SAKI

Saki, who took his pen name from the *Rubáiyát of Omar Khayyám*, was a master of what today would be called "black humor."

His real name was Hector Hugh Munro (1870–1916), and he was born of a Scottish family in Burma, where his father was inspector-general of police. His mother died before he was two, and he was sent to England to be reared by two aunts. After he finished grammar school, his father took him on many journeys through Europe, tutoring the boy all the while. At the age of twenty-three, Hector began service with the Burma police, but after a year with seven bouts of fever he returned to England and became a journalist. He acted for six years as a foreign correspondent. His first collection of stories appeared in 1904, and thereafter he turned out several other volumes, as well as a novel. At the beginning of World War I he enlisted as a private and fought in France. A brave soldier, he was killed during an attack in November, 1916.

Munro wrote some classic horror stories, but his main qualities were a sense of whimsy, love of animals, and high spirits. All these are shown in "Tobermory," one of a series of "chronicles" about a young Englishman named Clovis Sangrail, who enjoyed making fun of upper-class house parties and other boring social events. Once we make the assumption that a pet cat could learn to talk, the rest of this comic story follows naturally.

SAKI

Tobermory

*I*T WAS A CHILL, RAIN-WASHED AFTERNOON of a late August day, that indefinite season when partridges are still in security or cold storage, and there is nothing to hunt—unless one is bounded on the north by the Bristol Channel, in which case one may lawfully gallop after fat red stags. Lady Blemley's house party was not bounded on the north by the Bristol Channel, hence there was a full gathering of her guests round the tea table on this particular afternoon. And, in spite of the blankness of the season and the triteness of the occasion, there was no trace in the company of that fatigued restlessness which means a dread of the pianola and a subdued hankering for auction bridge. The undisguised open-mouthed attention of the entire party was fixed on the homely negative personality of Mr. Cornelius Appin. Of all her guests, he was the one who had come to Lady Blemley with the vaguest reputation. Someone had said he was "clever," and he had got his invitation in the moderate expectation, on the part of his hostess, that some portion at least of his cleverness would be contributed to the general entertainment. Until teatime that day she had been unable to discover in what direction, if any, his cleverness lay. He was neither a wit nor a croquet champion, a hypnotic force nor a begetter of amateur theatricals. Neither did his exterior suggest the sort of man in whom women are willing to pardon a generous measure of mental deficiency. He had subsided into mere Mr. Appin, and the Cornelius seemed a piece of transparent baptismal bluff. And now he was claiming to have launched on the world a discovery beside which the invention of gunpowder, of the printing press, and of steam locomotion were inconsiderable trifles. Science had made bewildering strides in many directions during recent decades, but this thing seemed to belong to the domain of miracle rather than to scientific achievement.

"And do you really ask us to believe," Sir Wilfrid was saying, "that you have discovered a means for instructing animals in the art of human speech, and that dear old Tobermory has proved your first successful pupil?"

"It is a problem at which I have worked for the last seventeen years," said Mr. Appin, "but only during the last eight or nine months have I been rewarded with glimmerings of success. Of course I have experimented with thousands of animals, but latterly only with cats, those wonderful creatures which have assimilated themselves so marvelously with our civilization while retaining all their highly developed feral instincts. Here and there among cats one comes across an outstanding superior intellect, just as one does among the ruck of human beings, and when I made the acquaintance of Tobermory a week ago I saw at once that I was in contact with a 'beyond-cat' of extraordinary intelligence. I had gone far along the road to success in recent experiments; with Tobermory, as you call him, I have reached the goal."

Mr. Appin concluded his remarkable statement in a voice which he strove to divest of a triumphant inflection. No one said "Rats," though Clovis' lips moved in a monosyllabic contortion which probably invoked those rodents of disbelief.

"And do you mean to say," asked Miss Resker, after a slight pause, "that you have taught Tobermory to say and understand easy sentences of one syllable?"

"My dear Miss Resker," said the wonder-worker patiently, "one teaches little children and savages and backward adults in that piecemeal fashion; when one has once solved the problem of making a beginning with an animal of highly developed intelligence one has no need for those halting methods. Tobermory can speak our language with perfect correctness."

This time Clovis very distinctly said, "Beyond-rats!" Sir Wilfrid was more polite, but equally sceptical.

"Hadn't we better have the cat in and judge for ourselves?" suggested Lady Blemley.

Sir Wilfrid went in search of the animal, and the company settled themselves down to the languid expectation of witnessing some more or less adroit drawing-room ventriloquism.

In a minute Sir Wilfrid was back in the room, his face white beneath its tan and his eyes dilated with excitement.

"By Gad, it's true!"

His agitation was unmistakably genuine, and his hearers started forward in a thrill of awakened interest.

Collapsing into an armchair he continued breathlessly: "I found him dozing in the smokingroom, and called out to him to come for his tea. He blinked at me in his usual way, and I said, 'Come on, Toby; don't keep us waiting'; and, by Gad! he drawled out in a most horribly natural voice that he'd come when he dashed well pleased! I nearly jumped out of my skin!"

Appin had preached to absolutely incredulous hearers; Sir Wilfrid's statement carried instant conviction. A Babellike chorus of startled exclamation arose, amid which the scientist sat mutely enjoying the first fruit of his stupendous discovery.

In the midst of the clamor Tobermory entered the room and made his way with velvet tread and studied unconcern across to the group seated round the tea table.

A sudden hush of awkwardness and constraint fell on the company. Somehow there seemed an element of embarrassment in addressing on equal terms a domestic cat of acknowledged mental ability.

"Will you have some milk, Tobermory?" asked Lady Blemley in a rather strained voice.

"I don't mind if I do," was the response, couched in a tone of even indifference. A shiver of suppressed excitement went through the listeners, and Lady Blemley might be excused for pouring out the saucerful of milk rather unsteadily.

"I'm afraid I've spilt a good deal of it," she said apologetically.

"After all, it's not my Axminster," was Tobermory's rejoinder.

Another silence fell on the group, and then Miss Resker, in her best district-visitor manner, asked if the human language had been difficult to learn. Tobermory looked squarely at her for a moment and then fixed his gaze serenely on the middle distance. It was obvious that boring questions lay outside his scheme of life.

"What do you think of human intelligence?" asked Mavis Pellington lamely.

"Of whose intelligence in particular?" asked Tobermory coldly.

"Oh, well, mine for instance," said Mavis, with a feeble laugh.

"You put me in an embarrassing position," said Tobermory, whose tone and attitude certainly did not suggest a shred of embarrassment. "When your inclusion in this house party was suggested Sir Wilfred protested that you were the most brainless woman of his acquaintance, and that there was a wide distinction between hospitality and the care of the feeble minded. Lady Blemley replied that your lack of brain

Tobermory

power was the precise quality which had earned you your invitation, as you were the only person she could think of who might be idiotic enough to buy their old car. You know, the one they call 'The Envy of Sisyphus,' because it goes quite nicely uphill if you push it."

Lady Blemley's protestations would have had greater effect if she had not casually suggested to Mavis only that morning that the car in question would be just the thing for her down at her Devonshire home.

Major Barfield plunged in heavily to effect a diversion.

"How about your carryings-on with the tortoiseshell puss up at the stables, eh?"

The moment he had said it everyone realized the blunder.

"One does not usually discuss these matters in public," said Tobermory frigidly. "From a slight observation of your ways since you've been in this house I should imagine you'd find it inconvenient if I were to shift the conversation on to your own little affairs."

The panic which ensued was not confined to the Major.

"Would you like to go and see if cook has got your dinner ready?" suggested Lady Blemley hurriedly, affecting to ignore the fact that it wanted at least two hours to Tobermory's dinnertime.

"Thanks," said Tobermory, "not quite so soon after my tea. I don't want to die of indigestion."

"Cats have nine lives, you know," said Sir Wilfrid heartily.

"Possibly," answered Tobermory; "but only one liver."

"Adelaide!" said Mrs. Cornett, "do you mean to encourage that cat to go out and gossip about us in the servants' hall?"

The panic had indeed become general. A narrow ornamental balustrade ran in front of most of the bedroom windows at the Towers, and it was recalled with dismay that this had formed a favorite promenade for Tobermory at all hours, whence he could watch the pigeons—and heaven knew what else besides. If he intended to become reminiscent in his present outspoken strain, the effect would be something more than disconcerting. Mrs. Cornett, who spent much time at her toilet table, and whose complexion was reputed to be of a nomadic though punctual disposition, looked as ill at ease as the Major. Miss Scrawen, who wrote fiercely sensuous poetry and led a blameless life, merely displayed irritation; if you are methodical and virtuous in private you don't necessarily want everyone to know it. Bertie van Tahn, who was so depraved at seventeen that he had long ago given up trying to be any worse, turned a dull shade of gardenia white, but he did not commit the error of dashing out of the room like Odo Finsberry, a young gentleman who was understood to be reading for the Church and who was possibly disturbed at the thought of scandals he might hear concerning other people. Clovis had the presence of mind to maintain a composed exterior; privately he was calculating how long it would take to procure a box of fancy mice through the agency of the Exchange and Mart as a species of hush money.

Even in a delicate situation like the present, Agnes Resker could not endure to remain too long in the background.

"Why did I ever come down here?" she asked dramatically.

Tobermory immediately accepted the opening.

"Judging by what you said to Mrs. Cornett on the croquet lawn yesterday, you were out for food. You described the Blemleys as the dullest people to stay with that you knew, but said they were clever enough to employ a first-rate cook; otherwise they'd find it difficult to get anyone to come down a second time."

"There's not a word of truth in it! I appeal to Mrs. Cornett—" exclaimed the discomfited Agnes.

"Mrs. Cornett repeated your remark afterwards to Bertie van Tahn," continued Tobermory, "and said, 'That woman is a regular Hunger Marcher; she'd go anywhere for four square meals a day,' and Bertie van Tahn said—"

At this point the chronicle mercifully ceased. Tobermory had caught a glimpse of the big yellow Tom from the Rectory working his way through the shrubbery towards the stable wing. In a flash he had vanished through the open French window.

With the disappearance of his too brilliant pupil Cornelius Appin found himself beset by a hurricane of bitter upbraiding, anxious inquiry, and frightened entreaty. The responsibility for the situation lay with him, and he must prevent matters from becoming worse. Could Tobermory impart his dangerous gift to other cats? was the first question he had to answer. It was possible, he replied, that he might have initiated his intimate friend the stable puss into his new accomplishment, but it was unlikely that his teaching could have taken a wider range as yet.

"Then," said Mrs. Cornett, "Tobermory may be a valuable cat and a great pet; but I'm sure you'll agree, Adelaide, that both he and the stable cat must be done away with without delay."

"You don't suppose I've enjoyed the last quarter of an hour, do you?" said Lady Blemley bitterly. "My husband and I are very fond of Tobermory—at least, we were before this horrible accomplishment was infused into him; but now, of course, the only thing is to have him destroyed as soon as possible."

"We can put some strychnine in the scraps he always gets at dinnertime," said Sir Wilfrid, "and I will go and drown the stable cat myself. The coachman will be very sore at losing his pet, but I'll say a very catching form of mange has broken out in both cats and we're afraid of it spreading to the kennels."

"But my great discovery!" expostulated Mr. Appin; "after all my years of research and experiment—"

"You can go and experiment on the shorthorns at the farm, who are under proper control," said Mrs. Cornett, "or the elephants at the Zoological Gardens. They're said to be highly intelligent, and they have this recommendation, that they don't come creeping about our bedrooms and under chairs, and so forth."

An archangel ecstatically proclaiming the Millennium, and finding that it clashed unpardonably with Henley and would have to be indefinitely postponed, could hardly have felt more crestfallen than Cornelius Appin at the reception of his wonderful achievement. Public opinion, however, was against him—in fact, had the general voice been consulted on the subject it is probable that a strong minority vote would have been in favor of including him in the strychnine diet.

Defective train arrangements and a nervous desire to see matters brought to a finish prevented an immediate dispersal of the party, but dinner that evening was not a social success. Sir Wilfrid had had rather a trying time with the stable cat and subsequently with the coachman. Agnes Resker ostentatiously limited her repast to a morsel of dry toast, which she bit as though it were a personal enemy; while Mavis Pellington maintained a vindictive silence throughout the meal. Lady Blemley kept up a flow of what she hoped was conversation, but her attention was fixed on the doorway. A plateful of carefully dosed fish scraps was in readiness on the sideboard, but sweets and savory and dessert went their way, and no Tobermory appeared either in the dining room or kitchen.

The sepulchral dinner was cheerful compared with the subsequent vigil in the smoking room. Eating and drinking had at least supplied a distraction and cloak to the prevailing embarrassment. Bridge was out of the question in the general tension of nerves and tempers, and after Odo Finsberry had given a lugubrious rendering of "Melisande in the Wood" to a frigid audience, music was tacitly avoided. At eleven the servants went to bed, announcing that the small window in the pantry had been left open as usual for Tobermory's private use. The guests read steadily through the current batch of magazines, and fell back gradually on the Badminton Library and bound volumes of *Punch.* Lady Blemley made periodic visits to the pantry, returning each time with an expression of listless depression which forestalled questioning.

At two o'clock Clovis broke the dominating silence.

"He won't turn up tonight. He's probably in the local newspaper office at the present moment, dictating the first installment of his reminiscences."

Love in the South Seas

W. SOMERSET MAUGHAM

Wherever he went, Maugham saw people who inspired him to imagine their life stories, and to write them in realistic, crystal-clear style.

William Somerset Maugham (1874–1965), son of an English couple, was born in Paris and spoke French before he spoke English. Both parents died before he was ten and he went to live with his father's brother, a clergyman in Kent. Much of his unhappy early life was used as material for his masterpiece, *Of Human Bondage*. Like Maupassant, he qualified as a doctor, but Maugham never practiced. He spent ten years in Paris, starving while teaching himself to write well. Thereafter he became during his long life a famous dramatist, novelist, and short-story author. His methods are well described in his little book, *The Summing Up* (1938). He died in the south of France at the age of eighty-one, having turned out a lengthy shelf of books.

As a vacation from his work as a British secret agent during World War I, Maugham spent several months in 1916 and 1917 visiting various islands in the Pacific. These places provided him with material for part of a novel, *The Moon and Sixpence* (1919), and half a dozen fine stories collected in *The Trembling of a Leaf* (1921). Among them is "Rain," his most notorious, and "Red," which he considered his most successful.

Maugham had wanted to go to the South Seas, he said, "ever since as a youth I had read *The Ebb-Tide* and *The Wrecker* [by Robert Louis Stevenson and Lloyd Osbourne]. . . . It was not only the beauty of the islands that took me; Herman Melville and Pierre Loti had prepared me for that . . . What excited me was to meet one person after another who was new to me . . . I filled my notebook with brief descriptions of their appearance and their character, and presently, my imagination excited by these multitudinous impressions, from a hint or incident or a happy invention, stories began to form themselves round certain of the most vivid of them." His story "Red," first printed in 1921, gives a feeling of what the South Seas were really like during the period of Maugham's visit. It is a love story, but a cruel one, and although the pace may seem slow, it marches steadily toward its incisive conclusion.

W. SOMERSET MAUGHAM

Red

*T*HE SKIPPER THRUST HIS HAND into one of his trouser pockets and with difficulty, for they were not at the sides but in front and he was a portly man, pulled out a large silver watch. He looked at it and then looked again at the declining sun. The Kanaka at the wheel gave him a glance, but did not speak. The skipper's eyes rested on the island they were approaching. A white line of foam marked the reef. He knew there was an opening large enough to get his ship through, and when they came a little nearer he counted on seeing it. They had nearly an hour of daylight still before them. In the lagoon the water was deep and they could anchor comfortably. The chief of the village which he could already see among the coconut trees was a friend of the mate's, and it would be pleasant to go ashore for the night. The mate came forward at that minute and the skipper turned to him.

"We'll take a bottle of booze along with us and get some girls in to dance," he said.

"I don't see the opening," said the mate.

He was a Kanaka, a handsome, swarthy fellow, with somewhat the look of a later Roman emperor, inclined to stoutness; but his face was fine and clean-cut.

"I'm dead sure there's one right here," said the captain, looking through his glasses. "I can't understand why I can't pick it up. Send one of the boys up the mast to have a look."

The mate called one of the crew and gave him the order. The captain watched the Kanaka climb and waited for him to speak. But the Kanaka shouted down that he could see nothing but the unbroken line of foam. The captain spoke Samoan like a native, and he cursed him freely.

"Shall he stay up there?" asked the mate.

"What the hell good does that do?" answered the captain. "The blame fool can't see worth a cent. You bet your sweet life I'd find the opening if I was up there."

He looked at the slender mast with anger. It was all very well for a native who had been used to climbing up coconut trees all his life. He was fat and heavy.

"Come down," he shouted. "You're no more use than a dead dog. We'll just have to go along the reef till we find the opening."

It was a seventy-ton schooner with paraffin auxiliary, and it ran, when there was no head wind, between four and five knots an hour. It was a bedraggled object; it had been painted white a very long time ago, but it was now dirty, dingy, and mottled. It smelt strongly of paraffin and of the copra which was its usual cargo. They were within a hundred feet of the reef now and the captain told the steersman to run along it till they came to the opening. But when they had gone a couple of miles he realized that they had missed it. He went about and slowly worked back again. The white foam of the reef continued without interruption and now the sun was setting. With a curse at the stupidity of the crew the skipper resigned himself to waiting till next morning.

"Put her about," he said. "I can't anchor here."

They went out to sea a little and presently it was quite dark. They anchored. When the sail was furled the ship began to roll a good deal. They said in Apia that one day she would roll right over; and the owner, a German-American who managed one of the largest stores, said that no money was big enough to induce him to go out in her. The cook, a Chinese in white trousers, very dirty and ragged, and a thin white tunic, came to say that supper was ready, and when the skipper went into the cabin he found the engineer already seated at table. The engineer was a long, lean man with a scraggy neck. He was dressed in blue overalls and a sleeveless jersey which showed his thin arms tattooed from elbow to wrist.

"Hell, having to spend the night outside," said the skipper.

The engineer did not answer, and they ate their supper in silence. The cabin was lit by a dim oil lamp. When they had eaten the canned apricots with which the meal finished the Chink brought them a cup of tea. The skipper lit a cigar and went on the upper deck. The island now was only a darker mass against the night. The stars were very bright. The only sound was the ceaseless breaking of the surf. The skipper sank into a deck chair and smoked idly. Presently three or four members of the crew came up and sat down. One of them had a banjo and another a concertina. They began to play, and one of them sang. The native song sounded strange on these instruments. Then to the singing a couple began to dance. It was a barbaric dance, savage and primeval, rapid, with quick movements of the hands and feet and contortions of the body; it was sensual, sexual even, but sexual without passion. It was very animal, direct, weird without mystery, natural in short, and one might almost say childlike. At last they grew tired. They stretched themselves on the deck and slept, and all was silent. The skipper lifted himself heavily out of his chair and clambered down the companion. He went into his cabin and got out of his clothes. He climbed into his bunk and lay there. He panted a little in the heat of the night.

But next morning, when the dawn crept over the tranquil sea, the opening in the reef which had eluded them the night before was seen a little to the east of where they lay. The schooner entered the lagoon. There was not a ripple on the surface of the water. Deep down among the coral rocks you saw little colored fish swim. When he had anchored his ship the skipper ate his breakfast and went on deck. The sun shone from an unclouded sky, but in the early morning the air was grateful and cool. It was Sunday, and there was a feeling of quietness, a silence as though nature were at rest, which gave him a peculiar sense of comfort. He sat, looking at the wooded coast, and felt lazy and well at ease. Presently a slow smile moved his lips and he threw the stump of his cigar into the water.

"I guess I'll go ashore," he said. "Get the boat out."

He climbed stiffly down the ladder and was rowed to a little cove. The coconut trees came down to the water's edge, not in rows, but spaced out with an ordered formality. They were like a ballet of spinsters, elderly but flippant, standing in affected attitudes with the simpering graces of a bygone age. He sauntered idly through them, along a path that could be just seen winding its tortuous way, and it led him presently to a broad creek. There was a bridge across it, but a bridge constructed of single trunks of coconut trees, a dozen of them, placed end to end and supported where they met by a forked branch driven into the bed of the creek. You walked on a smooth, round surface, narrow and slippery, and there was no support for the hand. To cross such a bridge required sure feet and a stout heart. The skipper hesitated. But he saw on the other side, nestling among the trees, a white man's house; he made up his mind and, rather gingerly, began to walk. He watched his feet carefully, and where one trunk joined on to the next and there was a difference of level, he tottered a little. It was with a gasp of relief that he reached the last tree and finally set his feet on the firm ground of the other side. He had been so intent on the difficult crossing that he never noticed anyone was watching him, and it was with surprise that he heard himself spoken to.

"It takes a bit of nerve to cross these bridges when you're not used to them."

He looked up and saw a man standing in front of him. He had evidently come out of the house which he had seen.

"I saw you hesitate," the man continued, with a smile on his lips, "and I was watching to see you fall in."

"Not on your life," said the captain, who had now recovered his confidence.

"I've fallen in myself before now. I remember, one evening I came back from shooting, and I fell in, gun and all. Now I get a boy to carry my gun for me."

He was a man no longer young, with a small beard, now somewhat grey, and a thin face. He was dressed in a singlet, without arms, and a pair of duck trousers. He wore neither shoes nor socks. He spoke English with a slight accent.

"Are you Neilson?" asked the skipper.

"I am."

"I've heard about you. I thought you lived somewhere round here."

The skipper followed his host into the little bungalow and sat down heavily in the chair which the other motioned him to take. While Neilson went out to fetch whisky and glasses he took a look round the room. It filled him with amazement. He had never seen so many books. The shelves reached from floor to ceiling on all four walls, and they were closely packed. There was a grand piano littered with music, and a large table on which books and magazines lay in disorder. The room made him feel embarrassed. He remembered that Neilson was a queer fellow. No one knew very much about him, although he had been in the islands for so many years, but those who knew him agreed that he was queer. He was a Swede.

"You've got one big heap of books here," he said, when Neilson returned.

"They do no harm," answered Neilson with a smile.

"Have you read them all?" asked the skipper.

"Most of them."

"I'm a bit of a reader myself. I have the *Saturday Evening Post* sent to me regler."

Neilson poured his visitor a good stiff glass of whisky and gave him a cigar. The skipper volunteered a little information.

"I got in last night, but I couldn't find the opening, so I had to anchor outside. I never been this run before, but my people had some stuff they wanted to bring over here. Gray, d'you know him?"

"Yes, he's got a store a little way along."

"Well, there was a lot of canned stuff that he wanted over, an' he's got some copra. They thought I might just as well come over as lie idle at Apia. I run between Apia and Pago-Pago mostly, but they've got smallpox there just now, and there's nothing stirring."

He took a drink of his whisky and lit a cigar. He was a taciturn man, but there was something in Neilson that made him nervous, and his nervousness made him talk. The Swede was looking at him with large dark eyes in which there was an expression of faint amusement.

"This is a tidy little place you've got here."

"I've done my best with it."

"You must do pretty well with your trees. They look fine. With copra at the price it is now. I had a bit of a plantation myself once, in Upolu it was, but I had to sell it."

He looked round the room again, where all those books gave him a feeling of something incomprehensible and hostile.

"I guess you must find it a bit lonesome here though," he said.

"I've got used to it. I've been here for twenty-five years."

Now the captain could think of nothing more to say, and he smoked in silence. Neilson had apparently no wish to break it. He looked at his guest with a meditative eye. He was a tall man, more than six feet high, and very stout. His face was red and blotchy, with a network of little purple veins on the cheeks, and his features were sunk into its fatness. His eyes were bloodshot. His neck was buried in rolls of fat. But for a fringe of long curly hair, nearly white, at the back of his head, he was quite bald; and that immense, shiny surface of forehead, which might have given him a false look of intelligence, on the contrary gave him one of peculiar imbecility. He wore a blue flannel shirt, open at the neck and showing his fat chest covered with a mat of reddish hair, and a very old pair of blue serge trousers. He sat in his chair in a heavy ungainly attitude, his great belly thrust forward and his fat legs uncrossed. All elasticity had gone from his

Red

limbs. Neilson wondered idly what sort of man he had been in his youth. It was almost impossible to imagine that this creature of vast bulk had ever been a boy who ran about. The skipper finished his whisky, and Neilson pushed the bottle towards him.

"Help yourself."

The skipper leaned forward and with his great hand seized it.

"And how come you in these parts anyways?" he said.

"Oh, I came out to the islands for my health. My lungs were bad and they said I hadn't a year to live. You see they were wrong."

"I meant, how come you to settle down right here?"

"I am a sentimentalist."

"Oh!"

Neilson knew that the skipper had not an idea what he meant, and he looked at him with an ironical twinkle in his dark eyes. Perhaps just because the skipper was so gross and dull a man the whim seized him to talk further.

"You were too busy keeping your balance to notice, when you crossed the bridge, but this spot is generally considered rather pretty."

"It's a cute little house you've got here."

"Ah, that wasn't here when I first came. There was a native hut, with its beehive roof and its pillars, overshadowed by a great tree with red flowers; and the croton bushes, their leaves yellow and red and golden, made a pied fence around it. And then all about were the coconut trees, as fanciful as women, and as vain. They stood at the water's edge and spent all day looking at their reflections. I was a young man then—Good Heavens, it's a quarter of a century ago—and I wanted to enjoy all the loveliness of the world in the short time allotted to me before I passed into the darkness. I thought it was the most beautiful spot I had ever seen. The first time I saw it I had a catch at my heart, and I was afraid I was going to cry. I wasn't more than twenty-five, and though I put the best face I could on it, I didn't want to die. And somehow it seemed to me that the very beauty of this place made it easier for me to accept my fate. I felt when I came here that all my past life had fallen away, Stockholm and its University, and then Bonn: it all seemed the life of somebody else, as though now at last I had achieved the reality which our doctors of philosophy—I am one myself, you know—had discussed so much. 'A year,' I cried to myself. 'I have a year. I will spend it here and then I am content to die.'

"We are foolish and sentimental and melodramatic at twenty-five, but if we weren't perhaps we should be less wise at fifty.

"Now drink, my friend. Don't let the nonsense I talk interfere with you."

He waved his thin hand towards the bottle, and the skipper finished what remained in his glass.

"You ain't drinking nothin'," he said, reaching for the whisky.

"I am of a sober habit," smiled the Swede. "I intoxicate myself in ways which I fancy are more subtle. But perhaps that is only vanity. Anyhow, the effects are more lasting and the results less deleterious."

"They say there's a deal of cocaine taken in the States now," said the captain.

Neilson chuckled.

"But I do not see a white man often," he continued, "and for once I don't think a drop of whisky can do me any harm."

He poured himself out a little, added some soda, and took a sip.

"And presently I found out why the spot had such an unearthly loveliness. Here love had tarried for a moment like a migrant bird that happens on a ship in mid-ocean and for a little while folds its tired wings. The fragance of a beautiful passion hovered over it like the fragrance of hawthorn in May in the meadows of my home. It seems to me that the places where men have loved or suffered keep about them always some faint aroma of something that has not wholly died. It is as though they had acquired a spiritual significance which mysteriously affects those who pass. I wish I could make myself clear." He smiled a little. "Though I cannot imagine that if I did you would understand."

He paused.

"I think this place was beautiful because here I had been loved beautifully." And now he shrugged his shoulders. "But perhaps it is only that my aesthetic sense is gratified by the happy conjunction of young love and a suitable setting."

Even a man less thick-witted than the skipper might have been forgiven if he were bewildered by Neilson's words. For he seemed faintly to laugh at what he said. It was as though he spoke from emotion which his intellect found ridiculous. He had said himself that he was a sentimentalist, and when sentimentality is joined with scepticism there is often the devil to pay.

He was silent for an instant and looked at the captain with eyes in which there was a sudden perplexity.

"You know, I can't help thinking that I've seen you before somewhere or other," he said.

Red

"I couldn't say as I remember you," returned the skipper.

"I have a curious feeling as though your face were familiar to me. It's been puzzling me for some time. But I can't situate my recollection in any place or at any time."

The skipper massively shrugged his heavy shoulders.

"It's thirty years since I first come to the islands. A man can't figure on remembering all the folk he meets in a while like that."

The Swede shook his head.

"You know how one sometimes has the feeling that a place one has never been to before is strangely familiar. That's how I seem to see you." He gave a whimsical smile. "Perhaps I knew you in some past existence. Perhaps, perhaps you were the master of a galley in ancient Rome and I was a slave at the oar. Thirty years have you been here?"

"Every bit of thirty years."

"I wonder if you knew a man called Red?"

"Red?"

"That is the only name I've ever known him by. I never knew him personally. I never even set eyes on him. And yet I seem to see him more clearly than many men, my brothers, for instance, with whom I passed my daily life for many years. He lives in my imagination with the distinctness of a Paolo Malatesta or a Romeo. But I daresay you have never read Dante or Shakespeare?"

"I can't say as I have," said the captain.

Neilson, smoking a cigar, leaned back in his chair and looked vacantly at the ring of smoke which floated in the still air. A smile played on his lips, but his eyes were grave. Then he looked at the captain. There was in his gross obesity something extraordinarily repellent. He had the plethoric self-satisfaction of the very fat. It was an outrage. It set Neilson's nerves on edge. But the contrast between the man before him and the man he had in mind was pleasant.

"It appears that Red was the most comely thing you ever saw. I've talked to quite a number of people who knew him in those days, white men, and they all agree that the first time you saw him his beauty just took your breath away. They called him Red on account of his flaming hair. It had a natural wave and he wore it long. It must have been of that wonderful color that the pre-Raphaelites raved over. I don't think he was vain of it, he was much too ingenuous for that, but no one could have blamed him if he had been. He was tall, six feet and an inch or two—in the native house that used to stand here was the mark of his height cut with a knife on the central trunk that supported the roof

—and he was made like a Greek god, broad in the shoulders and thin in the flanks; he was like Apollo, with just that soft roundness which Praxiteles gave him, and that suave, feminine grace which has in it something troubling and mysterious. His skin was dazzling white, milky, like satin; his skin was like a woman's."

"I had kind of a white skin myself when I was a kiddie," said the skipper, with a twinkle in his bloodshot eyes.

But Neilson paid no attention to him. He was telling his story now and interruption made him impatient.

"And his face was just as beautiful as his body. He had large blue eyes, very dark, so that some say they were black, and unlike most red-haired people he had dark eyebrows and long dark lashes. His features were perfectly regular and his mouth was like a scarlet wound. He was twenty."

On these words the Swede stopped with a certain sense of the dramatic. He took a sip of whisky.

"He was unique. There never was anyone more beautiful. There was no more reason for him than for a wonderful blossom to flower on a wild plant. He was a happy accident of nature.

"One day he landed at that cove into which you must have put this morning. He was an American sailor, and he had deserted from a man-of-war in Apia. He had induced some good-humored native to give him a passage on a cutter that happened to be sailing from Apia to Safoto, and he had been put ashore here in a dugout. I do not know why he deserted. Perhaps life on a man-of-war with its restrictions irked him, perhaps he was in trouble, and perhaps it was the South Seas and these romantic islands that got into his bones. Every now and then they take a man strangely, and he finds himself like a fly in a spider's web. It may be that there was a softness of fiber in him, and these green hills with their soft airs, this blue sea, took the northern strength from him as Delilah took the Nazarite's. Anyhow, he wanted to hide himself, and he thought he would be safe in this secluded nook till his ship had sailed from Samoa.

"There was a native hut at the cove and as he stood there, wondering where exactly he should turn his steps, a young girl came out and invited him to enter. He knew scarcely two words of the native tongue and she as little English. But he understood well enough what her smiles meant, and her pretty gestures, and he followed her. He sat down on a mat and she gave him slices of pineapple to eat. I can speak of Red only from hearsay, but I saw the girl three years after he first met her, and she was scarcely nineteen then. You cannot imagine how

Red

exquisite she was. She had the passionate grace of the hibiscus and the rich color. She was rather tall, slim, with the delicate features of her race, and large eyes like pools of still water under the palm trees; her hair, black and curling, fell down her back, and she wore a wreath of scented flowers. Her hands were lovely. They were so small, so exquisitely formed, they gave your heart-strings a wrench. And in those days she laughed easily. Her smile was so delightful that it made your knees shake. Her skin was like a field of ripe corn on a summer day. Good Heavens, how can I describe her? She was too beautiful to be real.

"And these two young things, she was sixteen and he was twenty, fell in love with one another at first sight. That is the real love, not the love that comes from sympathy, common interests, or intellectual community, but love pure and simple. That is the love that Adam felt for Eve when he awoke and found her in the garden gazing at him with dewy eyes. That is the love that draws the beasts to one another, and the gods. That is the love that makes the world a miracle. That is the love which gives life its pregnant meaning. You have never heard of the wise, cynical French duke who said that with two lovers there is always one who loves and one who lets himself be loved; it is a bitter truth to which most of us have to resign ourselves; but now and then there are two who love and two who let themselves be loved. Then one might fancy that the sun stands still as it stood when Joshua prayed to the God of Israel.

"And even now after all these years, when I think of these two, so young, so fair, so simple, and of their love, I feel a pang. It tears my heart just as my heart is torn when on certain nights I watch the full moon shining on the lagoon from an unclouded sky. There is always pain in the contemplation of perfect beauty.

"They were children. She was good and sweet and kind. I know nothing of him, and I like to think that then at all events he was ingenuous and frank. I like to think that his soul was as comely as his body. But I daresay he had no more soul than the creatures of the woods and forests who made pipes from reeds and bathed in the mountain streams when the world was young, and you might catch sight of little fawns galloping through the glade on the back of a bearded centaur. A soul is a troublesome possession and when man developed it he lost the Garden of Eden.

"Well, when Red came to the island it had recently been visited by one of those epidemics which the white man has brought to the South Seas, and one third of the inhabitants had died. It seems that the girl had lost all her near kin and she lived now in the house of distant cousins. The household consisted of two ancient crones, bowed and wrinkled, two younger women, and a man and a boy. For a few days he stayed there. But perhaps he felt himself too near the shore, with the possibility that he might fall in with white men who would reveal his hiding place; perhaps the lovers could not bear that the company of others should rob them for an instant of the delight of being together. One morning they set out, the pair of them, with the few things that belonged to the girl, and walked along a grassy path under the coconuts, till they came to the creek you see. They had to cross the bridge you crossed, and the girl laughed gleefully because he was afraid. She held his hand till they came to the end of the first tree, and then his courage failed him and he had to go back. He was obliged to take off all his clothes before he could risk it, and she carried them over for him on her head. They settled down in the empty hut that stood here. Whether she had any rights over it (land tenure is a complicated business in the islands), or whether the owner had died during the epidemic, I do not know, but anyhow no one questioned them, and they took possession. Their furniture consisted of a couple of grass mats on which they slept, a fragment of looking-glass, and a bowl or two. In this pleasant land that is enough to start housekeeping on.

"They say that happy people have no history, and certainly a happy love has none. They did nothing all day long and yet the days seemed all too short. The girl had a native name, but Red called her Sally. He picked up the easy language very quickly, and he used to lie on the mat for hours while she chattered gaily to him. He was a silent fellow, and perhaps his mind was lethargic. He smoked incessantly the cigarettes which she made him out of the native tobacco and pandanus leaf, and he watched her while with deft fingers she made grass mats. Often natives would come in and tell long stories of the old days when the island was disturbed by tribal wars. Sometimes he would go fishing on the reef, and bring home a basket full of colored fish. Sometimes at night he would go out with a lantern to catch lobster. There were plantains round the hut and Sally would roast them for their frugal meal. She knew how to make delicious messes from coconuts, and the breadfruit tree by the side of the creek gave them its fruit. On feast-days they killed a little pig and cooked it on hot stones. They bathed together in the creek; and in the evening they went down to the lagoon and paddled about in a dugout, with its great outrigger. The sea was deep blue, wine-colored at sundown, like the sea of Homeric Greece; but in the lagoon the color had an infinite variety, aquamarine and amethyst and emerald; and the setting sun turned it for a short moment to liquid gold. Then there was the color of the coral, brown, white, pink, red, purple; and the shapes it took were marvellous. It was like a magic garden, and the hurrying fish were like butterflies. It strangely lacked reality. Among the coral were pools with a floor of white sand and here, where the water was dazzling clear, it was very good to bathe. Then, cool and happy, they wandered back in the gloaming over the soft grass road to the creek, walking hand in hand, and now the myna birds filled the coconut trees with their clamor. And then the night, with that great sky shining with gold, that seemed to stretch more widely than the skies of Europe, and the soft airs that blew gently through the open hut, the long night again was all too short. She was sixteen and he was barely twenty. The dawn crept in among the wooden pillars of the hut and looked at those lovely children sleeping in one another's arms. The sun hid behind the great tattered leaves of the plantains so that it might not disturb them, and then, with playful malice, shot a golden ray, like the outstretched paw of a Persian cat, on their faces. They opened their sleepy eyes and they smiled to welcome another day. The weeks lengthened into months, and a year passed. They seemed to love one another as—I hesitate to say passionately, for passion has in it always a shade of sadness, a touch of bitterness or anguish, but as wholeheartedly, as simply and naturally as on that first day on which, meeting, they had recognized that a god was in them.

"If you had asked them I have no doubt that they would have thought it impossible to suppose their love could ever cease. Do we not know that the essential element of love is a belief in its own eternity? And yet perhaps in Red there was already a very little seed, unknown to himself and unsuspected by the girl, which would in time have grown to weariness. For one day one of the natives from the cove told them that some way down the coast at the anchorage was a British whaling ship.

" 'Gee,' he said, 'I wonder if I could make a trade of some nuts and plantains for a pound or two of tobacco.'

"The pandanus cigarettes that Sally made him with untiring hands were strong and pleasant enough to smoke, but they left him unsatisfied; and he yearned on a sudden for real tobacco, hard, rank, and pungent. He had not smoked a pipe for many months. His mouth watered at the thought of it. One would have thought some premonition of harm would have made Sally seek to dissuade him, but love possessed her so completely that it never occurred to her any power on earth could take him from her. They went into the hills together and gathered a great basket of wild oranges, green, but sweet and juicy; and they picked plantains from around the hut, and coconuts from their trees, and breadfruit and mangoes; and they carried them down to the cove. They loaded the unstable canoe with them, and Red and the native boy who had brought them the news of the ship paddled along outside the reef.

"It was the last time she ever saw him.

"Next day the boy came back alone. He was all in tears. This is the story he told. When after their long paddle they reached the ship and Red hailed it, a white man looked over the side and told them to come on board. They took the fruit they had brought with them and Red piled it up on the deck. The white man and he began to talk, and they seemed to come to some agreement. One of them went below and brought up tobacco. Red took some at once and lit a pipe. The boy imitated the zest with which he blew a great cloud of smoke from his mouth. Then they said something to him and he went into the cabin. Through the open door the boy, watching curiously, saw a bottle brought out and glasses. Red drank and smoked. They seemed to ask him something, for he shook his head and laughed. The man, the first man who had spoken to them, laughed too, and he filled Red's glass once more. They went on talking and drinking, and presently, growing tired of watching a sight that meant nothing to him, the boy curled himself upon the deck and slept. He was awakened by a kick; and, jumping to his feet, he saw that the ship was slowly sailing out of the lagoon. He caught sight of Red seated at the table, with his head resting heavily on his arms, fast asleep. He made a movement towards him, intending to wake him, but a rough hand seized his arm, and a man, with a scowl and words which he did not understand, pointed to the side. He shouted to Red, but in a moment he was seized and flung overboard. Helpless, he swam round to his canoe which was drifting a little way off, and pushed it onto the reef. He climbed in and, sobbing all the way, paddled back to shore.

"What had hapened was obvious enough. The whaler, by desertion or sickness, was short of hands, and the captain when Red came aboard had asked him to sign on; on his refusal he had made him drunk and kidnapped him.

"Sally was beside herself with grief. For three days she screamed and cried. The natives did what they could to comfort her, but she would not be comforted. She would not eat. And then, exhausted, she sank into a sullen apathy. She spent long days at the cove, watching

Red

the lagoon, in the vain hope that Red somehow or other would manage to escape. She sat on the white sand, hour after hour, with the tears running down her cheeks, and at night dragged herself wearily back across the creek to the little hut where she had been happy. The people with whom she had lived before Red came to the island wished her to return to them, but she would not; she was convinced that Red would come back, and she wanted him to find her where he had left her. Four months later she was delivered of a stillborn child, and the old woman who had come to help her through her confinement remained with her in the hut. All joy was taken from her life. If her anguish with time became less intolerable it was replaced by a settled melancholy. You would not have thought that among these people, whose emotions, though so violent, are very transient, a woman could be found capable of so enduring a passion. She never lost the profound conviction that sooner or later Red would come back. She watched for him, and every time someone crossed this slender little bridge of coconut trees she looked. It might at last be he."

Neilson stopped talking and gave a faint sigh.

"And what happened to her in the end?" asked the skipper.

Neilson smiled bitterly.

"Oh, three years afterwards she took up with another white man."

The skipper gave a fat, cynical chuckle.

"That's generally what happens to them," he said.

The Swede shot him a look of hatred. He did not know why that gross, obese man excited in him so violent a repulsion. But his thoughts wandered and he found his mind filled with memories of the past. He went back five and twenty years. It was when he first came to the island, weary of Apia, with its heavy drinking, its gambling and coarse sensuality, a sick man, trying to resign himself to the loss of the career which had fired his imagination with ambitious thoughts. He set behind him resolutely all his hopes of making a great name for himself and strove to content himself with the few poor months of careful life which was all that he could count on. He was boarding with a half-caste trader who had a store a couple of miles along the coast at the edge of a native village; and one day, wandering aimlessly along the grassy paths of the coconut groves, he had come upon the hut in which Sally lived. The beauty of the spot had filled him with a rapture so great that it was almost painful, and then he had seen Sally. She was the loveliest creature he had ever seen, and the sadness in those dark, magnificent eyes of hers affected him strangely. The Kanakas were a handsome race, and beauty was not rare among them, but it was the beauty of shapely animals. It was empty. But those tragic eyes were dark with mystery, and you felt in them the bitter complexity of the groping, human soul. The trader told him the story and it moved him.

"Do you think he'll ever come back?" asked Neilson.

"No fear. Why, it'll be a couple of years before the ship is paid off, and by then he'll have forgotten all about her. I bet he was pretty mad when he woke up and found he'd been shanghaied, and I shouldn't wonder but he wanted to fight somebody. But he'd got to grin and bear it, and I guess in a month he was thinking it the best thing that had ever happened to him that he got away from the island."

But Neilson could not get the story out of his head. Perhaps because he was sick and weakly, the radiant health of Red appealed to his imagination. Himself an ugly man, insignificant of appearance, he prized very highly comeliness in others. He had never been passionately in love, and certainly he had never been passionately loved. The mutual attraction of those two young things gave him a singular delight. It had the ineffable beauty of the Absolute. He went again to the little hut by the creek. He had a gift for languages and an energetic mind, accustomed to work, and he had already given much time to the study of the local tongue. Old habit was strong in him and he was gathering together material for a paper on the Samoan speech. The old crone who shared the hut with Sally invited him to come in and sit down. She gave him kava to drink and cigarettes to smoke. She was glad to have someone to chat with and while she talked he looked at Sally. She reminded him of the Psyche in the museum at Naples. Her features had the same clear purity of line, and though she had borne a child she had still a virginal aspect.

It was not till he had seen her two or three times that he induced her to speak. Then it was only to ask him if he had seen in Apia a man called Red. Two years had passed since his disappearance, but it was plain that she still thought of him incessantly.

It did not take Neilson long to discover that he was in love with her. It was only by an effort of will now that he prevented himself from going every day to the creek, and when he was not with Sally his thoughts were. At first, looking upon himself as a dying man, he asked only to look at her, and occasionally hear her speak, and his love gave him a wonderful happiness. He exulted in its purity. He wanted nothing from her but the opportunity to weave around her graceful person a web of beautiful fancies. But the open air, the equable temperature, the rest, the simple fare, began to have an unexpected effect on his health. His temperature did not soar at night to such alarming heights, he coughed less and began to put on weight; six months passed without his having a hemorrhage; and on a sudden he saw the possibility that he might live. He had studied his disease carefully, and the hope dawned upon him that with great care he might arrest its course. It exhilarated him to look forward once more to the future. He made plans. It was evident that any active life was out of the question, but he could live on the islands, and the small income he had, insufficient elsewhere, would be ample to keep him. He could grow coconuts; that would give him an occupation; and he would send for his books and a piano; but his quick mind saw that in all this he was merely trying to conceal from himself the desire which obsessed him.

He wanted Sally. He loved not only her beauty, but that dim soul which he divined behind her suffering eyes. He would intoxicate her with his passion. In the end he would make her forget. And in an ecstasy of surrender he fancied himself giving her too the happiness which he had thought never to know again, but had now so miraculously achieved.

He asked her to live with him. She refused. He had expected that and did not let it depress him, for he was sure that sooner or later she would yield. His love was irresistible. He told the old woman of his wishes, and found somewhat to his surprise that she and the neighbors, long aware of them, were strongly urging Sally to accept his offer. After all, every native was glad to keep house for a white man, and Neilson according to the standards of the island was a rich one. The trader with whom he boarded went to her and told her not to be a fool; such an opportunity would not come again, and after so long she could not still believe that Red would ever return. The girl's resistance only increased Neilson's desire, and what had been a very pure love now became an agonizing passion. He was determined that nothing should stand in his way. He gave Sally no peace. At last, worn out by his persistence and the persuasions, by turns pleading and angry, of everyone around her, she consented. But the day after when, exultant, he went to see her he found that in the night she had burnt down the hut in which she and Red had lived together. The old crone ran towards him full of angry abuse of Sally, but he waved her aside; it did not matter; they would build a bungalow on the place where the hut had stood. A European house would really be more convenient if he wanted to bring out a piano and a vast number of books.

And so the little wooden house was built in which he had now lived for many years, and Sally became his wife. But after the first few weeks of rapture, during which he was satisfied with what she gave him, he had known little happiness. She had yielded to him, through weariness, but she had only yielded what she set no store on. The soul which he had dimly glimpsed escaped him. He knew that she cared nothing for him. She still loved Red, and all the time she was waiting for his return. At a sign from him, Neilson knew that, notwithstanding his love, his tenderness, his sympathy, his generosity, she would leave him without a moment's hesitation. She would never give a thought to his distress. Anguish seized him and he battered at that impenetrable self of hers which sullenly resisted him. His love became bitter. He tried to melt her heart with kindness, but it remained as hard as before; he feigned indifference, but she did not notice it. Sometimes he lost his temper and abused her, and then she wept silently. Sometimes he thought she was nothing but a fraud, and that soul simply an invention of his own, and that he could not get into the sanctuary of her heart because there was no sanctuary there. His love became a prison from which he longed to escape, but he had not the strength merely to open the door—that was all it needed—and walk out into the open air. It was torture and at last he became numb and hopeless. In the end the fire burnt itself out and, when he saw her eyes rest for an instant on the slender bridge, it was no longer rage that filled his heart but impatience. For many years now they had lived together bound by the ties of habit and convenience, and it was with a smile that he looked back on his old passion. She was an old woman, for the women on the islands age quickly, and if he had no love for her any more, he had tolerance. She left him alone. He was contented with his piano and his books.

His thoughts led him to a desire for words.

"When I look back now and reflect on that brief passionate love of Red and Sally, I think that perhaps they should thank the ruthless fate that separated them when their love seemed still to be at its height. They suffered, but they suffered in beauty. They were spared the real tragedy of love."

"I don't know exactly as I get you," said the skipper.

"The tragedy of love is not death or separation. How long do you think it would have been before one or the other of them ceased to care? Oh, it is dreadfully bitter to look at a woman whom you have loved with all your heart and soul, so that you felt you could not bear to let her out of your sight, and realize that you would not mind if you never saw her again. The tragedy of love is indifference."

But while he was speaking a very extraordinary thing happened. Though he had been addressing the skipper he had not been talking to him, he had been putting his thoughts into words for himself, and with his eyes fixed on the man in front of him he had not seen him. But now an image presented itself to them, an image not of the man he saw, but of another man. It was as though he were looking into one of those distorting mirrors that make you extraordinarily squat or outrageously elongate, but here exactly the opposite took place, and in the obese, ugly old man he caught the shadowy glimpse of a stripling. He gave him now a quick, searching scrutiny. Why had a haphazard stroll brought him just to this place? A sudden tremor of his heart made him slightly breathless. An absurd suspicion seized him. What had occurred to him was impossible, and yet it might be a fact.

"What is your name?" he asked abruptly.

The skipper's face puckered and he gave a cunning chuckle. He looked then malicious and horribly vulgar.

"It's such a damned long time since I heard it that I almost forget it myself. But for thirty years now in the islands they've always called me Red."

His huge form shook as he gave a low, almost silent laugh. It was obscene. Neilson shuddered. Red was hugely amused, and from his bloodshot eyes tears ran down his cheeks.

Neilson gave a gasp, for at that moment a woman came in. She was a native, a woman of somewhat commanding presence, stout without being corpulent, dark, for the natives grow darker with age, with very grey hair. She wore a black Mother Hubbard, and its thinness showed her heavy breasts. The moment had come.

She made an observation to Neilson about some household matter and he answered. He wondered if his voice sounded as unnatural to her as it did to himself. She gave the man who was sitting in the chair by the window an indifferent glance, and went out of the room. The moment had come and gone.

Neilson for a moment could not speak. He was strangely shaken. Then he said:

"I'd be very glad if you'd stay and have a bit of dinner with me. Pot luck."

"I don't think I will," said Red. "I must go after this fellow Gray. I'll give him his stuff and then I'll get away. I want to be back in Apia tomorrow."

"I'll send a boy along with you to show you the way."

"That'll be fine."

Red heaved himself out of his chair, while the Swede called one of the boys who worked on the plantation. He told him where the skipper wanted to go, and the boy stepped along the bridge. Red prepared to follow him.

"Don't fall in," said Neilson.

"Not on your life."

Neilson watched him make his way across and when he had disappeared among the coconuts he looked still. Then he sank heavily in his chair. Was that the man whom Sally had loved all these years and for whom she had waited so desperately? It was grotesque. A sudden fury seized him so that he had an instinct to spring up and smash everything around him. He had been cheated. They had seen each other at last and had not known it. He began to laugh, mirthlessly, and his laughter grew till it became hysterical. The gods had played him a cruel trick. And he was old now.

At last Sally came in to tell him dinner was ready. He sat down in front of her and tried to eat. He wondered what she would say if he told her now that the fat old man sitting in the chair was the lover whom she remembered still with the passionate abandonment of her youth. Years ago, when he hated her because she made him so unhappy, he would have been glad to tell her. He wanted to hurt her then as she hurt him, because his hatred was only love. But now he did not care. He shrugged his shoulders listlessly.

"What did that man want?" she asked presently.

He did not answer at once. She was old too, a fat old native woman. He wondered why he had ever loved her so madly. He had laid at her feet all the treasures of his soul, and she had cared nothing for them. Waste, what waste! And now, when he looked at her, he felt only contempt. His patience was at last exhausted. He answered her question.

"He's the captain of a schooner. He's come from Apia."

"Yes."

"He brought me news from home. My eldest brother is very ill and I must go back."

"Will you be gone long?"

He shrugged his shoulders.

The Young Dancer and the Fat Man

KATHERINE MANSFIELD

Mistress of the impressionistic story in which, at a crucial moment, a whole life is revealed, Katherine Mansfield markedly influenced the trend of the short story.

Kathleen Mansfield Beauchamp (1888–1923) was born in Wellington, New Zealand, and much of her fiction describes her girlhood in that South Pacific member of the British Commonwealth. Her first story was published when she was nine. She went to school in London from 1903 to 1906, and after returning home went to Europe in 1908 to study music and work as a writer for the rest of her short life. She married J. Middleton Murray, writer and editor, in 1918. Her later years were overshadowed by a fatal case of tuberculosis.

"Her First Ball" might be called, in William Blake's words, a "song of innocence," in contrast with Katherine Mansfield's later and darker "songs of experience." No one has excelled her in writing about the emotions of young people. Like Anton Chekhov and James Joyce, she was chiefly interested in character revelation rather than a complex plot. Most of her stories give the feeling that spontaneous and fresh impressions were quickly put down, but her flowing prose, with overtones of poetry, was the result of careful revision. She lived as well as wrote, and as she once said: "To be rooted in life, that's what I want." Katherine Anne Porter, writing in 1937, said of her: "She states no belief, gives no motive, airs no theories, but simply presents to the reader a situation, a place, and a character, and there it is; and the emotional content is present as implicitly as the germ in a grain of wheat."

KATHERINE MANSFIELD

Her First Ball

*E*XACTLY WHEN THE BALL began Leila would have found it hard to say. Perhaps her first real partner was the cab. It did not matter that she shared the cab with the Sheridan girls and their brother. She sat back in her own little corner of it, and the bolster on which her hand rested felt like the sleeve of an unknown young man's dress suit; and away they bowled, past waltzing lampposts and houses and fences and trees.

"Have you really never been to a ball before, Leila? But, my child, how too weird—" cried the Sheridan girls.

"Our nearest neighbor was fifteen miles," said Leila softly, gently opening and shutting her fan.

Oh, dear, how hard it was to be indifferent like the others! She tried not to smile too much; she tried not to care. But every single thing was so new and exciting . . . Meg's tuberoses, Jose's long loop of amber, Laura's little dark head, pushing above her white fur like a flower through snow. She would remember forever. It even gave her a pang to see her cousin Laurie throw away the wisps of tissue paper he pulled from the fastenings of his new gloves. She would like to have kept those wisps as a keepsake, as a remembrance. Laurie leaned forward and put his hand on Laura's knee.

"Look here, darling," he said. "The third and the ninth as usual. Twig?"

Oh, how marvellous to have a brother! In her excitement Leila felt that if there had been time, if it hadn't been impossible, she couldn't have helped crying because she was an only child, and no brother had ever said "Twig?" to her; no sister would ever say, as Meg said to Jose that moment, "I've never known your hair to go up more successfully than it has tonight!"

Her First Ball

But, of course, there was no time. They were at the drill hall already; there were cabs in front of them and cabs behind. The road was bright on either side with moving fanlike lights, and on the pavement gay couples seemed to float through the air; little satin shoes chased each other like birds.

"Hold on to me, Leila; you'll get lost," said Laura.

"Come on, girls, let's make a dash for it," said Laurie.

Leila put two fingers on Laura's pink velvet cloak, and they were somehow lifted past the big golden lantern, carried along the passage, and pushed into the little room marked "Ladies." Here the crowd was so great there was hardly space to take off their things; the noise was deafening. Two benches on either side were stacked high with wraps. Two old women in white aprons ran up and down tossing fresh armfuls. And everybody was pressing forward trying to get at the little dressing table and mirror at the far end.

A great quivering jet of gas lighted the ladies' room. It couldn't wait; it was dancing already. When the door opened again and there came a burst of tuning from the drill hall, it leaped almost to the ceiling.

Dark girls, fair girls were patting their hair, tying ribbons again, tucking handkerchiefs down the fronts of their bodices, smoothing marble-white gloves. And because they were all laughing it seemed to Leila that they were all lovely.

"Aren't there any invisible hairpins?" cried a voice. "How most extraordinary! I can't see a single invisible hairpin."

"Powder my back, there's a darling," cried someone else.

"But I must have a needle and cotton. I've torn simply miles and miles of the frill," wailed a third.

Then, "Pass them along, pass them along!" The straw basket of programs was tossed from arm to arm. Darling little pink-and-silver programs, with pink pencils and fluffy tassels. Leila's fingers shook as she took one out of the basket. She wanted to ask someone, "Am I meant to have one too?" but she had just time to read: "Waltz 3. *Two, Two in a Canoe.* Polka 4. *Making the Feathers Fly,*" when Meg cried, "Ready, Leila?" and they pressed their way through the crush in the passage towards the big double doors of the drill hall.

Dancing had not begun yet, but the band had stopped tuning, and the noise was so great it seemed that when it did begin to play it would never be heard. Leila, pressing close to Meg, looking over Meg's shoulder, felt that even the little quivering colored flags strung across the ceiling were talking. She quite forgot to be shy; she forgot how in the middle of dressing she had sat down on the bed with one shoe off and one shoe on and begged her mother to ring up her cousins and say she couldn't go after all. And the rush of longing she had had to be sitting on the veranda of their forsaken up-country home, listening to the baby owls crying "More pork" in the moonlight, was changed to a rush of joy so sweet that it was hard to bear alone. She clutched her fan, and, gazing at the gleaming, golden floor, the azaleas, the lanterns, the stage at one end with its red carpet and gilt chairs and the band in a corner, she thought breathlessly, "How heavenly; how simply heavenly!"

All the girls stood grouped together at one side of the doors, the men at the other, and the chaperones in dark dresses, smiling rather foolishly, walked with little careful steps over the polished floor towards the stage.

"This is my little country cousin Leila. Be nice to her. Find her partners; she's under my wing," said Meg, going up to one girl after another.

Strange faces smiled at Leila—sweetly, vaguely. Strange voices answered, "Of course, my dear." But Leila felt the girls didn't really see her. They were looking towards the men. Why didn't the men begin? What were they waiting for? There they stood, smoothing their gloves, patting their glossy hair, and smiling among themselves. Then, quite suddenly, as if they had only just made up their minds that that was what they had to do, the men came gliding over the parquet. There was a joyful flutter among the girls. A tall, fair man flew up to Meg, seized her program, scribbled something; Meg passed him on to Leila. "May I have the pleasure? He ducked and smiled. There came a dark man wearing an eyeglass, then cousin Laurie with a friend, and Laura with a little freckled fellow whose tie was crooked. Then quite an old man—fat, with a big bald patch on his head—took her program and murmured, "Let me see, let me see!" And he was a long time comparing his program, which looked black with names, with hers. It seemed to give him so much trouble that Leila was ashamed. "Oh, please don't bother," she said eagerly. But instead of replying the fat man wrote something, glanced at her again. "Do I remember this bright little face?" he said softly. "Is it known to me of yore?" At that moment the band began playing; the fat man disappeared. He was tossed away on a great wave of music that came flying over the gleaming floor, breaking the groups up into couples, scattering them, sending them spinning. . . .

Leila had learned to dance at boarding school. Every Saturday afternoon the boarders were hurried off to a little corrugated iron mission hall where Miss Eccles (of London) held her "select" classes.

But the difference between that dusty-smelling hall—with calico texts on the walls, the poor terrified little woman in a brown velvet toque with rabbit's ears thumping the cold piano, Miss Eccles poking the girls' feet with her long white wand—and this was so tremendous that Leila was sure if her partner didn't come and she had to listen to the marvelous music and to watch the others sliding, gliding over the golden floor, she would die at least, or faint, or lift her arms and fly out of one of those dark windows that showed the stars.

"Ours, I think——" Someone bowed, smiled, and offered her his arm; she hadn't to die after all. Someone's hand pressed her waist, and she floated away like a flower that is tossed into a pool.

"Quite a good floor, isn't it?" drawled a faint voice close to her ear.

"I think it's most beautifully slippery," said Leila.

"Pardon!" The faint voice sounded surprised. Leila said it again And there was a tiny pause before the voice echoed, "Oh, quite!" and she was swung round again.

He steered so beautifully. That was the great difference between dancing with girls and men, Leila decided. Girls banged into each other, and stamped on each other's feet; the girl who was gentleman always clutched you so.

The azaleas were separate flowers no longer; they were pink and white flags streaming by.

"Were you at the Bells' last week?" the voice came again. It sounded tired. Leila wondered whether she ought to ask him if he would like to stop.

"No, this is my first dance," said she.

Her partner gave a little gasping laugh. "Oh, I say," he protested.

"Yes, it is really the first dance I've ever been to." Leila was most fervent. It was such a relief to be able to tell somebody. "You see, I've lived in the country all my life up until now. . . ."

At that moment the music stopped, and they went to sit on two chairs against the wall. Leila tucked her pink satin feet under and fanned herself, while she blissfully watched the other couples passing and disappearing through the swing doors.

"Enjoying yourself, Leila?" asked Jose, nodding her golden head.

Laura passed and gave her the faintest little wink; it made Leila wonder for a moment whether she was quite grown up after all. Certainly her partner did not say very much. He coughed, tucked his handkerchief away, pulled down his waistcoat, took a minute thread off his sleeve. But it didn't matter. Almost immediately the band started, and her second partner seemed to spring from the ceiling.

"Floor's not bad," said the new voice. Did one always begin with the floor? And then, "Were you at the Neaves' on Tuesday?" And again Leila explained. Perhaps it was a little strange that her partners were not more interested. For it was thrilling. Her first ball! She was only at the beginning of everything. It seemed to her that she had never known what the night was like before. Up till now it had been dark, silent, beautiful very often—oh, yes—but mournful somehow. Solemn. And now it would never be like that again—it had opened dazzling bright.

"Care for an ice?" said her partner. And they went through the swing doors, down the passage, to the supper room. Her cheeks burned, she was fearfully thirsty. How sweet the ices looked on little glass plates, and how cold the frosted spoon was, iced too! And when they came back to the hall there was the fat man waiting for her by the door. It gave her quite a shock again to see how old he was; he ought to have been on the stage with the fathers and mothers. And when Leila compared him with her other partners he looked shabby. His waistcoat was creased, there was a button off his glove, his coat looked as if it was dusty with French chalk.

"Come along, little lady," said the fat man. He scarcely troubled to clasp her, and they moved away so gently, it was more like walking than dancing. But he said not a word about the floor. "Your first dance, isn't it?" he murmured.

"How *did* you know?"

"Ah," said the fat man, "that's what it is to be old!" He wheezed faintly as he steered her past an awkward couple. "You see, I've been doing this kind of thing for the last thirty years."

"Thirty years?" cried Leila. Twelve years before she was born!

"It hardly bears thinking about, does it?" said the fat man gloomily. Leila looked at his bald head, and she felt quite sorry for him.

"I think it's marvelous to be still going on," she said kindly.

"Kind little lady," said the fat man, and he pressed her a little closer, and hummed a bar of the waltz. "Of course," he said, "you can't hope to last anything like as long as that. No-o," said the fat man, "long before that you'll be sitting up there on the stage, looking on, in your nice black velvet. And these pretty arms will have turned into little short fat ones, and you'll beat time with such a different kind of fan—a black bony one." The fat man seemed to shudder. "And you'll smile away like the poor old dears up there, and point to your daughter, and tell the elderly lady next to you how some dreadful man tried to kiss her at the club ball. And your heart will ache, ache"—the fat

Her First Ball

man squeezed her closer still, as if he really was sorry for that poor heart—"because no one wants to kiss you now. And you'll say how unpleasant these polished floors are to walk on, how dangerous they are. Eh, Mademoiselle Twinkletoes?" said the fat man softly.

Leila gave a light little laugh, but she did not feel like laughing. Was it—could it all be true? It sounded terribly true. Was this first ball only the beginning of her last ball after all? At that the music seemed to change; it sounded sad, sad; it rose upon a great sigh. Oh, how quickly things changed! Why didn't happiness last forever? Forever wasn't a bit too long.

"I want to stop," she said in a breathless voice. The fat man led her to the door.

"No," she said, "I won't go outside. I won't sit down. I'll just stand here, thank you." She leaned against the wall, tapping with her foot, pulling up her gloves and trying to smile. But deep inside her a little girl threw her pinafore over her head and sobbed. Why had he spoiled it all:

"I say, you know," said the fat man, "you mustn't take me seriously, little lady."

"As if I should!" said Leila, tossing her small dark head and sucking her underlip. . . .

Again the couples paraded. The swing doors opened and shut. Now new music was given out by the bandmaster. But Leila didn't want to dance any more. She wanted to be home, or sitting on the veranda listening to those baby owls. When she looked through the dark windows at the stars, they had long beams like wings. . . .

But presently a soft, melting, ravishing tune began, and a young man with curly hair bowed before her. She would have to dance, out of politeness, until she could find Meg. Very stiffly she walked into the middle; very haughtily she put her hand on his sleeve. But in one minute, in one turn, her feet glided, glided. The lights, the azaleas, the dresses, the pink faces, the velvet chairs, all became one beautiful flying wheel. And when her next partner bumped her into the fat man and he said, "Par*don,*" she smiled at him more radiantly than ever. She didn't even recognize him again.

Purely What Really Happened

ERNEST HEMINGWAY

Hemingway's revolutionary return to the simple style made him quite possibly the most influential writer of English prose in our century, and he was widely imitated in many countries.

Ernest Miller Hemingway (1898–1961) was born in Oak Park, Illinois, the son of a doctor. He attempted to excel in many sports, often getting injured through his zeal. After high school, he skipped college and became a reporter on the Kansas City *Star*. Thereafter he prided himself on being an outstanding journalist, and much of his fiction has the terseness demanded by a wide readership. He volunteered in 1917 for service in World War I, and was assigned to combat duty with the Italians on their front. Recovering from many dangerous wounds received when a mortar shell hit his post in July, 1918, he returned to news reporting and became one of the famed expatriates in post-war Paris. Later he spent much time as a sportsman and traveler, and was an outstanding correspondent during the Spanish Civil War of 1936–39 and World War II. He lived a violent life and died a violent death, and much of his writing expresses the perilousness of twentieth-century existence and the need for courage "in our time."

The award of the Nobel Prize for literature that went to him in 1954 for "forceful and style-making mastery of the art of modern narration" was a recognition that his rather narrow shelf of stories, novels, and travel books had made him an international figure.

"My Old Man," first published in France when he was twenty-five, reveals between the lines feeling that is the opposite of sentimentality. Although he struck his readers as original, many writings influenced Hemingway, including the rule-book for reporters on his newspapers and the King James version of the Bible. Some writers to whom he was indebted were Mark Twain, Stephen Crane, Gertrude Stein, Sherwood Anderson, F. Scott Fitzgerald, and Ivan Turgenev. But he wrote as he thought; in his case the style certainly was the man. His creed as an author was "to know what you really felt, to put down purely what really happened, what the actual things were that produced the emotions you experienced."

ERNEST HEMINGWAY

My Old Man

I GUESS looking at it, now, my old man was cut out for a fat guy, one of those regular little roly fat guys you see around, but he sure never got that way, except a little toward the last, and then it wasn't his fault, he was riding over the jumps only and he could afford to carry plenty of weight then. I remember the way he'd pull on a rubber shirt over a couple of jerseys and a big sweat shirt over that, and get me to run with him in the forenoon in the hot sun. He'd have, maybe, taken a trial trip with one of Razzo's skins early in the morning after just getting in from Torino at four o'clock in the morning and beating it out to the stables in a cab and then with the dew all over everything and the sun just starting to get going, I'd help him pull off his boots and he'd get into a pair of sneakers and all these sweaters and we'd start out.

"Come on, kid," he'd say, stepping up and down on his toes in front of the jock's dressing room, "let's get moving."

Then we'd start off jogging around the infield once, maybe, with him ahead, running nice, and then turn out the gate and along one of those roads with all the trees along both sides of them that run out from San Siro. I'd go ahead of him when we hit the road and I could run pretty stout and I'd look around and he'd be jogging easy just behind me and after a little while I'd look around again and he'd begun to sweat. Sweating heavy and he'd just be dogging it along with his eyes on my back, but when he'd catch me looking at him he'd grin and say, "Sweating plenty?" When my old man grinned, nobody could help but grin too. We'd keep right on running out toward the mountains and then my old man would yell, "Hey, Joe!" and I'd look back and he'd be sitting under a tree with a towel he'd had around his waist wrapped around his neck.

I'd come back and sit down beside him and he'd pull a rope out of his pocket and start skipping rope out in the sun with the sweat pouring off his face and him skipping rope out in the white dust with the rope going cloppetty, cloppetty, clop, clop, clop, and the sun hotter, and him working harder up and down a patch of the road. Say, it was a treat to see my old man skip rope, too. He could whirr it fast or lop it slow and fancy. Say, you ought to have seen wops look at us sometimes, when they'd come by, going into town walking along with big white steers hauling the cart. They sure looked as though they thought the old man was nuts. He'd start the rope whirring till they'd stop dead still and watch him, then give the steers a cluck and a poke with the goad and get going again.

When I'd sit watching him working out in the hot sun I sure felt fond of him. He sure was fun and he done his work so hard and he'd finish up with a regular whirring that'd drive the sweat out of his face like water and then sling the rope at the tree and come over and sit down with me and lean back against the tree with the towel and a sweater wrapped around his neck.

"Sure is hell keeping it down, Joe," he'd say and lean back and shut his eyes and breathe long and deep, "it ain't like when you're a kid." Then he'd get up before he started to cool and we'd jog along back to the stables. That's the way it was keeping down to weight. He was worried all the time. Most jocks can just about ride off all they want to. A jock loses about a kilo every time he rides, but my old man was sort of dried out and he couldn't keep down his kilos without all that running.

I remember once at San Siro, Regoli, a little wop, that was riding for Buzoni, came out across the paddock going to the bar for something cool; and flicking his boots with his whip, after he'd just weighed in and my old man had just weighed in too, and came out with the saddle under his arm looking red-faced and tired and too big for his silks and he stood there looking at young Regoli standing up to the outdoors bar, cool and kid-looking, and I says, "What's the matter, Dad?" 'cause I thought maybe Regoli had bumped him or something, and he just looked at Regoli and said, "Oh, to hell with it," and went on to the dressing room.

Well, it would have been all right, maybe, if we'd stayed in Milan and ridden at Milan and Torino, 'cause if there ever were any easy courses, it's those two. "Pianola, Joe," my old man said when he dismounted in the winning stall after what the wops thought was a

My Old Man

hell of a steeplechase. I asked him once. "This course rides itself. It's the pace you're going at that makes riding the jumps dangerous, Joe. We ain't going any pace here, and they ain't any really bad jumps either. But it's the pace always—not the jumps that makes the trouble."

San Siro was the swellest course I'd ever seen but the old man said it was a dog's life. Going back and forth between Mirafiore and San Siro and riding just about every day in the week with a train ride every other night.

I was nuts about the horses, too. There's something about it, when they come out and go up the track to the post. Sort of dancy and tight-looking with the jock keeping a tight hold on them and maybe easing off a little and letting them run a little going up. Then once they were at the barrier it got me worse than anything. Especially at San Siro with that big green infield and the mountains way off and the fat wop starter with his big whip and the jocks fiddling them around and then the barrier snapping up and that bell going off and them all getting off in a bunch and then commencing to string out. You know the way a bunch of skins gets off. If you're up in the stand with a pair of glasses all you see is them plunging off and then that bell goes off and it seems like it rings for a thousand years and then they come sweeping round the turn. There wasn't ever anything like it for me.

But my old man said one day, in the dressing room, when he was getting into his street clothes, "None of these things are horses, Joe. They'd kill that bunch of skates for their hides and hoofs up at Paris." That was the day he'd won the Premio Commercio with Lantorna shooting her out of the field the last hundred meters like pulling a cork out of a bottle.

It was right after the Premio Commercio that we pulled out and left Italy. My old man and Holbrook and a fat wop in a straw hat that kept wiping his face with a handkerchief were having an argument at a table in the Galleria. They were all talking French and the two of them were after my old man about something. Finally he didn't say anything any more but just sat there and looked at Holbrook, and the two of them kept after him, first one talking and then the other, and the fat wop always butting in on Holbrook.

"You go out and buy me a *Sportsman,* will you, Joe?" my old man said, and handed me a couple of soldi without looking away from Holbrook.

So I went out of the Galleria and walked over to in front of the Scala and bought a paper, and came back and stood a little way away because I didn't want to butt in and my old man was sitting back in his chair looking down at his coffee and fooling with a spoon and Holbrook and the big wop were standing and the big wop was wiping his face and shaking his head. And I came up and my old man acted just as though the two of them weren't standing there and said, "Want an ice, Joe?" Holbrook looked down at my old man and said slow and careful, "You son of a b———," and he and the fat wop went out through the tables.

My old man sat there and sort of smiled at me, but his face was white and he looked sick as hell and I was scared and felt sick inside because I knew something had happened and I didn't see how anybody could call my old man a son of a b———, and get away with it. My old man opened up the *Sportsman* and studied the handicaps for a while and then he said, "You got to take a lot of things in this world, Joe." And three days later we left Milan for good on the Turin train for Paris, after an auction sale out in front of Turner's stables of everything we couldn't get into a trunk and a suitcase.

We got into Paris early in the morning in a long, dirty station the old man told me was the Gare de Lyon. Paris was an awful big town after Milan. Seems like in Milan everybody is going somewhere and all the trams run somewhere and there ain't any sort of a mix-up, but Paris is all balled up and they never do straighten it out. I got to like it, though, part of it, anyway, and say, it's got the best racecourses in the world. Seems as though that were the thing that keeps it all going and about the only thing you can figure on is that every day the buses will be going out to whatever track they're running at, going right out through everything to the track. I never really got to know Paris well, because I just came in about once or twice a week with the old man from Maisons and he always sat at the Café de la Paix on the Opera side with the rest of the gang from Maisons and I guess that's one of the busiest parts of the town. But, say, it is funny that a big town like Paris wouldn't have a Galleria, isn't it?

Well, we went out to live at Maisons-Lafitte, where just about everybody lives except the gang at Chantilly, with a Mrs. Meyers that runs a boardinghouse. Maisons is about the swellest place to live I've ever seen in all my life. The town ain't so much, but there's a lake and a swell forest that we used to go off bumming in all day, a couple of us kids, and my old man made me a slingshot and we got a lot of things with it but the best one was a magpie. Young Dick Atkinson shot a rabbit with it one day and we put it under a tree and were all sitting around and Dick had some cigarettes and all of a sudden the rabbit jumped up and beat it into the brush and we chased it but we couldn't

My Old Man

find it. Gee, we had fun at Maisons. Mrs. Meyers used to give me lunch in the morning and I'd be gone all day. I learned to talk French quick. It's an easy language.

As soon as we got to Maisons, my old man wrote to Milan for his license and he was pretty worried till it came. He used to sit around the Café de Paris in Maisons with the gang, there were lots of guys he'd known when he rode up at Paris, before the war, lived at Maisons, and there's a lot of time to sit around because the work around a racing stable, for the jocks, that is, is all cleaned up by nine o'clock in the morning. They take the first batch of skins out to gallop them at 5:30 in the morning and they work the second lot at 8 o'clock. That means getting up early all right and going to bed early, too. If a jock's riding for somebody too, he can't go boozing around, because the trainer always has an eye on him, if he's a kid and if he ain't a kid he's always got an eye on himself. So mostly if a jock ain't working he sits around the Café de Paris with the gang and they can all sit around about two or three hours in front of some drink like a vermouth and seltz and they talk and tell stories and shoot pool and it's sort of like a club or the Galleria in Milan. Only it ain't really like the Galleria because there everybody is going by all the time and there's everybody around at the tables.

Well, my old man got his license all right. They sent it through to him without a word and he rode a couple of times. Amiens, up country and that sort of thing, but he didn't seem to get any engagement. Everybody liked him and whenever I'd come in to the Café in the forenoon I'd find somebody drinking with him because my old man wasn't tight like most of these jockeys that have got the first dollar they made riding at the World's Fair in St. Louis in nineteen ought four. That's what my old man would say when he'd kid George Burns. But it seemed like everybody steered clear of giving my old man any mounts.

We went out to wherever they were running every day with the car from Maisons and that was the most fun of all. I was glad when the horses came back from Deauville and the summer. Even though it meant no more bumming in the woods, 'cause then we'd ride to Enghien or Tremblay or St. Cloud and watch them from the trainers' and jockeys' stand. I sure learned about racing from going out with that gang and the fun of it was going every day.

I remember once out at St. Cloud. It was a big two hundred thousand franc race with seven entries and Kzar a big favorite. I went around to the paddock to see the horses with my old man and you never saw such horses. This Kzar is a great big yellow horse that looks like just nothing but run. I never saw such a horse. He was being led around the paddocks with his head down and when he went by me I felt all hollow inside, he was so beautiful. There never was such a wonderful, lean, running-built horse. And he went around the paddock putting his feet just so and quiet and careful and moving easy, like he knew just what he had to do and not jerking and standing up on his legs and getting wild-eyed like you see these selling platers with a shot of dope in them. The crowd was so thick I couldn't see him again except just his legs going by and some yellow and my old man started out through the crowd and I followed him over to the jock's dressing room back in the trees and there was a big crowd around there, too, but the man at the door in a derby nodded to my old man and we got in and everybody was sitting around and getting dressed and pulling shirts over their heads and pulling boots on and it all smelled hot and sweaty and linimenty and outside was the crowd looking in.

The old man went over and sat down beside George Gardner that was getting into his pants and said, "What's the dope, George?" just in an ordinary tone of voice 'cause there ain't any use him feeling around because George either can tell him or he can't tell him.

"He won't win," George says very low, leaning over and buttoning the bottoms of his pants.

"Who will?" my old man says, leaning over close so nobody can hear.

"Kircubbin," George says, "and if he does, save me a couple of tickets."

My old man says something in a regular voice to George and George says, "Don't ever bet on anything, I tell you," kidding like, and we beat it out and through all the crowd that was looking in over to the hundred franc mutuel machine. But I knew something big was up because George is Kzar's jockey. On the way he gets one of the yellow odds-sheets with the starting prices on and Kzar is only paying five for ten. Cefisidote is next at three to one and fifth down the list this Kircubbin at eight to one. My old man bets five thousand on Kircubbin to win and puts on a thousand to place and we went around back of the grandstand to go up the stairs and get a place to watch the race.

We were jammed in tight and first a man in a long coat with a gray tall hat and a whip folded up in his hand came out and then one after another the horses, with the jocks up and a stable boy holding the bridle on each side and walking along, followed the old guy. That big yellow horse Kzar came first. He didn't look so big when you first looked at him until you saw the length of his legs and the whole way

My Old Man

he's built and the way he moves. Gosh, I never saw such a horse. George Gardner was riding him and they moved along slow, back of the old guy in the gray tall hat that walked along like he was the ringmaster in a circus. Back of Kzar, moving along smooth and yellow in the sun, was a good-looking black with a nice head with Tommy Archibald riding him; and after the black was a string of five more horses all moving along slow in a procession past the grandstand and the pesage. My old man said the black was Kircubbin and I took a good look at him and he was a nice-looking horse, all right, but nothing like Kzar.

Everybody cheered Kzar when he went by and he sure was one swell-looking horse. The procession of them went around on the other side past the pelouse and then back up to the near end of the course and the circus master had the stable boys turn them loose one after another so they could gallop by the stands on their way up to the post and let everybody have a good look at them. They weren't at the post hardly any time at all when the gong started and you could see them way off across the infield all in a bunch, starting on the first swing like a lot of little toy horses. I was watching them through the glasses and Kzar was running well back, with one of the bays making the pace. They swept down and around and came pounding past and Kzar was way back when they passed us and this Kircubbin horse in front and going smooth. Gee, it's awful when they go by you and then you have to watch them go farther away and get smaller and smaller and then all bunched up on the turns and then come around towards into the stretch and you feel like swearing and goddamming worse and worse. Finally they made the last turn and came into the straightaway with this Kircubbin horse way out in front. Everybody was looking funny and saying "Kzar" in sort of a sick way and them pounding nearer down the stretch, and then something came out of the pack right into my glasses like a horse-headed yellow streak and everybody began to yell "Kzar" as though they were crazy. Kzar came on faster than I'd ever seen anything in my life and pulled up on Kircubbin that was going fast as any black horse could go with the jock flogging hell out of him with the gad and they were right dead neck and neck for a second but Kzar seemed going about twice as fast with those great jumps and that head out—but it was while they were neck and neck that they passed the winning post and when the numbers went up in the slots the first one was 2 and that meant Kircubbin had won.

I felt all trembly and funny inside, and then we were all jammed in with the people going downstairs to stand in front of the board where they'd post what Kircubbin paid. Honest, watching the race I'd forgot how much my old man had bet on Kircubbin. I'd wanted Kzar to win so damned bad. But now it was all over it was swell to know we had the winner.

"Wasn't it a swell race, Dad?" I said to him.

He looked at me sort of funny with his derby on the back of his head. "George Gardner's a swell jockey, all right," he said. "It sure took a great jock to keep that Kzar horse from winning."

Of course I knew it was funny all the time. But my old man saying that right out like that sure took the kick all out of it for me and I didn't get the real kick back again ever, even when they posted the numbers up on the board and the bell rang to pay off and we saw that Kircubbin paid 67.50 for 10. All round people were saying, "Poor Kzar! Poor Kzar!" And I thought, I wish I were a jockey and could have rode him instead of that son of a b———. And that was funny, thinking of George Gardner as a son of a b——— because I'd always liked him and besides he'd given us the winner, but I guess that's what he is, all right.

My old man had a big lot of money after that race and he took to coming into Paris oftener. If they raced at Tremblay he'd have them drop him in town on their way back to Maisons, and he and I'd sit out in front of the Café de la Paix and watch the people go by. It's funny sitting there. There's streams of people going by and all sorts of guys come up and want to sell you things, and I loved to sit there with my old man. That was when we'd have the most fun. Guys would come by selling funny rabbits that jumped if you squeezed a bulb and they'd come up to us and my old man would kid with them. He could talk French just like English and all those kind of guys knew him 'cause you can always tell a jockey—and then we always sat at the same table and they got used to seeing us there. There were guys selling matrimonial papers and girls selling rubber eggs that when you squeezed them a rooster came out of them and one old wormy-looking guy that went by with postcards of Paris, showing them to everybody, and, of course, nobody ever bought any, and then he would come back and show the underside of the pack and they would all be smutty postcards and lots of people would dig down and buy them.

Gee, I remember the funny people that used to go by. Girls around supper time looking for somebody to take them out to eat and they'd speak to my old man and he'd make some joke at them in French and they'd pat me on the head and go on. Once there was an American woman sitting with her kid daughter at the next table to us and they were both eating ices and I kept looking at the girl and she was awfully

My Old Man

good-looking and I smiled at her and she smiled at me, but that was all that ever came of it because I looked for her mother and her every day and I made up ways that I was going to speak to her and I wondered if I got to know her if her mother would let me take her out to Auteuil or Tremblay but I never saw either of them again. Anyway, I guess it wouldn't have been any good, anyway, because looking back on it I remember the way I thought out would be best to speak to her was to say, "Pardon me, but perhaps I can give you a winner at Enghien today?" and, after all, maybe she would have thought I was a tout instead of really trying to give her a winner.

We'd sit at the Café de la Paix, my old man and me, and we had a big drag with the waiter because my old man drank whisky and it cost five francs, and that meant a good tip when the saucers were counted up. My old man was drinking more than I'd ever seen him, but he wasn't riding at all now and besides he said that whisky kept his weight down. But I noticed he was putting it on, all right, just the same. He'd busted away from his old gang out at Maisons and seemed to like just sitting around on the boulevard with me. But he was dropping money every day at the track. He'd feel sort of doleful after the last race, if he'd lost on the day, until we'd get to our table and he'd have his first whisky and then he'd be fine.

He'd be reading the *Paris-Sport* and he'd look over at me and say, "Where's your girl, Joe?" to kid me on account I had told him about the girl that day at the next table. And I'd get red, but I liked being kidded about her. It gave me a good feeling. "Keep your eye peeled for her, Joe," he'd say, "she'll be back."

He'd ask me questions about things and some of the things I'd say he'd laugh. And then he'd get started talking about things. About riding down in Egypt, or at St. Moritz on the ice before my mother died, and about during the war when they had regular races down in the south of France without any purses, or betting or crowd or anything just to keep the breed up. Regular races with the jocks riding hell out of the horses. Gee, I could listen to my old man talk by the hour, especially when he'd had a couple or so of drinks. He'd tell me about when he was a boy in Kentucky and going coon hunting, and the old days in the States before everything went on the bum there. And he'd say, "Joe, when we've got a decent stake, you're going back there to the States and go to school."

"What've I got to go back there to go to school for when everything's on the bum there?" I'd ask him.

"That's different," he'd say and get the waiter over and pay the pile of saucers and we'd get a taxi to the Gare St. Lazare and get on the train out to Maisons.

One day at Auteuil, after a selling steeplechase, my old man bought in the winner for thirty thousand francs. He had to bid a little to get him but the stable let the horse go finally and my old man had his permit and his colors in a week. Gee, I felt proud when my old man was an owner. He fixed it up for stable space with Charles Drake and cut out coming in to Paris, and started his running and sweating out again, and him and I were the whole stable gang. Our horse's name was Gilford; he was Irish bred and a nice, sweet jumper. My old man figured that training him and riding him, himself, he was a good investment. I was proud of everything and I thought Gilford was as good a horse as Kzar. He was a good, solid jumper, a bay, with plenty of speed on the flat, if you asked him for it, and he was a nice-looking horse, too.

Gee, I was fond of him. The first time he started with my old man up, he finished third in a 2,500-meter hurdle race and when my old man got off him, all sweating and happy in the place stall, and went in to weigh, I felt as proud of him as though it was the first race he'd ever placed in. You see, when a guy ain't been riding for a long time, you can't make yourself really believe that he has ever rode. The whole thing was different now, 'cause down in Milan, even big races never seemed to make any difference to my old man, if he won he wasn't ever excited or anything, and now it was so I couldn't hardly sleep the night before a race and I knew my old man was excited, too, even if he didn't show it. Riding for yourself makes an awful difference.

Second time Gilford and my old man started, was a rainy Sunday at Auteuil, in the Prix du Marat, a 4,500-meter steeplechase. As soon as he'd gone out I beat it up in the stand with the new glasses my old man had bought for me to watch them. They started way over at the far end of the course and there was some trouble at the barrier. Something with goggle blinders on was making a great fuss and rearing around and busted the barrier once, but I could see my old man in our black jacket, with a white cross and a black cap, sitting up on Gilford, and patting him with his hand. Then they were off in a jump and out of sight behind the trees and the gong going for dear life and the parimutuel wickets rattling down. Gosh I was so excited, I was afraid to look at them, but I fixed the glasses on the place where they would come out back of the trees and then out they came with the old black jacket going third and they all sailing over the jump like birds. Then

My Old Man

they went out of sight again and then they came pounding out and down the hill and all going nice and sweet and easy and taking the fence smooth in a bunch, and moving away from us all solid. Looked as though you could walk across on their backs, they were all so bunched and going so smooth. Then they bellied over the big double Bullfinch and something came down. I couldn't see who it was, but in a minute the horse was up and galloping free and the field, all bunched still, sweeping around the long left turn into the straightaway. They jumped the stone wall and came jammed down the stretch toward the big water-jump right in front of the stands. I saw them coming and hollered at my old man as he went by, and he was leading by about a length and riding way out, and light as a monkey, and they were racing for the water-jump. They took off over the big hedge of the water-jump in a pack, and then there was a crash, and two horses pulled sideways out off it, and kept on going and three others were piled up. I couldn't see my old man anywhere. One horse kneed himself up and the jock had hold of the bridle and mounted and went slamming on after the place money. The other horse was up and away by himself, jerking his head and galloping with the bridle rein hanging and the jock staggered over to one side of the track against the fence. Then Gilford rolled over to one side off my old man and got up and started to run on three legs with his off hoof dangling and there was my old man laying there on the grass flat out with his face up and blood all over the side of his head. I ran down the stand and bumped into a jam of people and got to the rail and a cop grabbed me and held me and two big stretcher-bearers were going out after my old man and around on the other side of the course I saw three horses, strung way out, coming out of the trees and taking the jump.

My old man was dead when they brought him in and while a doctor was listening to his heart with a thing plugged in his ears, I heard a shot up the track that meant they'd killed Gilford. I lay down beside my old man, when they carried the stretcher into the hospital room, and hung onto the stretcher and cried and cried, and he looked so white and gone and so awfully dead, and I couldn't help feeling that if my old man was dead maybe they didn't need to have shot Gilford. His hoof might have got well. I don't know. I loved my old man so much.

Then a couple of guys came in and one of them patted me on the back and then went over and looked at my old man and then pulled a sheet off the cot and spread it over him; and the other was telephoning in French for them to send the ambulance to take him out to

Maisons. And I couldn't stop crying, crying and choking, sort of, and George Gardner came in and sat down beside me on the floor and put his arm around me and says, "Come on, Joe, old boy. Get up and we'll go out and wait for the ambulance."

George and I went out to the gate and I was trying to stop bawling and George wiped off my face with his handkerchief and we were standing back a little ways while the crowd was going out of the gate and a couple of guys stopped near us while we were waiting for the crowd to get through the gate and one of them was counting a bunch of mutuel tickets and he said, "Well, Butler got his, all right."

The other guy said, "I don't give a good goddam if he did, the crook. He had it coming to him on the stuff he's pulled."

"I'll say he had," said the other guy, and tore the bunch of tickets in two.

And George Gardner looked at me to see if I'd heard and I had all right and he said, "Don't you listen to what those bums said, Joe. Your old man was one swell guy."

But I don't know. Seems like when they get started they don't leave a guy nothing.

A Young Idyll of Japan

YASUNARI KAWABATA

Of all the contemporary Japanese authors, Yasunari was the last with the ability to resist the oncoming wave of realism and to evoke the lyrical spirit of old Japan.

Yasunari Kawabata was born in Osaka in 1899. His father, a doctor who enjoyed literature and art, died when the child was three; his mother died the following year. Yasunari was then brought up by his grandparents. In his early school days he wanted to become a painter, but at about the age of fifteen decided to become a writer of fiction instead. His *Diary of a Sixteen-Year Old* was later published. He entered the English Literature Department of Tokyo Imperial University and founded, with other students, a magazine to which he contributed. He joined the staff of a leading literary magazine in 1923, a year before graduation. The following year he began editing a magazine of his own, *Bungei Jidai*, starting the literary movement of neo-sensualism, which revolted against the colorless reporting of the naturalists and the propaganda of the proletarians. Kawabata became an important literary critic as well as a novelist, and befriended many new writers. He was appointed chairman of the Japanese Center of the P.E.N. Club and was elected to the Japan Academy. He was awarded the Nobel Prize for Literature in 1968.

"The Izu Dancer," first published in *Bungei Jidai* in 1925, is considered the masterpiece of Kawabata's earlier period. In a vacation setting on Izu, a peninsula on the south-central side of the main island of Honshu, a "melancholy" student finds that infatuation may mature into friendship.

YASUNARI KAWABATA

The Izu Dancer

I

A SHOWER SWEPT toward me from the foot of the mountain, touching the cedar forests white, as the road began to wind up into the pass. I was nineteen and traveling alone through the Izu Peninsula. My clothes were of the sort students wear, dark kimono, high wooden sandals, a school cap, a book sack over my shoulder. I had spent three nights at hot springs near the center of the peninsula, and now, my fourth day out of Tokyo, I was climbing toward Amagi Pass and South Izu. The autumn scenery was pleasant enough, mountains rising one on another, open forests, deep valleys, but I was excited less by the scenery than by a certain hope. Large drops of rain began to fall. I ran on up the road, now steep and winding, and at the mouth of the pass I came to a teahouse. I stopped short in the doorway. It was almost too lucky; the dancers were resting inside.

The little dancing girl turned over the cushion she had been sitting on and pushed it politely toward me.

"Yes," I murmured stupidly, and sat down. Surprised and out of breath, I could think of nothing more appropriate to say.

She sat near me; we were facing each other. I fumbled for tobacco and she handed me the ashtray in front of one of the other women. Still I said nothing.

She was perhaps sixteen. Her hair was swept up in mounds after an old style I hardly know what to call. Her solemn, oval face was dwarfed under it, and yet the face and the hair went well together,

The Izu Dancer

rather as in the pictures one sees of ancient beauties with their exaggerated rolls of hair. Two other young women were with her, and a man of twenty-four or twenty-five. A stern-looking woman of about forty presided over the group.

I had seen the little dancer twice before. Once I passed her and the other two young women on a long bridge half way down the peninsula. She was carrying a big drum. I looked back and looked back again, congratulating myself that here finally I had the flavor of travel. And then my third night at the inn I saw her dance. She danced just inside the entrance, and I sat on the stairs enraptured. On the bridge then, here tonight, I had said to myself: tomorrow over the pass to Yugano, and surely somewhere along those fifteen miles I will meet them—that was the hope that had sent me hurrying up the mountain road. But the meeting at the teahouse was too sudden. I was taken quite off balance.

A few minutes later the old woman who kept the teahouse led me to another room, one apparently not much used. It was open to a valley so deep that the bottom was out of sight. My teeth were chattering and my arms were covered with gooseflesh. I was a little cold, I said to the old woman when she came back with tea.

"But you're soaked. Come in here and dry yourself." She led me to her living room.

The heat from the open fire struck me as she opened the door. I went inside and sat back behind the fire. Steam rose from my kimono, and the fire was so warm that my head began to ache.

The old woman went out to talk to the dancers. "Well, now. So this is the little girl you had with you before, so big already. Why, she's practically a grown woman. Isn't that nice. And so pretty, too. Girls do grow up in a hurry, don't they?"

Perhaps an hour later I heard them getting ready to leave. My heart pounded and my chest was tight, and yet I could not find the courage to get up and go off with them. I fretted on beside the fire. But they were women, after all; granted that they were used to walking, I ought to have no trouble overtaking them even if I fell a half mile or a mile behind. My mind danced off after them as though their departure had given it license.

"Where will they stay tonight?" I asked the woman when she came back.

"People like that, how can you tell where they'll stay? If they find someone who will pay them, that's where it will be. Do you think they know ahead of time?"

335

Her open contempt excited me. If she is right, I said to myself, then the dancing girl will stay in my room tonight.

The rain quieted to a sprinkle, the sky over the pass cleared. I felt I could wait no longer, though the woman assured me that the sun would be out in another ten minutes.

"Young man, young man." The woman ran up the road after me. "This is too much. I really can't take it." She clutched at my book sack and held me back, trying to return the money I had given her, and when I refused it she hobbled along after me. She must at least see me off up the road, she insisted. "It's really too much. I did nothing for you—but I'll remember, and I'll have something for you when you come this way again. You will come again, won't you? I won't forget."

So much gratitude for one fifty-sen piece was rather touching. I was in a fever to overtake the little dancer, however, and her hobbling only held me back. When we came to the tunnel I finally shook her off.

II

Lined on one side by a white fence, the road twisted down from the mouth of the tunnel like a streak of lightning. Near the bottom of the jagged figure were the dancer and her companions. Another half mile and I had overtaken them. Since it hardly seemed graceful to slow down at once to their pace, however, I moved on past the women with a show of coolness. The man, walking some ten yards ahead of them, turned as he heard me come up.

"You're quite a walker. . . . Isn't it lucky the rain has stopped."

Rescued, I walked on beside him. He began asking questions, and the women, seeing that we had struck up a conversation, came tripping up behind us. The man had a large wicker trunk strapped to his back. The older woman held a puppy in her arms, the two young women carried bundles, and the girl had her drum and its frame. The older woman presently joined in the conversation.

"He's a high-school boy," one of the young women whispered to the little dancer, giggling as I glanced back.

"Really, even I know that much," the girl retorted. "Students come to the island often."

They were from Oshima in the Izu Islands, the man told me. In the spring they left to wander over the peninsula, but now it was getting cold and they had no winter clothes with them. After ten days or so at Shimoda in the south they would sail back to the islands. I glanced again at those rich mounds of hair, at the little figure all the more romantic now for being from Oshima. I questioned them about the islands.

"Students come to Oshima to swim, you know," the girl remarked to the young woman beside her.

"In the summer, I suppose." I looked back.

She was flustered. "In the winter too," she answered in an almost inaudible little voice.

"Even in the winter?"

She looked at the other women and laughed uncertainly.

"Do they swim even in the winter?" I asked again.

She flushed and nodded very slightly, a serious expression on her face.

"The child is crazy," the older woman laughed.

From six or seven miles above Yugano the road followed a river. The mountains had taken on the look of the South from the moment we descended the pass. The man and I became firm friends, and as the thatched roofs of Yugano came in sight below us I announced that I would like to go on to Shimoda with them. He seemed delighted.

In front of a shabby old inn the older woman glanced tentatively at me as if to take her leave. "But this gentleman would like to go on with us," the man said.

"Oh, would he?" she answered with simple warmth. " 'On the road a companion, in life sympathy,' they say. I suppose even poor things like us can liven up a trip. Do come in—we'll have a cup of tea and rest ourselves."

We went up to the second floor and laid down our baggage. The straw carpeting and the doors were worn and dirty. The little dancer brought up tea from below. As she came to me the teacup clattered in its saucer. She set it down sharply in an effort to save herself, but she succeeded only in spilling it. I was hardly prepared for confusion so extreme.

"Dear me. The child's come to a dangerous age," the older woman said, arching her eyebrows as she tossed over a cloth. The girl wiped tensely at the tea.

The remark somehow startled me. I felt the excitement aroused by the old woman at the teahouse begin to mount.

An hour or so later the man took me to another inn. I had thought till then that I was to stay with them. We climbed down over rocks and stone steps a hundred yards or so from the road. There was a public hot spring in the river bed, and just beyond it a bridge led to the garden of the inn.

We went together for a bath. He was twenty-three, he told me, and his wife had had two miscarriages. He seemed not unintelligent. I had assumed that he had come along for the walk—perhaps like me to be near the dancer.

A heavy rain began to fall about sunset. The mountains, gray and white, flattened to two dimensions, and the river grew yellower and muddier by the minute. I felt sure that the dancers would not be out on a night like this, and yet I could not sit still. Two and three times I went down to the bath, and came restlessly back to my room again.

Then, distant in the rain, I heard the slow beating of a drum. I tore open the shutters as if to wrench them from their grooves and leaned out the window. The drumbeat seemed to be coming nearer. The rain, driven by a strong wind, lashed at my head. I closed my eyes and tried to concentrate on the drum, on where it might be, whether it could be coming this way. Presently I heard a *samisen,* and now and then a woman's voice calling to someone, a loud burst of laughter. The dancers had been called to a party in the restaurant across from their inn, it seemed. I could distinguish two or three women's voices and three or four men's voices. Soon they will be finished there, I told myself, and they will come here. The party seemed to go beyond the harmlessly gay and to approach the rowdy. A shrill woman's voice came across the darkness like the crack of a whip. I sat rigid, more and more on edge, staring out through the open shutters. At each drumbeat I felt a surge of relief. "Ah, she's still there. Still there and playing the drum." And each time the beating stopped the silence seemed intolerable. It was as though I were being borne under by the driving rain.

For a time there was a confusion of footsteps—were they playing tag, were they dancing? And then complete silence. I glared into the darkness. What would she be doing, who would be with her the rest of the night?

I closed the shutters and got into bed. My chest was painfully tight. I went down to the bath again and splashed about violently. The rain stopped, the moon came out; the autumn sky, washed by the rain, shone like crystalline into the distance. I thought for a moment of running out barefoot to look for her. It was after two.

III

The man came by my inn at nine the next morning. I had just gotten up, and I invited him along for a bath. Below the bathhouse the river, high from the rain, flowed warm in the South Izu autumn sun. My

The Izu Dancer

anguish of last night no longer seemed very real. I wanted even so to hear what had happened.

"That was a lively party you had last night."

"You could hear us?"

"I certainly could."

"Natives. They make a lot of noise, but there's not much to them really."

He seemed to consider the event quite routine, and I said no more.

"Look. They've come for a bath, over there across the river. Damned if they haven't seen us. Look at them laugh." He pointed over at the public bath, where six or seven naked figures showed through the steam.

One small figure ran out into the sunlight and stood for a moment at the edge of the platform calling something to us, arms raised as though for a plunge into the river. It was the little dancer. I looked at her, at the young legs, at the sculptured white body, and suddenly a draught of fresh water seemed to wash over my heart. I laughed happily. She was a child, a mere child, a child who could run out naked into the sun and stand there on her tiptoes in her delight at seeing a friend. I laughed on, a soft, happy laugh. It was as though a layer of dust had been cleared from my head. And I laughed on and on. It was because of her too-rich hair that she had seemed older, and because she was dressed like a girl of fifteen or sixteen. I had made an extraordinary mistake indeed.

We were back in my room when the older of the two young women came to look at the flowers in the garden. The little dancer followed her halfway across the bridge. The old woman came out of the bath frowning. The dancer shrugged her shoulders and ran back, laughing as if to say that she would be scolded if she came any nearer. The older young woman came up to the bridge.

"Come on over," she called to me.

"Come on over," the younger woman echoed, and the two of them turned back toward their inn.

The man stayed on in my room till evening.

I was playing chess with a traveling salesman that night when I heard the drum in the garden. I started to go out to the veranda.

"How about another?" asked the salesman. "Let's have another game." But I laughed evasively and after a time he gave up and left the room.

Soon the younger women and the man came in.

339

"Do you have somewhere else to go tonight?" I asked.

"We couldn't find any customers if we tried."

They stayed on till past midnight, playing away at checkers.

I felt clearheaded and alive when they had gone. I would not be able to sleep, I knew. From the hall I called in to the salesman:

"Fine, fine." He hurried out ready for battle.

"It's an all-night match tonight. We'll play all night." I felt invincible.

We were to leave Yugano at eight the next morning. I poked my school cap into my book sack, put on a hunting cap I had bought in a shop not far from the public bath, and went up to the inn by the highway. I walked confidently upstairs—the shutters on the second floor were open—but I stopped short in the hall. They were still in bed.

The dancing girl lay almost at my feet, beside the youngest of the women. She flushed deeply and pressed her hands to her face with a quick flutter. Traces of makeup were left from the evening before, rouge on her lips and dots of rouge at the corners of her eyes. A thoroughly appealing little figure. I felt a bright surge of happiness as I looked down at her. Abruptly, still hiding her face, she rolled over, slipped out of bed, and bowed low before me in the hall. I stood dumbly wondering what to do.

The man and the older of the young women were sleeping together. They must be married—I had not thought of it before.

"You will have to forgive us," the older woman said, sitting up in bed. "We meant to leave today, but it seems there is to be a party tonight, and we thought we'd see what could be done with it. If you really must go, perhaps you can meet us in Shimoda. We always stay at the Koshya Inn—you should have no trouble finding it."

I felt deserted.

"Or maybe you could wait till tomorrow," the man suggested. "She says we have to stay today. . . . But it's good to have someone to talk to on the road. Let's go together tomorrow."

"A splendid idea," the woman agreed. "It seems a shame, now that we've gotten to know you . . . and tomorrow we start out no matter what happens. Day after tomorrow it will be forty-nine days since the baby died. We've meant all along to have a service in Shimoda to show that we at least remember, and we've been hurrying to get there in time. It would really be very kind of you. . . . I can't help thinking there's a reason for it all, our getting to be friends this way."

I agreed to wait another day, and went back down to my inn. I sat in the dirty little office talking to the manager while I waited for them

The Izu Dancer

to dress. Presently the man came by and we walked out to a pleasant bridge not far from town. He leaned against the railing and talked about himself. He had for a long time belonged to a theater company in Tokyo. Even now he sometimes acted in plays in Oshima, while at parties on the road he could do imitations of actors if called upon to. The strange, leglike bulge in one of the bundles was a stage sword, he explained, and the wicker trunk held both household goods and costumes.

"I made a mistake and ruined myself. My brother has taken over for the family in Kofu and I'm really not much use there."

"I thought you came from the inn at Nagaoka."

"I'm afraid not. That's my wife, the older of the two women. She's a year younger than you. She lost her second baby on the road this summer—it only lived a week—and she isn't really well yet. The old woman is her mother, and the girl is my sister.'

"You said you had a sister thirteen?"

"That's the one. I've tried to think of ways of keeping her out of this business, but there were all sorts of reasons why it couldn't be helped."

He said his own name was Eikichi, his wife was Chiyoko, the dancer, his sister, was Kaoru. The other girl, Yuriko, was a sort of maid. She was sixteen, and the only one among them who was really from Oshima. Eikichi became very sentimental. He gazed down at the river, and for a time I thought he was about to weep.

IV

On the way back, just off the road, we saw the little dancer petting a dog. She had washed away her makeup.

"Come on over to the inn," I called as we passed.

"I couldn't very well by myself."

"Bring your brother."

"Thank you. I'll be right over."

"Where are the others?"

"They couldn't get away from mother."

But the three of them came clattering across the bridge and up the stairs while we were playing checkers. After elaborate bows they waited hesitantly in the hall.

Chiyoko came in first. "Please, please," she called gaily to the others. "You needn't stand on formality in *my* room."

An hour or so later they all went down for a bath. I must come along, they insisted; but the idea of a bath with three young women was somewhat overwhelming, and I said I would go in later. In a moment the little dancer came back upstairs.

"Chiyoko says she'll wash your back for you if you come down now."

Instead she stayed with me, and the two of us played checkers. She was suprisingly good at it. I am better than most and had little trouble with Eikichi and the others, but she came very near beating me. It was a relief not to have to play a deliberately bad game. A model of propriety at first, sitting bolt upright and stretching out her hand to make a play, she soon forgot herself and was leaning intently over the board. Her hair, so rich it seemed unreal, almost brushed against my chest. Suddenly she flushed crimson.

"Excuse me. I'll be scolded for this," she exclaimed, and ran out with the game half finished. The older woman was standing beside the public bath across the river. Chiyoko and Yuriko clattered out of the bath downstairs at almost the same moment and retreated across the bridge without bothering to say good-bye.

Eikichi spent the day at my inn again, though the manager's wife, a solicitous sort of woman, had pointed out that it was a waste of good food to invite such people in for meals.

The dancer was practicing the *samisen* when I went up to the inn by the highway that evening. She put it down when she saw me, but at the older woman's order took it up again.

Eikichi seemed to be reciting something on the second floor of the restaurant across the street, where we could see a party in progress.

"What in the world is that?"

"That? He's reading a *Noh* play."

"An odd sort of thing to be doing."

"He has as many wares as a dime store. You can never guess what he'll do next."

The girl shyly asked me to read her a piece from a storyteller's collection. I took up the book happily, a certain hope in my mind. Her head was almost at my shoulder as I started to read, and she looked up at me with a serious, intent expression, her eyes bright and unblinking. Her large eyes, almost black, were easily her best feature. The lines of the heavy lids were indescribably graceful. And her laugh was like a flower's laugh. A flower's laugh—the expression does not seem strained when I think of her.

I had read only a few minutes when the maid from the restaurant across the street came for her. "I'll be right back," she said as she

The Izu Dancer

smoothed out her clothes. "Don't go away. I want to hear the rest."

She knelt in the hall to take her leave formally.

We could see the girl as though in the next room. She knelt beside the drum, her back toward us. The slow rhythm filled me with a clean excitement.

"A party always picks up speed when the drum begins," the woman said.

Chiyoko and Yuriko went over to the restaurant a little later, and in an hour or so the four of them came back.

"This is all they gave us." The dancer casually dropped fifty sen from her clenched fist into the older woman's hand. I read more of the story, and they talked of the baby that had died.

I was not held to them by curiosity, and I felt no condescension toward them. Indeed I was no longer conscious that they belonged to that low order, traveling performers. They seemed to know it and to be moved by it. Before long they decided that I must visit them on Oshima.

"We can put him in the old man's house." They planned everything out. "That should be big enough, and if we move the old man out it will be quiet enough for him to study as long as he can stay."

"We have two little houses, and the one on the mountain we can give to you."

It was decided, too, that I should help with a play they would give on Oshima for the New Year.

I came to see that the life of a traveling performer was not the forbidding one I had imagined. Rather it was easy-going, relaxed, carrying with it the scent of meadows and mountains. Then, too, this troupe was held together by close family affection. Only Yuriko, the hired girl—perhaps she was at a shy age—seemed uncomfortable before me.

It was after midnight when I left their inn. The girls saw me to the door, and the little dancer turned my sandals so that I could step into them without twisting. She leaned out and gazed up at the clear sky. "Ah, the moon is up. And tomorrow we'll be in Shimoda. I love Shimoda. We'll say prayers for the baby, and mother will buy me the comb she promised, and there are all sorts of things we can do after that. Will you take me to a movie?"

Something about Shimoda seems to have made it a home along the road for performers who wander the region of the Izu and Sagami hot springs.

V

The baggage was distributed as on the day we came over Amagi Pass. The puppy, cool as a seasoned traveler, lay with its forepaws on the older woman's arms. From Yugano we entered the mountains again. We looked out over the sea at the morning sun, warming our mountain valley. At the mouth of the river a beach opened wide and white.

"That's Oshima."

"So big! You really will come, won't you?" the dancer said.

For some reason—was it the clearness of the autumn sky that made it seem so?—the sea where the sun rose over it was veiled in a springlike mist. It was some ten miles to Shimoda. For a time the mountains hid the sea. Chiyoko hummed a song, softly, lazily.

The road forked. One way was a little steep, but it was more than a mile shorter than the other. Would I have the short, steep way, or the long, easy way? I took the short way.

The road wound up through a forest, so steep now that climbing it was like climbing hand-over-hand up a wall. Dead leaves laid it over with a slippery coating. As my breathing became more painful I felt a perverse recklessness, and I pushed on faster and faster, pressing my knee down with my fist at each step. The others fell behind, until presently I could only hear their voices through the trees; but the dancer, skirts tucked high, came after me with tiny little steps. She stayed always a couple of yards behind, neither trying to come nearer nor letting herself fall farther back. Sometimes I would speak to her, and she would stop and answer with a startled little smile. And when she spoke I would pause, hoping that she would come up even with me, but always she waited until I had started out again, and followed the same two yards behind. The road grew steeper and more twisted. I pushed myself on faster, and on she came, two yards behind, climbing earnestly and intently. The mountains were quiet. I could no longer hear the voices of the others.

"Where do you live in Tokyo?"

"In a dormitory. I don't really live in Tokyo."

"I've been in Tokyo. I went there once to dance, when the cherries were in bloom. I was very little, though, and I don't remember anything about it."

"Are your parents living?" she would take up again, or, "Have you ever been to Kofu?" She talked of the movies in Shimoda, of the dead baby.

The Izu Dancer

We came to the summit. Laying her drum on a bench among the dead autumn weeds, she wiped her face with a handkerchief. After that she turned her attention to her feet, then changed her mind and bent down instead to dust off the skirt of my kimono. I drew back surprised, and she fell to one knee. When she had brushed me off front and back, bent low before me, she stood up to lower her skirts—they were still tucked up for walking. I was breathing heavily. She invited me to sit down.

A flock of small birds flew up beside the bench. The dead leaves rustled as they landed, so quiet was the air. I tapped the drum a couple of times with my finger, and the birds started up in alarm.

"I'm thirsty."

"Shall I see if I can find you some water?" But a few minutes later she came back empty-handed through the yellowing trees.

"What do you do with yourself on Oshima?"

She mentioned two or three girls' names that meant nothing to me, and rambled on with a string of reminiscences. She was talking not of Oshima but of Kofu, apparently, of a grammar school she had been in for the first and second grades. She talked artlessly on as the memories of her friends came back to her.

The two younger women and Eikichi came up about ten minutes later, and the older woman ten minutes later still. On the way down I purposely stayed behind talking to Eikichi, but after two hundred yards or so the little dancer came running back up. "There's a spring below. They're waiting for you to drink first."

I ran down with her. The water bubbled clear and clean from shady rocks. The women were standing around it. "Have a drink. We waited for you. We didn't think you would want to drink after we had stirred it up."

I drank from my cupped hands. The women were slow to leave. They wet their handkerchiefs and washed the perspiration from their faces.

At the foot of the slope we came out on the Shimoda highway. Down the highway, sending up columns of smoke here and there, were the fires of the charcoal makers. We stopped to rest on a pile of wood. The dancing girl began to curry the puppy's shaggy coat with a pinkish comb.

"You'll break the teeth," the older woman warned.

"That's all right. I'm getting a new one in Shimoda."

It was the comb she wore in her hair, and even back in Yugano I

345

had planned to ask for it when we got to Shimoda. I was a little upset to find her combing the dog with it.

Eikichi and I walked on ten or fifteen yards ahead of them.

"But all he would have to do would be to get a gold tooth. Then you'd never notice," the dancer's voice came to me suddenly. I looked back.

They were obviously talking about my crooked teeth. Chiyoko must have brought the matter up, and the little dancer suggested a gold tooth for me. I felt no resentment at being talked about and no particular need to hear more. The conversation was subdued for a time.

"He's nice, isn't he," the girl's voice came again.

"He seems to be very nice."

"He really is nice. I like having someone so nice."

She had an open way of speaking, a youthful, honest way of saying exactly what came to her, that made it possible for me to think of myself as, frankly, "nice." I looked up anew at the mountains, so bright that they made my eyes ache a little. I had come at nineteen to think of myself as a misanthrope, a lonely misfit, and it was my depression at the thought that had driven me to this Izu trip. And now I was able to look upon myself as "a nice person" in the everyday sense of the expression. I find no way to describe what this meant to me. The mountains grew brighter—we were getting near Shimoda and the sea.

Now and then, on the outskirts of a village, we would see a sign: "Vagrant performers keep out."

The Koshuya was a cheap inn at the northern edge of Shimoda. I went up behind the rest to an atticlike room on the second floor. There was no ceiling, and the roof sloped down so sharply that at the window overlooking the street one could not sit comfortably upright.

"Your shoulder isn't stiff?" The older woman was fussing over the girl. "Your hands aren't sore?"

The girl went through the graceful motions of beating a drum. "They're not sore. I won't have any trouble. They're not sore at all."

"Good. I was worried."

I lifted the drum. "Heavy!"

"It's heavier than you'd think," she laughed. "It's heavier than that pack of yours."

They exchanged greetings with the other guests. The hotel was full of peddlers and wandering performers—Shimoda seemed to be a migrants' nest. The dancer handed out pennies to the inn children, who darted in and out. When I started to leave she ran to arrange my sandals for me in the doorway.

The Izu Dancer

"You will take me to a movie, won't you?" she whispered, almost to herself.

Eikichi and I, guided part way by a rather disreputable-looking man from the Koshuya, went on to an inn said to belong to an ex-mayor. We had a bath together and lunch, fish new from the sea.

I handed him a little money as he left. "Buy some flowers for the services tomorrow," I said. I had explained that I would have to go back to Tokyo on the morning boat. I was, as a matter of fact, out of money, but I told them I had to be back in school.

"Well, we'll see you this winter in any case," the older woman said. "We'll all come down to the boat to meet you. You must let us know when you're coming. You're to stay with us—we couldn't think of letting you go to a hotel. We're expecting you, remember, and we'll all be down at the boat."

When the others had left the room I asked Chiyoko and Yuriko to go to a movie with me. Chiyoko, pale and tired, lay with her hands pressed to her abdomen. "I couldn't, thank you. I'm simply not up to so much walking."

Yuriko stared stiffly at the floor.

The little dancer was downstairs playing with the inn children. When she saw me come down she ran off and began wheedling the older woman for permission to go to the movies. She came back looking distant and crestfallen.

"I don't see anything wrong. Why can't she go with him by herself?" Eikichi argued. I found it hard to understand myself, but the woman was unbending. The dancer sat out in the hall petting a dog when I left the inn. I could not bring myself to speak to her, so chilling was this new formality, and she seemed not to have the strength to look up.

I went to the movies alone. A woman read the dialogue by a small flashlight. I left almost immediately and went back to my inn. For a long time I sat looking out, my elbows on the windowsill. The town was dark. I thought I could hear a drum in the distance. For no very good reason I found myself weeping.

VI

Eikichi called up from the street while I was eating breakfast at seven the next morning. He had on a formal kimono, in my honor it seemed. The women were not with him. I was suddenly lonesome.

"They all wanted to see you off," he explained when he came up to my room, "but we were out so late last night that they couldn't get themselves out of bed. They said to apologize and tell you they'd be waiting for you this winter."

An autumn wind blew cold through the town. On the way to the ship he brought me fruit and tobacco and a bottle of cologne called "Kaoru." "Because her name's Kaoru," he smiled. "Oranges are bad on a ship, but persimmons you can eat. They help seasickness."

"Why don't I give you this?" I put my hunting cap on his head, pulled my school cap out of my pack, and tried to smooth away a few of the wrinkles. We both laughed.

As we came to the pier I saw with a quick jump of the heart that the little dancer was sitting at the water's edge. She did not move as we came up, only nodded a silent greeting. On her face were the traces of makeup I found so engaging, and the rather angry red at the corners of her eyes seemed to give her a fresh young dignity.

"Are the others coming?" Eikichi asked.

She shook her head.

"They're still in bed?"

She nodded.

Eikichi went to buy ship and lighter tickets. I tried to make conversation, but she only stared silently at the point where the canal ran into the harbor. Now and then she would nod a quick little nod, always before I had finished speaking.

The lighter pitched violently. The dancer stared fixedly ahead, her lips pressed tight together. As I started up the rope ladder to the ship I looked back. I wanted to say good-by, but I only nodded again. The lighter pulled off. Eikichi waved the hunting cap, and as the town retreated into the distance the girl began to wave something white.

I leaned against the railing and gazed out at Oshima until the southern tip of the Izu Peninsula was out of sight. It seemed a long while before I had said good-by to the little dancer. I went inside and on to my stateroom. The sea was so rough that it was hard even to sit up. A crewman came around to pass out metal basins for the seasick. I lay down with my book sack for a pillow, my mind clear and empty. I was no longer conscious of the passage of time. I wept silently, and when my cheek began to feel chilly I turned my book sack over. A young boy lay beside me. He was the son of an Izu factory owner, he explained, and he was going to Tokyo to get ready for high school entrance examinations. My school cap had attracted him.

"Is something wrong?" he asked after a time.

The Izu Dancer

"No. I've just said good-bye to someone." I saw no need to disguise the truth, and I was quite unashamed of my tears. I thought of nothing. It was as though I were slumbering in a sort of quiet fulfillment. I did not know when evening came, but there were lights on when we passed Atami. I was hungry and a little chilly. The boy opened his lunch and I ate as though it were mine. Afterwards I covered myself with part of his cape. I floated in a beautiful emptiness, and it seemed natural that I should take advantage of his kindness. Everything sank into an enfolding harmony.

The lights went out, the smell of the sea and of the fish in the hold grew stronger. In the darkness, warmed by the boy beside me, I gave myself up to my tears. It was as though my head had turned to clear water, it was falling pleasantly away drop by drop; soon nothing would remain.

A Broken Home in China

LU HSUN

Probably the most widely read author in China today, Lu Hsun is the greatest of the modern Chinese short-story writers.

Chou Shu-jen (1881–1936), to give his real name, was born in Chekiang province. His grandfather was an official in the Mandarin court who fell from grace and was imprisoned. The boy was brought up in bitter poverty, an experience that turned him early toward a burning desire for reform in China and a sympathy for the underprivileged people of the earth. He became a naval cadet, and then went to Japan in the early years of the twentieth century to study medicine. There he was much impressed by modern Western literature, and, after returning to China in 1915, he devoted himself to teaching and writing. He lectured on Chinese literature at Peking University, then strongly influenced by Russian ideas, and he admired Russian authors, some of whom he translated into Chinese. He was forced to flee from Peking to Shanghai in 1926 for political reasons.

Most of his stories, which he wrote slowly and painfully, reject the outworn customs of China. His best-known character is "Ah Q," a fumbling, stupid wanderer who is imposed upon by everyone.

Lu Hsun had a high sense of moral justice, and forced his readers to face realistically the need for change in Chinese life. As he once said: "It is high time for our writers to take off their masks, look life honestly, penetratingly, and boldly in the face, and write of flesh and blood."

"Divorce," first published in 1926, is a subtle story of the clash between the traditional way of Chinese life and modern ideas introduced from the Occident. It was one of the first pieces of fiction to stress social protest in his big country, and the movement thus started dominated the literary scene there even after the Communists took over in 1949.

LU HSUN

Divorce

"*A*H, UNCLE MU! Happy New Year and good health to you!"
"How are you, Pa San? Happy New Year!"
"So . . . Aiku's here too."
"Hello, Uncle Mu! Good to see you!" A din of voices greeted the old man and his daughter as they stepped onto the boat from the Magnolia Bridge Wharf. Some of the passengers clasped their hands and bowed; others made space for the newcomers on the benches in the cabin. Uncle Mu waved a welcome to all and sat down, leaning his long pipe against the side of the boat. Aiku took a place to his left, across the cabin from Pa San, her sickle-shaped feet fanning out to form a V.
"Going to the city, Uncle Mu?" asked a fellow, his complexion reddish like the shell of a crab.
"Not to the city," the old man replied. The weathered, deep lines in his face showed no outward sign of emotion, yet his voice betrayed just a tinge of regret. "We're going to Pang Village."
Suddenly everyone fell silent. One after another, they turned to stare at the old man and his daughter.
"It's the Aiku affair again," suggested Pa San.
"It is, and it will be the death of me. For three years now it's dragged on; quarreling one day, making up the next, and still there's no end to it."
"You'll go back to Honorable Wei's house again, eh?"
"That's right. Of course he's tried many times to patch things up between Aiku and her husband, but I've never agreed to his terms.

This time he thinks it will be different. The family is getting together for the New Year; even the Great Lord will be there."

"The Great Lord?" Pa San's eyes bulged. "So he'll take a hand in this matter too?"

"Yes. But what's he to do? Since we ruined their kitchen stove last year we've more or less gotten even. Besides, there's really no point in Aiku's going back to him now. It's too late."

Uncle Mu lowered his head as if in resignation.

"Well, I'm not going back," Aiku said defiantly. "I'm just doing this to spite them. When you think of it, that young animal of a husband finds himself a widow and then decides to rid himself of me. It isn't going to be as simple as he thinks. And to see his father encourage him in his loose ways, even trying to kick me out too . . . As if it were that easy! As for the Great Lord—just because he and the county magistrate are like brothers—does that mean he'll be unjust? I'm certain he's no fool like Mr. Wei. That man's only suggestion so far has been to say: 'Separate, better separate.' I'll just explain to him what I've put up with all these years and we'll see who the Great Lord decides is right."

Pa San shrugged in tacit agreement and became silent.

The others followed suit and no sound was heard save the splash of water against the bow of the boat. Uncle Mu took his pipe and began filling it.

A fat man sitting across the way, next to Pa San, dug into his girdle and came out with a flint. He struck it and held the flame out to Uncle Mu.

"Many thanks, many thanks," said Uncle Mu, nodding to him.

"Although this is our first meeting," said the fat man in a tone of respect, "I've heard your name mentioned many times. Indeed, who is there in the region of the eighteen villages by the sea who does not know of Uncle Mu? Everyone's been aware for a long time that young Shih has been carrying on with that little widow. Last year when you took your six sons and destroyed their kitchen stove—who was there to say that you weren't without cause? You have access to the houses of the great and you are a man respected and revered by all . . . Why fear them?"

"This man understands well," agreed Aiku. "But I haven't had the honor—"

"Wang Te-kuei," answered the fat man quickly.

"They can't just throw me out," Aiku began again. "I don't care whether they call in the Great Lord or the 'Greatest' Lord. I'll go on making trouble until their family is ruined and I see every one of them

Divorce

dead. Mr. Wei has had four chances to bring about a settlement, hasn't he? Even father has been a bit giddy over the size of the money he's proposed in settlement."

Uncle Mu swore softly under his breath

"But Uncle Mu, didn't the Shih family send Honorable Wei many wonderful delicacies for the great feast last year?" asked the crab-faced man.

"So what," answered Mu. "Will a little food turn a man away from justice? If so, then what would happen when somebody offered him more? No! Scholars know the truth. With them justice always prevails. A scholar is always the first to come to the defense of the ill-treated. Last year one of the men from my village returned from Peking. Now he's been around a lot, not like us. He told me that a certain Madame Kuang, who's the finest—"

"Wang Jetty!" shouted the boatman. "Anyone for Wang Jetty?"

"Here, me!" The fat man snatched up his pipe and darted from the cabin. He leapt ashore as the boat touched land, then turned back for a moment to nod a farewell to the others.

Once more the boat began to move and once more the passengers became still; there followed a quiet broken only now and then by the splash of the boatman's oars. Pa San, his eyes focused on Aiku's feet, sagged in his seat and his mouth began to slide open. Two old women in the forward section of the cabin began chanting softly, praying and counting on their beads. They would glance at Aiku, nod knowingly, all the while continuing to pucker their lips in prayer.

Aiku stared at the awning above her. She laid her plans. There were ways and means to cause trouble for her husband and his family. She practiced their ruination by idle design. As for Mr. Wei, he wasn't to be feared. Twice she had seen him: a fat little man with a round face and a round head. In her own village there were plenty like him, only, perhaps, they were a bit darker in complexion.

Uncle Mu finished his tobacco and the oil in his pipe began to sputter, but he continued to puff away. Next stop was Pang Village. He knew that only too well. Uncle Mu could not help but see the Literary Star Tower form in his mind's eye. He had visited the village many times over and it, like Mr. Wei, was all too familiar. There was nothing to fear there. His thoughts turned to his daughter, Aiku. He remembered how she had come home weeping, how she had told him about the brutal treatment she had received at the hands of her husband and his father and how, later, they had gotten the better of him. On other days, when he had thought back on all these things, he would concentrate on the time he destroyed their kitchen stove and punished them and, always, a thin smile would form on his lips. But not this time. The fat figure of the Great Lord had somehow managed to break into his train of thought; changing, confusing the picture.

The boat continued on. Only the singsong of the Buddhist prayers broke the stillness now. Everyone, just like Aiku and her father, was gathered up in his own thoughts.

"Here you are, Uncle Mu. Pang Village. Hustle your venerable bones ashore."

Torn from his daydreams, Mu looked up to see the outline of the Literary Star Tower rise before him. Hurriedly, he took Aiku and jumped ashore. Father and daughter started off for Mr. Wei's house. They turned south, passed thirty doors, then went around a corner. The house came into view. Four boats, each with a black awning over it, lay moored at the front gate. The two entered through a great, black-lacquered arch into the gatehouse. At two tables spread out in the gatehouse were many boatmen and farmhands. Aiku dared not stare at them; only a quick, furtive glance around to assure herself that her husband and father-in-law were not present.

A servant appeared and offered them soup and sweet cakes. Without knowing why, Aiku began to feel ill at ease. "Just because the Great Lord is a close friend to the county magistrate doesn't mean he won't be fair, does it?" she asked herself. "He's a scholar, one who knows the truth. He will stick up for the just. I'll tell the Great Lord everything, beginning with the day I married at the age of fifteen ... "

When they had finished their soup, Aiku knew that their time would soon come. Within moments she found herself following one of the servants. He led Aiku and her father across the main hall; they rounded a corner, finally entering the majestic reception room. The room was so crammed with furnishings and tapestries that Aiku had no time to take everything in. Many guests were present too. Their short satin jackets of purple and blue made the room come alive in a blaze of color. In the center of all this splendor was a man Aiku at once thought must be the Great Lord. Fat and round of face like Mr. Wei and the others, only much taller and much, much fatter. His eyes sat in his huge face like two narrow slits and beneath his squat nose a wispy black mustache glistened. Though he was completely bald, his complexion was ruddy, his skin soft, silken, and smooth. Aiku puzzled at the reason for this satin like texture. She finally decided that he rubbed his skin with the grease of a pig.

Divorce

"This is an anus block," the Great Lord was proudly announcing. He was holding a worn piece of jade up all to see. "It was used in ancient burials," he said, at the same time rubbing his nose several times over the jade. "Unfortunately it comes from a recent excavation, probably not much before the Han Dynasty. Still it's worth having; here, look at its mercury stain. The ancients, you know, believed that the anus block painted with mercury slowed a corpse's decay."

The jade was at once the center of attention of several heads, one of which, of course, was Mr. Wei. The others, sons of rich families, were obscured from Aiku's view by the massive figure of the Great Lord.

Aiku understood little of what was being said. She cared nothing about such matters. She took advantage of the diversion to glance about the room. Her husband and father-in-law, she noticed, were standing directly behind her, by the door close to the wall. It had been a year and a half since she had last seen them. Both looked older, more tired, than she had remembered. The young animal together with the old beast, she thought.

Attention on the piece of jade flagged abruptly. It passed from the Great Lord to the hands of Mr. Wei. He sat down and, stroking it with his finger, looked up at Uncle Mu.

"Only the two of you came?" he asked.

"Just us."

"Why didn't you bring your sons along?"

"They were occupied with other matters."

"We wouldn't have troubled you on New Years if it weren't for this affair. I'm sure you are sick of it by now. Been going on for two years, hasn't it?"

Wei continued on without waiting for a reply. "It's better, I say, to undo old knots than to tie new ones. Since Aiku and her husband can't get along, and his parents hold no love for her as well, better to accept my recommendation and separate. Of course I haven't the face to convince you of this. . . . But the Great Lord, as you well know, is the champion of justice. And his conclusion is the same as mine. However, he does suggest that both sides give in a little. He's instructed the Shih family to add another ten dollars to the settlement fee. That makes it a total of ninety dollars."

Uncle Mu made no move to answer.

"It's ninety dollars! You could carry the case to the Emperor himself and you wouldn't get such fine terms. Only the Great Lord would come up with such a handsome offer."

At this point the Great Lord widened the slits of his eyes and, looking at Uncle Mu, nodded his head.

Aiku saw at once that the situation was desperate. She was angered over her father's silence, and to think he was a man held in such high regard by all the families on the seacoast. He hadn't said a word in her defense. There was no reason for his timidity. Yet the Great Lord with all his talk of jade and the ancients was a pleasant surprise. He appeared to be a kindly soul, not nearly as frightening as she had imagined.

"The Great Lord is a scholar who knows the truth," Aiku broke in boldy. "He's not like us country folk. Much wrong has been done me and I appeal to the Great Lord for justice. Throughout my marriage I tried to be a loyal, faithful wife. I bowed my head as I came and went and I did not fail even once in my wifely duties. But the Shih family kept finding fault with me—each one picked on me. One year the weasel killed a big cock; they all accused me of not closing the door to the chicken coop. That mangy dog of theirs, the rotten beast, was the one who pushed open the door. He wanted to get the rice husks. But my own husband, that young animal, wouldn't even try to hear my side of it. He just slapped me."

The Great Lord's eyes focused on Aiku.

"There's a reason for their actions, I'm sure," Aiku continued. "The Great Lord must see this too, for he is a scholar, a man of great learning and wisdom, and he will be able to distinguish truth from falsehood. My husband was taken to that bitch, and his passion led him to drive me from his house. We were married properly. There were the 'three teas and the six gifts' before we were betrothed. And I was even carried to his house in an elegant bridal sedan chair! Are you going to let him toss me aside so easily? I mean to show them and I don't care if I have to go to court. If the district court won't give me satisfaction, I'll carry it to the prefecture—"

"The Great Lord knows all this," interrupted Mr. Wei. "Your attitude, Aiku, will gain you nothing. I can see you haven't changed one bit. Look how sensible your father is. It's a shame you and your brothers aren't more like him. Suppose you do take this matter to the prefecture, won't he consult with the Great Lord here? Then, of course, the case will also be public. Nobody's feelings will be spared. So—"

"I'll risk my life if I have to, even if it means the ruination of both families—"

"Such desperate measures are not needed here," said the Great Lord in a slow, measured voice. "You are still young. . . . We should

Divorce

all seek to bring about a peaceful settlement. It's peace that breeds wealth, you know. Now I've agreed to ten more dollars; that's generous. If your father-in-law and mother-in-law tell you: 'Get out!', then you must go. Let's hear no more talk of the prefecture. It would be the same there as it would be in Shanghai, Peking, or even in some foreign country. But don't take my word for it, ask him!"

With this, the Great Lord turned to a young man with a narrow, pointed chin. "He's newly returned from studying at a foreign school in Peking. Am I not correct?" the Great Lord asked the student.

"A-B-S-O-L-U-T-E-L-Y!" the young man answered. He had come to attention and he acted pleased at being consulted on so important a matter.

It was then that Aiku realized she stood alone. Her father refused to speak, her brothers had been afraid to come, and Mr. Wei had always sided with "them." And now the Great Lord had failed her. Even this student, with his worldly appearance and pompous ways, was merely mouthing what was expected of him. Pressed back as she was, Aiku was still determined to make one last plea: "Even the Great Lord has not understood!" Her eyes showed a mixture of surprise and disappointment. "It's true, we are only stupid country bumpkins. My father does not know how to deal with your kind. He's to blame; he's lost his wits completely. He let my husband and his family get the upper hand on every occasion. And as for them, they will resort to any form of trickery, however low and despicable, to court the favor of those above them—"

"Just look at her, Great Lord," her husband joined in. "She dares to act like this, even in your honored presence. When she was in my house we had no peace. You've heard her call me a young animal. She also calls my father an old beast and, sometimes, she even refers to me as a bastard. She's accused my mother of having ten times ten thousand lovers."

"Who in the hell has called you a bastard?" Aiku screamed at her husband. Abruptly she turned back to the Great Lord. "Now that this is out, let's set the record straight before everyone. He's always treated me rotten. It's either slut or bitch all the time. After he started up with that whore, he even cursed my ancestors. It's your duty to find out who is right, Great Lord."

Aiku began to add to this but suddenly her words faltered. The Great Lord motioned with his eyes; his round face turned dark. A shrill call came from his lips.

"LOI-A—A! Come here!" he called to a servant.

Aiku's heart missed a beat, then began to pound. She had lost, she knew, and now it appeared that everyone was against her. She'd risked speaking and failed. Only she was to blame.

The servant, dressed in a blue gown and black jacket, snapped to attention and moved to the Great Lord's side. The Great Lord whispered something into the man's ear. Though everyone tried, none save the two could tell what was being said. The servant seemed struck by the impact of the Great Lord's words. He twitched two times over and his face showed awe, even disbelief.

"Very well, sire," he said.

The servant backed away several steps, turned, and left the room.

Aiku sensed that something unexpected and utterly unforeseen was about to happen. It was something she was powerless to prevent. Only now did she realize the full power of the Great Lord. She had made a tragic mistake; acted too rashly, too rudely. She repented bitterly and suddenly found herself saying:

"But I've always intended to accept the Great Lord's decision. . . . "

The room was quiet and, although she had spoken in a soft, subservient voice, her words seemed to crash into silence. And, they fell onto the ears of Mr. Wei.

He leaped to his feet. "Good!" he exclaimed approvingly. "The Great Lord is truly just and Aiku is truly reasonable. Now it appears that even Uncle Mu can't object, since his own daughter has given her consent. I assume you both brought the wedding certificates. Now let both sides bring them forth."

Aiku watched as her father fumbled in his girdle. Meanwhile the servant had returned to the room. He handed the Great Lord a small, flat, jet-black object shaped like a tortoise. Aiku feared the worst. She glanced quickly at her father, but he was busily opening a bundle of blue cloth that had been given him by Mr. Wei. From it he withdrew some silver coins.

The Great Lord removed the head from the tortoiselike object and poured something from its body into the palm of his hand. Afterwards he returned the object to the servant. He rubbed one finger in his palm, then stuffed it up each nostril. A bright, yellow smear stained his nose and upper lip. He wrinkled his nose as if to sneeze.

Uncle Mu meanwhile counted out a pile of silver coins on a nearby table. Mr. Wei took back those not counted and returned them to her father-in-law. This done, Mr. Wei exchanged the red and green marriage certificates, returning each to its original owner.

Divorce

"Put them away," he commanded. "Make certain you have the right amount, Uncle Mu. This is no joking matter. All this silver. . . . "

"Ah-chooo!"

Though Aiku knew that it was only the Great Lord sneezing, she couldn't help but turn to look at him. His mouth was wide open and his nose twitched. He was still clutching the small object "used in the ancient burials" between his two fingers. Now he was rubbing the sides of his nose with it.

With some difficulty, Uncle Mu finished his count. Both sides put away the red and green marriage certificates. The tension seemed to leave the room then, and everyone appeared more relaxed. It was as though a certain harmony had returned.

"Excellent! This affair has been concluded satisfactorily," Mr. Wei said. Seeing that Uncle Mu and Aiku were about to leave, he breathed a sigh of relief. "Well, there's nothing more to be done. Congratulations on unraveling this knot! Must you leave? Stay and share the New Year feast with us. This is an important occasion."

"We can't stay," answered Aiku. "We'll come and drink with you next year."

"Thank you, Mr. Wei. We won't drink just now. We have other matters to attend to," her father chimed in. Uncle Mu and Aiku bowed and began to withdraw from the room.

"What? Not a single drop of wine before you go?" Mr. Wei called out to Aiku who brought up the rear.

"Really, we can't. But thanks, Mr. Wei."

Betrayal in Mexico

KATHERINE ANNE PORTER

"My one aim is to tell a straight story and to give true testimony" Miss Porter once said; but her method is sometimes confusing because of her heavy use of subtle symbols.

Born in 1890 in the small town of Indian Creek, Texas, on the Mexican border, Katherine Anne Porter was reared by a vigorous grandmother, who had lived in luxury in Kentucky before the Civil War but later was forced to bring up children and grandchildren in poverty. After attending southern convent schools, Katherine began to wander for many years in search of a spiritual home—to Mexico, Paris, Berlin. Many of her stories are based on her own life, and she is often a participant in them under the name of "Miranda." She began publishing around 1925, and her first collection, *Flowering Judas* (1930), brought acclaim for her concentration of style, which was made to serve her vision of life. Her output was not large, but as she wrote: "Now and again thousands of memories converge, harmonize, arrange themselves around a central idea in a coherent form, and I write a story."

"Flowering Judas," first published in 1930, was considered by Miss Porter to be her best. Like other Porter stories, it may at first offer a baffling experience to the reader who expects a strong plot. The action is psychological, and the outcome may be revealed merely in a bad dream. As with Chekhov and Katherine Mansfield, "character suspense" is what keeps us reading. We want to know chiefly not what these individuals *do,* but what they are really *like* and whether they are saved or damned. This is a story about faith, betrayal, and the kinds of love that might save or damn the people concerned. The theme of this story about Laura in Mexico, as suggested by Ray B. West, Jr., in his essay "Symbol and Theme in 'Flowering Judas' " is "Man cannot live divided by materialistic and spiritual values, nor can he live in the modern world by either, without faith and love."

KATHERINE ANNE PORTER

Flowering Judas

*B*RAGGIONI SITS HEAPED upon the edge of a straight-backed chair much too small for him, and sings to Laura in a furry, mournful voice. Laura has begun to find reasons for avoiding her own house until the latest possible moment, for Braggioni is there almost every night. No matter how late she is, he will be sitting there with a surly, waiting expression, pulling at his kinky yellow hair, thumbing the strings of his guitar, snarling a tune under his breath. Lupe the Indian maid meets Laura at the door, and says with a flicker of a glance towards the upper room, "He waits."

Laura wishes to lie down; she is tired of her hairpins and the feel of her long tight sleeves, but she says to him, "Have you a new song for me this evening?" If he says yes, she asks him to sing it. If he says no, she remembers his favorite one, and asks him to sing it again. Lupe brings her a cup of chocolate and a plate of rice, and Laura eats at the small table under the lamp, first inviting Braggioni, whose answer is always the same: "I have eaten, and besides, chocolate thickens the voice."

Laura says, "Sing, then," and Braggioni heaves himself into song. He scratches the guitar familiarly as though it were a pet animal, and sings passionately off key, taking the high notes in a prolonged painful squeal. Laura, who haunts the markets listening to the ballad singers, and stops every day to hear the blind boy playing his reed flute in Sixteenth of September Street, listens to Braggioni with pitiless courtesy, because she dares not smile at his miserable performance. Nobody dares to smile at him. Braggioni is cruel to everyone, with a kind of specialized insolence, but he is so vain of his talents, and so sensitive to slights, it would require a cruelty and vanity greater than his own to lay a finger on the vast cureless wound of his self-esteem. It would require courage, too, for it is dangerous to offend him, and nobody has this courage.

Braggioni loves himself with such tenderness and amplitude and eternal charity that his followers—for he is a leader of men, a skilled revolutionist, and his skin has been punctured in honorable warfare —warm themselves in the reflected glow, and say to each other: "He has a real nobility, a love of humanity raised above mere personal affections." The excess of this self-love has flowed out, inconveniently for her, over Laura, who, with so many others, owes her comfortable situation and her salary to him. When he is in a very good humor, he tells her, "I am tempted to forgive you for being a *gringa. Gringita!*" and Laura, burning, imagines herself leaning forward suddenly, and with a sound backhanded slap wiping the suety smile from his face. If he notices her eyes at these moments he gives no sign.

She knows what Braggioni would offer her, and she must resist tenaciously without appearing to resist, and if she could avoid it she would not admit even to herself the slow drift of his intention. During these long evenings which have spoiled a long month for her, she sits in her deep chair with an open book on her knees, resting her eyes on the consoling rigidity of the printed page when the sight and sound of Braggioni singing threaten to identify themselves with all her remembered afflictions and to add their weight to her uneasy premonitions of the future. The gluttonous bulk of Braggioni has become a symbol of her many disillusions, for a revolutionist should be lean, animated by heroic faith, a vessel of abstract virtues. This is nonsense; she knows it now and is ashamed of it. Revolution must have leaders, and leadership is a career for energetic men. She is, her comrades tell her, full of romantic error, for what she defines as cynicism in them is merely "a developed sense of reality." She is almost too willing to say, "I am wrong, I suppose I don't really understand the principles," afterward she makes a secret truce with herself, determined not to surrender her will to such expedient logic. But she cannot help feeling that she has been betrayed irreparably by the disunion between her way of living and her feeling of what life should be, and at times she is almost contented to rest in this sense of grievance as a private store of consolation. Sometimes she wishes to run away, but she stays. Now she longs to fly out of this room, down the narrow stairs, and into the street where the houses lean together like conspirators under a single mottled lamp, and leave Braggioni singing to himself.

Flowering Judas

Instead she looks at Braggioni, frankly and clearly, like a good child who understands the rules of behavior. Her knees cling together under sound blue serge, and her round white collar is not purposely nunlike. She wears the uniform of an idea, and has renounced vanities. She was born Roman Catholic, and in spite of her fear of being seen by someone who might make a scandal of it, she slips now and again into some crumbling little church, kneels on the chilly stone, and says a Hail Mary on the gold rosary she bought in Tehuantepec. It is no good and she ends by examining the altar with its tinsel flowers and ragged brocades, and feels tender about the battered doll-shape of some male saint whose white, lace-trimmed drawers hang limply around his ankles below the hieratic dignity of his velvet robe. She has encased herself in a set of principles derived from her early training, leaving no detail of gesture or of personal taste untouched, and for this reason she will not wear lace made on machines. This is her private heresy, for in her special group the machine is sacred, and will be the salvation of the workers. She loves fine lace, and there is a tiny edge of fluted cobweb on this collar, which is one of twenty precisely alike, folded in blue tissue paper in the upper drawer of her clothes chest.

Braggioni catches her glance solidly as if he had been waiting for it, leans forward, balancing his paunch between his spread knees, and sings with tremendous emphasis, weighing his words. He has, the song relates, no father and no mother, nor even a friend to console him; lonely as a wave of the sea he comes and goes, lonely as a wave. His mouth opens round and yearns sideways, his balloon cheeks grow oily with the labor of song. He bulges marvelously in his expensive garments. Over his lavender collar, crushed upon a purple necktie, held by a diamond hoop: over his ammunition belt of tooled leather worked in silver, buckled cruelly around his gasping middle: over the tops of his glossy yellow shoes Braggioni swells with ominous ripeness, his mauve silk hose stretched taut, his ankles bound with the stout leather thongs of his shoes.

When he stretches his eyelids at Laura she notes again that his eyes are the true tawny yellow cat's eyes. He is rich, not in money, he tells her, but in power, and this power brings with it the blameless ownership of things, and the right to indulge his love of small luxuries. "I have a taste for the elegant refinements," he said once, flourishing a yellow silk handkerchief before her nose. "Smell that? It is Jockey Club, imported from New York." Nonetheless he is wounded by life. He will say so presently. "It is true everything turns to dust in the hand, to gall on the tongue." He sighs and his leather belt creaks like a saddle girth. "I am disappointed in everything as it comes. Everything." He shakes his head. "You, poor thing, you will be disappointed too. You are born for it. We are more alike than you realize in some things. Wait and see. Some day you will remember what I have told you, you will know that Braggioni was your friend."

Laura feels a slow chill, a purely physical sense of danger, a warning in her blood that violence, mutilation, a shocking death, wait for her with lessening patience. She has translated this fear into something homely, immediate, and sometimes hesitates before crossing the street. "My personal fate is nothing, except as the testimony of a mental attitude," she reminds herself, quoting from some forgotten philosophic primer, and is sensible enough to add, "Anyhow, I shall not be killed by an automobile if I can help it."

"It may be true I am as corrupt, in another way, as Braggioni," she thinks in spite of herself, "as callous, as incomplete," and if this is so, any kind of death seems preferable. Still she sits quietly, she does not run. Where could she go? Uninvited she has promised herself to this place; she can no longer imagine herself as living in another country, and there is no pleasure in remembering her life before she came here.

Precisely what is the nature of this devotion, its true motives, and what are its obligations? Laura cannot say. She spends part of her days in Xochimilco, near by, teaching Indian children to say in English, "The cat is on the mat." When she appears in the classroom they crowd about her with smiles on their wise, innocent, clay-colored faces, crying, "Good morning, my titcher!" in immaculate voices, and they make of her desk a fresh garden of flowers every day.

During her leisure she goes to union meetings and listens to busy important voices quarreling over tactics, methods, internal politics. She visits the prisoners of her own political faith in their cells, where they entertain themselves with counting cockroaches, repenting of their indiscretions, composing their memoirs, writing out manifestoes and plans for their comrades who are still walking about free, hands in pockets, sniffing fresh air. Laura brings them food and cigarettes and a little money, and she brings messages disguised in equivocal phrases from the men outside who dare not set foot in the prison for fear of disappearing into the cells kept empty for them. If the prisoners confuse night and day, and complain, "Dear little Laura, time doesn't pass in this infernal hole, and I won't know when it is time to sleep unless I have a reminder," she brings them their favorite narcotics, and says in a tone that does not wound them with pity, "Tonight will really be night for you," and though her Spanish amuses them, they find her comforting, useful. If they lose patience and all faith, and curse the slowness of their friends in coming to their rescue with money and influence, they trust her not to repeat everything, and if she inquires, "Where do you think we can find money, or influence?" they are certain to answer, "Well, there is Braggioni, why doesn't he do something?"

She smuggles letters from headquarters to men hiding from firing squads in back streets in mildewed houses, where they sit in tumbled beds and talk bitterly as if all Mexico were at their heels, when Laura knows positively they might appear at the band concert in the Alameda on Sunday morning, and no one would notice them. But Braggioni says, "Let them sweat a little. The next time they may be careful. It is very restful to have them out of the way for a while." She is not afraid to knock on any door in any street after midnight, and enter in the darkness, and say to one of these men who is really in danger: "They will be looking for you—seriously—tomorrow morning after six. Here is some money from Vicente. Go to Vera Cruz and wait."

She borrows money from the Rumanian agitator to give to his bitter enemy the Polish agitator. The favor of Braggioni is their disputed territory, and Braggioni holds the balance nicely, for he can use them both. The Polish agitator talks love to her over café tables, hoping to exploit what he believes is her secret sentimental preference for him, and he gives her misinformation which he begs her to repeat as the solemn truth to certain persons. The Rumanian is more adroit. He is generous with his money in all good causes, and lies to her with an air of ingenuous candor, as if he were her good friend and confidant. She never repeats anything they may say. Braggioni never asks questions. He has other ways to discover all that he wishes to know about them.

Nobody touches her, but all praise her gray eyes, and the soft, round underlip which promises gaiety, yet is always grave, nearly always firmly closed: and they cannot understand why she is in Mexico. She walks back and forth on her errands, with puzzled eyebrows, carrying her little folder of drawings and music and school papers. No dancer dances more beautifully than Laura walks, and she inspires some amusing, unexpected ardors, which cause little gossip, because nothing comes of them. A young captain who had been a soldier in Zapata's army attempted, during a horseback ride near Cuernavaca, to express his desire for her with the noble simplicity befitting a rude folk hero: but gently, because he was gentle. This gentleness was his defeat, for when he alighted, and removed her foot from the stirrup, and essayed to draw her down into his arms, her horse, ordinarily a tame one, shied fiercely, reared and plunged away. The young hero's horse careered blindly after his stable mate, and the hero did not return to the hotel until rather late that evening. At breakfast he came to her table in full charro dress, gray buckskin jacket and trousers with strings of silver buttons down the leg, and he was in a humorous, careless mood. "May I sit with you?" and "You are a wonderful rider. I was terrified that you might be thrown and dragged. I should never have forgiven myself. But I cannot admire you enough for your riding!"

"I learned to ride in Arizona," said Laura.

"If you will ride with me again this morning, I promise you a horse that will not shy with you," he said. But Laura remembered that she must return to Mexico City at noon.

Next morning the children made a celebration and spent their playtime writing on the blackboard, "We lov ar ticher," and with tinted chalks they drew wreaths of flowers around the words. The young hero wrote her a letter: "I am a very foolish, wasteful, impulsive man. I should have first said I love you, and then you would not have run away. But you shall see me again." Laura thought, "I must send him a box of colored crayons," but she was trying to forgive herself for having spurred her horse at the wrong moment.

A brown, shock-haired youth came and stood in her patio one night and sang like a lost soul for two hours, but Laura could think of nothing to do about it. The moonlight spread a wash of gauzy silver over the clear spaces of the garden, and the shadows were cobalt blue. The scarlet blossoms of the Judas tree were dull purple, and the names of the colors repeated themselves automatically in her mind, while she watched not the boy, but his shadow, fallen like a dark garment across the fountain rim, trailing in the water. Lupe came silently and whispered expert counsel in her ear: "If you will throw him one little flower, he will sing another song or two and go away." Laura threw the flower, and he sang a last song and went away with the flower tucked in the band of his hat. Lupe said, "He is one of the organizers of the Typographers Union, and before that he sold *corridos* in the Merced market, and before that, he came from Guanajuato, where I was born. I would not trust any man, but I trust least those from Guanajuato."

She did not tell Laura that he would be back again the next night, and the next, nor that he would follow her at a certain fixed distance

Flowering Judas

around the Merced market, through the Zócolo, up Francisco I. Madero Avenue, and so along the Paseo de la Reforma to Chapultepec Park, and into the Philosopher's Footpath, still with that flower withering in his hat, and an indivisible attention in his eyes.

Now Laura is accustomed to him, it means nothing except that he is nineteen years old and is observing a convention with all propriety, as though it were founded on a law of nature, which in the end it might well prove to be. He is beginning to write poems which he prints on a wooden press, and he leaves them stuck like handbills in her door. She is pleasantly disturbed by the abstract, unhurried watchfulness of his black eyes, which will in time turn easily towards another object. She tells herself that throwing the flower was a mistake, for she is twenty-two years old and knows better; but she refuses to regret it, and persuades herself that her negation of all external events as they occur is a sign that she is gradually perfecting herself in the stoicism she strives to cultivate against that disaster she fears, though she cannot name it.

She is not at home in the world. Every day she teaches children who remain strangers to her, though she loves their tender round hands and their charming opportunist savagery. She knocks at unfamiliar doors not knowing whether a friend or a stranger shall answer, and even if a known face emerges from the sour gloom of that unknown interior, still it is the face of a stranger. No matter what this stranger says to her, nor what her message to him, the very cells of her flesh reject knowledge and kinship in one monotonous word. No. No. No. She draws her strength from this one holy talismanic word which does not suffer her to be led into evil. Denying everything, she may walk anywhere in safety, she looks at everything without amazement.

No, repeats this firm unchanging voice of her blood; and she looks at Braggioni without amazement. He is a great man, he wishes to impress this simple girl who covers her great round breasts with thick dark cloth, and who hides long, invaluably beautiful legs under a heavy skirt. She is almost thin except for the incomprehensible fullness of her breasts, like a nursing mother's, and Braggioni, who considered himself a judge of women, speculates again on the puzzle of her notorious virginity, and takes the liberty of speech which she permits without a sign of modesty, indeed, without any sort of sign, which is disconcerting.

"You think you are so cold, *gringita!* Wait and see. You will surprise yourself some day! May I be there to advise you!" He stretches his eyelids at her, and his ill-humored cat's eyes waver in a separate glance for the two points of light marking the opposite ends of a smoothly drawn path between the swollen curve of her breasts. He is not put off by that blue serge, nor by her resolutely fixed gaze. There is all the time in the world. His cheeks are bellying with the wind of song. "Oh girl with the dark eyes," he sings, and reconsiders. "But yours are not dark. I can change all that. Oh girl with the green eyes, you have stolen my heart away!" then his mind wanders to the song, and Laura feels the weight of his attention being shifted elsewhere. Singing thus, he seems harmless, he is quite harmless, there is nothing to do but sit patiently and say "No," when the moment comes. She draws a full breath, and her mind wanders also, but not far. She dares not wander too far.

Not for nothing has Braggioni taken pains to be a good revolutionist and a professional lover of humanity. He will never die of it. He has the malice, the cleverness, the wickedness, the sharpness of wit, the hardness of heart, stipulated for loving the world profitably. *He will never die of it.* He will live to see himself kicked out from his feeding trough by other hungry world saviors. Traditionally he must sing in spite of his life which drives him to bloodshed, he tells Laura, for his father was a Tuscany peasant who drifted to Yucatan and married a Maya woman: a woman of race, an aristocrat. They gave him the love and knowledge of music, thus: and under the rip of his thumbnail, the strings of the instrument complain like exposed nerves.

Once he was called Delgadito by all the girls and married women who ran after him; he was so scrawny all his bones showed under his thin cotton clothing, and he could squeeze his emptiness to the very backbone with his two hands. He was a poet and the revolution was only a dream then; too many women loved him and sapped away his youth, and he could never find enough to eat anywhere, anywhere! Now he is a leader of men, crafty men who whisper in his ear, hungry men who wait for hours outside his office for a word with him, emaciated men with wild faces who waylay him at the street gate with a timid, "Comrade, let me tell you ... " and they blow the foul breath from their empty stomachs in his face.

He is always sympathetic. He gives them handfuls of small coins from his own pocket, he promises them work, there will be demonstrations, they must join the unions and attend the meetings, above all they must be on the watch for spies. They are closer to him than his own brothers, without them he can do nothing—until tomorrow, comrade!

Until tomorrow. "They are stupid, they are lazy, they are treacherous, they would cut my throat for nothing," he says to Laura. He has good food and abundant drink, he hires an automobile and drives in the Paseo on Sunday morning, and enjoys plenty of sleep in a soft bed beside a wife who dares not disturb him, and he sits pampering his bones in easy billows of fat, singing to Laura, who knows and thinks these things about him. When he was fifteen, he tried to drown himself because he loved a girl, his first love, and she laughed at him. "A thousand women have paid for that," and his tight little mouth turns down at the corners. Now he perfumes his hair with Jockey Club, and confides to Laura: "One woman is really as good as another for me, in the dark. I prefer them all."

His wife organizes unions among the girls in the cigarette factories, and walks in picket lines, and even speaks at meetings in the evening. But she cannot be brought to acknowledge the benefits of true liberty. "I tell her I must have my freedom, net. She does not understand my point of view." Laura has heard this many times. Braggioni scratches the guitar and meditates. "She is an instinctively virtuous woman, pure gold, no doubt of that. If she were not, I should lock her up, and she knows it."

His wife, who works so hard for the good of the factory girls, employs part of her leisure lying on the floor weeping because there are so many women in the world, and only one husband for her, and she never knows where nor when to look for him. He told her: "Unless you can learn to cry when I am not here, I must go away for good." That day he went away and took a room at the Hotel Madrid.

It is this month of separation for the sake of higher principles that has been spoiled not only for Mrs. Braggioni, whose sense of reality is beyond criticism, but for Laura, who feels herself bogged in a nightmare. Tonight Laura envies Mrs. Braggioni, who is alone, and free to weep as much as she pleases about a concrete wrong. Laura has just come from a visit to the prison, and she is waiting for tomorrow with a bitter anxiety as if tomorrow may not come, but time may be caught immovably in this hour, with herself transfixed, Braggioni singing on forever, and Eugenio's body not yet discovered by the guard.

Braggioni says: "Are you going to sleep?" Almost before she can shake her head, he begins telling her about the May-Day disturbances coming on in Morelia, for the Catholics hold a festival in honor of the Blessed Virgin, and the Socialists celebrate their martyrs on that day. "There will be two independent processions, starting from either end of town, and they will march until they meet, and the rest depends . . ." He asks her to oil and load his pistols. Standing up, he unbuckles his ammunition belt, and spreads it laden across her knees. Laura sits with the shells slipping through the cleaning cloth dipped in oil, and he says again he cannot understand why she works so hard for the revolutionary idea unless she loves some man who is in it. "Are you not in love with someone?" "No," says Laura. "And no one is in love with you?" "No." "Then it is your own fault. No woman need go begging. Why, what is the matter with you? The legless beggar woman in the Alameda has a perfectly faithful lover. Did you know that?"

Laura peers down the pistol barrel and says nothing, but a long, slow faintness rises and subsides in her; Braggioni curves his swollen fingers around the throat of the guitar and softly smothers the music out of it, and when she hears him again he seems to have forgotten her, and is speaking in the hypnotic voice he uses when talking in small rooms to a listening, close-gathered crowd. Some day this world, now seemingly so composed and eternal, to the edges of every sea shall be merely a tangle of gaping trenches, of crashing walls and broken bodies. Everything must be torn from its accustomed place where it has rotted for centuries, hurled skyward and distributed, cast down again clean as rain, without separate identity. Nothing shall survive that the stiffened hands of poverty have created for the rich and no one shall be left alive except the elect spirits destined to procreate a new world cleansed of cruelty and injustice, ruled by benevolent anarchy: "Pistols are good, I love them, cannon are even better, but in the end I pin my faith to good dynamite," he concludes, and strokes the pistol lying in her hands. "Once I dreamed of destroying this city, in case it offered resistance to General Ortíz, but it fell into his hands like an overripe pear."

He is made restless by his own words, rises and stands waiting. Laura holds up the belt to him: "Put that on, and go kill somebody in Morelia, and you will be happier," she says softly. The presence of death in the room makes her bold. "Today, I found Eugenio going into a stupor. He refused to allow me to call the prison doctor. He had taken all the tablets I brought him yesterday. He said he took them because he was bored."

"He is a fool, and his death is his own business," says Braggioni, fastening his belt carefully.

"I told him if he had waited only a little while longer, you would have got him set free," says Laura. "He said he did not want to wait."

"He is a fool and we are well rid of him," says Braggioni, reaching for his hat.

He goes away. Laura knows his mood has changed, she will not see him any more for a while. He will send word when he needs her to

Flowering Judas

go on errands into strange streets, to speak to the strange faces that will appear, like clay masks with the power of human speech, to mutter their thanks to Braggioni for his help. Now she is free, and she thinks, I must run while there is time. But she does not go.

Braggioni enters his own house where for a month his wife has spent many hours every night weeping and tangling her hair upon her pillow. She is weeping now, and she weeps more at the sight of him, the cause of all her sorrows. He looks about the room. Nothing is changed, the smells are good and familiar, he is well acquainted with the woman who comes toward him with no reproach except grief on her face. He says to her tenderly: "You are so good, please don't cry any more, you dear good creature." She says, "Are you tired, my angel? Sit here and I will wash your feet." She brings a bowl of water, and kneeling, unlaces his shoes, and when from her knees she raises her sad eyes under her blackened lids, he is sorry for everything, and bursts into tears. "Ah, yes, I am hungry, I am tired, let us eat something together," he says, between sobs. His wife leans her head on his arm and says, "Forgive me!" and this time he is refreshed by the solemn, endless rain of her tears.

Laura takes off her serge dress and puts on a white linen nightgown and goes to bed. She turns her head a little to one side, and lying still, reminds herself that it is time to sleep. Numbers tick in her brain like little clocks, soundless doors close of themselves around her. If you would sleep, you must not remember anything, the children will say tomorrow, good morning, my teacher, the poor prisoners who come every day bringing flowers to their jailor. 1-2-3-4-5 it is monstrous to confuse love with revolution, night with day, life with death—ah, Eugenio!

The tolling of the midnight bell is a signal, but what does it mean? Get up, Laura, and follow me: come out of your sleep, out of your bed, out of this strange house. What are you doing in this house? Without a word, without fear she rose and reached for Eugenio's hand, but he eluded her with a sharp, sly smile and drifted away. This is not all, you shall see—Murderer, he said, follow me, I will show you a new country, but it is far away and we must hurry. No, said Laura, not unless you take my hand, no; and she clung first to the stair rail, and then to the topmost branch of the Judas tree that bent down slowly and set her upon the earth, and then to the rocky ledge of a cliff, and then to the jagged wave of a sea that was not water but a desert of crumbling stone. Where are you taking me? she asked in wonder but without fear. To death, and it is a long way off, and we must hurry, said Eugenio. No, said Laura, not unless you take my hand. Then eat these flowers, poor prisoner, said Eugenio in a voice of pity, take and eat: and from the Judas tree he stripped the warm bleeding flowers, and held them to her lips. She saw that his hand was fleshless, a cluster of small white petrified branches, and his eye sockets were without light, but she ate the flowers greedily, for they satisfied both hunger and thirst. Murderer! said Eugenio, and Cannibal! This is my body and my blood. Laura cried No! and at the sound of her own voice, she awoke trembling, and was afraid to sleep again.

*Dream
Ponies in
the Moonlight*

WILLIAM FAULKNER

Faulkner, a great writer about the South, was awarded the Nobel Prize in 1949 "for his powerful and artistically independent contribution to the new American novel."

Born of a middle-class family with deep roots in the South even before the Civil War, William Faulkner (1897-1962) spent nearly all of his life at Oxford, Mississippi, site of the University of Mississippi. Most of his books deal with this town and the surrounding countryside, which he made famous as "Yoknapatawpha County." During World War I he served in 1918 in Canada as a lieutenant in the British Air Force. He returned to Oxford, serving for a short time as postmaster, and took a number of courses at the University.

Faulkner drifted to New Orleans, where, by the help of Sherwood Anderson, another fiction writer, he had his first poem published and began writing novels. After wandering to New York and Europe, he went home to Oxford and took a job shoveling coal on the night shift at a power plant. Here he rewrote his best novels, and after 1931 was able to support himself by turning out books and motionpicture scenarios. He lived with his wife and their children outside of town as a gentleman farmer, and spent much time hunting and fishing. Many of his novels and stories deal not only with his home region, but with the same people and families, and he drew upon his own ancestry for a number of incidents. He is recognized today as one of the world's most powerful storytellers. One of his main themes is the decline of decency and humanity exemplified by people like Flem Snopes and his clan.

"Spotted Horses" first appeared in *Scribner's Magazine* for June, 1931, and later was lengthened, changed, and used as a part of Faulkner's novel *The Hamlet* (1940). Easily classified as a "tall tale" deriving from the American tradition of frontier humor, it shows beneath the grim comedy a compassion and grief for those who are victimized by dreams.

WILLIAM FAULKNER

Spotted Horses

I

YES, SIR. FLEM SNOPES has filled that whole country full of spotted horses. You can hear folks running them all day and all night, whooping and hollering, and the horses running back and forth across them little wooden bridges ever now and then kind of like thunder. Here I was this morning pretty near half way to town, with the team ambling along and me setting in the buckboard about half asleep, when all of a sudden something come swurging up outen the bushes and jumped the road clean, without touching hoof to it. It flew right over my team big as a billboard and flying through the air like a hawk. It taken me thirty minutes to stop my team and untangle the harness and the buckboard and hitch them up again.

That Flem Snopes. I be dog if he ain't a case, now. One morning about ten years ago the boys was just getting settled down on Varner's porch for a little talk and tobacco, when here come Flem out from behind the counter, with his coat off and his hair all parted, like he might have been clerking for Varner for ten years already. Folks all knowed him; it was a big family of them about five miles down the bottom. That year, at least. Sharecropping. They never stayed on any place over a year. Then they would move on to another place, with the chap or maybe the twins of that year's litter. It was a regular nest of them. But Flem. The rest of them stayed tenant farmers, moving ever year, but here come Flem one day, walking out from behind Jody Varner's counter like he owned it. And he wasn't there but a year or two before folks knowed that if him and Jody was both still in that

Spotted Horses

store in ten years more it would be Jody clerking for Flem Snopes. Why, that fellow could make a nickel where it wasn't but four cents to begin with. He skun me in two trades myself, and the fellow that can do that, I just hope he'll get rich before I do; that's all.

All right. So here Flem was, clerking at Varner's, making a nickel here and there and not telling nobody about it. No, sir. Folks never knowed when Flem got the better of somebody lessen the fellow he beat told it. He'd just set there in the store chair, chewing his tobacco and keeping his own business to hisself, until about a week later we'd find out it was somebody else's business he was keeping to hisself—provided the fellow he trimmed was mad enough to tell it. That's Flem.

We give him ten years to own ever thing Jody Varner had. But he never waited no ten years. I reckon you-all know that gal of Uncle Billy Varner's, the youngest one; Eula. Jody's sister. Ever Sunday ever yellow-wheeled buggy and curried riding horse in that country would be hitched to Bill Varner's fence, and the young bucks setting on the porch, swarming around Eula like bees around a honey pot. One of these here kind of big, soft-looking gals that could giggle richer than plowed new-ground. Wouldn't none of them leave before the others, and so they would set there on the porch until time to go home, with some of them with nine and ten miles to ride and then get up tomorrow and go back to the field. So they would all leave together and they would ride in a clump down to the creek ford and hitch them curried horses and yellow-wheeled buggies and get out and fight one another. Then they would get in the buggies again and go on home.

Well, one day about a year ago, one of them yellow-wheeled buggies and one of them curried saddle horses quit this country. We heard they was heading for Texas. The next day Uncle Billy and Eula and Flem come into town in Uncle Bill's surrey, and when they come back, Flem and Eula was married. And on the next day we heard that two more of them yellow-wheeled buggies had left the country. They mought have gone to Texas, too. It's a big place.

Anyway, about a month after the wedding, Flem and Eula went to Texas, too. They was gone pretty near a year. Then one day last month, Eula come back, with a baby. We figured up, and we decided that it was as well-growed a three-months-old baby as we ever see. It can already pull up on a chair. I reckon Texas makes big men quick, being a big place. Anyway, if it keeps on like it started, it'll be chewing tobacco and voting time it's eight years old.

And so last Friday here come Flem himself. He was on a wagon with another fellow. The other fellow had one of these two-gallon hats and a ivory-handled pistol and a box of gingersnaps sticking out of his hind pocket, and tied to the tail gate of the wagon was about two dozen of them Texas ponies, hitched to one another with barbed wire. They was colored like parrots and they was quiet as doves, and ere a one of them would kill you quick as a rattlesnake. Nere a one of them had two eyes the same color, and nere a one of them had ever see a bridle, I reckon; and when that Texas man got down offen the wagon and walked up to them to show how gentle they was, one of them cut his vest clean offen him, same as with a razor.

Flem had done already disappeared; he had went on to see his wife, I reckon, and to see if that ere baby had done gone on to the field to help Uncle Billy plow, maybe. It was the Texas man that taken the horses on to Mrs. Littlejohn's lot. He had a little trouble at first, when they come to the gate, because they hadn't never see a fence before, and when he finally got them in and taken a pair of wire cutters and unhitched them and got them into the barn and poured some shell corn into the trough, they durn nigh tore down the barn. I reckon they thought that shell corn was bugs, maybe. So he left them in the lot and he announced that the auction would begin at sunup tomorrow.

That night we was setting on Mrs. Littlejohn's porch. You-all mind the moon was nigh full that night, and we could watch them spotted varmints swirling along the fence and back and forth across the lot same as minnows in a pond. And then now and then they would all kind of huddle up against the barn and rest themselves by biting and kicking one another. We would hear a squeal, and then a set of hoofs would go Bam! against the barn, like a pistol. It sounded just like a fellow with a pistol, in a nest of cattymounts, taking his time.

II

It wasn't ere a man knowed yet if Flem owned them things or not. They just knowed one thing: that they wasn't never going to know for sho if Flem did or not, or if maybe he didn't just get on that wagon at the edge of town, for the ride or not. Even Eck Snopes didn't know, Flem's own cousin. But wasn't nobody surprised at that. We knowed that Flem would skin Eck quick as he would ere a one of us.

They was there by sunup next morning, some of them come twelve and sixteen miles, with seed money tied up in tobacco sacks in their overalls, standing along the fence, when the Texas man come out of Mrs. Littlejohn's after breakfast and clumb onto the gate post with that ere white pistol butt sticking outen his hind pocket. He taken a new box of gingersnaps outen his pocket and bit the end offen it like

Spotted Horses

a cigar and spit out the paper, and said the auction was open. And still they was coming up in wagons and a horse and muleback and hitching the teams across the road and coming to the fence. Flem wasn't nowhere in sight.

But he couldn't get them started. He begun to work on Eck, because Eck holp him last night to get them into the barn and feed them that shell corn. Eck got out just in time. He come outen that barn like a chip on the crest of a busted dam of water, and clumb into the wagon just in time.

He was working on Eck when Henry Armstid come up in his wagon. Eck was saying he was skeered to bid on one of them, because he might get it, and the Texas man says, "Them ponies? Them little horses?" He clumb down offen the gatepost and went toward the horses. They broke and run, and him following them, kind of chirping to them, with his hand out like he was fixing to catch a fly, until he got three or four of them cornered. Then he jumped into them, and then we couldn't see nothing for a while because of the dust. It was a big cloud of it, and them bare-eyed, spotted things swoaring outen it twenty foot to a jump, in forty directions without counting up. Then the dust settled and there they was, that Texas man and the horse. He had its head twisted clean around like a owl's head. Its legs was braced and it was trembling like a new bride and groaning like a sawmill, and him holding its head wrung clean around on its neck so it was snuffing sky. "Look it over," he says, with his heels dug too and that white pistol sticking outen his pocket and his neck swole up like a spreading adder's until you could just tell what he was saying, cussing the horse and talking to us all at once: "Look him over, the fiddle-headed son of fourteen fathers. Try him, buy him; you will get the best—" Then it was all dust again, and we couldn't see nothing but spotted hide and mane, and that ere Texas man's boot heels like a couple of walnuts on two strings, and after a while that two-gallon hat come sailing out like a fat old hen crossing a fence.

When the dust settled again, he was just getting outen the far fence corner, brushing himself off. He come and got his hat and brushed it off and come and clumb onto the gatepost again. He was breathing hard. The hammerhead horse was still running round and round the lot like a merry-go-round at a fair. That was when Henry Armstid come shoving up to the gate in them patched overalls and one of them dangle-armed shirts of hisn. Hadn't nobody noticed him until then. We was all watching the Texas man and the horses. Even Mrs. Littlejohn; she had done come out and built a fire under the washpot in her backyard, and she would stand at the fence a while and then go back into the house and come out again with a arm full of wash and stand at the fence again. Well, here come Henry shoving up, and then we see Mrs. Armstid right behind him, in that ere faded wrapper and sunbonnet and them tennis shoes. "Git on back to that wagon," Henry says.

"Henry," she says.

"Here, boys," the Texas man says; "make room for missus to git up and see. Come on, Henry," he says; "here's your chance to buy that saddle horse missus has been wanting. What about ten dollars, Henry?"

"Henry," Mrs. Armstid says. She put her hand on Henry's arm. Henry knocked her hand down.

"Git on back to that wagon, like I told you," he says.

Mrs. Armstid never moved. She stood behind Henry, with her hands rolled into her dress, not looking at nothing. "He hain't no more despair than to buy one of them things," she says. "And us not five dollars ahead of the pore house, he hain't no more despair." It was the truth, too. They ain't never made more than a bare living offen that place of theirs, and them with four chaps and the very clothes they wears she earns by weaving by the firelight at night when Henry's asleep.

"Shut your mouth and git on back to that wagon," Henry says. "Do you want I taken a wagon stake to you here in the big road?"

Well, that Texas man taken one look at her. Then he begun on Eck again; like Henry wasn't even there. But Eck was skeered. "I can git me a snapping turtle or a water moccasin for nothing. I ain't going to buy none."

So the Texas man said he would give Eck a horse. "To start the auction, and because you holp me last night. If you'll start the bidding on the next horse," he says, "I'll give you that fiddle-head horse."

I wish you could have seen them, standing there with their seed-money in their pockets, watching that Texas man give Eck Snopes a live horse, all fixed to call him a fool if he taken it or not. Finally Eck says he'll take it. "Only I just starts the bidding," he says. "I don't have to buy the next one lessen I ain't overtopped." The Texas man said all right, and Eck bid a dollar on the next one, with Henry Armstid standing there with his mouth already open, watching Eck and the Texas man like a mad dog or something. "A dollar," Eck says.

The Texas man looked at Eck. His mouth was already open too, like he had started to say something and what he was going to say had up and died on him. "A dollar? You mean, *one* dollar, Eck?"

"Durn it," Eck says; "two dollars, then."

Well, sir, I wish you could a seen that Texas man. He taken out that gingersnap box and held it up and looked into it, careful, like it might have been a diamond ring in it, or a spider. Then he throwed it away and wiped his face with a bandanna. "Well," he says. "Well. Two dollars. Two dollars. Is your pulse all right, Eck?" he says, "Do you have ager sweats at night, maybe?" he says. "Well," he says, "I got to take it. But are you boys going to stand there and see Eck get two horses at a dollar a head?"

That done it. I be dog if he wasn't nigh as smart as Flem Snopes. He hadn't no more than got the words outen his mouth before here was Henry Armstid, waving his hand. "Three dollars," Henry says. Mrs. Armstid tried to hold him again. He knocked her hand off, shoving up to the gatepost.

"Mister," Mrs. Armstid says, "we got chaps in the house and no corn to feed the stock. We got five dollars I earned my chaps a-weaving after dark, and him snoring in the bed. And he hain't no more despair."

"Henry bids three dollars," the Texas man says. "Raise him a dollar, Eck, and the horse is yours."

"Henry," Mrs. Armstid says.

"Raise him, Eck," the Texas man says.

"Four dollars," Eck says.

"Five dollars," Henry says, shaking his fist. He shoved up right under the gatepost. Mrs. Armstid was looking at the Texas man too.

"Mister," she says, "if you take that five dollars I earned my chaps a-weaving for one of them things, it'll be a curse onto you and yourn during all the time of man."

But it wasn't no stopping Henry. He had shoved up, waving his fist at the Texas man. He opened it; the money was in nickels and quarters, and one dollar bill that looked like a cow's cud. "Five dollars," he says. "And the man that raises it'll have to beat my head off, or I'll beat his'n."

"All right," the Texas man says. "Five dollars is bid. But don't you shake your hand at me."

III

It taken till nigh sundown before the last one was sold. He got them hotted up once and the bidding got up to seven dollars and a quarter, but most of them went around three or four dollars, him setting on the gatepost and picking the horses out one at a time by mouth-word, and Mrs. Littlejohn pumping up and down at the tub and stopping and coming to the fence for a while and going back to the tub again. She had done got done too, and the wash was hung on the line in the backyard, and we could smell supper cooking. Finally they was all sold; he swapped the last two and the wagon for a buckboard.

We was all kind of tired, but Henry Armstid looked more like a mad dog than ever. When he bought, Mrs. Armstid had went back to the wagon, setting in it behind them two rabbit-sized, bonepore mules, and the wagon itself looking like it would fall all to pieces soon as the mules moved. Henry hadn't even waited to pull it outen the road; it was still in the middle of the road and her setting in it, not looking at nothing, ever since this morning.

Henry was right up against the gate. He went up to the Texas man. "I bought a horse and I paid cash," Henry says. "And yet you expect me to stand around here until they are all sold before I can get my horse. I'm going to take my horse outen that lot."

The Texas man looked at Henry. He talked like he might have been asking for a cup of coffee at the table. "Take your horse," he says.

Then Henry quit looking at the Texas man. He begun to swallow, holding onto the gate. "Ain't you going to help me?" he says.

"It ain't my horse," the Texas man says.

Henry never looked at the Texas man again, he never looked at nobody. "Who'll help me catch my horse?" he says. Never nobody said nothing. "Bring the plowline," Henry says. Mrs. Armstid got outen the wagon and brought the plowline. The Texas man got down offen the post. The woman made to pass him, carrying the rope.

"Don't you go in there, missus," the Texas man says.

Mrs. Armstid wasn't looking at nobody, neither, with her hands across her middle, holding the rope. "I reckon I better," she says. Her and Henry went into the lot. The horses broke and run. Henry and Mrs. Armstid followed.

"Git him into the corner," Henry says. They got Henry's horse cornered finally, and Henry taken the rope, but Mrs. Armstid let the horse get out. They hemmed it up again, but Mrs. Armstid let it get out again, and Henry turned and hit her with the rope. "Why didn't you head him back?" Henry says. He hit her again. "Why didn't you?" It was about that time I looked around and see Flem Snopes standing there.

It was the Texas man that done something. He moved fast for a big man. He caught the rope before Henry could hit the third time, and Henry whirled and made like he would jump at the Texas man. But he never jumped. The Texas man went and taken Henry's arm and let him outen the lot. Mrs. Armstid come behind them and the Texas man taken some money outen his pocket and he give it into Mrs. Armstid's hand. "Get him into the wagon and take him on home," the Texas man says, like he might have been telling them he enjoyed his supper.

Then here come Flem. "What's that for, Buck?" Flem says.

"Thinks he bought one of them ponies," the Texas man says. "Get him on away, missus."

But Henry wouldn't go. "Give him back that money," he says. "I bought that horse and I aim to have him if I have to shoot him."

And there was Flem, standing there with his hands in his pockets, chewing, like he had just happened to be passing.

"You take your money and I take my horse," Henry says. "Give it back to him," he says to Mrs. Armstid.

"You don't own no horse of mine," the Texas man says. "Get him on home, missus."

Then Henry seen Flem. "You got something to do with these horses," he says. "I bought one. Here's the money for it." He taken the bill outen Mrs. Armstid's hand. He offered it to Flem. "I bought one. Ask him. Here. Here's the money," he says, giving the bill to Flem.

When Flem taken the money, the Texas man dropped the rope he had snatched outen Henry's hand. He had done sent Eck Snopes's boy up to the store for another box of gingersnaps, and he taken the box outen his pocket and looked into it. It was empty and he dropped it on the ground. "Mr. Snopes will have your money for you tomorrow," he says to Mrs. Armstid. "You can get it from him tomorrow. He don't own no horse. You get him into the wagon and get him on home." Mrs. Armstid went back to the wagon and got in. "Where's that ere buckboard I bought?" the Texas man says. It was after sundown then. And then Mrs. Littlejohn come out on the porch and rung the supper bell.

IV

I come on in and et supper. Mrs. Littlejohn would bring in a pan of bread or something, then she would go out to the porch a minute and come back and tell us. The Texas man had hitched his team to the buckboard he had swapped them last two horses for, and him and Flem had gone, and then she told that the rest of them that never had ropes had went back to the store with I. O. Snopes to get some ropes, and wasn't nobody at the gate but Henry Armstid, and Mrs. Armstid setting in the wagon in the road, and Eck Snopes and that boy of hisn. "I don't care how many of them fool men gets killed by them things,"

Mrs. Littlejohn says, "But I ain't going to let Eck Snopes take that boy into that lot again." So she went down to the gate, but she come back without the boy or Eck neither.

"It ain't no need to worry about that boy," I says. He's charmed. He was right behind Eck last night when Eck went to help feed them. The whole drove of them jumped clean over that boy's head and never touched him. It was Eck that touched him. Eck snatched him into the wagon and taken a rope and frailed the tar outen him.

So I had done et and went to my room and was undressing, long as I had a long trip to make next day, I was trying to sell a machine to Mrs. Bundren up past Whiteleaf when Henry Armstid opened that gate and went in by hisself. They couldn't make him wait for the balance of them to get back with their ropes. Eck Snopes said he tried to make Henry wait, but Henry wouldn't do it. Eck said Henry walked right up to them and that when they broke, they run clean over Henry like a haymow breaking down. Eck said he snatched that boy of hisn out of the way just in time and that them things went through that gate like a creek flood and into the wagons and teams hitched side the road, busting wagon tongues and snapping harness like it was fishing-line, with Mrs. Armstid still setting in their wagon in the middle of it like something carved outen wood. Then they scattered, wild horses and tame mules with pieces of harness and singletrees dangling offen them, both ways up and down the road.

"There goes ourn, paw!" Eck says his boy said. "There it goes, into Mrs. Littlejohn's house." Eck says it run right up the steps and into the hourse like a boarder late for supper. I reckon so. Anyway, I was in my room, in my underclothes, with one sock on and one sock in my hand, leaning out the window when the commotion busted out, when I heard something run into the melodeon in the hall; it sounded like a railroad engine. Then the door to my room come sailing in like when you throw a tin bucket top into the wind and I looked over my shoulder and see something that looked like a fourteen-foot pinwheel a-blaring its eyes at me. It had to blare them fast, because I was already done jumped out the window.

I reckon it was anxious, too. I reckon it hadn't never seen barbed wire or shell corn before, but I know it hadn't never seen underclothes before, or maybe it was a sewing-machine agent it hadn't never seen. Anyway, it whirled and turned to run back up the hall and outen the house, when it met Eck Snopes and that boy just coming in, carrying a rope. It swirled again and run down the hall and out the back door

Spotted Horses

just in time to meet Mrs. Littlejohn. She had just gathered up the clothes she had washed, and she was coming onto the back porch with a armful of washing in one hand and a scrubbing board in the other, when the horse skidded up to her, trying to stop and swirl again. It never taken Mrs. Littlejohn no time a-tall.

"Git outen here, you son," she says. She hit it across the face with the scrubbing board; that ere scrubbing board split as neat as ere a axe could have done it, and when the horse swirled to run back up the hall, she hit it again with what was left of the scrubbing board, not on the head this time. "And stay out," she says.

Eck and that boy was half-way down the hall by this time. I reckon that horse looked like a pinwheel to Eck too. "Git to hell outen here, Ad!" Eck says. Only there wasn't time. Eck dropped flat on his face, but the boy never moved. The boy was about a yard tall maybe, in overalls just like Eck's; that horse swoared over his head without touching a hair. I saw that, because I was just coming back up the front steps, still carrying that ere sock and still in my underclothes, when the horse come onto the porch again. It taken one look at me and swirled again and run to the end of the porch and jumped the banisters and the lot fence like a hen hawk and lit in the lot running and went out the gate again and jumped eight or ten upside-down wagons and went on down the road. It was a full moon then. Mrs. Armstid was still setting in the wagon like she had done been carved outen wood and left there and forgot.

That horse. It ain't never missed a lick. It was going about forty miles a hour when it come to the bridge over the creek. It would have had a clear road, but it so happened that Vernon Tull was already using the bridge when it got there. He was coming back from town; he hadn't heard about the auction; him and his wife and three daughters and Mrs. Tull's aunt, all setting in chairs in the wagon bed, and all asleep, including the mules. They waked up when the horse hit the bridge one time, but Tull said the first he knew was when the mules tried to turn the wagon around in the middle of the bridge and he seen that spotted varmint run right twixt the mules and run up the wagon tongue like a squirrel. He said he just had time to hit it across the face with his whipstock, because about that time the mules turned the wagon around on that ere one-way bridge and that horse clumb across onto the bridge again and went on, with Vernon standing up in the wagon and kicking at it.

Tull said **the** mules turned in the harness and clumb back into the wagon too, with Tull trying to beat them out again, with the reins wrapped around his wrist. After that he says all he seen was overturned chairs and womenfolks' legs and white drawers shining in the moonlight, and his mules and that spotted horse going on up the road like a ghost.

The mules jerked Tull outen the wagon and drug him a spell on the bridge before the reins broke. They thought at first that he was dead, and while they was kneeling around him, picking the bridge splinters outen him, here come Eck and that boy, still carrying the rope. They was running and breathing a little hard. "Where'd he go?" Eck says.

V

I went back and got my pants and shirt and shoes on just in time to go and help get Henry Armstid outen the trash in the lot. I be dog if he didn't look like he was dead, with his head hanging back and his teeth showing in the moonlight, and a little rim of white under his eyelids. We could still hear them horses, here and there; hadn't none of them got more than four—five miles away yet, not knowing the country, I reckon. So we could hear them and folks yelling now and then: "Whooey. Head him!"

We toted Henry into Mrs. Littlejohn's. She was in the hall; she hadn't put down the armful of clothes. She taken one look at us, and she laid down the busted scrubbing board and taken up the lamp and opened a empty door. "Bring him in here," she says.

We toted him in and laid him on the bed. Mrs. Littlejohn set the lamp on the dresser, still carrying the clothes. "I'll declare, you men," she says. Our shadows was way up the wall, tiptoeing too; we could hear ourselves breathing. "Better get his wife," Mrs. Littlejohn says. She went out, carrying the clothes.

"I reckon we had," Quick says. "Go get her, somebody."

"Whyn't you go?" Winterbottom says.

"Let Ernest git her," Durley says. "He lives neighbors with them."

Ernest went to fetch her. I be dog if Henry didn't look like he was dead. Mrs. Littlejohn come back, with a kettle and some towels. She went to work on Henry, and then Mrs. Armstid and Ernest come in. Mrs. Armstid come to the foot of the bed and stood there, with her hands rolled into her apron, watching what Mrs. Littlejohn was doing, I reckon.

"You men get outen the way," Mrs. Littlejohn says. "Git outside," she says. "See if you can't find something else to play with that will kill some more of you."

Spotted Horses

"Is he dead?" Winterbottom says.

"It ain't your fault if he ain't," Mrs. Littlejohn says. "Go tell Will Varner to come up here. I reckon a man ain't so different from a mule, come long come short. Except maybe a mule's got more sense."

We went to get Uncle Billy. It was a full moon. We could hear them, now and then, four miles away: "Whooey. Head him." The country was full of them, one on every wooden bridge in the land, running across it like thunder: "Whooey. There he goes. Head him."

We hadn't got far before Henry begun to scream. I reckon Mrs. Littlejohn's water had brung him to; anyway, he wasn't dead. We went on to Uncle Billy's. The house was dark. We called to him, and after a while the window opened and Uncle Billy put his head out, peart as a peckerwood, listening. "Are they still trying to catch them durn rabbits?" he says.

He come down, with his britches on over his nightshirt and his suspenders dangling, carrying his horse-doctoring grip. "Yes, sir," he says, cocking his head like a woodpecker; "they're still a-trying."

We could hear Henry before we reached Mrs. Littlejohn's. He was going Ah-Ah-Ah. We stopped in the yard. Uncle Billy went on in. We could hear Henry. We stood in the yard, hearing them on the bridges, this-a-way and that: "Whooey. Whooey."

"Eck Snopes ought to caught hisn," Ernest says.

"Looks like he ought," Winterbottom said.

Henry was going Ah-Ah-Ah steady in the house; then he begun to scream. "Uncle Billy's started," Quick says. We looked into the hall. We could see the light where the door was. Then Mrs. Littlejohn come out.

"Will needs some help," she says. "You, Ernest. You'll do." Ernest went into the house.

"Hear them?" Quick said. "That one was on Four Mile bridge." We could hear them; it sounded like thunder a long way off; it didn't last long:

"Whooey."

We could hear Henry: "Ah-Ah-Ah-Ah-Ah."

"They are both started now," Winterbottom says. "Ernest too."

That was early in the night. Which was a good thing, because it taken a long night for folks to chase them things right and for Henry to lay there and holler, being as Uncle Billy never had none of this here chloryfoam to set Henry's leg with. So it was considerate in Flem to get them started early. And what do you reckon Flem's comment was?

That's right. Nothing. Because he wasn't there. Hadn't nobody see him since that Texas man left.

VI

That was Saturday night. I reckon Mrs. Armstid got home about daylight, to see about the chaps. I don't know where they thought her and Henry was. But lucky the oldest one was a gal, about twelve, big enough to take care of the little ones. Which she did for the next two days. Mrs. Armstid would nurse Henry all night and work in the kitchen for hern and Henry's keep, and in the afternoon she would drive home (it was about four miles) to see to the chaps. She would cook up a pot of victuals and leave it on the stove, and the gal would bar the house and keep the little ones quiet. I would hear Mrs. Littlejohn and Mrs. Armstid talking in the kitchen. "How are the chaps making out?" Mrs. Littlejohn says.

"All right," Mrs. Armstid says.

"Don't they git skeered at night?" Mrs. Littlejohn says.

"Ina May bars the door when I leave," Mrs. Armstid says. "She's got the axe in bed with her. I reckon she can make out."

I reckon they did. And I reckon Mrs. Armstid was waiting for Flem to come back to town—hadn't nobody seen him until this morning—to get her money the Texas man said Flem was keeping for her. Sho. I reckon she was.

Anyway, I heard Mrs. Armstid and Mrs. Littlejohn talking in the kitchen this morning while I was eating breakfast. Mrs. Littlejohn had just told Mrs. Armstid that Flem was in town. "You can ask him for that five dollars," Mrs. Littlejohn says.

"You reckon he'll give it to me?" Mrs. Armstid says.

Mrs. Littlejohn was washing dishes, washing them like a man, like they was made out of iron. "No," she says. "But asking him won't do no hurt. It might shame him. I don't reckon it will, but it might."

"If he wouldn't give it back, it ain't no use to ask," Mrs. Armstid says.

"Suit yourself," Mrs. Littlejohn says. "It's your money."

I could hear the dishes.

"Do you reckon he might give it back to me?" Mrs. Armstid says. "That Texas man said he would. He said I could get it from Mr. Snopes later."

"Then go and ask him for it," Mrs. Littlejohn says.

I could hear the dishes.

"He won't give it back to me," Mrs. Armstid says.

"All right," Mrs. Littlejohn says. "Don't ask him for it, then."

Spotted Horses

I could hear the dishes; Mrs. Armstid was helping. "You don't reckon he would, do you?" she says. Mrs. Littlejohn never said nothing. It sounded like she was throwing the dishes at one another. "Maybe I better go and talk to Henry about it," Mrs. Armstid says.

"I would," Mrs. Littlejohn says. I be dog if it didn't sound like she had two plates in her hands, beating them together. "Then Henry can buy another five-dollar horse with it. Maybe he'll buy one next time that will out and out kill him. If I thought that, I'd give you back the money, myself."

"I reckon I better talk to him first," Mrs. Armstid said. Then it sounded like Mrs. Littlejohn taken up all the dishes and throwed them at the cookstove, and I come away.

That was this morning. I had been up to Bundren's and back, and I thought that things would have kind of settled down. So after breakfast, I went up to the store. And there was Flem, setting in the store chair and whittling, like he might not have ever moved since he come to clerk for Jody Varner. I. O. was leaning in the door, in his shirt sleeves and with his hair parted too, same as Flem was before he turned the clerking job over to I. O. It's a funny thing about them Snopes: they all looks alike, yet there ain't ere a two of them that claims brothers. They're always just cousins, like Flem and Eck and Flem and I. O. Eck was there too, squatting against the wall, him and that boy, eating cheese and crackers outen a sack; they told me that Eck hadn't been home a-tall. And that Lon Quick hadn't got back to town, even. He followed his horse clean down to Samson's Bridge, with a wagon and a camp outfit. Eck finally caught one of hisn. It run into a blind lane at Freeman's and Eck and the boy taken and tied their rope across the end of the lane, about three foot high. The horse come to the end of the lane and whirled and run back without ever stopping. Eck says it never seen the rope a-tall. He says it looked just like one of these here Christmas pinwheels. "Didn't it try to run again?" I says.

"No," Eck says, eating a bite of cheese offen his knife blade. "Just kicked some."

"Kicked some?" I says.

"It broke its neck," Eck says.

Well, they was squatting there, about six of them, talking, talking at Flem; never nobody knowed yet if Flem had ere a interest in them horses or not. So finally I come right out and asked him. "Flem's done skun all of us so much," I says, "that we're proud of him. Come on, Flem," I says, "how much did you and that Texas man make offen them horses? You can tell us. Ain't nobody here but Eck that bought one of them; the others ain't got back to town yet, and Eck's your own cousin; he'll be proud to hear, too. How much did you-all make?"

They was all whittling, not looking at Flem, making like they was studying. But you could a heard a pin drop. And I. O. He had been rubbing his back up and down on the door, but he stopped now, watching Flem like a pointing dog. Flem finished cutting the sliver offen his stick. He spit across the porch, into the road. "Twarn't none of my horses," he says.

I. O. cackled, like a hen, slapping his legs with both hands. "You boys might just as well quit trying to get ahead of Flem," he said.

Well, about that time I see Mrs. Armstid come outen Mrs. Littlejohn's gate, coming up the road. I never said nothing. I says, "Well, if a man can't take care of himself in a trade, he can't blame the man that trims him."

Flem never said nothing, trimming at the stick. He hadn't seen Mrs. Armstid. "Yes, sir," I says. "A fellow like Henry Armstid ain't got nobody but hisself to blame."

"Course he ain't," I. O. says. He ain't seen her, either. "Henry Armstid's a born fool. Always is been. If Flem hadn't a got his money, somebody else would."

We looked at Flem. He never moved. Mrs. Armstid come on up the road.

"That's right," I says. "But come to think of it, Henry never bought no horse." We looked at Flem; you could a heard a match drop. "That Texas man told her to get that five dollars back from Flem next day. I reckon Flem's done already taken that money to Mrs. Littlejohn's and give it to Mrs. Armstid."

We watched Flem. I. O. quit rubbing his back against the door again. After a while Flem raised his head and spit across the porch, into the dust. I. O. cackled, just like a hen. "Ain't he a beating fellow, now?" I. O. says.

Mrs. Armstid was getting closer, so I kept on talking, watching to see if Flem would look up and see her. But he never looked up. I went on talking about Tull, about how he was going to sue Flem, and Flem setting there, whittling his stick, not saying nothing else after he said they wasn't none of his horses.

Then I. O. happened to look around. He seen Mrs. Armstid. "Pssst!" he says. Flem looked up. "Here she comes!" I. O. says. "Go out the back. I'll tell her you done went in to town today."

Spotted Horses

But Flem never moved. He just set there, whittling, and we watched Mrs. Armstid come up onto the porch, in that ere faded sunbonnet and wrapper and them tennis shoes that made a kind of hissing noise on the porch. She come onto the porch and stopped, her hands rolled into her dress in front, not looking at nothing.

"He said Saturday," she says, "that he wouldn't sell Henry no horse. He said I could get the money from you."

Flem looked up. The knife never stopped. It went on trimming off a sliver same as if he was watching it. "He taken that money off with him when he left," Flem says.

Mrs. Armstid never looked at nothing. We never looked at her, neither, except that boy of Eck's. He had a half-et cracker in his hand, watching her, chewing.

"He said Henry hadn't bought no horse," Mrs. Armstid says. "He said for me to get the money from you today."

"I reckon he forgot about it," Flem said. "He taken that money off with him Saturday." He whittled again. I. O. kept on rubbing his back, slow. He licked his lips. After a while the woman looked up the road, where it went on up the hill, toward the graveyard. She looked up that way for a while, with that boy of Eck's watching her and I. O. rubbing his back slow against the door. Then she turned back toward the steps.

"I reckon it's time to get dinner started," she says.

"How's Henry this morning, Mrs. Armstid?" Winterbottom says.

She looked at Winterbottom; she almost stopped. "He's resting, I thank you kindly," she says.

Flem got up, outen the chair, putting his knife away. He spit across the porch. "Wait a minute, Mrs. Armstid," he says. She stopped again. She didn't look at him. Flem went on into the store, with I. O. done quit rubbing his back now, with his head craned after Flem, and Mrs. Armstid standing there with her hands rolled into her dress, not looking at nothing. A wagon come up the road and passed; it was Freeman, on the way to town. Then Flem come out again, with I. O. still watching him. Flem had one of these little striped sacks of Jody Varner's candy; I bet he still owes Jody that nickel, too. He put the sack into Mrs. Armstid's hand, like he would have put it into a hollow stump. He spit again across the porch. "A little sweetening for the chaps," he says.

"You're right kind," Mrs. Armstid says. She held the sack of candy in her hand, not looking at nothing. Eck's boy was watching the sack, the half-et cracker in his hand; he wasn't chewing now. He watched

Mrs. Armstid roll the sack into her apron. "I reckon I better get on back and help with dinner," she says. She turned and went back across the porch. Flem set down in the chair again and opened his knife. He spit across the porch again, past Mrs. Armstid where she hadn't went down the steps yet. Then she went on, in that ere sunbonnet and wrapper all the same color, back down the road toward Mrs. Littlejohn's. You couldn't see her dress move, like a natural woman walking. She looked like a old snag still standing up and moving along on a high water. We watched her turn in at Mrs. Littlejohn's and go outen sight. Flem was whittling. I. O. begun to rub his back on the door. Then he begun to cackle, just like a durn hen.

"You boys might just as well quit trying," I. O. says. "You can't git ahead of Flem. You can't touch him. Ain't he a sight, now?"

I be a dog if he ain't. If I had brung a herd of wild cattymounts into town and sold them to my neighbors and kinfolks, they would have lynched me. Yes, sir.

A Father in the Philippines

JOSÉ GARCÍA VILLA

The leading Filipino short-story writer of his day found much material among the people of his Pacific islands.

José García Villa was born in Manila. His father was a doctor who had been chief of staff for General Emilio Aguinaldo, leader of the Filipino insurgents against both Spain and the United States. The father wanted José to become a doctor as well, but the young man left the University of Manila and came to the United States in 1930 to attain greater freedom to express himself. Before graduating he began publishing his work, as well as editing a little magazine, *Clay*. Several of his stories appeared in the annual series of *Best Short Stories* edited by Edward J. O'Brien; the 1932 volume was dedicated to Villa. He collected his stories in *Footnote to Youth* (1933) and later turned to writing highly experimental poetry.

One of a number of fine writers in English in the Philippines, where this language is still standard in most schools, Villa made use in "The Son of Rizal" of the national hero of that country, Dr. José Rizal, whose two novels inspired the rebellion against Spanish rule. The theme of "the search for a father" is widespread and is still being used today.

JOSÉ GARCÍA VILLA

The Son of Rizal

*L*AST DECEMBER THIRTIETH I boarded the last afternoon train for Lucena, Tayabas. I had waited until the afternoon to leave, for in the morning my wife, my children, and I had gone to the Luneta to view the annual Rizal Day parade. On the morning of the thirty-first I had to close an important land deal in Lucena.

From my compartment in the train I could see that the third-class cars were filling with returning provincials who had come to the city —Manila—to celebrate the day. They formed a motley, obstreperous group and crowded both the station platform and the steps of the cars. They bustled and palavered loudly like little children. Some were students going home for a day or two, and they were easily distinguishable from the rest by their modern, flashy clothes. There was a short, ducklike fellow among them who hummed "Ramona," but nobody listened to him, for another was cracking a joke about women.

There was much pushing and jostling on the steps to the cars, and a woman whose feet had been stepped on issued a string of shrill invectives: "Goats! Pigs! Brutes!" she cried to those about her: did they have no regard for women, did they have no conscience, and oh! of what advantage being a woman if you had to be trampled upon like a mat!

But there was one person especially of all this crowd who caught my attention—or was it a feeling of pity? I felt guilty that I should think myself so superior as to bestow compassion on a fellow creature. Yet there I was, feeling it, and unable to help myself. He was a small, bark-colored man, lugging a long, narrow buri bag, which in the native tongue is called *bayong*. He found difficulty in pushing through the group on the steps to the car, and finally retreated quietly to the platform. On his thin face was written a fear that the train might start before he had got on. Then the locomotive bell began to ring its slow, annunciative notes, and the man got more and more nervous.

In my pocket I had two tickets, for not quite fifteen minutes ago my eldest son had insisted on going along with me, but had later on decided not to. The tickets had been bought, and I could not find the nerve to return the other. In such little things I am most sensitive, and would feel myself brazen and shameless if I returned with indifference the things already paid for. Compassionately again (and I hated myself for it) I thought of offering the other ticket to the man.

Half guiltily I whistled to him, and he glanced confusedly in my direction. I beckoned him to approach, which I saw he was reluctant to do—so afraid was he that he would lose more time and not get on the train at all. But I raised my two tickets for him to see, and I surmised that he understood my intention, for he hobbled hurriedly to my window. In brief words I explained to him that I had an extra ticket, and would he be kind enough to share my company in my compartment? I was alone, I said. Timidly yet eagerly he accepted my invitation.

The steps to the first-class cars are often, if not always, clear, and soon he was at the door of my compartment. He mumbled a deferential greeting, removing his black-green hat. I told him to step in, and he did so, silently lifting the buri bag and depositing it on the iron net above our heads; beside it he placed the hat. Then he settled himself awkwardly on the seat opposite mine, and regarded me with soft, pathetic eyes. The train started.

He was sparely built and poorly dressed. He wore the poor man's *camisa-chino,* but it was clean and freshly starched. He had on white drill trousers and red velvet slippers.

He smiled shyly at me and I smiled in return.

"You see, I've got my ticket," he tried to explain, pulling it out of his *camisa-chino's* pocket, "but it was hard to get in. I cannot afford to ride in *here,* you know," he confessed, half embarrassed. His thick lips moved slowly, docilely, and his voice was thin, slow, and sad. His melancholy eyes lowered in humility.

I told him I was glad to help him. I said I was bound for Lucena, and he where?

"Calamba. That is where I live. I have three children—two little girls and a boy. Their mother—she died at childbirth."

I expressed my sympathy and told him I hoped the children were well.

"They are good children," he said contentedly.

We fell into a warm, friendly chat. He was well-mannered in speech, and although he did not talk fluently—sometimes he was tongue-tied—yet he managed to convey his thoughts.

We became confidential, and I spoke to him of my business. I said I was married and had more children than he had, and was a commercial agent. I said I was tired of the work but was not sure I should be more successful in other lines.

In return he spoke to me about himself and his trade. His name was Juan Rizal and he was a shoemaker. He had a little shop in the front of his house. "It is not a big house," he said.

I said, "You have a good name—Juan Rizal."

"My father is Rizal," he answered.

"Then maybe you are a relative of the hero," I said inferentially. "Near relation, I suppose."

"No. Rizal is my *father*," he said. "Rizal. Doctor Rizal," he emphasized, and I saw a brilliant light of pride in his small buttonlike eyes. "Yes," he affirmed himself with not a little bombast.

I said I had not heard and did not know that Rizal had a son.

"Yes, he *has*," he said matter-of-factly. "I am *he*." And he looked at me superiorly.

"The books do not speak of Rizal having a son," I said.

"They don't know," he negated with perfect self-confidence. "They don't know, at all. I *am* the son of Rizal."

As he said this, he set himself erect, lifted his chest out, and plaited together his fingers on his lap. He was little and thin, and when he stretched himself to look great and dignified, he became pathetically distorted. Now he looked elongated, disconcertingly elongated, like an extending, crawling leech.

And I was moved, and I lied:

"I am glad to know you, I am glad to know the son of Rizal."

"Rizal had only *one* son," he explained. "*I* am he, that son—yes, *I* am he. But people won't believe me. They are envious of me."

There was a slight whispering, protesting note in his voice. His thick lips quivered and a film covered his eyes. I thought he was going to cry and I began to feel uncomfortable.

"They are *envious* of me," he repeated, and could not say more. A choking emotion had seized him. He swayed slightly as though he would fall.

I realized the intensity of his feeling and I kept quiet. When he returned to himself, he asked me in a half fearful, half apologetic tone:

"Do you believe me?"

"Yes," I said, but faltering a little.

A happy light beamed in his doglike eyes.

He said, "Thank you. Thank you. Thank you."

There were minutes of silence, and we looked through the window at the passing scenes. The greenery in the soft sunlight was beautiful and healthy, imparting to the eyes a sense of coolness, of vastness. The air, though rather warm, we felt cool and soothing. The train moved smoothly, like a vessel on a very peaceful sea.

It was I who broke the silence. I said I had gone to the Luneta that morning to see the parade. The sun had been hot, and my wife, the children, and I had perspired a lot. "It is a trial, waiting for and watching a parade," I said.

He said I was right and that he too had seen the parade. He had come to Manila for that purpose only. "I go once a year. It is a sort of —pilgrimage. But—I love my father, you see."

It was a naïve, full-souled statement. His eyes ceased for the moment being dull and inexpressive. The soft warmth of gentleness, of a supreme devotional love, filled them. They became the eyes of a dove.

"I love my father," he repeated wistfully, softly, as though he were chanting a most sacred song.

But I (and may God punish me for my cruelty!) remarked inadvertently that he didn't look like his father.

A look of immeasurable hurt stole into his eyes, and he looked at me imploringly, questioned me with those small, melancholy eyes that but a moment ago had been so happy, so inspired, so tender. Struggling out of impending defeat, clamoring to be saved, to be believed in, those eyes looked at me so that a lump rose unwillingly in my throat.

But as though he bore me no grudge at all for my cruel remark, he said softly, lowly, as though in solemn prayer: "I take—after my mother."

Yet he was disturbed, completely broken by my remark, I realized. It had cut him deeply, although he wanted to appear composed. But his efforts were futile. His unrest was visible everywhere in his person: his eyes grew painfully feverish, his nostrils quivered, his lips trembled. And he gave it up with a twitch of his lips, let himself be as he felt, and talked, to dispel my doubts, about his mother and his birth:

"My father and my mother—they lived together before they were married. They lived in Talisay, during my father's deportation, but I was born in Dapitan. People don't know that. When I was born they thought I was dead. Dead. But that is not true. I was *alive*. People thought I was born so, because when my mother was in a delicate condition before my birth, my father played a prank on her and she sprang forward and struck against an iron stand. She became sick. I was born prematurely. But I was alive. Do you understand? I was born, and alive—and I lived." There was galvanic energy in his excited voice. "My mother, she was Irish—Josefina Bracken." He gazed deeper into my eyes. "I don't remember her well," he said. "I don't remember her. She had brown eyes and a little nose." He blew his nose with a cheap, colored handkerchief.

"My father liked her but maybe he did not love her. He loved Leonora. Leonora was his cousin. They were separated when my father went to Europe. Leonora's mother intercepted his letters. She withheld them from Leonora. When my father came back she was married." He stopped and brooded.

"I ran away from my mother when I was old enough to do so. I ran away to Calamba. My father was born there. I wanted to go there, to live there. I have lived there ever since. Have you ever been to Calamba?"

"No," I said.

"My father married my mother on the morning of his execution." he pursued. "My father was brave," he said. "He was not afraid of the Spaniards. He fell forward when they shot him. They wanted to shoot him in the back, but he turned around and fell forward."

He was greatly excited. His face was flushed. "They shot him—my father—the white scoundrels! They shot my father—as they would a dog!" He was indignant. His thin, sticklike fingers closed and opened frantically. He was so vituperative I was afraid he did not realize what he was saying.

I stretched a comforting hand to his to calm him down. He looked at me with quivering lips and I realized his helplessness. He told me that he had not meant to upset me. He begged tearfully for my forgiveness, clutching my hands tightly in his. "Please forgive me," he said. "Please forgive me."

I was afraid he would kneel down; so I moved over to his side and said I understood.

"Do you?" he said. "Do you?" His voice was pleading, full of pain.

"I do," I said.

He quieted down. He turned his face away from mine, ashamed that he had let his feelings run loose.

We were silent again. Only the chug-chug-chug of the train could be heard, and the wind-tossed laughter of those in the neighboring compartments. The air had grown cooler, dusk was fast approaching,

The Son of Rizal

and only a lone bird fluttered in the sky. There was a sweet, flowing sound as we crossed a rivulet.

My companion turned to me and made me understand that he was desirous of asking a question. I encouraged him.

"His books—you have read my father's books, the *Noli* and the *Filibusterismo?*" There was still a tremor in his voice, and he mispronounced the last title, calling it "Plisterismo."

"Only the *Noli,*" I said. "I have not had the time to read the other."

We were approaching the station of Calamba, Laguna.

"We are nearing your place," I said.

"Yes," he said, and a sadness was now in his voice. "I wish," he murmured, "I could invite you home."

"I will drop in some day."

The train slackened speed and finally stopped.

I helped the son of Rizal lift the buri bag from the net.

"For my children," he explained, smiling. "I bought them fruits."

He asked me before he alighted:

"Do you really believe me?"

"I do."

He was very happy and shook my hands effusively.

"Good-bye," he said.

"Good-bye."

The train moved again.

The following month I went to Calamba on the invitation of a friend. It had been a long time, about six years, since we had last met in the city, and now I was to be godfather to his first-born. The choosing of a name depended on me, he had written. Aside from the customary baptismal gift, I brought with me a plaster bust of Rizal which I intended to present to Juan Rizal.

After the ceremony I asked my host if he knew anything about Juan Rizal.

"Yes," he said. "You mean Juan Kola."

I told him to explain.

"He is a shoemaker—owns a little shop near the edge of the town. The children call him Juan Sirá. You know what that means: nutty."

"Tell me more."

"Well, he calls himself Juan Rizal—tells that to people whom he meets. There is a sad story behind it. I will tell it to you:

"When Juan Kola was a small boy, his father was very cruel to him. He used to beat him for any or no reason at all. Naturally the boy grew to dislike his father—learned to hate him as much as he feared him.

But when the boy was twelve or thereabouts, the father died. The boy knew no happiness so great; so he cried. Otherwise the boy would not have wept. He was so used to his father's meanness and cruelty that any sorrow, any pain, could not make him cry. He had forgotten how to cry, had learned to stifle that surging in the breast that brings tears to the eyes, and he would merely whine, dry-eyed, like a puppy that is kicked. But this time he wept, and for a long time afterwards you could see him in the streets crying. And when people asked him why he cried, he replied, 'I don't know. I just want to cry.' He was not evading the truth; the boy simply had no words for it. But the people knew.

"Then the boy began thinking of Rizal. Rizal was born here, you know, and that makes him closer to us than to you who live elsewhere. Rizal to us is a reality, a magnificent, potent reality, but to you he is only a myth, a golden legend. He is to you a star, faraway, bright, unreachable. To us he is not unreachable, for he is among us. We feel him, breathe with him, live with him. *Juan Kola lived with him—lives with him.* In his young untutored mind he knew that if Rizal were his father he would be a good father, a supremely beautiful father, and he, Juan Kola, would always be happy. And so Juan Kola, the little unhappy boy, made José Rizal his father.

"He was a poor boy, Juan Kola, and he could not go to school. He had to work and earn his living. He does not read or write, but he knows much about Rizal's life from the schoolteacher who boarded with the shoemaker to whom he was apprenticed. Of nights, when work was over, he would go to her, to this teacher, and ask her questions, and she, filled with sympathy for the boy, gave him of her time.

"When Juan's father died, he destroyed all his father's things. There was a picture left of his father, but he burned it, not wishing to remember anything of his true parent. He wanted to be fully the son of his adopted father. From then on he was the son of Rizal.

"And that," concluded my friend, "is the story of Juan Sirá. The children have misnamed him. It is cruel, unjust. He who can dream of beautiful things, and live in them, surely he is great—and wise."

"Take me to Juan Rizal," I said.

I presented my gift to Juan Rizal in his shabby little nipa home. Juan Rizal was exultant when he opened the package containing Rizal's bust. "I have always wanted one, but I could not afford it," he said with tremulous lips and adoring eyes.

The Girl and the Doctor

WILLIAM CARLOS WILLIAMS

A busy doctor all his life in an industrial town, Williams was also a celebrated American poet, essayist, and storyteller.

William Carlos Williams (1883–1963) was born in Rutherford, New Jersey, of ancestors of several European stocks, but in appearance was a "typical" professional American. He went to school in his birthplace and in Geneva, Switzerland. He earned the degree of Doctor of Medicine at the University of Pennsylvania, interned for two years in New York City, studied pediatrics at the University of Leipzig in Germany, and in 1920 began his long career as a doctor specializing in diseases of children. His life was not physically adventurous, but he explored through his writing the exciting possibilities of a new poetry and a new prose in the American idiom.

"The Use of Force," first collected in 1932, is outwardly merely a casual anecdote, but closer examination shows that its strong theme arouses many questions. The doctor, the most noble image of civilization, in the pursuit of his duty resorts to force, and confesses his emotions as the "battle" progresses to get a child, representing unconforming nature, to open her mouth because she is suspected of being stricken with a deadly disease.

Dr. Williams appears to be showing that a resort to force, even in the most noble cause, always corrupts the humanity of the person who uses this means to his end. Perhaps this small story is even a parable of the national and international world of today, where groups proclaiming admirable goals try to force their will upon other groups by violent means.

WILLIAM CARLOS WILLIAMS

The Use of Force

THEY WERE NEW PATIENTS to me, all I had was the name, Olson. Please come down as soon as you can, my daughter is very sick.

When I arrived I was met by the mother, a big startled looking woman, very clean and apologetic who merely said, Is this the doctor? and let me in. In the back, she added. You must excuse us, doctor, we have her in the kitchen where it is warm. It is very damp here sometimes.

The child was fully dressed and sitting on her father's lap near the kitchen table. He tried to get up, but I motioned for him not to bother, took off my overcoat and started to look things over. I could see that they were all very nervous, eyeing me up and down distrustfully. As often, in such cases, they weren't telling me more than they had to; it was up to me to tell them; that's why they were spending three dollars on me.

The child was fairly eating me up with her cold, steady eyes, and no expression to her face whatever. She did not move and seemed, inwardly, quiet; an unusually attractive little thing, and as strong as a heifer in appearance. But her face was flushed, she was breathing rapidly, and I realized that she had a high fever. She had magnificent blonde hair, in profusion. One of those picture children often reproduced in advertising leaflets and the photogravure sections of the Sunday papers.

She's had a fever for three days, began the father, and **we don't know** what it comes from. My wife has given her things, you **know**, like people do, but it don't do no good. And there's been a lot of

The Use of Force

sickness around. So we thought you'd better look her over and tell us what is the matter?

As doctors often do I took a trial shot at it as a point of departure. Has she had a sore throat?

Both parents answered me together, No . . . No, she says her throat don't hurt her.

Does your throat hurt you? added the mother to the child. But the little girl's expression didn't change, nor did she move her eyes from my face.

Have you looked?

I tried to, said the mother, but I couldn't see.

As it happens, we had been having a number of cases of diphtheria in the school to which this child went during that month and we were all, quite apparently, thinking of that, though no one had as yet spoken of the thing.

Well, I said, suppose we take a look at the throat first. I smiled in my best professional manner and asking for the child's first name I said, come on, Mathilda, open your mouth and let's take a look at your throat.

Nothing doing.

Aw, come on, I coaxed, just open your mouth wide and let me take a look. Look, I said opening both hands wide, I haven't anything in my hands. Just open up and let me see.

Such a nice man, put in the mother. Look how kind he is to you. Come on, do what he tells you to. He won't hurt you.

At that I ground my teeth in disgust. If only they wouldn't use the word "hurt" I might be able to get somewhere. But I did not allow myself to be hurried or disturbed, but speaking quietly and slowly I approached the child again.

As I moved my chair a little nearer, suddenly with one catlike movement both her hands clawed instinctively for my eyes and she almost reached them too. In fact she knocked my glasses flying and they fell, though unbroken, several feet away from me on the kitchen floor.

Both the mother and father almost turned themselves inside out in embarrassment and apology. You bad girl, said the mother, taking her and shaking her by one arm. Look what you've done. The nice man. . . .

For heaven's sake, I broke in. Don't call me a nice man to her. I'm here to look at her throat on the chance that she might have diphtheria and possibly die of it. But that's nothing to her. Look here, I said to the child, we're going to look at your throat. You're old enough to understand what I'm saying. Will you open it now by yourself or shall we have to open it for you?

Not a move. Even her expression hadn't changed. Her breaths however were coming faster and faster. Then the battle began. I had to do it. I had to have a throat culture for her own protection. But first I told the parents that it was entirely up to them. I explained the danger but said that I would not insist on a throat examination so long as they would take the responsibility.

If you don't do what the doctor says you'll have to go to the hospital, the mother admonished her severely.

Oh yeah? I had to smile to myself. After all, I had already fallen in love with the savage brat, the parents were contemptible to me. In the ensuing struggle they grew more and more abject, crushed, exhausted while she surely rose to magnificent heights of insane fury of effort bred of her terror of me.

The father tried his best, and he was a big man but the fact that she was his daughter, his shame at her behavior and his dread of hurting her made him release her just at the critical moment several times when I had almost achieved success, till I wanted to kill him. But his dread also that she might have diptheria made him tell me to go on, go on though he himself was almost fainting, while the mother moved back and forth behind us raising and lowering her hands in an agony of apprehension.

Put her in front of you on your lap, I ordered, and hold both her wrists.

But as soon as he did the child let out a scream. Don't, you're hurting me. Let go of my hands. Let them go I tell you. Then she shrieked terrifyingly, hysterically. Stop it! Stop it! You're killing me!

Do you think she can stand it, doctor! said the mother.

You get out, said the husband to his wife. Do you want her to die of diphtheria?

Come on now, hold her, I said.

Then I grasped the child's head with my left hand and tried to get the wooden tongue depressor between her teeth. She fought, with clenched teeth, desperately! But now I also had grown furious—at a child. I tried to hold myself down but I couldn't. I know how to expose a throat for inspection. And I did my best. When finally I got the wooden spatula behind the last teeth and just the point of it into the mouth cavity, she opened up for an instant but before I could see

The Use of Force

anything she came down again and gripping the wooden blade between her molars she reduced it to splinters before I could get it out again.

Aren't you ashamed, the mother yelled at her. Aren't you ashamed to act like that in front of the doctor?

Get me a smooth-handled spoon of some sort, I told the mother. We're going through with this. The child's mouth was already bleeding. Her tongue was cut and she was screaming in wild hysterical shrieks. Perhaps I should have desisted and come back in an hour or more. No doubt it would have been better. But I have seen at least two children lying dead in bed of neglect in such cases, and feeling that I must get a diagnosis now or never I went at it again. But the worst of it was that I too had got beyond reason. I could have torn the child apart in my own fury and enjoyed it. It was a pleasure to attack her. My face was burning with it.

The damned little brat must be protected against her own idiocy, one says to one's self at such times. Others must be protected against her. It is social necessity. And all these things are true. But a blind fury, a feeling of adult shame, bred of a longing for muscular release are the operatives. One goes on to the end.

In a final unreasoning assault I overpowered the child's neck and jaws. I forced the heavy silver spoon back of her teeth and down her throat till she gagged. And there it was—both tonsils covered with membrane. She had fought valiantly to keep me from knowing her secret. She had been hiding that sore throat for three days at least and lying to her parents in order to escape just such an outcome as this.

Now truly she *was* furious. She had been defensive before but now she attacked. Tried to get off her father's lap and fly at me while tears of defeat blinded her eyes.

Questions

Numbers in parentheses refer to topics in Appendix A, "Main Questions for the Study of a Story." For comments exemplifying these points see the same numbers in Appendix B, "Analysis of 'The Man Who Would Be King.'"

E. T. W. HOFFMANN / PAGE 1

1. What is the narrator's main motive for concentrating so passionately on the old house? Why does he term it "accursed information" when he is told that it is used as part of the property of a pastry cook? Why should he become excited when he learns that this information is false?
2. There is motivated action *(3)* in this story, but it is certainly not the well-crafted story of later writers. Can you briefly narrate the main points of the plot? Is *coincidence* used to further the action or to hamper it, or is it used for its own sake?
3. Does Hoffmann evoke atmosphere to convince us that the outcome is a natural result of the setting? Can you compare Hoffmann's plausibility *(9)* in his use of a supernatural setting with that of Poe in "The Fall of the House of Usher," written later?
4. This is a romantic story of the supernatural, in which the main character builds "a thousand castles in Spain" at the sight of an old house, and is fascinated by talk of "dreams, hallucinations, and trances." Does Hoffmann make convincing the behavior of the various persons? Do we really believe this story could happen, or is it pure fantasy?
5. What purpose is served by the discussion at the evening gathering, especially the story of the Italian colonel?
6. Is any rational explanation given for the magical qualities of the mirror purchased from a peddler?
7. What is the point of having Gabrielle's baby stolen? Why was it returned?
8. Who is the mysterious gypsy woman? Does she have a plot function in the story?

QUESTIONS

9. We are told at the end that the Countess Edwina, niece of the mad old woman, was the living figure seen by the narrator. How do you account for the fact that her picture appeared in the mirror when the narrator visited the office of the doctor?
10. At the ending, the narrator, instead of pursuing his living "ideal" young lady, leaves the town. What accounts for such behavior contrary to the expected courting actions?

ALEXANDER PUSHKIN / PAGE 17

1. What is Silvio's principal trait *(2)*? What is the Count's main trait? Do they necessarily oppose each other strongly and create conflict *(3)*?
2. Why do the soldiers assume that Silvio is a coward?
3. Is Silvio admirable or unadmirable? At one time he appears like a "fiend"; at another, his face is "hideous." Is he a hero or a villain, or just a person who is the victim of a passion for revenge?
4. What causes Silvio to change his mind in the first duel? In the second?
5. Is this a story of achievement or decision *(3)*?
6. In some cases, may it be as dramatic to refrain from action as to act?
7. Is the tone *(5)* of the author amusing, sarcastic, serious, grotesque, pensive, gay, casual, tragic, or what?
8. The narrator *(6)* is a character in the story but takes no action and merely listens to the stories of the principals. Would it be better to have Silvio tell the whole story? Or could the Count be a better narrator? Does the method used by Pushkin lend more plausibility *(9)* to a strange series of events?
9. The structure *(7)* of the story breaks into two parts. The first part raises a question, the second answers it. Do you think it would be better if the story started at the beginning with the first duel of Silvio?
10. Does the picture on the Count's wall containing two bullet holes arouse suspense *(8)*?
11. In comparison with "The Mystery of the Deserted House," is there anything unrealistic in "The Pistol Shot"?

NATHANIEL HAWTHORNE / PAGE 30

1. The theme *(1)* is much more profound than simple admonitions such as "Beware of evil companions" or "Don't attend strange meetings at night." Can you state the main theme in a sentence or two? Scholars have written many essays on this story, and some of their explanations are extremely complicated and differ one from the other. Granting that Hawthorne may

QUESTIONS

have implied much more in this story than he intended, do you think he wrote it merely to confuse the reader concerning his main idea?
2. Tell everything you know about this young man's character *(2)*. What was his motive in entering the forest?
3. What does the encounter with the strange old man in the forest tell us about Brown?
4. Brown's blighting experience results from his opinions about various townspeople. Name them and state his relationship. His most important feelings, however, revolve around his wife Faith. What do they reveal concerning his need for "faith"?
5. Hawthorne often uses contrasts of light and dark in his fiction. Do you find any such contrasts in this story of good and evil, of appearance and reality?
6. Which is the "night of all nights in the year" when a good Christian should not leave the town and enter the depths of a forest?
7. Faith, the name of Brown's wife, is clearly *allegorical*. What other allegories do you find in this story?
8. Some people accept the existence of evil; others embrace it; others refuse to believe in it. Would you say that Brown does none of these, but is merely stupefied by his awareness of evil? Is his name symbolic of this attitude?
9. The climax *(7)* of the story comes just after the meeting of the witches in the forest. How does Hawthorne reinforce his theme *(1)* by the use of this evil setting?
10. Brown is willing to lend his soul to the devil for a night, but refuses to allow anyone else this experience. What is the lifelong result of this attitude?
11. The modern author would probably avoid writing a final paragraph like that in this story, in which Hawthorne reports Brown's later life. Do you believe it would have been better for Hawthorne to show us the gloomy effect on Brown rather than merely tell us that it happened?

EDGAR ALLAN POE / PAGE 43

1. Is this merely a horror story which we enjoy by suspending our disbelief for the sake of a few shudders, or does it have a larger theme *(1)*?
2. What is Usher's main trait *(2)*? He seems to be isolated from society, to look inward upon himself, and to suffer from an abnormal sensitivity. Are these qualities usually found together?
3. Would you say that Madeline, Roderick's twin sister, is merely a mirror reflection of her brother, and that her fate foreshadows his own yielding to death? Is Roderick a split personality?

QUESTIONS

4. The conflict *(3)* in this story has been termed by one writer as that between life-reason and death-madness. Can you find incidents which reveal this conflict?
5. Do Roderick and Madeline literally cause each other's death? If so, is there any larger significance to this fact?
6. This is primarily a story of atmosphere *(4)* in which the setting seems to impel the outcome of the action. What details reinforce the tone of remoteness, decay, horrible gloom, and despair?
7. What is the function of the unnamed narrator *(6)*? Is he merely a stand-in for the reader, or does his attitude contrast with that of Usher? What practical aid does he give to help Usher's condition?
8. What parts of the story do you consider implausible *(9)*? Is coincidence used too heavily, thus creating melodrama?
9. What is the meaning and function of the song "The Haunted Palace," which Usher sings? Does the story reveal more than the poem by itself would reveal? If so, what?
10. What is the value of listing the books in Usher's library? Do these books seem to have anything in common?

HERMAN MELVILLE / PAGE 61

1. Although the casual reader might assume that Bartleby is the main character *(2)*, a second look will show that it is really the lawyer-narrator who is most affected by the events. Moreover, his character *develops* during the action. Can you show the stages by which the safe, prudent, methodical man of law becomes more and more involved, until he is committed to the side of a withdrawn madman and feels that he is "his brother's keeper"?
2. Bartleby probably could not tell his own story. The unnamed narrator *(6)*, by telling it in the first person, gains some sympathy from us. Is he a reliable reporter of his own motives, or do we finally know more about his character than he himself does?
3. What are the main traits *(2)* of the three fellow copyists—Turkey, Nippers, and Ginger Nut? Are they really much more sane than Bartleby?
4. Melville was an admiring friend of Hawthorne, to whom he dedicated *Moby Dick*. Hawthorne felt that the "unpardonable sin" was withdrawal from humanity. Do you see any resemblance between the fates of Young Goodman Brown and Bartleby?
5. The narrator, on hearing at the end that Bartleby is asleep, responds: "With kings and counselors." Does this allusion to the Bible (Job, 3:14) reveal that the narrator sees a connection between the tribulations of Bartleby and Job?

QUESTIONS

6. Symbolism appears in this story—that is, objects suggest more than their literal meaning. Bartleby is a shut-in personality, whose withdrawal brings on his death. Note the use of "Wall Street" (a real place which also connotes the idea of being pent up), the prisonlike office, the Tombs (a New York prison), and the discovery that Bartleby had previously worked in the dead letter office. Can you find other examples of symbolism in the story?
7. Do the final words—"Ah, Bartleby! Ah, humanity!"—imply that everyone shares this miserable man's attitude? If not, what does Melville mean? Or does he raise a serious question here without giving an easy answer?

PEDRO ANTONIO DE ALARCÓN / PAGE 95

1. Wherein lies the conflict *(3)* in this story? Does the main trait of the villain directly oppose the main trait of the hero?
2. Is this a story of achievement or decision *(3)*?
3. Wherein lies the humor of this story? What type of humor is it—wit, comedy, satire, or what?
4. Such tender care of each plant might seem implausible *(9)* to many readers. How does Alarcón build up the reader's belief in the main character?

BJÖRNSTJERNE BJÖRNSON / PAGE 101

1. This is the briefest story in this collection; however, it has the main ingredients of fiction—theme, characterization, action, and setting. Can you state all these four for "The Father"?
2. The narration *(6)* is third-person omniscient. Do you feel that it would be an improvement if the narrator shared his feelings with us, or if the story were told either by the priest or by Thord?
3. During the first three visits to the priest, Thord asks for something on his own account, reflecting his pride in his son. How do these visits differ from the final one? Why is it that only during the last scene does the priest feel that the son has brought a blessing to his father?

GUY DE MAUPASSANT / PAGE 105

1. The beginning *(7)* gives the setting *(4)* almost as if it were merely a motion picture of a market-day scene. Does the selection of details give, however, a tone that foreshadows the character of Hauchecorne through depicting his neighbors and his town?

QUESTIONS

2. Do common expressions like "He protests too much" and "Where there's smoke, there's fire" have anything to do with the theme *(1)*?
3. The main character *(2)* might well be considered unsympathetic to us. He was perhaps capable of stealing a pocketbook and even boasting of the deed. What redeeming qualities, if any, do you find in the old man?
4. Hauchecorne is not strongly individualized. Does this lack suggest that, in his place, many people might do what he does?
5. Irony *(12)* appears when the pocketbook is found and the old man thinks his troubles are over. What other ironies do you find?

SHOLEM ALEICHEM / PAGE 113

1. There is a gap between the adult world and that of the boy. What details reveal this separation?
2. Does the stranger's repeated interest in Rikal the maid foreshadow the climax *(7)*?
3. Are there any ironies of situation *(12)* in this story?
4. The adults are fooled in this story as well as is the boy. What qualities in them make it easy for an impostor to take advantage of them all? At the end, what has the boy lost that the parents do not lose?

HENRY JAMES / PAGE 152

1. At their first meeting, the artist assumes that the couple have come to pay him to paint their portraits. What does this initial misconception add to the story?
2. How is the contrast between the amateur and the expert shown in the frequent use of the words "real thing," "same thing," and "ideal thing"?
3. What was the quality in Miss Churm that made her superior to Mrs. Monarch as a model?
4. A contrast is made in the story between photography and drawing. What might a good drawing supply that a photograph lacks? Is there any connection as well between telling a "true story" and trying to put a real incident into a piece of fiction?
5. Near the end, the narrator says: "If my servants were my models, then my models might be my servants." This reversal shows irony of situation *(12)*. If there were no stronger meaning to the story than this, however, "The Real Thing" would be merely a trick with an ending of the O. Henry sort. Do you believe that in the sentence in the text prior to this one, James comes closest to expressing briefly his main theme *(1)*?

QUESTIONS

6. What purpose is served by the artist's friend, Jack Hawley?
7. The narrator in his final sentence says he is content to have paid the price for the memory. What aspect of this memory do you think was worth the price of a possible permanent harm?

SELMA LAGERLÖF / PAGE 176

1. It is usually impossible in a short story to have two main characters. Who is the main character *(2)* in this story—Berg the peasant, or Tord the fisher boy? If Tord is the main one, why does the author give a strong impression early in the story of Berg's wild behavior during the search?
2. Can you contrast the main traits *(2)* of the two outlaws? If they are so different, what binds them together?
3. Was Tord really a thief?
4. The structure *(7)* of this story is scrambled; the events are not told in the order in which they occur. If it is about the awakening of conscience in the fisher boy, does this rearrangement help us to understand better the stages in this awakening?
5. Are the qualities in Berg that would lead him to kill a monk but later to convert a pagan boy to Christianity so different that we feel the character is inconsistent?
6. Do you approve or disapprove of Tord's act in betraying Berg and killing him with his own hands? Justify your answer.
7. Do the final words of the story, when Tord says that he killed Berg because he taught him that "the foundation of the world is justice," have a strong connection with the main theme?
8. Can you chart the emotions *(10)* through which Tord passes during his transition from crude paganism to what might be considered a mercy killing of his companion?

JOSEPH CONRAD / PAGE 193

1. The theme *(1)* is a general conclusion about life made by Marlow. What is this conclusion? Do you agree with it? Does the theme necessarily derive from the events of the main story?
2. What are the main contrasts here between the young Marlow and his older self? What is the chief quality that makes the young man respond more strongly to the voyage than do the old captain and the first mate?
3. Sailors are often superstitious, and omens in this story foreshadow the fate of the *Judea*. What are some of these omens?

QUESTIONS

4. This is a perfect example of the frame story; a setting is given, a person tells the main narrative, and then the reader is returned to the opening scene. What is the value of having this story told by an older man recollecting his younger days? Would it be better to have a different type of narrator *(6)*?
5. "Youth" marks the first appearance in Conrad's writings of the loquacious narrator Marlow, who is used in several other short stories as well as in novels. Do you think Marlow is Conrad himself, or a character created to fill an artistic function? What seems to be Marlow's main trait *(2)* in his youth? In the later time when he tells the story of the early voyage?
6. Why are Marlow's listeners individualized so carefully, since they take no part in the story?
7. Is there any pattern *(11)* in the various delays that keep Marlow from fulfilling his romantic mission?

ANTON CHEKHOV / PAGE 221

1. Would you say that the main character trait *(2)* of Olenka is a *lack* of character?
2. This story, although it might appear merely a character sketch, has a plot *(3)*. Can you state it briefly?
3. Is the unity of the story in plot *(3)* or in character *(2)*, or in both?
4. Do Olenka's early admirations for her father, her French master, and her aunt foreshadow her later admirations?
5. During her life, Olenka has four strong attachments which reveal pattern *(11)*. What are the similarities and differences in each attachment? Are they all merely that of the stock character of the merry widow?
6. Although, as Chekhov says, Olenka could not get through a year without being in love with someone, nobody thinks ill of her for this trait. Why?
7. What does Olenka give to her various lovers? What does she take?
8. What is the significance of the fact that Olenka's third love is a married man?
9. What is the effect on Olenka's health and happiness when she does not have someone to love?
10. This is a story about love. What different kinds of love are revealed?
11. What seems to be the attitude of the author toward his characters— pitying, ridiculing, objective, or something else?
12. Why do women as well as men admire the darling?
13. Why does Olenka, who never had a child, attach herself so strongly at the end to little Sasha?

QUESTIONS

JAMES JOYCE / PAGE 233

1. The main character *(2)*, Gabriel Conroy, during one evening finds that his barriers of egotism are steadily broken down. After hearing his wife tell of an earlier love, his jealousy is dissolved in a realization of the spiritual brotherhood that unites all the living and the dead. Is this a narrow theme *(1)* or a quite broad one?
2. Why does the story open on the commonplace level with a focus on Lily the maid? Does the scene between Conroy and Lily begin the process of breaking down his self-assurance when he resents her right to live in a world of her own?
3. How does the argument with Miss Ivors continue the process of weakening Gabriel's self-assurance?
4. Gretta Conroy comes from the west of Ireland, associated in Gabriel's mind with wildness and lack of respectability. Can you find incidents in which he seems to fear the West? The final paragraph includes the words: "The time had come for him to set out on his journey westward." Although "going west" is a common synonym for death, do you believe Gabriel is dying?
5. Gretta's dead lover is named Michael Furey. Is this a more passionate-sounding name than Gabriel? Is there a contrast in these names between fiery young love and amiable respectability?
6. What is the significance of the title? Does it fit in with Joyce's often-expressed idea that the dead do not stay buried? Note that the important figure of Michael Furey appears only through Gretta's remarks.
7. The structure *(7)* consists of a series of scenes at the party, and a final scene in the hotel. Can you show the bearing of each scene in revealing the change in attitude of Gabriel?
8. The snow is clearly a symbol, which changes during the story. It is not here a symbol of death. What does it signify at the end, falling "upon all the living and the dead"?

E. M. FORSTER / PAGE 271

1. Surbiton is a rather dull, modern suburb of London. Would it be better for the story if the boy lived in a region with a more romantic name, such as Blackfriars or Knightsbridge?
2. The naughty young men who put up the sign "To Heaven" were romantic poets; Shelley in particular is named. Would their heaven be a religious paradise or a poet's paradise?
3. The boy's mother protests that they are not "Philistines." What is a

QUESTIONS

Philistine in this connection? Do you believe her protest? Why do the boy's parents refuse to go with him when he returns to urge them?

4. How does Mr. Bons ("snob" spelled backward) reveal his snobbishness?
5. In what sense could the world of poetic make-believe be more real than Surbiton?
6. The first driver of the omnibus is Sir Thomas Browne, a noted seventeenth-century author who was also a doctor. Does Forster risk anything by having Browne speak in the same latinate, ponderous way in which he wrote?
7. The three girls in the pool are the Rhine maidens, who appear in the cycle of German operas by Richard Wagner. Why do they call up: "Truth in the depth, truth on the height"?
8. "Dan someone" is Dante, the greatest Italian poet, and his three horses represent the three parts of his *Divine Comedy*. What does he mean when he tells Bons: "I am the means and not the end. I am the food and not the life"? Does he imply that poetry, while a good in itself, is also a means toward a richer spiritual existence?
9. Why at the end (Telos) does Achilles elevate the boy upon his famous shield and crown him with a laurel wreath, while ignoring the pompous Mr. Bons?
10. Forster seems to imply that literature should be approached with the innocence of a child rather than with prideful scholarship. Probably it is true that the ability, so easily shown by children, to experience strongly the reality of the world of fiction is better than the approach of painful study. Does this idea, however, rule out the possibility that deeper appreciation might be gained by study and by discussing literature with others?

SAKI / PAGE 286

1. What does this story imply about the hypocrisy of most people?
2. Who is the main character *(2)*? If, as suggested by the title, it is Tobermory, what is his main trait?
3. Are there any patterns *(11)* in the revelations of the weaknesses of the various guests?
4. Is the language of the talking cat a parody on that of the guests with whom he talks?
5. After the revelations of their weaknesses, the guests seem to make a feeble effort to reform; but what is their drastic plan for dealing with the situation?

QUESTIONS

W. SOMERSET MAUGHAM / PAGE 294

1. Who is the main character *(2)*? Although the story opens with the skipper of the trading schooner, do not overlook Neilson.
2. Contrast the qualities of the skipper and Neilson. What might cause the same woman to devote herself to such different lovers?
3. Just what qualities of South Sea life might eventually pall on such a man as Neilson?
4. It is ironical *(12)* that the two famous lovers should meet again after many years, and not even recognize each other. If this were the main plot *(3)*, however, this would be merely another trick story of reversal and probably an unsuccessful one, for the shrewd reader guesses the identity of Red fairly early. Would you say that the story avoids anticlimax by having it end with Neilson's decision to leave the islands?
5. The setting *(4)* is one that is not familiar to most readers. What words and passages make it clear that Maugham is writing about an island in the South Pacific?
6. The main plot question is not raised early in the story. What substitute questions does Maugham bring up that would arouse some suspense *(8)*?
7. How does Maugham handle the exposition, the narration of earlier events which makes it possible for the reader to understand what happens later in the story?
8. What special contributions *(13)* does Maugham offer the reader of this story?
9. If this is a story mainly about love, what do you think is the author's attitude toward this emotion?

KATHERINE MANSFIELD / PAGE 314

1. Would you be surprised to find that the theme *(1)* of this apparently uneventful story might deal with youth and age, with life and time, with reflection and activity, with happiness and sadness, and with awareness and forgetfulness?
2. This story intends to do more than describe the feelings of a country girl at her first real party. What does it intend?
3. In what way is Leila's first ball the beginning of her last ball?
4. The tone *(5)* of the story is apparently gay, but there are profound overtones. What details suggest the seriousness of life?
5. Does the story have immediacy—that is, do we feel we are living along with Leila and sharing all her thoughts?
6. Leila is sorry for the fat man. Is he sorry for her?
7. What is the irony *(12)* at the end, when Leila doesn't even recognize the

QUESTIONS

fat man who foretold her dreary future? Do people often refuse to remember unpleasant truths?

ERNEST HEMINGWAY / PAGE 321

1. About how old is the narrator? Do all his expressions seem to fit this particular boy, or does he ever say anything that sounds more adult than he is?
2. What are the boy's main traits *(2)*, as revealed by his self-characterization?
3. This is a growing-up story, about initiation into the real world. What parts of the boy's narrative show that he is attaining some maturity? For example, does he begin to question some of the values and codes with which he has been brought up?
4. Are the qualities the boy admires in horses the same qualities he admires in the people he knows?
5. Does the boy usually say less, or more, than he feels?
6. Are you bothered by the use of profanity, of slang (using "skins" for horses, and other racetrack jargon), or of terms such as "wop" for Italian? Do such expressions seem to be inserted for their shock value, or are they natural in the contexts?
7. Is there any contrast between Joe's fun with the other boys at Maisons and his remarks about the people he met at the Café de la Paix?
8. Is there irony *(12)* at the end when George Gardner, a crooked jockey, says: "Your old man was one swell guy"?
9. Is the ending—the death of the father and his horse—inevitable, or is this climax dragged in for the sake of sensation?

YASUNARI KAWABATA / PAGE 334

1. Can you chart the successive stages of the action *(3)* showing the student's approach to the dancing girl?
2. Does the mention in the first paragraph of "a certain hope" arouse suspense *(8)*? What is the hope?
3. What is the value of delaying the naming of the members of the troupe of players?
4. What is, exactly, the ending *(7)*? What has the narrator learned that makes him weep?
5. Is there a gap of class distinction between the student and his new friends? What details show the differences? Note that at the entrance to villages near Shimoda are signs: "Vagrant performers keep out."

QUESTIONS

LU HSUN / PAGE 351

1. Who is the main character *(2)*? What does he or she want? Does this character succeed in attaining the desired goal? Are we satisfied with the outcome?
2. Mu's daughter, Aiku, says at the hearing: "I'll risk my life if I have to, even if it means the ruination of both families." Do you feel that her attitude is excessive in this situation?
3. Is there any suggestion of bribery in the story? If so, where?
4. Since ancient times, the most unifying force in China has been the family. The highest ideal was that this unity should be preserved, even though it might be the custom that a bride must be ruled by her husband and his family. Do you believe the author approved of Aiku's attitude?

KATHERINE ANNE PORTER / PAGE 361

1. Does the title give a clue to the theme? Note that it is the name of a tree popularly known as the Judas tree, because Judas, the betrayer of Christ, hanged himself on it and the red buds come from the body of Judas. Eating the buds of this tree would be a sacrament not of faith but of betrayal.
2. What is Laura's main trait *(2)*?
3. Laura is attractive, but in the story her virginity is notorious and no one touches her. What are her relations with the young captain, the organizer of the typographer's union, Braggioni, and Eugenio?
4. The events of the story are not told in the order in which they happen. We first hear of Eugenio as a corpse; later we learn, at the most fitting time, of the manner of his death. Why is such a rearrangement effective?
5. May both Braggioni and Eugenio be considered as symbols of Christ?
6. In just what ways is Laura a betrayer?
7. Laura is shown as unable to participate in three kinds of love: Christian (she prays but feels guilty); humanitarian (she cannot share the ardor of the revolutionists she is serving); and passionate (she is cool to all her suitors). Would you say that lacking faith—as Judas lacked faith—she is incapable of love and even of an awareness of life?

WILLIAM FAULKNER / PAGE 374

1. Who is the main character *(2)*? Flem Snopes is obviously the villain. The narrator, although a sympathetic participant, takes no direct action against Snopes. Henry Armstid is a self-centered victim who brings a terrible burden on his family. Is Mrs. Armstid the one who learns most about life in this story?

QUESTIONS

2. Flem Snopes speaks seldom. By what actions is this figure characterized *(2)*?
3. What is the function in the story of Mrs. Littlejohn? Is she merely a typical woman, impatient with the folly of men, or does her character underline the isolation of Mrs. Armstid?
4. What does the Texan's refusal to accept Henry Armstid's money reveal about the inhumanity of Snopes?
5. The bare plot *(3)* of this story is that an evil person plays upon the dreams of decent, hard-working human beings and makes a profit. What is the value of reading a story in which virtue does not triumph?
6. How does the author reconcile the tones *(5)* of humor and brutality?
7. What danger does Faulkner run by having a story told in the dialect of a certain region? How does he keep the language from being a cheap imitation of comic-strip hillbilly speech?
8. Wherein does the humor of this story lie? Does the Texan's use of understatement, for example, add to the comedy?

JOSÉ GARCIÁ VILLA / PAGE 392

1. The story appears to be little more than a report of a real encounter. Does it, however, have a theme *(1)*?
2. Why does "Juan Rizal" tell lies? Do you believe he is insane?
3. Is the narrator *(6)* merely a means of telling the story, or does he take part in the action *(3)*?
4. What details show that the setting *(4)* is in the Philippines?
5. What are the differences between Juan's real father and his imagined father?
6. Do you agree with the narrator's friend when he says: "He who can dream of beautiful things, and live in them, surely he is great—and wise"?

WILLIAM CARLOS WILLIAMS / PAGE 400

1. Although the author gives some names, the characters *(2)* might merely be labeled The Mother, The Father, The Child, and The Doctor. In a brief story with a strong theme, is it necessary to individualize the characters greatly?
2. The conflict on the lowest level is the practical need, the social necessity to protect the girl and others. But does not the ending reveal a disease of human nature which is defined by the use of force?
3. At what stages does the doctor change his cool, professional attitude in the course of the story? What actions by the parents affect this attitude? Do their threats and false promises help or hinder him?

QUESTIONS

4. The doctor, representing "civilization," shows growing respect for his enemy, the "savage brat," who denies his status even when it is supported by her parents. Would you say that he wins a victory or suffers a defeat in this encounter? What victory or what defeat?
5. Who is right, the doctor or the child?
6. The doctor admits: "It was a pleasure to attack her." Would you say that resorting to force, as shown by this story, opens up a blind fury, a drive toward conquest for its own sake, even a delight in cruelty?

Appendix A: Main Questions for the Study of a Story

1. THEME What is the theme? In other words, what important comment on life does the author make in the story? Can you state it in a single sentence, beginning with: "This story shows that . . . "? Do you think this theme is true or false? The theme might be called the main idea of the story. It is *not* a conclusion of fact, or a prescriptive or moral message. Theme should not be confused with characterization, plot, or setting. A great story should be rich in its comment on life. It may be hard to find a brief paraphrase of its complex and organic meaning, but unless we try to say what the story is about, we may go far astray on judging all the other qualities. Since almost any idea might be the theme of a story, it is impossible to classify even the greatest themes of fiction. Usually, a theme that has universality is likely to produce a better story than a narrow and too specific theme. Sometimes a theme is so rich that it embodies an entire philosophy.

The story should have unity of theme; that is, the one principal idea should emerge in all its implications as the story goes on, until finally the author's answer in this specific situation is clear and gives a single effect. There is no room in a short story for the presentation of a variety of complicated themes.

2. CHARACTERIZATION What does characterization contribute to the total effect? Fiction is essentially people doing things. In the short story there is not enough space to show much *development* of character, but the short story can give *revelation* of character. Now, who are the chief characters? What is each character like? What does each want (motivation)? Why does each do what he does? Do the characters succeed or fail in attaining their desires? Are their desires presented as admirable or unadmirable? What do their actions (including what they say or think) reveal about them? Are traits presented by mere description or statement, or do we assume them from actions? Who are the

APPENDIX A

minor characters, and what are they like? Do the characters seem to be individuals or individualized types, or are they mere straw men or personifications of abstractions? Do they seem to act because they must, or because they are puppets moved about by the author to fit the plot? Is the hero a superman and the villain a fiend, or are the characters presented with some virtues and some human failings? Does the story violate experience by having all the good people in one group and all the bad ones in the opposition group?

Most stories have unity of characterization; that is, there is one, and only one, main character, the one to whom the events of the story mean the most. Who is the main character to whom this story belongs? What does he want? What is the main conflict of the main character? Does he fail or succeed in attaining his purpose? This character is presented as having certain prominent traits and desires which carry him through the story; at the end, would you say that what happens to him is *inevitable* under these conditions? Are there any unnecessary characters in the cast? If the main character is a *type,* can he or she be classed, for example, as one of the following: prodigal son, Cinderella, romantic dreamer, Robin Hood, lucky simpleton, mastermind, clever weakling, enduring sufferer, Frankenstein? Is the main character an agent who does things, or is he a patient to whom others do things?

3. ACTION What does the action of the story contribute to the total effect? The action is the series of happenings in the story; these may be physical, mental, or emotional events. Action, when motivated, is called *plot.* In a well-planned story the plot makes the *main character* face a *problem* by going through *conflicts* or struggles which increase in importance and which result in some *crisis* and a final *significant event* which ends that line of conflict one way or another.

Plots may be considered to belong to two general types. The story of *decision* shows the main character faced with a necessity—preferably urgent—to choose among alternatives; the plot then shows the strong pressures on him to choose one or another alternative. The story of *achievement* assumes that the character has made a decision to seek a goal; the plot then shows him attempting to reach this goal, despite mounting opposition, and through the exercise of his main trait winning or losing his objective. The most satisfying achievement plot for most readers shows an admirable main character attempting to do something beneficial to others, and succeeding despite mounting obstacles. He may lose a material reward but win a moral victory. He need not always be a hero; a lesser character, such as the type of lovable rogue, may be admirable so long as his aims are not greedy or criminal. Many stories do not succeed in gaining the desired effect because the author plans a story of achievement but uses the plot line of the story of decision, or vice versa.

APPENDIX A

Plots may vary from a single incident to a highly complicated series of interlocking events; if characterization or setting is of high importance, the events need not be complex, whereas in a mystery story or one of dramatic action, the plot may be extremely complicated. Now, does the action of this story develop the theme and follow logically from the natures of the characters? Are there major and minor conflicts among the characters? Is this story about:

   a. A trivial incident?
   b. A representative incident?
   c. An apparently trivial incident which is actually important?
   d. An intrinsically important event in the lives of the main characters?

Is the action well motivated through characterization, or is there much action merely for the sake of action, resulting in farce or melodrama?

Conflicts are clashes of persons, forces, ideas, or emotions. The conflicts which arise during the action of a short story may be of the following kinds, and one or more of these kinds may appear in the same story: animal versus animal; man versus animal; man and animal versus animal; man and animal versus man and animal; man versus the forces of nature; man versus man in physical struggle, mental struggle or struggle of wits, and psychological struggle or struggle of wills; man versus society; man versus himself (dual personality, rival forces within the same man); man versus supernatural forces (ghosts, magic); and man versus fate. Which of these kinds of conflict do you find in the story?

The story should have unity of action. What is the most important conflict in the story, which exemplifies the theme and reveals the main trait or traits of the principal character? Does this main action carry through from a beginning to a logical conclusion? Is there too little action, or too much? Is there any incident that could be omitted without damaging the total effect?

4. SETTING What does the setting contribute to the total effect? The setting is the area in time and space in which the action goes on. The author's theme may hold good for various times and places, and then the setting need not be important. On the other hand, theme, characterization, and action may be made more significant by the choice of a proper time and place. Setting is important if it is unusual or if its details are a main part of the action or if it works upon the emotions of the characters. Within the brief limits of the short story, elaborate setting for its own sake is seldom justified. But if the setting is an active part of the story—so much so that it might be considered as a motivating force upon the characters—then a story of atmosphere or local

APPENDIX A

color results. Is this, then, an atmosphere or local-color story? Does the author avoid static description and weave the setting into the action? Does he avoid describing beyond the needs of the story? Are details chosen which are emotionally significant and which have suggestion value? Is there an appeal to senses other than sight?

The story should have unity of setting. Transitions of time and place within the story require some effort by the reader to perceive. The reader should not be shifted all over the map without need. Incidents and setting should work together to give an effect of consistency; certain happenings could occur more suitable in one place and time than in another. Is there any indication when the story takes place—century, day, season, hour? One story may cover only a few minutes of life; another may cover a much longer period.

5. STYLE Does the style of the story (including diction and dialogue) contribute consistently to the final effect? The style of a writer reveals his power of artistic composition—the best choice of words and sounds to fit his material. The style of good narrative need not be flowery or pedantic. It has many of the qualities of good poetic style—such as figures of speech, euphony, exact choice of words, skillful repetition, and use of selected, revealing details which have power to suggest—but these are used for storytelling purposes rather than for poetic purposes. *Diction* is the choice of words. *Dialogue* is the words the characters speak (in a first-person narrative, the entire story might be considered as a monologue in which the diction should be suited to the speaker). Do you think the story could be told better by using a higher or lower level of speech or style? If dialect appears, is it convincing and lively, and not too confusing? Does the diction avoid being commonplace, trite, discursive, or offensive through use of vulgar, brutal, or repulsive details?

A story should have unity of style. Is the style consistent with the desired effect, or does the writer seem to be jumping from one style to another? The style should be suitable throughout and fit the main tone of humor, tragedy, somberness, satire, seriousness, gaiety, or the like. This does not mean that the style should lack variety, but merely that the author should not damage his main effect by incongruous shifts in style, resulting in a patchwork of conflicting tones.

6. NARRATOR Who is the narrator, and what does the choice of this narrator add to the total effect? A story may be told by one or more of the following narrators:

    a. Main character in the story (in first person)
    b. Minor character who tells the story (in first person) as an observer
    c. Author who tells the story as an omniscient observer (in first person or, better, in third person), using the convention of knowing all about the actions and thoughts of:

APPENDIX A

1. The main character
2. A minor character
3. Several characters
d. Writers of diaries, letters or other documents

First-person stories lend an air of reality and human testimony, but it is hard for a hero to tell his own story without seeming boastful or conceited. A minor character or the author as a human observer may use the first person, but such a narrator must then be placed where he can witness all the important events of the story or be told about them. "How does he know this?" we ask ourselves—and this again may strain plausibility (see *9*). The interpretation of events told by such a narrator will be colored by personal bias; this can be harmful or useful to the story.

Using the convention of the omniscient observer—the author who is presumed to know everything and see everywhere—gives an air of unbiased and objective truth. This method, particularly when it sticks close to the viewpoint of one character in the story, lends immediacy and enables us to share closely in the feelings and thoughts of the character, who then becomes a central means of perception for us. Establishing and keeping such a means of perception throughout the story avoids baffling shifts from one character to another —shifts which strain the reader's attention and which require too much space for the short story.

Letters and other documents may sometimes be a good means of telling all or part of a story. A *frame* story is one which starts out (in either first- or third-person narrative) with a scene that sets the stage and then has a character in that scene tell the main story. A poor choice of the means of narrating may spoil an otherwise good story. Where surprise is important, as in a detective story, a human narrator like Sherlock Holmes's Dr. Watson, who does not properly interpret all the events, would be a good choice for the author.

7. STRUCTURE What is the structure of the story? Structure is the arrangement of the various elements in the story in order of presentation so as to give artistic continuity to the whole. One story may have a structure like that of a simple chain of events; another may be more like a play, with several scenes and rising dramatic interest; another may go in a circle and return to the starting place; another may have its incidents arranged in a steadily increasing intensity to the final line; another may end with a complete reversal of the situation, as in the common sort of surprise ending. The skillful author arranges the *pace* of presentation—summary, straight narrative, description, exposition, dramatic scene, dialogue, flashbacks, thoughts of a character, and so on—in order to lend variety and rising intensity to the structure. Some of these kinds of narrative require more space than others; is each worth the space it takes? For instance, a full scene treatment, with all dialogue and actions given,

APPENDIX A

takes up much space but may be worth it, particularly at the climax of the story. Summary is the most economical kind of narrative, but mere statement of what happened may be flat, unconvincing, and lacking in emotional value.

Aristotle's division of a work into beginning, middle, and end is still useful. Further consideration will here be given to three elements of structure —beginning, climaxes, and ending:

a. Does the *beginning* of the story skillfully set the action going, suggest the theme, sketch in the background, introduce the main characters and their problems, handle the exposition of previous events, arouse suspense, and hint at the probable outcome? Is the beginning too exciting, so that there must be a letdown after the opening and hence a drop in interest? Is the exposition of earlier events—what we must know in order to understand the situation the characters are facing—given in a lump of bare statement, or is it woven into the story and shown quickly through speech and action?

b. What is the *climax* of the story—the point of highest interest, at which the conflict is resolved and the outcome is clear? The climax should come at the "end of the middle" of the story and should be followed quickly by the end of the story. A climax may be merely a physical event, or it may be mental or emotional. Some readers are expert enough to pick out three kinds of climax rather than only one. The *climax of theme* is the point in the story at which full illumination comes to the reader concerning the main meaning of the story. The *climax of action* is the event which shows conclusively the final outcome of the main conflict. The *climax of character* is the point at which the fate of the main character becomes definitely clear. These three climaxes may or may not come at exactly the same point in the story.

c. Does the *ending* of the story come too quickly, or too slowly to cause the needed final effect? If the story does not end soon after the point of climax, it will suffer the letdown called anticlimax. Looking back, do you feel that the story ending was inevitable in this situation, or that it came by pure chance or coincidence? Do you believe that a valid answer has been given to the main problem raised, or do you feel that the author has either dodged the question or invented a fake answer which does not agree with common sense? If the ending is a surprise, is it one that might have been fairly foreseen by an astute reader?

8. SUSPENSE Is there suspense in the story which makes you continue to read with interest? Suspense may merely appeal to curiosity about answering a riddle that the author has propounded, or it may awaken deep concern regarding what the author has to say about life. Does the author arouse curiosity about any point without satisfying it later? Is all the suspense concentrated on the outcome of the main action, or does the author arouse and satisfy suspense concerning minor incidents of the story?

APPENDIX A

9. PLAUSIBILITY Is the story plausible? Does the author avoid the use of improbable events or strained coincidences? Do you feel, as you read, that the events of the story could really happen in this way? A good story need not be true to life in the sense that it supplies easily recognized or familiar characters, incidents, or settings. In the first place, only a person wholly familiar with the scene or character depicted would qualify as a judge of whether it is factually exact.

More important for judgment of the artistry of the story is this question: Does the story have a logic of its own and state some truth about human existence? Truth is stranger than fiction and sometimes harder to believe. What is wanted in fiction is verisimilitude—the appearance of truth. The reader who is unused to fiction may unfairly criticize a story because he reads it as if it were history or biography or seeks merely facts that fit his personal experience; he denies to the author, in Samuel Taylor Coleridge's words, a "willing suspension of disbelief." The story need not be true to life so long as it is true to fiction, for fiction is the world in which we look for the order that we seldom find in real life. Stories of fantasy and imagination, such as *Alice's Adventures in Wonderland,* might in this sense be "true." The skillful writer prepares the way for our belief by foreshadowing coming events, until we are ready to accept them as following logically.

10. EMOTIONS Which of the main human emotions or feelings are presented by the author in this story? Does he rely upon two or three obvious emotions (revenge, courage, fear) or does he deal with a wider range of emotions? On the other hand, does he concentrate on emotions which are too special to arouse universality of response? Does his presentation of emotion ring true to your experience? Is the story marred by sentimentality (the presentation of emotion that is much more intense than the situation warrants)? Do the emotions appeal to us through our own feelings—that is, does the author make us feel, or just tell us how we ought to feel? Note that there may be a difference between the emotions the character undergoes in the story and the emotion the reader feels while reading about the character (for instance, the character may feel despair; the reader then feels pity).

11. PATTERNS Are there any patterns in the story? Pattern is made by repetition of elements, usually repetition with variation. Its effect may be merely cumulative, or it may be climactic. Patterns may be found in theme statement, characterization, incidents of action, settings, diction, structure, or the like.

12. IRONY OF SITUATION Is there irony of situation in the story? An ironic outcome is one which is the reverse of what was expected or hoped—an outcome that is almost mockingly the opposite, contrasting promise and fulfillment, for example, or appearance and reality. Use of this contrast, which

APPENDIX A

may be heavy or subtle, often reveals much about the real beliefs of the author, and may give the effect that life is like that.

13. SPECIAL CONTRIBUTIONS Does the story offer you any special contributions? These might be: humor, lively dialogue, symbolism, allusions, historical fact, geographical information, scientific information, facts on social customs or manners, quotable passages, confirmation of your own ideas, moral opinions, or thoughts on current economic, political, or social problems.

14. LITERARY BACKGROUND Would your appreciation of this story be heightened by knowing its literary background (the author's life and times, other works by this author, works by other authors of this period or this type)? Such background knowledge may be very useful, so long as one remembers that biography is not criticism, although it may improve the soundness of criticism.

15. BLENDING Are the ingredients blended successfully in the right proportions, so that the reader gets the total effect? For example, do the characters, action, and setting best exemplify the theme? Does the action of the story spring logically from the characters? Does the setting help to make effective the theme, characterization, and action? Does the style suit the theme, characterization, action, and setting? Is the final story a well-unified whole?

Appendix B

Analysis of "The Man Who Would Be King"

To learn how to appreciate a good short story, it might be better to read one story fifteen times for different purposes, rather than to read fifteen stories in the usual, casual way. To try out the list of questions given in Appendix A, let us seek to apply them to one story, Kipling's "The Man Who Would Be King," in the hope that insights will emerge to reveal the richness of craftsmanship in fiction.

1. THEME This story shows that a man who would rule a nation must first rule himself, and that, paradoxically, a man may be most truly a king when he is no longer on his throne. This bare statement may sound trite or preachy, but it emerges slowly through the story and has many implications and qualifications which keep it from being too obvious. The theme seems quite universal if kingship can be extended to the idea of any important leadership. The author sticks quite well to his main theme throughout, so that a single effect is given at the end.

2. CHARACTERIZATION Kipling's characterizations contribute greatly to the total effect of the story. Unlike shorter narratives, there is room for development of character; the protagonist at the end is a quite different person than at the opening. This chief character is Daniel Dravot, the man who would be king. A beggar, who has not yet realized his full capacity for leadership, he decides to become head of an unruly mass of mountain tribes in a little-known region. He achieves this goal only to discover that success has brought new responsibilities he is unable to fulfill.

His desire to be a king is presented as admirable; at the time the story was written, during the Pax Britannica lasting from 1815 to 1914, several Englishmen became rulers of large domains which they added to the British Empire (the story mentions in particular James Brooke, Rajah of Sarawak). The traits of the various characters are presented both by what they say and do and by

APPENDIX B

what others say about them; Kipling's ability to sketch a minor character in a line is clearly seen (e.g., a bandit on the road to Kafirstan characterizes himself by saying, "If you are rich enough to buy, you are rich enough to rob.").

Other leading characters are the narrator (who properly keeps his own personality and judgments in the background) and Peachey Taliaferro Carnehan. Carnehan is an admiring ally of Dravot and the one who survives to tell of his fate. When the great crisis comes he is wiser than Dravot, yet does not join the opposition. The contrast between Carnehan's faithfulness to an ideal of self-control and Dravot's flaw is symbolized by their punishments. Dravot is allowed to signal his downfall, whereas Carnehan is crucified (a symbolic godlike agony) and after his "miraculous" survival is put in the temple, "because they said he was more of a god than old Daniel that was a man." Billy Fish, the Kafir chief who becomes a loyal convert to Dravot's program, is in a sense a foil to Dravot; he is a lesser leader who shows off to advantage a greater leader. No villain appears, for the opposition comes not from outside but from within the main character.

Minor characters, such as the bystanders in the Serai, the bandits, the people of Kafirstan (including Dravot's intended bride), and the Superintendent of the Asylum are properly kept in their places; they lack names and characterizing traits.

Character is destiny in this story, for the events that occur seem to grow naturally from the desires of Daniel Dravot, rather than to fit a preconceived complication of exciting events. He is not a superman, but possesses some human failings (his downfall is caused by a desire that is all too human). In the early part of the story he is shown as having some traits which are unadmirable, verging on the criminal; but these traits later are valuable when he decides that India is not big enough for such as he, and he goes out almost alone to win a kingdom. There is no simple division of the cast of characters into good guys and bad guys, a division contradicting our experience.

There is unity of characterization in this story. Although the narrator is the only one in possession of the available facts (Carnehan at the end is insane and unaware of the significance of his adventures), the narrator is not the main character. Dravot is the one to whom the events of the action mean the most, as we learn from his actions in the last days of his life. His entrance on the stage is properly delayed and prepared. He is described by Carnehan as "a big man with a red beard, and a great swell." His name is withheld for a time, but we find that it is Daniel, a name known to all Bible readers as that of a great prophet at the Persian court of Nebuchadnezzar, whose faith saved him from a lion's den. Daniel Dravot does not bear the name of a king, but his stature, his beard (often a symbol of power), and the redness of his complexion—suggesting both gold and blood—are all qualities associated with kingship.

APPENDIX B

Dravot, after having practised a number of trades, wants to be an absolute monarch. This is probably the dream of most men, but few take such strong steps to achieve it as does Dravot. He signs with Carnehan a contract (a document given in full) which denies them the two things that make life worth having. Through exercise of his varied experience and his gift for leadership, he fights his way to kingship, and through an apparent miracle is accorded godship.

His main conflict comes after he is crowned. He begins dreaming of becoming an emperor and handing over his domain to Queen Victoria. His downfall comes when he breaks his own contract and decides to take a wife. This act shows not only the quite human need for a companion but a desire to found a dynasty—the desire to have a son to carry on the ruler's responsibilities that has been the downfall of a number of kings. There is no question of love; the wedding must be public and the bride chosen for reasons of state. When this bride bites Dravot and draws blood, the priests decide that Dravot is neither god nor devil but a mortal man, and his downfall begins. That the girl would bite him is not inevitable. Sooner or later, however, Dravot's overweening desires would have brought out some other evidence of his mortality and his reign would have ended.

It is possible to consider him as a tragic hero comparable to those in Greek drama or in plays such as some of Shakespeare's. In many of these tragedies, a king suffers catastrophe because of a flaw in character, and the audience, by observing the action, is reassured that there is a moral order in their world which cannot be transgressed forever. Often the tragic flaw is the excess of a virtue; and Dravot's pride in developing his power pushes him beyond the bounds of the possible. Pride, one of the seven deadly Christian sins, by which Satan fell from Heaven, was also the main flaw in many Greek tragic heroes. The rather amused tone of the narrator, however, makes it clear that he at least does not consider Dravot's fate to be classically tragic.

3. ACTION Most of the events of "The Man Who Would Be King," although a detailed synopsis would be lengthy (and would be no substitute for the full story), contribute to the total effect. These events are not merely physical but also mental and emotional. The motives of the main characters appear quite plausible when examined (see *9*). The plot shows that the main character, Dravot, faces the problem of becoming a king. He surmounts an increasing number of obstacles which result in a final crisis that significantly puts an end to the conflict when he meets death.

This is a story of achievement. From the beginning Dravot shows no wavering in his determination to fulfill his decision to exercise royal power, even when Carnehan argues with him against the marriage. The plot therefore shows him attempting to reach the goal of his dreams, despite mounting opposition, and, through the exercise of his main trait, winning and then

APPENDIX B

losing his objective. This plot is satisfying to most readers in that it shows a main character whose chief motive is on the whole admirable (that is, to bring order and progress to a backward group who are of the same race as his own) and who struggles to achieve his ends. He gains these ends but later is forced to accept a moral rather than a material victory (he dies like a gentleman—or a king).

Since Dravot's dream of rulership is not an uncommon human aspiration, the author does not need to take much time to build up the motivation. As this is not a detective story or one with a surprise ending, the plot does not have to be tricky. The plot does, however, reveal the theme and seems to follow logically from the natures of the actors. The events are far from trivial; they are literally concerned with life and death. Kipling attains maximum dramatic effect by having Dravot start at the bottom before reaching the top. Is it not more exciting to have a beggar become a king than to have a prince become a king? Since the setting is strange to most readers, many actions might appear to be strongly sensational; but melodrama (unmotivated action) is avoided.

Action is kept lively through the use of several types of conflict. The two men fight the forces of nature to cross the mountains to Kafirstan. There is much physical struggle between them and the native people. They also use their minds to outwit or master others, and likewise there is a psychological conflict, in which the disillusion of the natives in Dravot's godship results in a struggle of will against will. The conflict between the loafers and society is shown as one motivation for their leaving India. The greatest conflict in the story, however, is that between two forces in the same man (Dravot's need for self-preservation versus his desire to marry a queen and found a dynasty). There is no suggestion of supernatural forces at work (the disappearance of Dravot's head can be explained rationally). Nor is this a story in which the action is motivated by fate; the characters appear to possess some freedom of will and are not victims of determinism.

The story, although long, does have unity of action. The most important conflict, as has been said, is that between two sides of Dravot's character, leading him to continue a course that is at least deadly, if not completely tragic. This crisis is led up to slowly, but there is plenty of action preceding it— perhaps so much that some readers may miss the importance of this crisis leading to a logical conclusion. Yet the chain of cause and effect results from the traits of the characters. Some incidents which might seem at first to be easily omitted actually have a part in the slow building of plausibility in this story of strange action in a distant land.

4. SETTING The setting in India and Kafirstan in the 1880s contributes heavily to the total effect of this story. Indeed, only a few places in the world could serve as the scene of the action; a beggar could not plausibly attain

APPENDIX B

kingship in a "civilized" region. The specific theme therefore requires that settings unfamiliar to most readers must be used, and full attention is given to helping us visualize the various scenes. Kipling does not, however, indulge in descriptions for their own sake. The narrator's terse and shocking account at the beginning, of what it is like to travel by Intermediate Class on a train in India, helps to characterize both himself and the vagabond who starts the chain of events. The facts he gives concerning the Native States may appear to be digressive; but the description of his work as a correspondent includes doing business with "divers Kings," so that we may consider him a reliable informant concerning royalty. Perhaps his two pages of description of the work of a journalist in an Indian newspaper office are more extensive than required by the theme. This description, however, mentions the newspaper's publication of information about kings and other world leaders, and also sets the stage for the two interviews during which most of the action of the story is brought out in dialogues.

Kipling's power of description in stripped prose has often been admired. He learned early to condense and delete, and his use of appeals to the various senses give us a strong feeling of immediacy, a feeling that we are ourselves on the scene. He depends not only upon the sense of sight. His writing so evokes the India of his birth that many readers of an earlier generation formed their main conception of this big country from their reading of Kipling. A few examples of sensory appeals are: "Sometimes I lay out upon the ground and devoured what I could get, from a plate made from a flapjack"; "It was horribly cold, because the wind was blowing off the sands"; "little black copy boys are whining 'copy wanted' like tired bees"; "the press machines are red-hot of touch"; "Now and again a spot of almost boiling water would fall on the dust with the flop of a frog."

Kipling did not need to invent Kafirstan, the one place in the world, Dravot believed, that was available for setting up his kingdom. Kafirstan is the old name for a mountainous region west of India. It was populated by Kafirs (a Persian word meaning "infidels") who were nature worshippers until they were forcibly converted to Islam in 1896 and made a part of northeastern Afghanistan under the name of Nuristan. Early writers believed that the tribes were blond descendants of the army of Alexander the Great; Kipling exaggerates this possibility by having the natives turn out to be strongly English in appearance. The narrator gives Dravot and Carnehan all the printed information on Kafirstan available in his office, and the fact that they have knowledge of the country makes their later task of conquest easier.

The story has unity of setting. The main scenes are limited to the railway carriage, the narrator's office, and the Serai. Settings on the journey to Kafirstan and in that country are given to us through Carnehan's dialogue, and hence we get them second hand; but his madness permits the author to give

APPENDIX B

only the essentials of these scenes, distorted by insane recollection. Enough is given, though, to enable us to picture the conquest and the downfall of the two adventurers.

Transitions from one place to another are handled quickly. The main time gap of two years, between the narrator's farewell to the two travelers and the reappearance of Carnehan in the office, is clearly shown to be a time lapse, even though the pressroom activities are apparently unchanged, and Carnehan remarks of the narrator, "You've been setting here ever since." Kipling's descriptions of time and space quickly indicate hour of the day, seasons, and places where action occurs.

5. STYLE Kipling's individualized prose style has been admired and imitated even by those who write about other regions or who do not share his opinions. Analysis of his sentences by the student would be greatly repaid. Kipling himself made a few comments on his style in his autobiography. He remarked on the importance of revision, especially omission of excess words. He used a strong black ink to make deletions in the manuscript; thus the pleasure he felt in blotting out words equaled the pleasure he originally felt in putting down words, and eased the pangs of cutting down a story to provide greater impact.

The style of Kipling, fresh and crisp, bearing few traces of the influence of earlier writers, brought to the world a new picture of India, which had been known to the English for several centuries but was now seen in a brightly colored light through the magic of his diction. Self-characterization is achieved by shrewd use of dialogue, which often includes slang or other colloquial terms. Note, however, that Kipling does not clutter his story with Indian expressions that need to be translated; in fact, only one phrase, "copy wanted," is given in a foreign language. He attains his local color while still writing English. Some of the terms he uses are vulgar or brutal, but he is speaking of vulgar or brutal things and aims by this use to attain shock value.

The style varies in different parts of the story to suit narrative needs, but the main tone is consistent. This tone, briefly, voices an ironic attitude toward a serio-comic adventure. The irony is emphasized because the style is not somber; the characters are treated as if their actions verged on comedy, and they are tenderly mocked. Kipling's style has the consistency of the born storyteller who does not spoil his yarn by incongruous shifts in manner or tone.

6. NARRATOR The choice of a narrator contributes well to the total effect. The narrator is clearly of Type B, a minor character who tells the story in first person as an observer. This is not a frame story, however, for the narrator (presumably Kipling himself) does more than make formal opening and closing remarks. He can plausibly obtain all the facts offered. He is personally

APPENDIX B

acquainted with the leading characters. He is a fellow Freemason and, responding to their appeal, does them a favor. He heads them off from an attempt at blackmail—an act which they consider a bad turn—but furnishes them with valuable knowledge to aid in their quest. He is a trained journalist who may be expected to record events professionally.

For all these reasons the reader trusts the veracity of this observer, who seems to give out the story almost as impartially as would an omniscient narrator, and who further adds the plausibility of one who was on the scene. This narrator is retained throughout, even though the critical action is told to him by Carnehan after his return from Kafirstan. This story could not properly be narrated by Dravot, since he dies. It could possibly be told by Carnehan alone, but he ends up insane and it would be easy to believe that the entire adventure was removed from reality. The use of a minor character as narrator adds additional depth which lends credibility to the whole story. The author has therefore chosen a suitable focus of narration.

7. STRUCTURE The author uses a series of different narrative devices to arrange the elements of his story in a continuity that varies the pace yet achieves a total effect. The chain of events is given chronologically as known to the narrator. He starts with an epigraph ("Brother to a Prince and fellow to a beggar if he be found worthy"), a device Kipling found useful in many other stories. The opening paragraph is exposition: personal reflection on the meaning of the story he has not yet told. The next two paragraphs are straight narration, using description as well, and preparing for the coming scene in the intermediate carriage. This scene, conducted mainly in dialogue as if it were on the stage, is worth the necessary space. Carnehan's scene problem is to persuade the narrator to do him a special favor; he succeeds by making an appeal to a fellow Mason (a password is exchanged, referring to the Square and to the Mother Lodge); and the outcome is that the narrator is persuaded to comply and as a sequel meets the main character.

The interim, during which the narrator acts as a newspaper correspondent in the native states, is covered quickly by exposition and synopsis, but contains references to kings and princes. The encounter with the red-bearded man, wherein the narrator fulfills his obligation, is handled in minimum space, but the first meeting with the main character is achieved. As a sequel, the narrator acts to keep the two adventurers out of trouble. He then returns to his office and exposition replaces narrative; but as has been mentioned under 5, the two pages of description are more than mere local color, and set the stage for the lengthy first scene in that office. Analysis of structure in the foregoing manner could be continued throughout the entire story, to show how the author has used the various devices of presentation to form a cohesive structure.

APPENDIX B

Dialogue is well used to lend immediacy. Even though the dialogue deals with past events, if an event is *told about* now, the reader is inclined to feel that it is *happening* now.

The *beginning* of the story, which runs up to the first scene in the newspaper office and which has already been briefly discussed, sets the action going in the second paragraph, suggests the theme of kingship a number of times in the epigraph and the first paragraph, sketches in the strange background, and hints at the outcome. Because Kipling does begin at the beginning, no exposition of earlier events is needed. Suspense is aroused when the strange loafer, on urgent business, makes an unusual request. The main character and his main problem are not introduced until the middle of the story, but a substitute suspense is aroused concerning the actions of the two mysterious men, so that the reader continues in the expectation that their goal is a higher one than blackmailing Indian rulers. This opening is, however, not so breathtaking that it creates a letdown by overshadowing later events.

The *middle* of the story, which takes up most of the space, contains the various climaxes, during which the conflicts are resolved and the outcome is clear. All these climaxes come during Carnehan's long dialogue. The *climax of action* comes when he says: "They took them without any sound." Thereafter the reader knows that Dravot has failed to win his goal, and death or destruction must follow. The *climax of character* comes when Dravot says: "D'you suppose I can't die like a gentleman?" No further development of his attitude can be expected thereafter. The *climax of theme* comes, accompanied by irony and shock, when Carnehan, like a carnival showman, reveals the dried, crowned head of Dravot. The final meaning of true kingship is strikingly brought home.

The *ending* comes soon thereafter, with Carnehan singing a hymn. The author could have stopped here, but a few loose ends remain to be tied up in a *sequel,* which adds further suspense as well as describing the death of Carnehan, the sole remaining witness of this adventure. Kipling avoids anticlimax, however, by having the high points of the narrative come near the end.

The ending, although perhaps not as inevitable as that of a Greek tragedy, comes through the working out of cause and effect rather than coincidence, and conclusively solves the main problem raised by the author. The story does not have a surprise ending with an unexpected reversal of expectations, but it has a final touch of mystery.

8. SUSPENSE The qualities that would make one want to finish this story, once he had begun it, are several: to get the final meaning, to understand the characters better, to enjoy the style, and so on. The usual suspense expected, however, is found in the episodes of the action and especially the final outcome. Although the ending is highly dramatic, the author early begins to build

APPENDIX B

suspense. Since we do not for some time become fully aware of the main theme, Kipling supplies substitute suspense (see 7). Our first question is not: "Can these beggars become kings?" but "Who are these strange men and what are they trying to do?" When this latter question is answered, we want to go on to the larger question. Answers to all the suspenseful questions are given by the author except, as has been hinted, what happened to Dravot's head.

9. PLAUSIBILITY Whether or not a story is convincing is a matter that each reader must judge for himself. Kipling supplies a number of statements, however, which make it easier for one to suspend disbelief in this story of adventure. It is set in a far place and in a now distant time, and we are willing to accept the possibility that strange things could have happened there and then. The "two strong men" have prepared themselves by making their livings in various ways; they are especially expert at drilling men to become soldiers who could bring order to a country. Dravot has spent fourteen years in India and can speak native languages The two are able masqueraders who can fool the narrator at the Serai. Their speech sounds convincing. The existence of Kafirstan is reinforced when the narrator in the office gives the men various named books and the encyclopedia.

Events are foreshadowed not only in the opening paragraph but elsewhere. The horse dealer in the Serai says of Dravot: "He will either be raised to honor or have his head cut off." Both predictions come true. The third clause of the "Contrack," which was put in because it looked "regular," was fulfilled when the men did conduct themselves with dignity and discretion.

The strongest use of coincidence, which often damages plausibility, occurs when the priest overturns the sacred stone and finds that the Master's Mark beneath is identical with that on Dravot's ritual apron. Carnehan refers twice to this event as an amazing miracle. (It is probable that the mark was a swastika in a circle, a device that Kipling later adopted for the jackets of all his books.) This coincidence may not be so miraculous if one knows that anthropologists have pointed out that much of the symbolism of modern Freemasonry seems to be derived from that of native cults of the Near East. The coincidence is fairly used by Kipling, however, because it does not offer an easy solution for the characters (or the author), but leads to a fatal complication—the conviction that the two are not men but gods.

Reflection on the climax of action in the story—the killing of Dravot because he is "Neither God nor Devil, but a man"—shows that such an event happened at least once in real life. Captain James Cook, discoverer of the Hawaiian Islands, was greeted by the natives as their god Lono, returned to them from the sea. He accepted their worship, and was killed during a skirmish on the beach after he was stabbed and groaned in pain. According to a Hawaiian chronicler, "Then the chief knew that he was a man and not a god, and, that mistake ended, he struck him dead." The events of the death of Cook were well known to Englishmen and might have been in the back of Kipling's mind when he wrote this story.

10. EMOTIONS A surprisingly wide range of human emotions is revealed by a close study of this story, considering that it appears at first reading to be merely about an odd adventure. The main emotions of the main character, Dravot, are successively shown as self-control, ambition, determination, curiosity, hopefulness, aggressiveness, domination, pride, overweening superiority, desire for a queen to begin a dynasty, rage against unwanted advice, fruitless anger verging on insanity, pain after being shot, and, finally, a return to self-control just before his death. These are not emotions that are too specialized to be shared by most readers. This is clearly not a love story, but throughout there are expressions of brotherhood and loyalty among men. Sentimentality is avoided by the matter-of-fact descriptions and by the somewhat mocking tone of the narrator toward the whole proceeding. The author does not tell us how we should feel; we respond to cues from what the characters say and do. Note that we may respond at second- or third-hand; we may react to what the narrator feels, and also to what the narrator feels about the feelings of a character.

11. PATTERNS A number of artistic repetitions, usually with variation, are found in this story. The main theme of kingship is echoed many times, lending unity. The epigraph includes the word prince. The opening paragraph repeats this word, and uses king twice and kingdom once, along with crown. After the narrator leaves the train, he does business with kings and princes. Back in his office, although there were no kings there, telephone reports come in about kings being killed on the continent, and after the sickness "the kings continue to divert themselves as selfishly as before." The narrator sits up late in his office on the night he meets the future kings of Kafirstan because a king or someone else of importance was going to do something. He hears the men declare that they are going to become kings in their own right. After seeing them off on the road, he would have prayed for them, "but, that night, a real king died in Europe." Carnehan's long account of how the two men became real kings contains a number of references to kings, a queen, an emperor, and golden crowns. Carnehan reveals the head with its crown. He then is found in the street singing a hymn, but the words are changed from the original church version. "The Son of God" has become "the son of man," and a "kingly crown" has become a "golden crown." The omission of the expected final reference to kingship emphasizes the word through its absence.

Patterns are found in characterization. Again and again Dravot's red beard is mentioned as his chief mark. It is symbolic of his royal power, and is associated with the colors red and gold. After Dravot makes his fatal decision

APPENDIX B

to marry, Carnehan describes him as "looking like a big red devil," and "the low sun hit his crown and beard on one side and the two blazed like hot coals." When Dravot's chosen bride bites his hand, it is "red with blood." The revelation of Dravot's dried head includes his red beard and golden crown. The revelation mentions the blood-red banner of the son of man. Characterization is thus reinforced by color symbolism.

Patterns are found in the actions of the cast. Each seems always in character, speaking and performing in his typical modes. The most marked pattern, perhaps, is in structure. The two scenes in the narrator's office are similar in some ways but different in others. They strongly and ironically contrast the expectation and the realization.

12. IRONY OF SITUATION A number of ironies can be found in this story. It is ironic that a real journalist should encounter a loafer who blackmails rajahs by pretending to be a newspaper correspondent. Prophetically, Dravot says: "It isn't so easy being a king as it looks." The two men, capable of kingship, appear to us disguised as loafers, and in the Serai are again disguised as priest and faithful servant. "They have no more knowledge of their real identity (nor has the narrator)," says Fussell, "than the crowds of amused native onlookers have of the external 'tramp' identity." It is certainly ironic that these beggars should actually attain to kingship. After the miracle of the Master's Mark, Dravot says, "We're more than safe now"; but his acceptance as a god ironically leads to his death as a man. The two kings are overpowered by the very weapons they have drilled their men to use.

It is ironic that the last words of the loafer Carnehan should be those of a Christian hymn, and that he is delivered casually to the nearest missionary, for Carnehan himself has been an active missionary of empire. A final large irony is the fact that the narrator, a reporter of news, cannot publish in his paper the biggest scoop coming his way—that two Englishmen had become kings of Kafirstan—because both his informant and the golden crown (sole evidence of the truth of the case) have vanished.

13. SPECIAL CONTRIBUTIONS Additional qualities that may add to the rewards of reading this story can be found. There is some mild humor, and the dialogue is striking. Although Kipling cannot be called a symbolist writer of the extreme type, such as James Joyce, he does use symbols for his purpose. Dravot's beard has been mentioned. The strongest symbolism is found in Kipling's use of Masonry, and especially of the Bible. He, like most people of his generation, was brought up on the Book of Books, and this reading imbued his style and furnished many of his allusions. Indeed, as Fussell says, we become aware that the two men are acting out a virtual parody of Biblical history: "From their initial appearance as 'gods' and lawgivers to the wicked tribes, to Dravot's 'redemption' and Peachey's crucifixion, their actions are

APPENDIX B

played before an ironic background constructed of the kingly acts, both temporal and spiritual, legalistic and symbolistic, Hebraic and Christian, of the Bible." "It's true," Carnehan says of his story. "True as Gospel."

History, geography (such as that of India, Afghanistan, and Kafirstan), manners and customs of people strange to us—all these factual details lend richness. Perhaps the strongest contribution, however, is arousing us to reflection on the meaning of this story in terms of current world events. All his life Kipling was labeled a loyal glorifier of British imperialism, and indeed he often spoke of "the white man's burden" and the duty of building colonies based on British culture. Yet even in his first book of poems, *Departmental Ditties*, he voiced the idea that the rightness of empire depends upon the rightness of the men who administer the law faithfully.

In "The Man Who Would Be King," one of Kipling's first important short stories, he is by no means a jingo, but on a high ethical basis examines what empire building does to the soul. After Prime Minister Harold Wilson announced in 1968 that England would abdicate the last of her overseas possessions east of Suez, Kipling's prophetic poem "Recessional"(1897), a strong warning against an overweening pride that could make the British Empire one with Nineveh and Tyre, was frequently quoted. This short story about Dravot could serve equally well in a discussion of the real meaning of world power.

14. LITERARY BACKGROUND Kipling, born in India and schooled in England, on his return to his native country was appointed sub-editor of the Lahore *Civil and Military Gazette*, and later wrote for the Allahabad *Pioneer*. To these papers he began contributing short stories which were later published in slim paperback volumes at a low price. "The Man Who Would Be King" appeared in one of these volumes, *The Phantom 'Rickshaw*, in 1888, when the author was only twenty-three years old. Three years earlier he had been initiated into a Masonic Lodge at Lahore. Like most writers, he wrote best about what he best knew. The use of shop talk and striking details in this short story shows his lifelong delight in writing about the day's work of men and women in many places and walks of life.

15. BLENDING The main ingredients of fiction are neatly intermingled in the fictional cake of this story. The theme is well presented through the persons chosen to enact the episodes in the setting created. The action seems to derive from their characters with the logic of fiction. The style unifies theme, characterization, and setting.